50 West Kellogg Boulevard
P.O. Box 3526
St. Paul, Minnesota 55165

Printed in the United States of America

Library of Congress Cataloging in Publication Data

Ferdico, John N
Criminal procedure for the law enforcement officer.
(Criminal justice series)
Includes index.
1. Criminal procedure—United States. I. Title. II. Series.
KF9619.F47 1979 345'.73'05 78-22096
ISBN 0-8299-0188-4

Ferdico Crim.Proc.Law Officer 2d Ed.
5th Reprint—1983

Criminal Procedure for the Law Enforcement Officer

SECOND EDITION

by

John N. Ferdico, J.D., M.U.A.

Member of the Maine and Massachusetts Bars

Former Assistant Attorney General
and Director of Law Enforcement Education
for the State of Maine

Criminal Justice Series

West Publishing Co.
St. Paul • New York • Los Angeles • San Francisco
1979

INTRODUCTION TO LAW ENFORCEMENT—Continued

Police Tactics in Hazardous Situations by the San Diego, California Police Department, 228 pages, 1976.

Law Enforcement Handbook for Police by Louis B. Schwartz, Professor of Law, University of Pennsylvania and Stephen R. Goldstein, Professor of Law, University of Pennsylvania, 333 pages, 1970.

Police Operations—Tactical Approaches to Crimes in Progress by Inspector Andrew Sutor, Philadelphia, Pennsylvania Police Department, 329 pages, 1976.

Introduction to Law Enforcement and Criminal Justice by Henry Wrobleski and Karen M. Hess, both Professors at Normandale Community College, Bloomington, Minnesota, 525 pages, 1979.

JUVENILE JUSTICE

Text and Selected Readings on Introduction to Juvenile Delinquency by Paul F. Cromwell, Jr., George G. Killinger, Rosemary C. Sarri, Professor, School of Social Work, The University of Michigan and H. N. Solomon, Professor of Criminal Justice, Nova University, 502 pages, 1978.

Juvenile Justice Philosophy: Readings, Cases and Comments 2nd Edition by Frederic L. Faust, Professor of Criminology, Florida State University and Paul J. Brantingham, Department of Criminology, Simon Fraser University, 467 pages, 1979.

Introduction to the Juvenile Justice System by Thomas A. Johnson, Professor of Criminal Justice, Washington State University, 492 pages, 1975.

Cases and Comments on Juvenile Law by Joseph J. Senna, Professor of Criminal Justice, Northeastern, University and Larry J. Siegel, Professor of Criminal Justice, Northeastern University, 543 pages, 1976.

MANAGEMENT AND SUPERVISION

Selected Readings on Managing the Police Organization by Larry K. Gaines and Truett A. Ricks, both Professors of Criminal Justice, Eastern Kentucky University, 527 pages, 1978.

Criminal Justice Management: Text and Readings by Harry W. More, Jr., 377 pages, 1977.

Effective Police Administration: A Behavioral Approach 2nd Edition by Harry W. More, Jr., Professor, San Jose State University, 360 pages, 1979.

Police Management and Organizational Behavior: A Contingency Approach by Roy R. Roberg, Professor of Criminal Justice, University of Nebraska at Omaha, 350 pages, 1979.

Police Administration and Management by Sam S. Souryal, Professor of Criminal Justice, Sam Houston State University, 462 pages, 1977.

Law Enforcement Supervision—A Case Study Approach by Robert C. Wadman, Rio Hondo Community College, Monroe J. Paxman, Brigham Young University and Marion T. Bentley, Utah State University, 224 pages, 1975.

POLICE—COMMUNITY RELATIONS

Readings on Police—Community Relations 2nd Edition by Paul F. Cromwell, Jr., and George Keefer, Professor of Criminal Justice, Southwest Texas State University, 506 pages, 1978.

West's Criminal Justice Series

PSYCHOLOGY

Interpersonal Psychology for Law Enforcement and Corrections by L. Craig Parker, Jr., Criminal Justice Dept. Director, University of New Haven and Robert D. Meier, Professor of Criminal Justice, University of New Haven, 290 pages, 1975.

VICE CONTROL

The Nature of Vice Control in the Administration of Justice by Robert W. Ferguson, 509 pages, 1974.

Cases, Text and Materials on Drug Abuse Law by Gerald F. Uelman, Professor of Law, Loyola University, Los Angeles and Victor G. Haddox, Professor of Criminology, California State University at Long Beach and Clinical Professor of Psychiatry, Law and Behavioral Sciences, University of Southern California School of Medicine, 564 pages, 1974.

To Angus and Fred

*

Preface to the Second Edition

The Second Edition of Criminal Procedure for the Law Enforcement Officer contains a discussion of all developments in the law of criminal procedure of importance to law enforcement officers through November 1978. In the material added since the publication of the First Edition, I have concentrated primarily on decisions of the United States Supreme Court. A limited number of lower court decisions were also selected for inclusion based on their significance, their discussion of new issues, or their lucid illustration of legal principles. I also included some earlier decided cases which have taken on added significance in light of recent developments.

Several sections of the First Edition have been substantially revised and several new sections have been added to reflect recent developments in the law. Noteworthy among the revisions are an updated treatment of resistance to arrest and an extended discussion of warrantless entry of dwellings to arrest in Chapter 1; a reorganization of the discussion of the establishment of probable cause through the use of informants in Chapter 3; an explanation in Chapter 4 of the changes in the rules on search incident to arrest resulting from the United States Supreme Court decision in United States v. Chadwick; a discussion in Chapter 7 of impoundment and inventory of motor vehicles as affected by the United States Supreme Court decision in South Dakota v. Opperman; a discussion of and presentation of guidelines for multiple interrogations under *Miranda* in Chapter 9; an elaboration of the discussion in Chapter 10 of the justification for stopping and frisking based on an informant's tip; an updating of the Check List for Lineup Identifications, the guidelines for photographic identifications, and the section on the effect of improper identification procedure in Chapter 9; and a rewritten section on habeas corpus in Chapter 13.

Some of the important new sections in the Second Edition are as follows: in Chapter 1, new forms for an arrest warrant, a complaint, and a summons; in Chapter 2, new sections entitled History, Multiple Affidavits, Anticipatory Search Warrants, Administrative Search Warrants, and Effect of Illegal Search and Seizure, and new forms for an affidavit for a search warrant, a search warrant, and a return and inventory; in Chapter 5, several new sections on indications of voluntariness of consent; in Chapter 7, several new sections on the operation of the *Carroll* doctrine; in Chapter 9, new sections dealing with the effect of Fourth Amendment violations on the admissibility of statements, statements obtained after the defendant is formally charged, and the effect of *Miranda* in court; in Chapter 11, new sections discussing the effects of the United States Supreme Court cases of Neil v. Biggers and Manson v. Brathwaite; in Chapter 13, a new indictment form; and in Chapter 14, a discussion of several additional exceptions to the hearsay rule.

In both the revised material and the new material I have attempted to highlight two major continuing trends affecting all aspects of criminal procedure law. These trends are the emphasis of all courts on the individual's reasonable expectation of privacy as the touchstone of the Fourth Amendment and the reliance of many state courts on their state constitutions to place greater restrictions on law enforcement officers than those mandated by the United States Supreme Court. Both of these trends have been visible characteristics of the regime of the so-called Burger Court and seem to show no signs of waning.

I would like to thank Maine Assistant Attorney General Michael D. Seitzinger for giving his time and expertise to reading over the second edition manuscript and making suggestions for its improvement. In addition, I would like to thank the following criminal justice instructors for their helpful comments on the second edition manuscript: Mr. Richard E. Givan of Eastern Kentucky University, Professor Edward H. Horney of Delaware Technical and Community College, Mr. Arnold M. Jochums of the University of Southern Illinois, and Professor James W. Vandellen of Owens Technical College in Ohio. I would also like to express my appreciation to West Publishing Company for its assistance and cooperation throughout the development of the second edition. And I would like to especially thank Mary Lou Leahy for her invaluable assistance in the preparation and editing of the manuscript.

JOHN N. FERDICO

Dresden, Maine
January, 1979

Preface to the First Edition

The law of criminal procedure is not only complex, but is constantly changing. The law enforcement officer is expected to understand these complexities and keep abreast of the changes. More importantly, he is required to apply the law to diverse situations which do not always neatly conform to the principles set out to guide him. To compound the law enforcement officer's problem, most court opinions on criminal procedure are written in a rambling, legalistic style that even lawyers and judges have trouble understanding. The result is a gap of communication and understanding between those who make the rules (judges) and those who must enforce them (law enforcement officers). Violation of rights of citizens by officers who are unaware or ignorant of court-imposed limitations on their activities is one of the main causes of the failure of many prosecutions and the reversal of many convictions.

This book is an attempt to bridge the gap of communication and understanding between judges and law enforcement officers. I believe that law enforcement officers need understandable guidelines for conducting arrests, searches and seizures, interrogations, and lineups. I also believe that law enforcement officers should be familiar with the language and reasoning of the courts in these areas. Officers, however, should not be expected to read through long involved opinions of every state and federal case that affects them and to extract principles of law to guide them in the execution of their duties. They already carry a heavy enough burden. Reading and interpreting the law is the job of an attorney. Therefore, I have tried in this book to reduce the complexity of the law of criminal procedure into simple straight-forward advice illustrated with examples of actual cases. I have also used quotations from cases, when I believed they were written in clear, understandable language.

Since much of the law of criminal procedure is based on decisions of the United States Supreme Court, I have concentrated heavily on the facts and reasoning of most of the major decisions of that court. These Supreme Court decisions, however, are interpreted and refined by lower federal courts and state courts. As a result, the law of criminal procedure in every state differs in some way from that in every other state. Since this book is designed for use nationwide, it cannot deal with the peculiarities of the law of criminal procedure in any one state. Therefore, I have selected decisions of lower federal courts and state courts which appear to reflect the prevailing view of the law nationwide, and which I believe are well-reasoned and illuminating. Also, I have attempted to set out the safest procedure for a law enforcement officer to follow when there is a significant difference in opinion on a point of law among the courts. Officers should, however, consult state statutes and court decisions or local prosecuting attorneys for advice and assistance in enforcing the laws of their state.

I hope that this book will prove useful not only as a criminal procedure text, but also as a legal reference book for officers in the field. In order to keep the book current with the changing law, I plan to update it by means of yearly supplements. I welcome all comments and suggestions for improvement from readers.

Finally, I would like to express my appreciation to all those who assisted me in any way in the research and preparation of this book. I owe special gratitude to Maine Attorney General Jon A. Lund and Deputy Attorney General Richard S. Cohen for their support and cooperation, to my colleagues, Assistant Attorneys General Peter Goranites and Michael Seitzinger for their help and encouragement, and to Edith Hary and her staff at the Maine State Law Library for their invaluable assistance. I would also like to thank James B. Zagel, Chief of the Criminal Justice Division of the Illinois Attorney General's Office, and Patrick F. Healy, Executive Director of the National District Attorneys Association for granting me permission to use the publication *Confessions and Interrogations After Miranda* in the preparation of this book. Most of all, I would like to thank Mary Lou Leahy for devoting her entire summer to editing, proofreading, and typing the manuscript, but more importantly, for providing inspiration and understanding when I needed it.

JOHN N. FERDICO

Augusta, Maine
March, 1975

Summary of Contents

PART FOUR

PREPARATION OF A CASE FOR COURT

Table of Contents

PART ONE

ARREST, SEARCH WARRANTS, AND PROBABLE CAUSE

PART TWO

EXCEPTIONS TO THE SEARCH WARRANT REQUIREMENT

Chapter 7. Search and Seizure of Vehicles Without a Warrant—C't'd

PART THREE

ADMISSIONS AND CONFESSIONS, STOP AND FRISK, AND PRE-TRIAL IDENTIFICATION PROCEDURES

Chapter 9. Admissions and Confessions—Continued

PART FOUR

PREPARATION OF A CASE FOR COURT

*

Criminal Procedure for the Law Enforcement Officer

SECOND EDITION

†

PART ONE

ARREST, SEARCH WARRANTS, AND PROBABLE CAUSE

1

ARREST

The power of arrest is the most important power that a law enforcement officer possesses. It enables him to deprive a person of his freedom to carry out his daily affairs, and it initiates against a person the processes of criminal justice, which may ultimately result in that person being fined or imprisoned. Since an arrest has a potentially awesome impact upon a person's life, the law provides severe limitations and restrictions on the law enforcement officer's exercise of the power of arrest. It is therefore essential for every law enforcement officer to fully understand the body of law governing the arrest procedure.

This body of arrest law is based upon guarantees embodied in the United States Constitution. The familiar Fourth Amendment to the U. S. Constitution provides as follows:

> The right of the people to be secure in their *persons*, houses, papers, and effects, against unreasonable searches and seizures, shall not be violated, and no Warrants shall issue, but upon probable cause, supported by Oath or affirmation, and particularly describing the place to be searched and the *persons* or things *to be seized.* (emphasis supplied) U.S.C.A.Const. Amend. IV.

There is a common belief among law enforcement personnel that the Fourth Amendment, quoted above, applies only to searches and seizures of material things and not of people. The word "persons" has been emphasized in the above passage to indicate clearly that this amendment is not so restricted, but that it also protects individuals from illegal seizures of their persons, i. e. illegal arrests. Furthermore, the U. S. Supreme Court has dispelled any lingering uncertainty as to the status of illegal arrest under the Fourth Amendment in the 1959 case of Henry v. U. S.:

> [I]t is the command of the Fourth Amendment that no warrants either for searches or *arrests* shall issue except "upon probable cause * * *" (emphasis supplied) 361 U.S. 98, 100, 80 S.Ct. 168, 170, 4 L.Ed.2d 134, 137 (1959).

Keeping in mind this basic requirement that law enforcement officers must respect the rights guaranteed by the Fourth Amendment in order for an arrest to be valid, we turn now to the task of formulating a precise definition of arrest and discussing authority, execution, and various other aspects of the law of arrest.

DEFINITION OF ARREST

Numerous attempts have been made to frame an all-inclusive definition of arrest which would be applicable in all situations. None of these have been entirely satisfactory because arrest is a term which eludes exact definition. In effect, it is a legal conclusion used to describe a complex series of events which have in fact taken place.

Nevertheless, we include here the Maine Supreme Judicial Court's definition of arrest, which is readily understandable and is substantially the same as definitions given by courts in other jurisdictions, both state and federal:

> An arrest in criminal law "signifies the apprehension or detention of the person of another in order that he may be forthcoming to answer for an alleged or supposed crime." State v. MacKenzie, 161 Me. 123, 137, 210 A.2d 24, 32–33 (Supreme Judicial Court of Maine, 1965).

The Maine court went on to set out the basic elements necessary to constitute an arrest. These elements are:

1. A purpose or intention to effect an arrest under real or pretended authority;
2. An actual or constructive seizure or detention of the person to be arrested by one having the present power to control him;
3. A communication by the arresting officer to the one whose arrest is sought of his intention or purpose then and there to make the arrest; and
4. An understanding by the person who is to be arrested that it is the intention of the arresting officer then and there to arrest and detain him.

Each of these elements will be discussed separately in some detail.

Intention to Arrest

To satisfy this first requirement, there must be an intent on the part of the law enforcement officer to take a person into the custody of the law, and to deprive him of his liberty and freedom of movement at the time the officer takes control of him. This intent of the arresting officer to take the person into the custody of the law is the basic element which distinguishes an arrest from lesser forms of detention.

Lesser forms of detention may result from the many and varied situations confronting a law enforcement officer in his daily duties, in which the officer does not intend to actually take anyone into the custody of the law but merely stops or detains a person. The following are examples of common situations in which a law enforcement officer may detain a person, but in which technically there is no arrest:

1. Restraining a person who is behaving in a manner which is dangerous either to himself or others;
2. Stopping a person to find out his identity or to seek information relating to a possible crime;
3. Service of a subpoena or other process such as a summons or notice to appear in court;
4. Restraining an insane person who is presenting an immediate danger either to himself or others;
5. Asking a suspect or material witness to appear at the station for questioning;
6. Stopping a vehicle to inspect license, equipment, or load.

Although this is not a complete list, it illustrates the type of situation in which there is no intent by the law enforcement officer to take the person into the custody of the law. Without further action on the part of the officer there is no arrest.

There is one further detention situation which deserves mention in this context. This is the situation where police stop a person under suspicious circumstances and conduct a brief, general on-the-scene investigation about the possible commission of a crime. If, accompanying this brief detention of the person, there is a limited search of the person for possible weapons, this situation would be commonly referred to as "stop and frisk." There has been much discussion and several court decisions in this area over the last few years. Because of its importance stop and frisk will be discussed separately in Chapter 10. For purposes of this chapter, it is important to note that the ordinary stop and frisk situation does not involve an intention to arrest and therefore does not constitute an arrest.

A further requirement of arrest is that the restraint of the person be exercised under the authority of the law enforcement officer whether it be real authority or pretended. An example of pretended authority would be the situation where an officer makes an arrest without authority to do so but he assumes wrongfully that he does have the authority. It is still technically an arrest despite the officer's error. This requirement distinguishes arrest from the situation in which a person might be seized and detained without any type of authority being apparent or claimed. An example would be a kidnapping, when a person is seized but no one claims any kind of authority to arrest him.

Seizure or Detention

To technically constitute an arrest, the arrested person must come within the actual custody and control of the law enforcement officer. There are two kinds of seizure or detention which will satisfy this requirement—actual and constructive.

An actual seizure or detention is the taking into custody of a person with the use of hands or with force, including the use of weapons. The ordinary situation would include the grabbing, holding, or handcuffing of a person to restrain his freedom of action. However, the mere touching of the person of the accused is also considered to be an actual seizure and may constitute an arrest if the other elements of arrest are present. Childress v. State, 227 Md. 41, 175 A.2d 18 (Maryland Supreme Court, 1961).

A constructive seizure may be accomplished when the person being arrested submits to the control of the law enforcement officer without any physical force whatsoever being applied. His peaceable submission eliminates the need for manual force and it satisfies the requirement of seizure or detention.

Mere words of the officer such as "You are under arrest," without anything else, will not be sufficient to satisfy the seizure or detention element of arrest. There must be, in addition, an actual physical seizure of the person or a submission by him to the officer's will and control. Furthermore, the seizure need only be momentary and if the other necessary elements of arrest are present, the arrest is completed, even if it is followed by an immediate escape. The person does not have to be permanently confined in order to satisfy the seizure or detention requirement.

Communication and Understanding

The final two elements of arrest can be considered together because they are two aspects of the same issue. Briefly stated, the law enforcement officer's actions in making an arrest must result in an understanding on the part of the arrested party that he is being arrested. This understanding is ordinarily shown when the officer notifies the person that he is arresting him. However, facts and circumstances may make it obvious to the suspect that he is being arrested, such as when he is being handcuffed or otherwise physically restrained. The officer may never say a word but the circumstances convey the idea.

There is one exception to the rule that understanding is an essential element of arrest. Despite the fact that a person arrested is unconscious, insane, or so drunk that he is incapable of understanding anything, he may still be placed technically under arrest when his body is actually seized and restrained, even though his understanding is delayed until he regains consciousness. State v. Cram, 176 Or. 577, 160 P.2d 283 (Oregon Supreme Court, 1945).

ARREST AUTHORITY UNDER A WARRANT

Despite the fact that the authority of law enforcement officers and private citizens to arrest without a warrant in proper circumstances has been recognized for a long time, arrests made under the authority of a warrant have always been preferred. The reason for favoring the warrant procedure is that it places the sometimes delicate decision of determining whether there is probable cause to justify an arrest in the hands of an impartial judicial authority. The U. S. Supreme Court has said that " 'the informed and deliberate determinations of magistrates empowered to issue warrants * * * are to be preferred over the hurried action of officers' " Aguilar v. Texas, 378 U.S. 108, 110–111, 84 S.Ct. 1509, 1512, 12 L.Ed.2d 723, 726 (1964). This preference for warrants attempts to avoid placing responsibility for determining probable cause upon law enforcement officers and private citizens with the resulting danger of rash and ill advised action on their part.

Furthermore, if a warrant is proper on its face and the officer does not abuse his authority in executing the arrest, the officer is protected against civil liability for false arrest or false imprisonment, even though it is later determined that the arrest was unjustified. The officer is not so protected when he arrests without a warrant.

The Arrest Warrant

The arrest warrant is a written order, issued by a proper authority upon probable cause, directing the arrest of a particular person or persons. A typical form for an arrest warrant appears on page 9. The person issuing the arrest warrant could be a judge, a magistrate, a complaint justice, a justice of the peace, or a clerk of the court. Every jurisdiction authorizes different judicial officers to issue warrants, and it is up to each law enforcement officer to know who has the authority in his jurisdiction. For the remainder of this chapter, the term "magistrate" will be used to designate the judicial officer authorized to issue arrest warrants. The warrant is issued on the basis of a sworn statement, called the complaint, charging that a particularly described accused has committed a described offense against the state or the United States. The person swearing out the complaint is often a law enforcement officer.

The Complaint

The complaint must state the essential facts constituting the offense charged, including the time and place of its commission and the name of the accused or a reasonably definite description if the name is not known. It must be sworn to and signed by the person charging the offense (the complainant). A warrant issued upon an unsworn statement is void, and any arrest made under such a warrant is illegal. A typical complaint form appears on page 10.

The complaint is discussed in further detail in Chapter 13.

Probable Cause

Whether or not the complainant has personal knowledge of the facts connected with the offense, probable cause must be established to the magistrate's satisfaction that the offense charged in the complaint was committed and that the accused committed it. Probable cause, although incapable of precise definition, should be a familiar concept to every law enforcement officer. Probable cause exists where the facts and circumstances within a person's knowledge and of which he has reasonably trustworthy information are sufficient in themselves to warrant a man of reasonable caution and prudence in the belief that an offense has been or is being committed. Draper v. U. S., 358 U.S. 307, 313, 79 S.Ct. 329, 333, 3 L.Ed.2d 327, 332 (U.S. Supreme Court, 1959). It means something less than certainty but more than mere suspicion, speculation, or possibility. The magistrate must be satisfied that probable cause exists before he is empowered

Warrant for Arrest of Defendant (Rev. 7-52) Cr. Form No. 12

United States District Court

FOR THE

____

UNITED STATES OF AMERICA
v.
} No.

To [1]

You are hereby commanded to arrest and bring h forthwith before the United States District Court for the District of in the city of to answer to an charging h with

in violation of

Dated at ...., *Clerk.*

on ....19........

By ...., *Deputy Clerk.*

Bail fixed at $..

RETURN

District of ss

Received the within warrant the day of 19 and executed same.

....,

By ....,

[1] Insert designation of officer to whom the warrant is issued, e. g., "any United States Marshal or any other authorized officer"; or "United States Marshal for .... District of ...."; or "any United States Marshal"; or "any Special Agent of the Federal Bureau of Investigation"; or "any United States Marshal or any Special Agent of the Federal Bureau of Investigation"; or "any agent of the Alcohol Tax Unit."

[B9580]

Form A.O. 91 (Rev. 12-1-68) **Complaint**

United States District Court
FOR THE

____

UNITED STATES OF AMERICA v	Magistrate's Docket No. Case No. COMPLAINT for VIOLATION of U.S.C. Title Section

BEFORE_______________________, _______________________________,
Name of Magistrate — Address of Magistrate

The undersigned complainant being duly sworn states:

That on or about , 19 , at

in the

District of

(1)

did(2)

And the complainant states that this complaint is based on

And the complainant further states that he believes that

are material witnesses in relation to this charge.

_______________________________,
Signature of Complainant.

_______________________________,
Official Title.

Sworn to before me, and subscribed in my presence, _______________, 19____.

_______________________________,
United States Magistrate.

(1) Insert name of accused.
(2) Insert statement of the essential facts constituting the offense charged.

[B9581]

to issue an arrest warrant. The meaning of probable cause will be discussed in detail in Chapter 3.

Because of the probable cause requirement, a separate affidavit or affidavits setting forth in detail the facts and circumstances upon which probable cause is to be based are often filed with the original complaint. If there is room for it, these facts may be set forth in the original complaint. A separate affidavit need not be prepared with any particular formality and may merely be a sworn recitation of the facts upon which the complainant relies in seeking the issuance of a warrant. The magistrate may require additional affidavits of other persons having pertinent and reliable information upon which probable cause can be based. In any case, all information upon which probable cause is based should appear either in the original sworn complaint or in additional affidavits. The reason for this is to maintain a record of the evidence produced before the magistrate issuing the warrant in case the validity of the warrant is called into question at a later date.

Requirements of Arrest Warrant

The arrest warrant, once issued, should conform to certain requirements as follows:

1. The warrant must bear the caption of the court or division of the court from which it issues.
2. The person to be arrested must be named in the warrant if his name is known. If not known, the warrant should contain any name or description by which he can be identified with reasonable certainty. In other words, the warrant must show on its face that it is directed toward a particular individual.
3. The warrant should describe the offense charged in the complaint. This description should be in the language of the appropriate statute or ordinance. The important consideration, however, is that the description be in words definite enough for the accused to readily understand the charge against him. Stating that he is charged merely with "a felony" or "a misdemeanor" is insufficient and will invalidate the warrant.
4. The time of issuance of the warrant should be stated.
5. The warrant should be directed to an appropriate officer or officers and should command that the defendant be brought before the proper judicial official.
6. The warrant must be signed by the issuing magistrate and must state what his official title is.

Summons

All law enforcement officers should be aware that a magistrate is empowered to issue a summons instead of an arrest warrant in certain situations. The requirements for a summons are the same as those for a warrant except that a summons directs the defendant to appear before a court at a stated time and place rather than ordering his arrest. Court rules and statutes usually provide that if a defendant fails to appear in response to a summons, a warrant shall issue for his arrest. A typical summons form appears on page 13.

The summons is usually used in instances where the offense charged in the complaint is a violation of a municipal ordinance or some other misdemeanor or petty offense. If the offender is a citizen with his "roots firmly established in the soil of the community" so that he can be easily found for service of a warrant if he ignores the summons, the summons procedure is a much easier and better way of inducing the accused to appear in court, rather than arresting him and locking him up.

There is some confusion about the meaning of the term "summons", because it is often used to describe a citation, ticket, or notice to appear issued by a law enforcement officer, especially in traffic cases. Such a notice is *not* a summons in the legal sense because it is not issued by a magistrate on the basis of a complaint. The citation, ticket, or notice to appear merely gives notice to the offender that he may be arrested if he does not voluntarily appear in court to answer the charge against him.

ARREST AUTHORITY WITHOUT A WARRANT

The law enforcement officer in his daily duties will often be faced with the decision whether to apply for an arrest warrant or to make an arrest without a warrant. Since an officer often has to make an immediate decision in this respect, the inexperienced or poorly trained officer will run into problems if he does not know his rights and limitations. It thus becomes important for the officer to have a clear working knowledge of the law governing arrest without a warrant.

In order to determine whether he has the authority to arrest without a warrant, the officer must first know the difference between a felony and a misdemeanor because his authority depends upon the distinction between the two. In most state statutes, a felony is defined as any crime which is or may be punished by death or imprisonment in a state prison. Since most states do not provide for imprisonment in

Form A. O. 83 (Rev. 1970)

Magistrate's Summons

United States District Court

FOR THE

Magistrate's Docket No. ________

Case No. ________

UNITED STATES OF AMERICA

v

SUMMONS

To

Name of Defendant

You are hereby summoned to appear before the undersigned United States Magistrate

, at place

on , 19 , at time o'clock M. to answer to a complaint charging you

with here describe offense charged in complaint

in violation of U.S.C. Title Section

Date , 19

United States Magistrate.

This summons was received by me at on

19

Defendant.

RETURN*

This summons was served by me on , 19 in the following manner:

Name.,

Title.,

*As to who may serve the summons and the manner of its service see Rule 4 (c) of the Federal Rules of Criminal Procedure and Rule 4 (c) of the Rules of Civil Procedure.

[B9582]

the state prison unless the term of the sentence is one year or more, it is generally agreed that an offense is not a felony unless the penalty is at least one year's incarceration. It should be noted that it is the punishment which *may* be imposed that determines whether an offense is a felony or misdemeanor, not the penalty which finally *is* imposed. *Therefore, a felony can be defined as any offense for which the punishment could possibly be imprisonment for a term of one year or more. All offenses which do not amount to a felony are classified as misdemeanors.*

States differ greatly as to which specific offenses are classified as felonies and which are misdemeanors. It is very important for each law enforcement officer to familiarize himself with the classifications of offenses into felonies and misdemeanors in his state.

Misdemeanors

In most states, unless otherwise provided by statute, a law enforcement officer may make an arrest without a warrant for a misdemeanor only when the misdemeanor is "committed in his presence." Ordinarily, committed in his presence means that the officer sees an offense being committed with his own eyes and he makes the arrest. However, it may be dark or the officer's sight may be blocked or restricted for other reasons, and he may have to rely on his other senses. Realizing this, courts have held that an offense is committed in the officer's presence if he is able to perceive it through any of his five senses—sight, hearing, touch, taste, and smell. People v. Bock Leung Chew, 142 Cal.App.2d 400, 298 P.2d 118 (California Court of Appeals, 1959). Furthermore, the officer may use any legal mechanical or electrical means to enhance his senses such as field glasses, hearing aids, etc. People v. Steinberg, 148 Cal.App.2d 855, 307 P.2d 634 (California Court of Appeals, 1957). His knowledge of the offense may even come to him through information received from the suspect himself through an admission or confession. Cornish v. State, 215 Md. 64, 137 A.2d 170 (Maryland Supreme Court, 1957).

However, the mere fact that a misdemeanor is actually taking place in the officer's presence is not enough in itself to give him the authority to make an arrest. The officer must *know* that an offense is being committed *before* he makes the arrest. State v. Pluth, 157 Minn. 145, 195 N.W. 789 (Minnesota Supreme Court, 1923). Therefore, if an officer makes an arrest on mere suspicion or chance that an offense is being committed, and he later proves to be right, the arrest is not justified and is illegal.

If an officer comes upon the scene of a misdemeanor after the offense has been completed, he may *not* arrest the alleged offender without a warrant. This is true even though the offender is still at the scene, because the offense was not *committed in the officer's presence.* The officer has two choices when the misdemeanor offense has terminated before he arrives.

1. Invite the offender to voluntarily submit to custody;
2. Identify the offender and then seek a warrant for his arrest.

There is *no* authority to arrest for a *past* misdemeanor without a warrant.

Misdemeanor Arrests on Probable Cause

In recent years, some state legislatures have enacted laws making exceptions to the general rule that arrest without warrant for a misdemeanor is only authorized for offenses committed in the officer's presence. These enactments have authorized arrests for certain types of misdemeanors, such as fish and game violations or liquor violations, on probable cause alone. Since the laws of each state are different, each law enforcement officer must determine for what misdemeanor offenses, if any, his state law allows arrests on probable cause.

Promptness of Arrest

Time is a very important factor in making an arrest without a warrant for a misdemeanor committed in the officer's presence. The arrest must be made promptly and without unnecessary delay. The officer must set out to make the arrest at the time of the offense and continue his efforts until the arrest is accomplished or abandoned. As stated by the Supreme Court of Mississippi in a leading case on the subject:

> The arrest for misdemeanors committed or attempted in the presence of officers must be made as quickly after the commission of the offense as the circumstances will permit. After an officer has witnessed a misdemeanor, it is his duty to then and there arrest the offender. Under some circumstances, there may be justification for delay, as for instance, when the interval between the commission of the offense and the actual arrest is spent by the officer in pursuing the offender, or in summoning assistance where such may reasonably appear to be necessary; * * * If, however, the officer witnesses the commission of an offense and does not arrest the offender, but departs on other business, or for other purposes, and afterwards returns, he cannot then arrest the offender without a warrant; for then the reasons for allowing the arrest to be made without a warrant have disappeared. Smith v. State, 228 Miss. 476, 480, 87 So.2d 917, 919 (1956).

Therefore, a reasonable delay in making a warrantless misdemeanor arrest, which is closely connected with the offense itself or with an attempted flight by the offender, will usually not invalidate the arrest. Examples of reasonable delays would be delays to summon assistance in making the arrest, to plan strategy to overcome the resistance to arrest, to pursue a fleeing offender, or to take safety precautions. If the officer delays a warrantless misdemeanor arrest to do something unconnected with the process of arrest, however, the arrest will be unlawful. Such delays require an officer to obtain a warrant and to make the arrest in accordance with the warrant.

Felonies

A law enforcement officer may make a warrantless public arrest for a felony if, at the time of arrest, he has probable cause to believe that a felony has been committed and that the person to be arrested is committing or has committed the felony. In U. S. v. Watson, 423 U.S. 411, 96 S.Ct. 820, 46 L.Ed.2d 598 (1976), the U.S. Supreme Court said:

> Law enforcement officers may find it wise to seek arrest warrants where practicable to do so, and their judgments about probable cause may be more readily accepted where backed by a warrant issued by a magistrate. * * * But we decline to transform this judicial preference into a constitutional rule when the judgment of the Nation and Congress has for so long been to authorize warrantless public arrests on probable cause rather than to encumber criminal prosecutions with endless litigation with respect to the existence of exigent circumstances, whether it was practicable to get a warrant, whether the suspect was about to flee, and the like. 423 U.S. at 423–424, 96 S.Ct. at 827–828, 46 L.Ed.2d at 608–609.

Some states, however, either by statute or by court interpretation of the state constitution, place greater restrictions on the arrest authority of law enforcement officers. In People v. Hoinville, 191 Colo. 357, 553 P.2d 777 (Colorado Supreme Court, 1976), the court held that a state statute providing that "[a]n arrest warrant should be obtained when practicable," required police officers to obtain a warrant whenever possible. Officers must determine whether their state has similar requirements and, if so, they must obey them.

Assuming that most states allow warrantless felony arrests on probable cause, the key terms the law enforcement officer must know to determine his authority are "felony" and "probable cause." "Felony" has already been defined in an earlier section of this chapter as any offense for which the punishment could possibly be imprisonment for a term of one year or more. It should only be noted that, in order to apply the definition of felony, the officer must have a thorough knowledge of the definitions and possible range of punishments for all crimes in his state.

Probable Cause

Probable cause has also been defined earlier in relation to the requirements for the issuance of an arrest warrant. It has the same meaning with respect to arrests without a warrant except that it is the law enforcement officer and not the magistrate who must be convinced that the offense was committed and that the suspect committed it. It should be emphasized that the officer must be in possession of concrete facts or information linking the suspect to the specific offense in question. With anything less, the officer takes his chances of having the arrest declared unlawful.

The basis for probable cause may arise through facts or information which the officer himself has personally observed or gathered. It may also be based upon apparently reliable information from third parties such as the victim, other police agencies, witnesses, reporters, informants, etc. The defendant's reputation or criminal record *alone*, without further suspicious circumstances, will *not* be enough to give an officer probable cause to justify an arrest. However, if there are other circumstances, combined with the defendant's reputation, then together they might be enough. U. S. ex rel. Coffey v. Fay, 344 F.2d 625 (2nd Circuit Court of Appeals, 1965).

It is important to note that probable cause is to be evaluated from the collective information of the police at the time of the arrest and not merely on the personal knowledge of the arresting officer. Therefore, if the knowledge of the police in its totality shows probable cause, a law enforcement officer who makes a warrantless arrest upon orders to do so is acting on probable cause, even though he personally does not have all the information upon which probable cause is based. State v. Smith, Me., 277 A.2d 481 (Supreme Judicial Court of Maine, 1971). Even if the collective knowledge of the police is not sufficient to establish probable cause, an officer arresting upon orders will be protected from civil and criminal liability. The arrest in this situation, however, would be unlawful, because it was not based on probable cause. Whiteley v. Warden, 401 U.S. 560, 91 S.Ct. 1031, 28 L.Ed.2d 306 (U.S. Supreme Court, 1971).

A law enforcement officer has probable cause to believe that a suspect has committed a particular felony if the officer knows that an arrest warrant has been issued and is still outstanding against the suspect for the commission of that felony. An officer with such knowledge has the authority to arrest the defendant despite the fact that he does not have nor does his department have the warrant. Bartlett v. U. S., 232 F.2d 135 (5th Circuit Court of Appeals, 1956).

If an officer making an arrest has probable cause to believe that a felony has been committed and that the defendant is the one who committed it, it makes no difference whether the officer was right or wrong in making the arrest or that the defendant was later acquitted of the crime for which he was arrested. The officer is still justified in making the arrest and it is a legal arrest. On the other hand, if the officer, on a hunch or intuition, makes a warrantless arrest without probable cause, it makes no difference whether the defendant is guilty or not. The arrest is still illegal. Therefore, probable cause is the main consideration in determining the validity of an arrest.

Probable cause will be discussed in detail in Chapter 3.

Promptness of Arrest

Unlike a warrantless arrest for a misdemeanor, which must be made immediately, a warrantless arrest for a felony may be made after some delay. This is true whether or not the felony was committed in the officer's presence. Carlo v. U. S., 282 F.2d 841 (2nd Circuit Court of Appeals, 1961). Delay may be justified for a variety of reasons, as long as the delay is not designed to prejudice the offender's constitutional rights. Thus an officer may postpone making an arrest to complete further undercover work, to avoid alerting other potential offenders, to protect the identity of undercover agents or informers, or for various other lawful reasons. As the U.S. Supreme Court has said:

> The police are not required to guess at their peril the precise moment at which they have probable cause to arrest a suspect, risking a violation of the Fourth Amendment if they act too soon, and a violation of the Sixth Amendment if they wait too long. Law enforcement officers are under no constitutional duty to call a halt to a criminal investigation the moment they have the minimum evidence to establish probable cause, a quantum of evidence which may fall far short of the amount necessary to support a criminal prosecution. Hoffa v. U. S., 385 U.S. 293, 310, 87 S.Ct. 408, 417, 17 L.Ed.2d 374, 386 (1966).

Nevertheless, an extended period of delay between the time of the offense and the time of arrest may be so great as to give rise to a presumption that the accused was prejudiced by it. Jackson v. U. S., 122 U.S.App.D.C. 124, 351 F.2d 821 (District of Columbia Court of Appeals, 1965). Therefore, unless there is good reason for delaying the arrest, it should be made as soon as possible after the offense.

EFFECTING THE ARREST

As stated earlier, in order to effect an arrest, a law enforcement officer must bring the accused under his power of control, or the accused must submit to the custody of the officer. The arrest may be made by actually laying hands on the accused. If there is such physical contact with the accused, only the slightest amount of touching or force is necessary. There does not have to be actual capture or retention of a person in order for there to be a legal arrest.

If there is no touching or physical contact with the accused, any action of the officer is sufficient which shows an intention of the officer to take the accused into custody, *provided* the accused submits to the direction of the officer. However, if the accused is not restrained of his liberty and brought within the power or control of the law, there is no arrest.

Notice Required by the Officer

When a law enforcement officer is making an arrest, he should, whenever possible, give notice of the following things to the person being arrested:

1. He should make known his authority by giving his identity if it is not obvious or already known to the suspect. An officer's uniform or a display of his badge is a sufficient indication of authority for this purpose. Wilson v. Superior Court, 46 Cal.2d 291, 294 P.2d 36 (Supreme Court of California, 1956).
2. He should announce his intention to take the suspect into custody. This may be done by simply telling the person that he is under arrest. State v. Parker, Mo., 378 S.W.2d 274 (Missouri Court of Appeals, 1964).
3. He should announce the correct grounds or reason for making the arrest. This does not need to be in technical language and need not precede the arrest. U. S. v. Robinson, 325 F.2d 391 (2nd Circuit Court of Appeals, 1963).

Failure to give notice of the grounds of arrest or stating the wrong grounds will not make an arrest illegal. It is therefore not an absolute requirement for a valid arrest. Gearing v. State, Miss., 185 So.2d 652 (Supreme Court of Mississippi, 1966). However, if the officer does not announce his authority, and his identity is unknown, the suspect has a right to resist the arrest as an unlawful assault on his person. The suspect has this right whether or not he is guilty of an offense. Daniel v. State, Fla.App., 132 So.2d 312 (District Court of Appeal of Florida, 1961).

There are certain situations in which it is not practical for the officer to give any notice when he is making an arrest. These situations are:

1. When it would endanger the officer to do so;
2. When it would adversely affect his making the arrest;
3. When the person to be arrested is in the act of committing the crime. Squadrito v. Griebsch, 1 N.Y.2d 471, 154 N.Y.S. 2d 37, 136 N.E.2d 504 (New York Court of Appeals, 1956);
4. When the person to be arrested is fleeing the scene of the crime.

Time of Arrest

An arrest, whether under authority of a warrant or lawfully made without a warrant, may be made on any day of the week and at any time of the day or night, unless otherwise provided in the warrant or by statute. However, common sense dictates that, if possible, arrests should not be made at unreasonable hours of the night or early morning or on the Sabbath.

Effecting the Arrest Under a Warrant

There are some additional considerations involved in effecting an arrest when under authority of a warrant. First of all, when an officer is directed to serve a warrant of arrest, any questions as to his reasonable belief in the guilt of the defendant or his personal knowledge of facts pertaining to the offense are immaterial. There is no requirement that the offense be committed in his presence or that he have reasonable grounds of suspicion that the defendant committed the offense. His duty and authority require him to carry out the command as stated in the warrant and the only questions which concern him are (1) whether the person arrested is the one for whom the warrant was issued, and (2) whether the warrant is valid or fair on its face.

When the accused is identified in the warrant by name, the law enforcement officer is required to exercise reasonable diligence to make sure that he is arresting the person designated in the warrant and no other. If the person being arrested denies his identity and there is a reasonably simple and direct means of checking, the officer may incur liability if he fails to check and goes ahead with the arrest. Wallner v. Fidelity & Deposit Co. of Maryland, 253 Wis. 66, 33 N.W.2d 215 (Supreme Court of Wisconsin, 1948). The same holds true where the warrant merely describes the person to be arrested without naming him. The officer must be very careful in determining whether the person arrested is the person identified in the warrant.

The requirement that the warrant be valid or fair on its face is important, because a warrant which is not valid on its face gives the officer no protection. He acts without authority insofar as such a warrant is concerned. Therefore, the officer is bound to examine the warrant and if it is obviously bad, he acts at his peril in carrying it out. While he is not concerned with the actual facts of the case, he is bound to know the law.

In order to determine whether a warrant is valid on its face, the officer must look to several things. First of all, if the court issuing the warrant clearly has no jurisdiction, the warrant is void on its face. Likewise, the warrant is void if it does not disclose any legal offense charged against the person to be arrested, or if it fails to name or describe any identifiable person. Gattus v. State, 204 Md. 589, 105 A.2d 661 (Court of Appeals of Maryland, 1954). A warrant that is not signed by the issuing magistrate is also void on its face.

Once it has been determined that the warrant is valid on its face, the officer must carry it out and serve it on the named individual. He no longer has any discretion of his own and is merely carrying out the command of the court:

> When the warrant purports to be for a matter within the jurisdiction of the justice (magistrate), the ministerial officer is obliged to execute it, and of course must be justified by it. He cannot inquire upon what evidence the judicial officer proceeded, or whether he committed an error or irregularity in his decision * * *, the constable has nothing to look to but the warrant as his guide * * *. Alexander v. Lindsey, 230 N.C. 663, 667, 55 S.E.2d 470, 473–74 (Supreme Court of North Carolina, 1949).

The officer executing the warrant must also check the warrant to see that he is either specifically named or comes within the class of officers designated to serve the warrant. If the warrant is directed to all law enforcement officers in the state, it is permissible for any authorized officer to execute it. If, however, the warrant is directed only to a sheriff of a certain county, for example, only that sheriff or his deputy can execute it.

Most states have statutes allowing arrest warrants for violations of state law to be executed at any place within the boundaries of the state. However, a law enforcement officer of one state may not go into another state to arrest under a warrant except in cases of fresh pursuit, which will be discussed later.

When actually making the arrest under the warrant, the officer should give the same notice that he would ordinarily give in making any arrest. Also the officer should have the warrant in his possession at the time of arrest and he should show the warrant to the party arrested. In some states, however, statutes provide that an officer may make a legal arrest pursuant to a warrant even though the warrant is not in his possession. If he does so, however, he must inform the defendant of the offense charged and of the fact that a warrant has been issued. If the defendant requests, the officer must show him the warrant as soon as possible.

It should be noted that, like a warrantless arrest for a felony, an arrest made under a warrant (for a felony or misdemeanor) need not be made immediately. The officer has considerable discretion as to the time and place of making an arrest under a warrant. He may have lawful strategic reasons for delay or he may wish to select a time when the arrest can be accomplished with the least difficulty. As one court stated:

> [O]rdinarily there is no legal requirement that a warrant of arrest must be executed immediately or at the first opportunity * * * While its execution should not be unreasonably delayed there may be perfectly valid reasons why further investigation should be made before the drastic step is taken of arresting a citizen on a criminal charge. Certainly there is no constitutional right to be arrested promptly or otherwise. U. S. v. Joines, 258 F.2d 471, 472–73 (3rd Circuit Court of Appeals, 1958).

In State v. Heyer, 16 Or.App. 22, 517 P.2d 314 (Oregon Court of Appeals, 1973), the court held that a sixteen-month delay before arresting the defendant was reasonable. The justification for the delay was that the informant was a girl in her junior year of high school, and revealing her identity would have made her known to the students whom she had been investigating.

The arrest warrant will usually direct the officer to make a return of the warrant and to explain what he has done in carrying out the command of the warrant. Officers should carefully comply with the instructions in the warrant and with any state statutory provisions dealing with the return of warrants. If neither the warrant nor a statute provides instructions on returning the warrant, the officers should still return the warrant to the judicial officer who issued it and explain what he has done in obedience to it or why he has done nothing. Unless prescribed by statute, no particular form of return is required.

If a law enforcement officer fails to make a return after executing a warrant, the arrest made under the warrant may be held invalid. The officer would then be unprotected by the warrant if he were sued for false arrest, false imprisonment, or some other wrongful act arising out of the arrest.

Service of Summons

As discussed above, a magistrate may, under certain circumstances, issue a summons instead of an arrest warrant. A summons is served upon a defendant by delivering a copy to him personally, or by leaving it at his dwelling house or usual place of abode with some person of suitable age and discretion who resides there. It may also be served by mailing it to the defendant's last known address. As with an arrest warrant, most states provide that a summons for a violation of state law may be served at any place within the state. Also, a summons must be returned by the officer serving it to the proper magistrate before the return date appearing on the summons.

Aid in Making the Arrest

A law enforcement officer may request a private citizen to aid him in making an arrest. The laws of some states require that any person so called upon by a law enforcement officer to assist him in the execution of his official duties, including the arrest of another person, is legally obligated to obey the officer. If the person refuses or neglects to aid the officer, he may be punished for his refusal. When a private citizen acts in aid of a known law enforcement officer, he has the same rights and privileges that the officer has. While so acting, he has the status of a temporary law enforcement officer. As such, he has the right to use force and to enter property. If the person called upon acts in good faith, he does not have to inquire into the authority of the officer making the arrest. He is protected from liability even if the officer was acting illegally:

> It would be manifestly unfair to impose civil liability upon a private person for doing that which the law declares it a misdemeanor for him to refuse to do. Peterson v. Robison, 43 Cal.2d 690, 697, 277 P.2d 19, 24 (Supreme Court of California, 1954).

Using Discretion in Deciding Not to Arrest

There are many situations in which a law enforcement officer clearly has the power and authority to arrest but good police practice indicates that he should not exercise that power. Although it is beyond the scope of this chapter to give detailed guidelines in this area, a brief discussion is necessary to set out general principles.

Most important, a law enforcement officer should be guided by the principle that his primary job is to protect the public at large. Therefore, when an arrest might either cause greater risk of harm to the public or would only cause embarrassment to an individual who poses no real threat to the community, proper police practice may call for a decision not to exercise the full extent of the officer's arrest powers.

For example, when a crowd is present, it is often unwise to arrest a person or persons who are creating a minor disturbance. There is always the danger of aggravating the disturbance and possibly precipitating a riot or civil disorder. If there is a less drastic way to handle the matter, it should be explored even though there may be actual legal grounds for an arrest. The same considerations apply to minor domestic disputes or the handling of intoxicated persons who are creating no danger and may need no more than an assist in getting home. *It should always be remembered that an arrest is a significant restraint on a person's freedom and should always be justified by circumstances.*

Some local law enforcement agencies have definite policies covering the behavior of officers in this area. If there are no such policies, the individual officer will be called upon to exercise his own common sense and good judgment. *In any case, the officer should realize that not all situations in which he may make an arrest are situations in which he necessarily should make an arrest.*

PLACE OF ARREST

Most states have statutes providing that a law enforcement officer, when acting under authority of a warrant, may make an arrest at any place within the state where the defendant may be found. Similarly, the officer may serve a summons at any place within the state.

However, an officer generally has no official authority to arrest *without* a warrant outside of the territorial or geographical limits of the county or district for which he has been elected or appointed. This area is usually referred to as his *bailiwick.* Thus, a sheriff may not arrest without a warrant beyond the county in which he has been elected, nor may a municipal police officer arrest without a warrant beyond the limits of the city in which he has been appointed. On the other hand, the authority of state law enforcement officers is statewide and their power to arrest without a warrant runs throughout the state.

A law enforcement officer of one state has no authority to arrest in another state except as a private citizen or when in fresh pursuit. Both of these exceptions will be discussed in further detail.

Citizen's Arrest Authority

The general rule limiting an officer's warrantless arrest powers to his own bailiwick does not completely prevent him from making an arrest without a warrant outside his bailiwick. As a private citizen, the officer has the same authority as any other private citizen to make an arrest without a warrant. This authority comes from the common law, which is a body of unwritten law, developed in England and based upon court decisions that receives its binding force from traditional usage, custom, and universal acceptance. Under the common law rule in force in most states, a private citizen has the authority to arrest any person whom he has probable cause to believe has committed a felony. However, he can justify the arrest only by further showing that the felony was *actually committed.* The citizen's arrest authority, therefore, differs significantly from the arrest authority of a law enforcement officer operating within his bailiwick. The private citizen acts at his peril if no felony was actually committed, whereas a law enforcement officer is protected as long as the arrest is based on probable cause.

A private citizen has the further authority under the common law, to arrest for felonies and "breach of peace" misdemeanors *committed in his presence.* In the case of a felony, exercise of the authority to arrest is not only a privilege but a duty. There is no clear definition of "breach of the peace" misdemeanors, but practically speaking, the misdemeanor must cause or threaten direct harm to the public. While this does not mean the harm must always be physical, this will usually be the case.

Therefore, the law enforcement officer may, in a state where the common law rule on citizen's arrest is followed, arrest without a warrant under the above circumstances anywhere in his state without regard to whether or not he is within his bailiwick. Furthermore, unless neighboring states have modified the common law rule regarding citizen's arrest, a law enforcement officer has further arrest authority outside the borders of his state as a private citizen. It would be wise, however, for every officer to be familiar with the laws of his state and of neighboring states before making a citizen's arrest, because several states have enacted statutes that differ from the common law.

Fresh Pursuit

Under the common law and most statutes, the area within which a law enforcement officer may make a lawful arrest without a warrant may also be extended beyond the borders of his bailiwick in cases of fresh pursuit. Fresh pursuit refers to the situation in which an officer is attempting to make an arrest for an offense within his bailiwick, and the offender flees into another jurisdiction to avoid arrest, with the officer immediately pursuing him. The common law allowed warrantless arrests in fresh pursuit only in felony cases, but today most state statutes allow such arrests both for felonies and misdemeanors. In order for the warrantless arrest made in fresh pursuit to be legal, the following conditions must be met:

1. The officer must have had valid authority to arrest for the offense in the first place;
2. The pursuit must be of a fleeing criminal attempting to avoid immediate capture; and
3. The pursuit must have been started promptly and maintained continuously.

The main thing to remember is that the pursuit should be fresh. It must flow out of the act of attempting to make an arrest and be a part of the continuous process of apprehension. This does not mean that the pursuit has to be instantaneous but it does have to be made without unreasonable delay or interruption. There should not be any side trips or diversions even for outside police business. However, the pursuit is not legally broken by unavoidable interruptions connected with the act of apprehension such as eating, sleeping, summoning assistance, or obtaining further information.

Outside State Boundaries

Fresh pursuit may sometimes carry the law enforcement officer outside the boundaries of his state. Ordinarily, an officer has no authority beyond that of a private citizen to make arrests in another state. However, many states have adopted the "Uniform Act on Fresh Pursuit" or similar legislation, which permits law enforcement officers from other states, entering their state in fresh pursuit, to make an arrest. The Uniform Fresh Pursuit Law of Iowa is typical and is quoted below:

> Any member of a duly organized state, county, or municipal law enforcement unit of another state of the United States who enters this state in fresh pursuit, and continues within this state in such fresh pursuit, of a person in order to arrest him on the ground that he is believed to have committed a felony in such other state, shall have the same authority to arrest and hold such person in custody, as has any member of any duly organized state, county or municipal law enforcement unit of this state to arrest and hold in custody a person on the ground that he is believed to have committed a felony in this state. Iowa Code Ann. § 756.1.

Since some states extend the privilege to out-of-state officers to make an arrest in fresh pursuit only on a reciprocity basis, it is important for law enforcement officers to be familiar not only with their state's statute, but also with the fresh pursuit statutes of all neighboring states.

A law enforcement officer who makes an arrest in fresh pursuit under such a statute in a neighboring state must take the person arrested before an appropriate court without unreasonable delay. The best procedure is to immediately contact law enforcement personnel in that state for advice and aid in locating the right court. Also, officers of every state which has adopted the Uniform Act or a similar act should be prepared to assist officers from other states who have made arrests in fresh pursuit in their state.

Some states allow an arresting officer from another state to take a person arrested in fresh pursuit back to the officer's home state after the arrested person is brought before an appropriate court. Other states allow removal of a person arrested by an out-of-state officer in fresh pursuit only upon extradition or waiver of extradition. Extradition is a procedure whereby authorities in one state (the demanding state) demand from another state (the asylum state) that a fugitive from justice in the demanding state, who is present in the asylum state, be delivered to the demanding state. Most states have adopted the Uniform Criminal Extradition Act, which provides uniform extradition procedures among the states.

USE OF FORCE

A law enforcement officer making an arrest has the right only to use that amount of force reasonably necessary to effect the arrest and to detain the arrestee. The officer may use reasonable force also to:

1. Overcome the offender's resistance to lawful arrest;
2. Prevent his escape;
3. Retake him if he escapes; and
4. Protect himself from bodily harm.

Of course, reasonable force depends upon all the facts and circumstances surrounding the arrest as they appear to the arresting officer, as a prudent and cautious man, before and at the time of making the arrest. Some of the facts and circumstances to be considered are the nature of the offense, the defendant's reputation, the available help, the presence of weapons, and the defendant's words or actions.

Under no circumstances, however, is an officer permitted to use unreasonable force or subject the offender to wanton violence in effecting an arrest. All law enforcement officers should remember that the sole purpose of an arrest is to bring the alleged offender before a court of law and not to given an officer the opportunity of wreaking public or personal vengeance upon the prisoner.

In general, the amount of force which may be used in making an arrest (outside of self defense) depends on whether the offense is a felony or a misdemeanor. The more serious the offense, usually the greater degree of latitude the officer has in using forcible means.

Felonies

Felonies are considered to be serious offenses and therefore, the use of strong measures may be justified to overcome resistance and effect an arrest. Stinnett v. Virginia, 55 F.2d 644 (4th Circuit Court of Appeals, 1932). Under the common law rule, the officer need not retreat or desist from his purpose to arrest in order to avoid the necessity of resorting to extreme measures, but he must stand his ground and use all necessary force to bring the offender into his custody. However, the use of deadly force is permitted only as a last resort where otherwise the officer would have to give up his attempts.

In this context, it is important to remember that the officer always has the right to summon aid. As mentioned above, some states require every private citizen by law to assist an officer in making an arrest, if so requested. Therefore, the officer will not be justified in using firearms or other deadly force if the arrest can be accomplished or flight prevented by summoning and using such assistance.

Furthermore, the law enforcement officer should have *actual knowledge* both that a felony has been or is being committed and that the person to be arrested committed it before using deadly force in making an arrest or preventing flight. *Although courts have differed in this area, it is clear that an officer uses deadly force at his own peril if the wrong person is injured or killed or no felony has been committed.* Even though the officer is justified in making an *arrest* on probable cause, if he is in fact proven wrong, he may *not* be able to legally justify a *killing or maiming* to effect that arrest.

It is worthy of note that there has been much criticism of the common law rule with regard to the use of deadly force in felony cases. In response to this criticism, the following change in the rule was proposed in Section 3.07(2)(b) of the Model Penal Code:

> The use of deadly force is not justifiable under this Section unless:
> (i) the arrest is for a felony; and
> (ii) the person effecting the arrest is authorized to act as a peace officer or is assisting a person whom he believes to be authorized to act as a peace officer; and
> (iii) the actor believes that the force employed creates no substantial risk of injury to innocent persons; and
> (iv) the actor believes that:
> (1) the crime for which the arrest is made involved conduct including the use or threatened use of deadly force; or

(2) there is substantial risk that the person to be arrested will cause death or serious bodily harm if his apprehension is delayed.

Some states may have adopted this section of the Model Penal Code or some other changes in the law, either by statute or by court decision. Officers should make sure they know the law in their state. Very serious consequences can arise from the unwarranted use of deadly force, such as death or injury to the officer or other persons, or liability of the officer both civilly and criminally.

Misdemeanors

In arresting for a misdemeanor, a law enforcement officer is entitled to use whatever physical force is reasonably necessary under the circumstances to make an arrest or prevent flight. However, except in cases of self-defense, the officer is *never* justified in using firearms or other deadly force to effect an arrest in a misdemeanor case. *The rule is that it is better that a misdemeanant escape rather than a human life be taken.* The reason for this rule is that usually, the security of life and property is not significantly endangered by a misdemeanant being at large, while the safety and security of society usually require the speedy arrest and containment of a felon. Holloway v. Moser, 193 N.C. 185, 136 S.E. 375 (Supreme Court of North Carolina, 1927). Shooting or using other deadly force toward a suspect in a misdemeanor case is excessive force constituting an assault. If the officer kills the suspect, he may be guilty of murder or manslaughter.

Self Defense

Regardless of whether the offense is a felony or misdemeanor, the law enforcement officer, in making a lawful arrest, may use whatever force is necessary under the circumstances, including deadly force, if the officer reasonably believes that the suspect is about to assault him and that the officer will thereby be placed in peril of death or serious injury. The duty of the officer is to be the aggressor and press forward to place the person under restraint. This cannot be accomplished by purely defensive action on the officer's part. Therefore, if the officer has lawful authority to make an arrest, he is not required to back down in the face of physical resistance to the arrest. State v. Williams, 29 N.J. 27, 148 A.2d 22 (New Jersey Supreme Court, 1959). When the officer is faced with the choice of abandoning the arrest or using deadly weapons in *self defense,* he has the right to use them if it becomes necessary to protect himself. Again, it is the officer's obligation to do his duty and continue his efforts, matching force with force, even to the extent of using deadly weapons if necessary.

Many law enforcement agencies have departmental policies with regard to self defense and these should be consulted and followed whenever possible.

Resistance to Arrest

In our discussion of the use of force, we must consider not only the use of force by law enforcement officers, but also the use of force against them. Probably the most common instance of use of force against law enforcement officers is resistance to arrest. Resistance to arrest means opposition by direct, forcible means against an officer's person in order to prevent him from taking the accused into custody. Under statutes defining the offense of resisting arrest, indirect interference or hindrance of an officer will usually not support a conviction. Resistance requires active opposition such as shooting, striking, pushing, or otherwise struggling with the officer. Therefore, mere flight, concealment, or other avoidance or evasion of arrest will not constitute resistance. In the language of the Virginia Supreme Court of Appeals:

> The fact that the accused sought to escape the officer by merely running away was not such an obstruction as the law contemplates. While it is the duty of every citizen to submit to a lawful arrest, yet flight is not such an offense as will make a person amenable to the charge of resisting or obstructing an officer who is attempting to make an arrest, as there is a broad distinction between avoidance and resistance or obstruction. Jones v. Commonwealth, 141 Va. 471, 478, 126 S.E. 74, 76–77 (1925).

Nor will verbal objections, protests, or threats unaccompanied by force or danger constitute resistance. (It should be noted, however, that such behavior may constitute a violation of some other statute prohibiting the hindrance, intimidation, or obstruction of a law enforcement officer.) If, however, a threat is of a serious nature, accompanied by the apparent ability and present intention to execute it, and the officer is prevented from acting because of his reasonable fear of serious bodily injury, the threat may constitute resistance to arrest.

Under the common law rule, the offense of resisting arrest requires that the arrest be lawful. If the arrest is unlawful, the person being arrested has the *right* to resist. Also, the person being arrested has a right to resist, if the person making the arrest is not an officer of the law, or if the officer does not proceed in a lawful manner in making the arrest. Therefore, it is very important for a law enforcement officer, when making an arrest

1. to establish his identity, if not already known or obvious, and
2. to explain his purpose and authority.

According to the common law rule, a person threatened with an illegal arrest may not only resist the arrest, but may use such force as may be reasonably necessary to defend himself and prevent an impending injury. State v. McGowan, 243 N.C. 431, 90 S.E.2d 703 (Supreme Court of North Carolina, 1956). Since the impending injury resulting from an arrest is ordinarily only a brief unlawful detention, the degree of force a person may use is strictly limited. If he uses more force than is reasonably necessary for the purpose, he may be guilty of an assault and battery on the officer. Deadly force is rarely justified to resist an unlawful arrest, except when a person has reasonable grounds to fear death or great bodily injury at the hands of an officer.

It should be noted that the law on resisting arrest and on other interferences with law enforcement officers is in a state of flux and differs from state to state. For example, some states do not allow a private citizen to use force to resist an arrest made by one who the citizen knows or has good reason to believe is an authorized police officer engaged in the performance of his duties, whether or not the arrest is illegal. If, however, the officer uses excessive and unnecessary force in effecting the arrest, the citizen may respond or counter with reasonable force to protect himself. As stated by the Supreme Court of New Jersey:

> Despite his duty to submit quietly without physical resistance to an arrest made by an officer acting in the course of his duty, even though the arrest is illegal, his right to freedom from unreasonable seizure and confinement can be protected, restored and vindicated through legal processes. However, the rule permitting reasonable resistance to excessive force of the officer, whether the arrest is lawful or unlawful, is designed to protect a person's bodily integrity and health and so permits resort to self-defense. Simply stated, the law recognizes that liberty can be restored through legal processes but life or limb cannot be repaired in a courtroom. And so it holds that the reason for outlawing resistance to an unlawful arrest and requiring disputes over its legality to be resolved in the courts has no controlling application on the right to resist an officer's excessive force. * * *
>
> Two qualifications on the citizen's right to defend against and to repel an officer's excessive force must be noticed. He cannot use greater force in protecting himself against the officer's unlawful force than reasonably appears to be necessary. If he employs such greater force, then he becomes the aggressor and forfeits the right to claim self-defense to a charge of assault and battery on the

> officer. * * * Furthermore, if he knows that if he desists from his physically defensive measures and submits to arrest the officer's unlawfully excessive force would cease, the arrestee must desist or lose his privilege of self-defense. State v. Mulvihill, 57 N.J. 151, 156–57, 270 A.2d 277, 280 (1970).

As illustrated by the *Mulvihill* case, the modern trend is away from the common law rule allowing resistance to any illegal arrest, because of the dangers inherent in the rule and because the consequences of an illegal arrest are at the most a brief period of detention during which the arrested person can resort to nonviolent legal remedies for regaining his liberty. It is important for each law enforcement officer to determine whether his state operates under the common law rule, some modification of that rule, or some newly created rule.

Entry of Dwellings

According to the common law, the right of a law enforcement officer to enter a dwelling to effect an arrest depends upon whether he has legal authority to arrest. If he has the legal authoity to arrest, whether with or without a warrant, he also has the authority to enter any dwelling house, forcibly if necessary, and search for the suspect when he has probable cause to believe that the person whom he seeks to arrest is in that dwelling house. As stated by the 9th Circuit Court of Appeals:

> An agent must have probable cause to believe that the person he is attempting to arrest, with or without a warrant, is in a particular building at the time in question before that agent can legitimately enter the building by ruse or any other means. To hold otherwise is to grant the agent a license to go from house to house employing ruse entries in violation of the right of privacy of the respective occupants. U. S. v. Phillips, 497 F.2d 1131, 1136 (1974).

This authority to enter a dwelling house to arrest applies even to misdemeanor cases if the officer has legal authority to make an arrest for a misdemeanor.

It is worthy of note that the rule allowing forcible entry of dwellings in all situations where there is legal authority to arrest has come under some criticism in recent years. The U. S. Supreme Court gave notice that a constitutional issue might be involved in a warrantless entry to arrest in the case of Jones v. U. S., 357 U.S. 493, 78 S.Ct. 1253, 2 L.Ed.2d 1514 (1958). The Court's opinion noted that "whether the forcible nighttime entry into a dwelling to arrest a person reasonably believed within, upon probable cause that he had committed a felony, under circumstances where no reason appears why an arrest warrant could not have been sought" raised a "grave constitutional question." 357 U.S. at 499–500, 78 S.Ct. at 1257, 2 L.Ed.2d at 1519. In the 1971 case of Coolidge v. New Hampshire, 403 U.S. 443, 91 S.Ct. 2022, 29 L.Ed.2d 564 (1971), the U. S. Supreme Court said:

> [T]he notion that the warrantless entry of a man's house in order to arrest on probable cause is *per se* legitimate is in fundamental conflict with the basic principle of Fourth Amendment law * * *. 403 U.S. at 477, 91 S.Ct. at 2044, 29 L.Ed.2d at 589.

The U. S. Supreme Court again dealt with the question of warrantless entry of dwellings to arrest in the case of U. S. v. Santana, 427 U.S. 38, 96 S.Ct. 2406, 49 L.Ed.2d 300 (1976). In that case, police officers drove to the defendant's house after receiving information that the defendant had in her possession marked money used to make a heroin buy arranged by an undercover agent. The defendant was standing in the doorway of her house holding a paper bag as the police pulled up within fifteen feet of her. The officers got out of the car, shouting "police", and the defendant retreated into the vestibule of her house where they caught her. When she tried to pull away, envelopes containing heroin fell to the floor from the paper bag. Some of the marked money was found on her person.

The Court held that the defendant, while standing in the doorway of her house, was in a "public place" for purposes of the Fourth Amendment. Since she was not in an area where she had any expectation of privacy and she was exposed to public view, speech, hearing, and touch, it was the same as if she had been standing completely outside her house. When police sought to arrest her, they merely intended to make a warrantless arrest in a public place upon probable cause. Under U. S. v. Watson, 423 U.S. 411, 96 S.Ct. 820, 46 L.Ed.2d 598 (U. S. Supreme Court, 1976), such an arrest did not violate the Fourth Amendment. By retreating into a private place, the defendant could not defeat an otherwise proper arrest that had been set in motion in a public place. Since the officers needed to act quickly to prevent the destruction of evidence, there was a true hot pursuit, even though there was only a very short chase. Thus the warrantless entry to make the arrest was justified, as was the search incident to that arrest.

Although the U. S. Supreme Court has not flatly banned warrantless entries of the home to arrest, some state courts have done so. The California Supreme Court in People v. Ramey, 16 Cal.3d 263, 127 Cal.Rptr. 629, 545 P.2d 1333, (1976), has ruled that "warrantless arrests in the home are per se unreasonable in the absence of exigent circumstances." 16 Cal.3d at 276, 127 Cal.Rptr. at 637, 545 P.2d at 1341. In that case the state court relied upon its state constitution to place greater restrictions on law enforcement officers than those imposed by the U. S. Supreme Court.

Other courts have allowed warrantless entries of dwellings to arrest under limited conditions. In Dorman v. U. S., 140 U.S.App.D.C. 313, 435 F.2d 385 (District of Columbia Circuit Court of Appeals, 1970), the court established standards to guide law enforcement officers in these situations. The court stated that there was no *general* exception to the warrant requirement simply because the entry was for the purpose of arresting a suspected felon. But under certain urgent conditions a warrantless entry to arrest could be justified. These conditions are:

1. A grave offense, especially a crime of violence, has been committed;
2. The suspect is reasonably believed to be armed;
3. Officers clearly have probable cause to arrest;
4. Officers have strong reason to believe that the suspect is in the dwelling;
5. The suspect is likely to escape if not swiftly apprehended;
6. Officers can enter the dwelling peaceably; and
7. Officers can enter at a reasonable time of day.

Law enforcement officers must determine whether their states have rules governing warrantless arrests in the home. Otherwise, unless there are exigent circumstances, the safest procedure for the officer is to obtain an arrest warrant before arresting any person in a home. In this context, exigent circumstances means "an emergency situation requiring swift action to prevent imminent danger to life or serious damage to property, or to forestall the imminent escape of a suspect or destruction of evidence." 16 Cal.3d at 276, 127 Cal.Rptr. at 637, 545 P.2d at 1341.

Assuming an officer has a right to make a warrantless entry of a dwelling to arrest someone inside, he must first knock on the door, announce his authority and purpose and then demand admittance. If this demand is refused or met with silence, the officer may enter forcibly after waiting a reasonable time under the circumstances. Masiello v. U. S., 115 U.S.App.D.C. 57, 317 F.2d 121 (District of Columbia Circuit Court of Appeals, 1963). In the words of the United States Supreme Court:

> The requirement of prior notice of authority and purpose before forcing entry into a home is deeply rooted in our heritage, and should not be given grudging application. * * * Every householder, the good and the bad, the guilty and the innocent, is entitled to the protection designed to secure the common interest against unlawful invasion of the house. The petitioner could not be lawfully arrested in his home by officers breaking in without first giving him notice of their authority and purpose. Because the petitioner

did not receive that notice before the officers broke the door to invade his home, the arrest was unlawful, and the evidence seized should have been suppressed. Miller v. U. S., 357 U.S. 301, 313–14, 78 S.Ct. 1190, 1198, 2 L.Ed.2d 1332, 1340–41 (1958).

Forcible entry of a dwelling, in this context, does not necessarily mean only the violent breaking down of a door or the smashing of a window. The United States Supreme Court stated that "[a]n unannounced intrusion into a dwelling * * * is no less an unannounced intrusion whether officers break down a door, force open a chain lock on a partially open door, open a locked door by use of a passkey, or * * * open a closed but unlocked door." Sabbath v. U. S., 391 U.S. 585, 590, 88 S.Ct. 1755, 1758, 20 L.Ed.2d 828, 834 (1968). Before making any entry of this type to arrest, officers must first knock, announce their authority and purpose, and demand admittance.

In certain situations, however, the failure to knock, announce, and demand admittance will be excused. These situations are as follows:

1. When the officer's purpose is already known to the offender or other person upon whom demand for entry is made. As the U. S. Supreme Court stated in the *Miller* case:

   > It may be that, without an express announcement of purpose, the facts known to officers would justify them in being virtually certain that the petitioner already knows their purpose so that an announcement would be a useless gesture. 375 U.S. at 310, 78 S.Ct. at 1196, 2 L.Ed.2d at 1338.

2. When the officer's personal safety might be imperiled by compliance with such requirements. Fairman v. Warden, 83 Nev. 332, 431 P.2d 660 (Supreme Court of Nevada, 1967).
3. When the incidental delay might defeat the arrest by permitting the offender to escape. State v. Fair, 45 N.J. 77, 211 A.2d 359 (Supreme Court of New Jersey, 1965).
4. When the preliminary warnings might permit destruction of important evidence by those inside the house. This situation often comes up in drug cases, in which the evidence is often small and easily destroyed or disposed of. In Ker v. California, 374 U.S. 23, 83 S.Ct. 1623, 10 L.Ed.2d 726 (1963), the U. S. Supreme Court held that the unannounced entry into the defendant's apartment was proper when otherwise evidence of narcotics activity would have been destroyed. However, the holding in the *Ker* case was limited to the particular facts of that case. There, officers not only reasonably believed that the defendant was in possession of narcotics, but defendant's furtive conduct in eluding them shortly be-

fore the arrest gave them grounds to believe that he might have been expecting the police.

In Meyer v. U. S., 386 F.2d 715 (9th Circuit Court of Appeals, 1967), the officers had nothing to justify their unannounced entry into a dwelling except the claim of a general propensity of narcotics violators to destroy evidence. The court held that the entry was unlawful:

> Under the Fourth Amendment, a specific showing must always be made to justify any kind of police action tending to disturb the security of the people in their homes. Unannounced forcible entry is in itself a serious disturbance of that security and cannot be justified on a blanket basis. Otherwise, the constitutional test of reasonableness would turn only on practical expediency, and the amendment's primary safe-guard—the requirement of particularity, would be lost. Just as the police must have sufficient particular reason to enter at all, so must they have some particular reason to enter in the manner chosen. 386 F.2d at 718.

DISPOSITION OF PRISONER

Initial Appearance Before the Magistrate

When a law enforcement officer has arrested a person, either with or without a warrant, it is his duty to take the prisoner before a magistrate, or deliver him according to the mandate of the warrant. State statutes require that this duty be done "immediately," "without unnecessary delay," "forthwith," or in some similar language. These state statutes confer a substantial right upon the defendant and create a corresponding duty upon the law enforcement officer. An arrested person has a constitutional right to reasonable access to the courts, and any denial or undue restriction of this right constitutes a denial of due process of law under the Fourteenth Amendment. In re Allison, 66 Cal.2d 282, 57 Cal.Rptr. 593, 425 P.2d 193 (Supreme Court of California, 1967).

The reasons behind the rule requiring an arrested person to be brought before a magistrate without unnecessary delay are as follows:

1. To advise the arrested person of the charge being made against him, so that he may prepare his defense;
2. To fully advise the arrested person of his rights, such as his right to a preliminary hearing, his right to counsel, and under some statutes, his right to remain silent;
3. To protect the arrested person from being abandoned in jail and forgotten or otherwise cut off from contact with people who can help him;

4. To prevent secret and extended interrogation of arrested persons by law enforcement officers;
5. To give the arrested person an early opportunity to secure his release on bail while awaiting the final outcome of the proceedings against him; and
6. To give the arrested person an opportunity, in petty misdemeanor cases, to speedily conclude the matter by pleading guilty to the charge, paying his fine, and going on his way.

Courts have been quite flexible in interpreting the meaning of "immediately," "without unnecessary delay," "forthwith," and like phrases in statutes requiring arrested persons to be brought before a magistrate. Courts have realized that a certain amount of delay is necessary for the officer to perform required duties and other unavoidable activities connected with the arrest such as booking the arrested person, routinely questioning and searching him (if legally allowed), and checking facts. As one court has said:

> The duty enjoined upon arresting officers to arraign "without unnecessary delay" indicates that the command does not call for automatic obedience. Circumstances may justify a brief delay between arrest and arraignment, as for instance, where the story volunteered by the accused is susceptible of quick verification through third parties. Williams v. U. S., 273 F.2d 781, 797–98 (9th Circuit Court of Appeals, 1959).

Officers may have to delay in bringing an arrested person before a magistrate, because the person is physically or mentally incapacitated by illness or for some other reason. Drunkenness of an arrested person may be a ground for delay, if the person's condition is such that he could not understand the proceedings. Finally, an officer may have to delay because a magistrate is not readily available, either because the courts are closed, or because the distance to be travelled to reach a magistrate is great.

Therefore, "immediately," "without unnecessary delay," "forthwith," or other similar statutory language, cannot be defined in terms of minutes and hours but must be interpreted in light of all the circumstances. If the officer brings the arrested person before a magistrate as soon as one is available, and does not detain him to coerce a confession from him or otherwise harass him, the requirements of the rule should be satisfied.

Protection and Welfare of the Prisoner

As indicated above, there will be occasions when a magistrate or bail commissioner is not available, thereby delaying the arrested person's appearance. Furthermore, delay may result from an officer's carrying out necessary duties, may be requested by the prisoner himself, or may be caused by his being sick, intoxicated or otherwise incapacitated. In these situations, it is the duty of the officer to keep the arrested person safely in custody for the necessary period of time until he can be brought before a magistrate. For this purpose, the officer may exercise such degree of control over the prisoner as may be necessary to prevent his escape, although he must not subject him to any greater restraint than is reasonably justified to keep him safely in custody.

It may become necessary for the law enforcement officer to physically confine the prisoner rather than keep him in the officer's personal custody. Ordinarily the place of confinement will be a jail, but the officer may choose any safe, suitable place if a jail is unavailable.

Once an officer has a prisoner in his custody, he has certain responsibilities toward the prisoner. He has the responsibility to take care of the life, health, and safety of the prisoner and may be liable in damages if he fails to do so. Therefore, if the defendant is sick or injured at the time of the arrest or later, it is the duty of the officer to see that he receives adequate medical attention. He may even have to take him to the hospital before taking him to jail if the defendant's condition requires it. The officer, however, is not personally liable for the expenses involved.

Any unnecessary force, violence or brutality used against a prisoner is unlawful and the officer may be liable for assault and battery. Furthermore, if the prisoner is assaulted or injured by other prisoners, and the officer either negligently or willfully allowed such assault, then the officer may be personally liable for the damages.

Handcuffing

One of the ways in which an officer may prevent the escape of a prisoner and also protect himself from harm is to handcuff the prisoner. The law leaves the decision whether or not to use handcuffs largely up to the discretion of the individual law enforcement officer. He will be held liable for assault or otherwise only in cases of clear abuse of this discretion.

The right to handcuff is freely recognized in cases involving felony arrests but it is not confined to such cases. Circumstances often justify such precautions in misdemeanor cases also, especially where a breach of the peace is involved. In deciding whether or not to use handcuffs, the officer is entitled to consider a variety of factors—the nature of the person arrested, his reputation or record, the time of day or night, the possibility of violence, the number of prisoners involved, and the distance to the jail. Again, if an individual department has a policy regarding handcuffing, it should be consulted and followed by the officers of that department.

Property of Prisoner

When a person is arrested, it is normal procedure before confinement for police to search his person for weapons and evidence and to place all his belongings in safekeeping for return to him when he is released.

Such a pre-incarceration search and seizure need not be conducted immediately upon the prisoner's arrival at the place of incarceration. For example, the U. S. Supreme Court held that a seizure of a prisoner's clothing in the morning, several hours after his arrest and incarceration the previous evening, was reasonable. No substitute clothing was available at the time of arrest and, therefore, the normal processes incident to arrest and custody had not been completed. The Court said:

> [O]nce the accused is lawfully arrested and is in custody, the effects in his possession at the place of detention that were subject to search at the time and place of his arrest may lawfully be searched and seized without a warrant even though a substantial period of time has elapsed between the arrest and subsequent administrative processing, on the one hand, and the taking of the property for use as evidence, on the other. U. S. v. Edwards, 415 U.S. 800, 807, 94 S.Ct. 1234, 1239, 39 L.Ed.2d 771, 778 (1974).

Sometimes, especially when a vehicle is involved, an officer may be required to take positive steps to protect the defendant's property or else he may become liable in damages for failure to do so. For example, in an often cited case, a trucker was arrested and taken to jail, leaving his truck standing in a docking area on the waterfront. Over the trucker's protests, the arresting officer and his superior refused to allow him to remove the truck to a place of safety and refused to take any steps themselves to protect it. While the defendant trucker was in jail, his truck was stripped and, in attempting to steal it, the thieves damaged the transmission. The officers were held liable for the damages. Whitehead v. Stringer, 106 Wash. 501, 180 P. 486 (Supreme Court of Washington, 1919).

In order to protect themselves from liability of this nature, many law enforcement agencies have a policy of impounding arrested persons' vehicles and making an inventory of their contents. For a further discussion of impoundment and inventory of vehicles, see Chapter 7 on Search and Seizure of Vehicles Without a Warrant.

Identification of Prisoner

Pre-trial procedures for identifying persons arrested for a crime take many different forms. One aspect of these identification procedures is the confrontation of the prisoner with victims or witnesses of the crime, sometimes accomplished through the use of a police lineup or showup. The arrestee has no right to object to being viewed by witnesses for identification purposes and also has no right to demand to be placed in a lineup. For a discussion of lineup techniques and the right to counsel, see Chapter 11 on Pre-trial Identification Procedures.

In addition, law enforcement officers clearly have the right to take fingerprints, footprints, or photographs of the arrested person for purposes of identification or evidence. These may even be taken by force if necessary. Schmerber v. California, 384 U.S. 757, 86 S. Ct. 1826, 16 L.Ed.2d 908 (U. S. Supreme Court, 1966). Photographs may be useful to show that at the time of arrest, the defendant had dyed hair or a beard, or to show bruises or scratches which might be evidence in crimes of violence. Courts have also held that law enforcement officers may obtain voice exemplars or have a dentist examine a defendant's mouth for a missing tooth for identification purposes:

> [T]he Supreme Court held in *Dionisio* [U. S. v. Dionisio, 410 U.S. 1, 93 S.Ct. 764, 35 L.Ed.2d 67 (1973)] that the Fourth Amendment does not protect "what a person knowingly exposes to the public even in his home or office. * * * Like a man's facial characteristics, or handwriting, his voice is repeatedly produced for others to hear. No person can have a reasonable expectation that others will not know the sound of his voice, any more than he can reasonably expect that his face will be a mystery to the world." This doctrine is applicable as well to a missing tooth. (material in brackets added) U. S. v. Holland, 378 F.Supp. 144, 155 (U. S. District Court, Eastern District of Pennsylvania, 1974).

Law enforcement officers also have the authority to make a physical examination of the defendant for measurements, scars, bruises, tattoos, etc. To enable this to be done, the defendant may be required to disrobe against his will:

> Such procedures and practices and tests may result in freeing an innocent man accused of crime, or may be part of a chain of facts and circumstances which help identify a person accused of a crime or connect a suspect or an accused with the crime of which he has been suspected or has been accused. The law is well settled that such actions, practices, and procedures do not violate any constitutional right. Commonwealth v. Aljoe, 420 Pa. 198, 202, 216 A.2d 50, 52–53 (Pennsylvania Supreme Court, 1966).

Courts have even allowed an examination of an arrested person's bodily cavities as long as the methods used did not amount to excessive force or brutality and did not "shock the conscience" or offend the sense of justice. Blackford v. U. S., 247 F.2d 745 (9th Circuit Court of Appeals, 1957). Furthermore, the U. S. Supreme Court has held that there is no denial of due process of law in taking a blood sample from a person who is unconscious and unable to give consent, and no unreasonable search and seizure or violation of his privilege against self incrimination when such specimen is taken from him without his consent while he is in lawful custody. Schmerber v. California, 384 U.S. 757, 86 S.Ct. 1826, 16 L.Ed.2d 908 (1966).

In the *Schmerber* case, the blood sample was taken in a hospital by a physician following accepted medical procedures. Also, there was a need for immediate action because the alcoholic content in the blood would quickly dissipate. The Court said:

> [W]e reach this judgment only on the facts in the present record. The integrity of an individual's person is a cherished value of our society. That we today hold that the Constitution does not forbid the State's minor intrusions into an individual's body under stringently limited conditions in no way indicates that it permits more substantial intrusions or intrusions under other conditions. 384 U.S. at 772, 86 S.Ct. at 1836, 16 L.Ed.2d at 920.

Courts have generally refused requests by the prosecution to allow surgery to remove a bullet from a person when the operation would pose a substantial risk to the person. Some courts, however, have allowed minor surgery to remove a bullet from a person when the surgical procedure posed no threat of serious bodily injury and the evidence was critical to the prosecution's case. Creamer v. State, 229 Ga. 511, 192 S.E.2d 350 (Supreme Court of Georgia, 1972).

Law enforcement officers should not attempt to arrange for the removal by surgery of bullets or other objects without first contacting a prosecuting attorney. Also, unless there is an emergency, a search warrant or court order must be obtained before such surgery will be allowed.

Release of Prisoner Prior to Appearance Before a Magistrate

After an arrest *without* a warrant has been made, further investigation sometimes indicates to the arresting officer that no offense actually has been committed, that the person arrested is innocent, or that the evidence against him is insufficient to justify making a formal charge. In such circumstances, it is the practice for law enforcement officers in some jurisdictions to use their own judgment in releasing the arrested person. There is little reason or justice in requiring that a person, now believed innocent, be held in custody until he can be taken before a magistrate.

Nevertheless, despite the obvious injustice of prolonging the detention of such persons, some courts have been slow to depart from the rule laid down in early cases, that the arresting officer has no right to dispose of his prisoner other than by taking him before the nearest magistrate without unnecessary delay. Therefore, in order to protect himself from liability, the wisest course for the officer to follow when he feels a prisoner should be released is to obtain a written waiver from him. Since it is the arrested person's right to go before a magistrate on the offense, he can waive that right, consent to his release, and the arresting officer is protected from any claim of damages for false arrest. It must be re-emphasized, however, that it is the arrested person's *right* to be taken before a magistrate and the officer may not release the person if he insists upon being taken to court to remove any possible stigma or suspicion connected with his arrest.

EFFECT OF ILLEGAL ARREST

Although a detailed discussion is beyond the scope of this chapter, law enforcement officers should be made aware of some of the possible consequences of an illegal arrest, both to themselves and to the prosecution of the person arrested.

First, it is an almost universal rule that jurisdiction to try a person actually before the court is in no way affected by the manner in which the person was brought before the court. Therefore, the fact that one is illegally arrested is not grounds for quashing the indictment, information, or complaint brought against him and does not preclude a trial on the charges, or affect the validity of the proceedings in any way. State v. Boynton, 143 Me. 313, 62 A.2d 182 (Supreme Judicial Court of Maine, 1948).

However, while an illegal arrest does not deprive the court of jurisdiction to try an offender, the exclusionary rule may be applicable and may affect the trial adversely. The exclusionary rule, as it relates to arrest, states that any evidence obtained by exploitation of an unlawful arrest will be inadmissible in court in a prosecution against the person arrested. Therefore, if the only evidence which the state has against an armed robbery suspect is a gun, stocking, and large roll of bills taken from his person during a search incident to an unlawful arrest, the offender will very likely go free because these items will be inadmissible in court. The exclusionary rule is discussed in further detail in Chapter 2 under Effect of Illegal Search and Seizure.

A confession obtained by exploitation of an illegal arrest will also be inadmissible in court. Officers cannot avoid the effect of the illegal arrest by simply giving the arrested person the *Miranda* warnings. Other factors indicating that the confession was sufficiently an act of free will must be present.

> The *Miranda* warnings are an important factor, to be sure, in determining whether the confession is obtained by exploitation of illegal arrest. But they are not the only factor to be considered. The temporal proximity of the arrest and the confession, the presence of intervening circumstances, * * * and, particularly, the purpose and flagrancy of the official misconduct are all relevant. Brown v. Illinois, 422 U.S. 590, 603–04, 95 S.Ct. 2254, 2261–62, 45 L.Ed.2d 416, 427 (U. S. Supreme Court, 1975).

Officers should take care to ensure that a confession obtained from an arrested person is a product of the person's free will, especially when there is concern about the legality of the arrest.

A consent search following an illegal arrest may also be declared invalid. The Supreme Court of California stated that, " '[a] search and seizure made pursuant to consent secured immediately following an illegal entry or arrest * * * is inextricably bound up with the illegal conduct and cannot be separated therefrom.' " People v. Johnson, 68 Cal.2d 629, 632, 68 Cal.Rptr. 441, 443, 440 P.2d 921, 923 (1968). An identification of a defendant by a witness may be declared inadmissible in court if it is caused by or is the result of an illegal arrest. State v. Brown, 50 Wis.2d 565, 185 N.W.2d 323 (Supreme Court of Wisconsin, 1971). In fact, it is safe to assume that any evidence gathering activity which follows closely upon and is closely related to an illegal arrest will result in any evidence obtained being declared inadmissible. The exclusionary rule is discussed in greater detail in Chapter 2.

Another possible consequence of an unlawful arrest, mentioned throughout this chapter, is that the arresting officer can be sued for false arrest or false imprisonment. All that is necessary to make out a case for false arrest or false imprisonment is that the individual be restrained of his liberty without legal justification. There does not have to be any malice or bad motive on the part of the arresting officer. As a practical matter, however, a person will be more likely to go to the trouble of suing an officer who had apparent ill feeling toward him or offended him either verbally or physically at the time of the illegal arrest.

Furthermore, depending upon the circumstances and the degree of force used, an officer's actions in making an *unlawful* arrest may give rise to a civil suit for damages or a criminal prosecution against him for anything from assault and battery to murder, the same as any other aggressor. In such cases, the officer is not entitled to the full right of self-defense if his acts are illegal.

It should again be noted in this context that an officer can be civilly and criminally liable even if the arrest is *lawful,* if he uses excessive and unreasonable force in making the arrest.

SUMMARY

The responsibility of the law enforcement officer is to enforce the laws of the community and protect the public at large. To enable him to do this, he is given power and authority beyond that of the ordinary citizen. One of these powers is the power to arrest and the incidental powers to use force, carry weapons, etc.

There are, however, very definite limitations on these powers, derived from the Fourth Amendment to the U. S. Constitution and expounded in court decisions and statutes. If the officer exceeds his authority, uses more force than is necessary, or is careless or reckless in performing his duties, the results can be devastating. The consequences of unlawful actions by an arresting officer can range from the loss of the prosecution's case to a suit for damages or prosecution against the officer for a variety of offenses.

It therefore becomes imperative that the law enforcement officer not only know the law of arrest but that he act in accordance with it. The successful prosecution of criminal offenders and the officer's own career in law enforcement could depend on the officer's proper compliance with the law.

2

SEARCH WARRANTS

Like the law of arrest, the law governing search warrants is based upon guarantees embodied in the United States Constitution. As a point of departure for the discussion of search warrants, the Fourth Amendment to the Constitution will be quoted again in full:

> The right of the people to be secure in their persons, houses, papers and effects, against unreasonable searches and seizures, shall not be violated, and no Warrants shall issue, but upon probable cause, supported by Oath or affirmation, and particularly describing the place to be searched and the persons or things to be seized. U.S.C.A. Const. Amend. IV.

Whereas, in the foregoing chapter on Arrest, the main concern was the *seizure* of the *person,* the discussion of search warrants will be concerned with a broader array of matters including the search of persons *and* places and the seizure of a variety of things.

Probable cause, which is a common aspect of both arrest and search and seizure law, will be discussed in full in Chapter 3.

HISTORY

The Fourth Amendment to the United States Constitution was adopted in response to abuses of governmental search and seizure authority originating in England in the 17th and 18th centuries. The early development of legally authorized searches and seizures under English common law is somewhat obscure. It appears that search warrants were first used in cases involving stolen property. Their use to recapture stolen goods became widespread and increasingly violative of citizens' privacy. Eventually, warrants were extended to the enforcement of other laws. For example, in the 18th century the government issued general warrants to enforce the strict libel laws. A general warrant is one which fails to specify the person or place to be searched or the person or item to be seized, and which leaves the time and manner of the search to the discretion of the searching officer. These general warrants were abused by law enforcement officers and soon no person or his property was free from unlimited search conducted at the whim of an officer on the mere suspicion that the person possessed literature critical of the King or of others in high places.

Despite their unpopularity with the citizenry, these abusive practices were transplanted to the American colonies. In mid-18th century, Parliament enacted legislation authorizing general searches, called writs of assistance, to be conducted against the colonists to enforce the Trade Acts. Writs of assistance authorized royal customs officers to search houses and ships at will in order to discover and seize smuggled goods or goods on which the required duties had not been paid. The reaction of the colonists against the writs of assistance was strong and was one of the major causes of the American Revolution. As stated in the 1886 United States Supreme Court case of Boyd v. U. S.:

> The practice had obtained in the colonies of issuing writs of assistance to the revenue officers, empowering them, in their discretion, to search suspected places for smuggled goods, which James Otis pronounced "the worst instrument of arbitrary power, the most destructive of English liberty and the fundamental principles of law, that ever was found in an English law book;" since they placed "the liberty of every man in the hands of every petty officer." This was in February, 1761, in Boston, and the famous debate in which it occurred was perhaps the most prominent event which inaugurated the resistance of the colonies to the oppressions of the mother country. "Then and there," said John Adams, "then and there was the first scene of the first act of opposition to the arbitrary claims of Great Britain. Then and there the child of Independence was born." 116 U.S. 616, 625, 6 S.Ct. 524, 528–29, 29 L.Ed. 746, 749.

The experiences of our founding fathers with general warrants and writs of assistance caused them to insist upon including in the basic charters of the states and of the nation suitable guarantees against unreasonable searches and seizures. A prohibition against searches conducted at the whim of a law enforcement officer without any restrictions on the person or place to be searched or the person or item to be seized was first embodied in the Virginia Bill of Rights adopted in 1776. By the close of the Revolutionary War, most of the states had adopted similar provisions. The present Fourth Amendment to the United States Constitution, with its emphasis on the protection of warrants issued upon probable cause, was included in the Bill of Rights in 1791. Today, the constitution of every state in the Union contains a similar provision.

DEFINITION

It is necessary to begin the discussion of search warrants with a clear definition. A search warrant is (1) an order in writing; (2) issued by a proper judicial authority; (3) in the name of the people; (4) directed to a law enforcement officer; (5) commanding him to search for certain personal property; and (6) bring it before the judicial authority named in the warrant. In many of its aspects, the search warrant is substantially the same as an arrest warrant, which, in effect, is an order to take a *person* into custody and bring him before the proper judicial authority. Throughout the course of this discussion, the terms of the above definition will be clarified and important relationships between search warrants and arrest warrants will be highlighted.

OBTAINING A SEARCH WARRANT

The law enforcement officer wishing to obtain a search warrant must follow proper procedures in applying for the warrant. If he does not, the warrant may not be issued or, if issued, may later be declared invalid, resulting in lost evidence and very likely a lost case. Search warrant procedures differ from state to state and are found in various statutes and court decisions. The procedures common to most states will be summarized and discussed in this chapter.

Who May Issue Search Warrants

The only persons authorized to issue search warrants are those judicial officers who have been specifically authorized to do so. Most states have statutes which give this authority to such officers as clerks of court, magistrates, complaint justices, justices of the peace, and judges. Every law enforcement officer should know which judicial officers are authorized to issue search warrants in his state. These judicial officers may not be the same as those authorized to issue arrest warrants. A search warrant issued by an officer without authority is of no legal effect, and a search made pursuant to such a warrant is unlawful. For convenience, the term "magistrate" will be used throughout the rest of this chapter to designate an official authorized to issue search warrants.

Form A. O. 106 (Rev. Apr. 1973)

Affidavit for Search Warrant

United States District Court

FOR THE

Docket No.________

UNITED STATES OF AMERICA

vs.

Case No.________

AFFIDAVIT FOR SEARCH WARRANT

BEFORE

Name of Judge[1] or Federal Magistrate — Address of Judge[1] or Federal Magistrate

The undersigned being duly sworn deposes and says:

That he has reason to believe that (on the person of) (on the premises known as)

in the District of

there is now being concealed certain property, namely

here describe property

which are

here give alleged grounds for search and seizure[2]

And that the facts tending to establish the foregoing grounds for issuance of a Search Warrant are as follows:[3]

______________________________,
Signature of Affiant.

______________________________,
Official Title, if any.

Sworn to before me, and subscribed in my presence, , 19

______________________________,
Judge[1] or Federal Magistrate.

[1]United States Judge or Judge of a State Court of Record.
[2]If a search is to be authorized "at any time in the day or night" pursuant to Rule 41(c), show reasonable cause therefor.
[3]If the warrant is to authorize execution pursuant to 21 U.S.C. § 879 without prior notice of authority or purpose, indicate the circumstances creating the need for such a warrant.

(B9583)

FPI LC 12-10-73 120M 7658

Grounds for Issuance

In order for the magistrate to issue a search warrant, he must have probable cause to believe that items subject to seizure are in a particular place or on a particular person at the time of the issuance of the warrant. It is the law enforcement officer's duty to provide the magistrate with the information upon which probable cause is based. The officer does this in his application for a search warrant by means of an affidavit, which must be supported by oath or affirmation. An affidavit is merely a written declaration or statement of facts sworn to before the magistrate. An example of a typical affidavit form appears on page 48.

Officers should note that if they knowingly and intentionally, or with reckless disregard for the truth, make false statements in an affidavit supporting a request for a search warrant, the warrant may not issue or evidence seized pursuant to the warrant may be suppressed. In Franks v. Delaware, 438 U.S. 154, 98 S.Ct. 2674, 57 L.Ed.2d 667 (1978), the United States Supreme Court held that a defendant may challenge the veracity of an affidavit used by the police to procure a search warrant. The Court said:

> [W]here the defendant makes a substantial preliminary showing that a false statement knowingly and intentionally, or with reckless disregard for the truth, was included by the affiant in the warrant affidavit, and if the allegedly false statement is necessary to the finding of probable cause, the Fourth Amendment requires that a hearing be held at the defendant's request. In the event that at the hearing the allegation of perjury or reckless disregard is established by the defendant by a preponderance of the evidence, and, with the affidavit's false material set to one side, the affidavit's remaining content is insufficient to establish probable cause, the search warrant must be voided and the fruits of the search excluded to the same extent as if probable cause was lacking on the face of the affidavit. 438 U.S. at 155–56, 98 S.Ct. at 2676–77, 57 L.Ed.2d at 672.

The following discussion will cover in detail the information which must be presented to the magistrate to enable him to issue a search warrant.

Probable Cause

Some states require that the sworn affidavit contain *all* the information upon which the magistrate is to base his finding of probable cause to issue a search warrant. State v. Hawkins, Me., 261 A.2d 255 (Supreme Judicial Court of Maine, 1970). Other states allow the showing of probable cause to be made by sworn oral testimony given before the magistrate supplementing the affidavit. State v. Oliveri, 261 Iowa 1140, 1145–46, 156 N.W.2d 688, 691 (Supreme Court of Iowa, 1968). It is strongly suggested that, whether or not state law requires it, each officer include *all* the information upon which probable cause is to be based in the affidavit. By writing the information down, the officer forces himself to think carefully about his case. Oftentimes, he may realize that his information is too weak to support a finding of probable cause, and he may save himself and the magistrate a great deal of time and trouble by not presenting the information. On the other hand, the officer may discover leads on how to further develop weak evidence until it is sufficient to support a finding of probable cause. Also, when all the information upon which probable cause is based is contained in the affidavit, a complete record is made available later to a court reviewing the decision of the magistrate, upon a motion to suppress evidence or on an appeal. For these reasons, and for ease of presentation, the remainder of this chapter will speak of the affidavit as the only vehicle for presenting information to the magistrate to obtain a search warrant.

The affidavit should indicate to the magistrate (1) that a criminal offense has been or is being committed; and (2) that seizable evidence relating to that offense is in a particular place at a particular time. The amount of proof required to convince the magistrate to issue the search warrant is essentially the same as that required for the issuance of an arrest warrant or that which is required before an officer may arrest without a warrant for a felony. The constitutional term used to describe this amount of proof is "probable cause." Probable cause means the same as "reasonable cause," "sufficient cause," or "reasonable cause to believe," as found in various statutes, constitutional provisions, and judicial opinions. In general, absolute certainty or "evidence beyond a reasonable doubt" is not required to establish probable cause. Something more than "mere suspicion" is required, however. Furthermore, the information supporting probable cause for the issuance of a search warrant need not be sufficient to support a verdict of guilty and will often even be inadmissible evidence at the trial. As stated by the U. S. Supreme Court, probable cause exists where the facts and circumstances shown are sufficent to justify an ordinarily prudent and cautious person in believing there is a reasonable basis for the search. Beck v. Ohio, 379 U.S. 89, 91, 85 S.Ct. 223, 225, 13 L.Ed.2d 142, 145 (U. S. Supreme Court, 1964).

Probable cause may arise through facts or information which the officer himself has personally observed or gathered. It may also be based upon reliable information from third parties such as the victim, other police agencies, witnesses, reporters, informants, or even information from the defendant himself. In recent years, there have been many decisions of state and federal courts and the U. S. Supreme Court dealing with various aspects of probable cause. A detailed discussion of these cases and of probable cause in general, appears in Chapter 3. The important thing for the officer to remember is that he must state in the affidavit the facts and circumstances upon which probable cause is based. Mere conclusions, statements of belief, or opinions of the law enforcement officer will not suffice.

It should further be noted that probable cause to search and probable cause to arrest will usually arise out of different sets of facts. In order to find probable cause to arrest, the magistrate must find sufficient facts to show that an offense was committed and that a particular suspect committed it. Probable cause to search, on the other hand, turns on facts tending to show that particular items are connected with criminal activity and that they will be found in a particular place.

Another difference between probable cause to arrest and probable cause to search is that time is a very important factor in determining probable cause to search. The items to be seized must be in the place or on the person to be searched at the time the application for a search warrant is made or, in the case of a warrantless search, at the time the search is executed. If too long a time passes between the time when the information upon which probable cause is based is gathered and execution of the search, there may no longer be good reason to believe that the property is still at the same location. Probable cause is said to be "stale" in such situations.

The length of time that an item of property is likely to remain at a given location depends upon the nature of the property, the nature of the criminal activity, the duration of the criminal activity, the criminal suspects, and many other factors. For example, in State v. Willey, Me., 363 A.2d 739 (Supreme Judicial Court of Maine, 1976), the court held that the fact that the informant had made three purchases of marijuana in one week from the defendant was insufficient to justify the conclusion that 31 days after the last purchase, marijuana was still at defendant's premises. In cases involving evidence that is likely to disappear or be moved, therefore, officers should apply for a warrant or conduct a warrantless search (in the proper circumstances) as soon as possible. If the items sought are not likely to disappear or be moved, like business records of an illegal real estate scheme, for example, the records will probably remain at their location for an extended period of time after the business transactions have taken place. The U. S. Supreme Court said:

> The business records sought were prepared in the ordinary course of petitioner's business in his law office or that of his real estate corporation. It is eminently reasonable to expect that such records would be maintained in those offices for a period of time and surely as long as the three months required for the investigation of a complex real estate scheme. Andresen v. Maryland, 427 U.S. 463, 479, n. 9, 96 S.Ct. 2737, 2747, n. 9, 49 L.Ed.2d 627, 641, n. 9 (1976).

Another court held that an affidavit stating that hand grenades had been observed at the defendant's residence within the past 30 days was not insufficient because of stale probable cause. The court said that "[u]nlike many other items of contraband, hand grenades are not, to the best of our knowledge, in great demand even by the criminal element in our society; and they do not lend themselves to rapid disposition in the marketplace." U. S. v. Dauphinee, 538 F.2d 1 (1st Circuit Court of Appeals, 1976).

Items Subject to Seizure

Most states have statutes stating that a warrant may be isued to search for and seize certain types of property. Although these statutes differ in many respects, the following list is typical of the types of property allowed to be seized:

1. Property stolen or embezzled; or
2. Property designed or intended for use or which is or has been used as a means of committing a criminal offense (instrumentalities); or
3. Property, the possession of which is unlawful (contraband); or
4. Property consisting of nontestimonial evidence which will aid in a particular apprehension or conviction.

The first three listed types of property should be self-explanatory. The fourth may need some discussion. This fourth type of property is sometimes called "mere evidence." Examples of mere evidence might be items of clothing, shoes, or business records. "Mere evidence" was added to the list by many states in accordance with the U. S. Supreme Court decision in 1967 in the case of Warden v. Hayden, 387 U.S. 294, 87 S.Ct. 1642, 18 L.Ed.2d 782 (1967). That decision did away with the previous proposition that search warrants could not be used as a means of gaining access to a man's house or office and papers solely for the purpose of making search to secure mere evidence to be used against him in a criminal proceeding. Nevertheless, even though mere evidence may now be seized, some statutes place certain limitations on its seizure.

One of these limitations is that the evidence to be seized must be nontestimonial. This requirement protects the individual from being compelled to be a witness against himself in violation of his Fifth Amendment rights. It was widely thought that private personal papers and business records could not be seized under this limitation because of their testimonial nature. The U. S. Supreme Court held, however, that a seizure of personal papers or business records from a person under a search warrant does not necessarily compel the person to be a witness against himself. Andresen v. Maryland, 427 U.S. 463, 96 S.Ct. 2737, 49 L.Ed.2d 627 (1976). In the *Andresen* case, the Court quoted an earlier case stating that " 'a party is privileged from producing the evidence, but not from its production.' " 427 U.S. at 473, 96 S.Ct. at 2745, 49 L.Ed.2d at 638. The Court held that the defendant in the *Andresen* case was not compelled to be a witness against himself because he was not required to say or to do anything during the search. If law enforcement authorities had attempted to subpoena the records, however, the defendant could have refused to give up the records by exercising his Fifth Amendment rights. The Court said:

> [A]lthough the Fifth Amendment may protect an individual from complying with a subpoena for the production of his personal records in his possession because the very act of production may constitute a compulsory authentication of incriminating information, * * * a seizure of the same materials by law enforcement officers differs in a crucial respect—the individual against whom the search is directed is not required to aid in the discovery, production, or authentication of incriminating evidence. 427 U.S. at 473–74, 96 S. Ct. at 2745, 49 L.Ed.2d at 638.

A person has even less protection against production of his bank records. The U. S. Supreme Court, in U. S. v. Miller, 425 U.S. 435, 96 S.Ct. 1619, 48 L.Ed.2d 71 (1976) held that a person's bank records are not private papers of the kind protected against compulsory production by the Fifth Amendment. By choosing to deal with a bank, a person loses his expectation of Fourth Amendment protection against government investigation:

> The checks are not confidential communications but negotiable instruments to be used in commercial transactions. All of the documents obtained, including financial statements and deposit slips, contain only information voluntarily conveyed to the banks and exposed to their employees in the ordinary course of business. 425 U.S. at 442, 96 S.Ct. at 1624, 48 L.Ed.2d at 79.

Although the *Miller* case concerned a subpoena, either a search warrant or subpoena could be used to obtain a person's bank records without violating his Fifth Amendment right against compulsory self-incrimination.

Both the *Andresen* and *Miller* cases serve to highlight a basic principle regarding the obtaining of papers as evidence in criminal cases: "There is no special sanctity in papers, as distinguished from other forms of property, to render them immune from search and seizure, if only they fall within the scope of the principles of the cases in which other property may be seized, and if they be adequately described in the affidavit and warrant." Gouled v. U. S., 255 U.S. 298, 309, 41 S.Ct. 261, 265, 65 L.Ed. 647, 652 (1921). Therefore, officers seizing items such as business records or personal papers under a warrant should refrain from requiring the defendant to assist them in any way. Otherwise the evidence may be suppressed in court because it was seized in violation of the defendant's Fifth Amendment rights.

The other limitation on the seizure of mere evidence is that the evidence to be seized must aid in a particular apprehension or conviction. The reason for this second requirement was stated by the United States Supreme Court:

> The requirements of the Fourth Amendment can secure the same protection of privacy whether the search is for "mere evidence" or for fruits, instrumentalities or contraband. There must of course be a nexus—automatically provided in the case of fruits, instrumentalities or contraband—between the item to be seized and criminal behavior. Thus in the case of "mere evidence," probable cause must be examined in terms of cause to believe that the evidence sought will aid in a particular apprehension or conviction. In doing so, consideration of police purposes will be served. Warden v. Hayden, 387 U.S. 294, 306–07, 87 S.Ct. 1642, 1650, 18 L.Ed.2d 782, 792 (1967).

Law enforcement officers are encouraged to indicate in every affidavit for a search warrant that the property they wish to seize falls within one of the types of property listed above or listed in their particular state's statute defining items subject to seizure. It is good practice to describe the property in the terms of the particular state statute.

Particular Description of Place or Person

The sworn affidavit for the search warrant must contain a description of the premises to be searched which particularly points to a definitely ascertainable place so as to exclude all others. It has been held that the description of premises is sufficient if "officers thereby are enabled to ascertain and identify the place intended by reasonable effort. * * * A technical description of the place to be searched is not necessary." State v. Brochu, Me., 237 A.2d 418, 422 (Supreme Judicial Court of Maine, 1967). The following examples will help to illustrate how courts have dealt with descriptions of premises in particular instances.

In the *Brochu* case cited above, the property to be searched was described as "the premises known as the dwelling of Armand A. Brochu located at 20 Forest Street, in the City/Town of Biddeford, County of York and State of Maine, said premises being owned/occupied by Armand A. Brochu." The court held that no one could have been misled by the description of the premises in the warrant. Furthermore the description was held to cover not only the dwelling house but also the garage and any other buildings generally associated with and included within a house or home.

Where the place to be searched is a multiple-occupancy dwelling such as an apartment house, hotel, or rooming house, the affidavit must go beyond merely stating the location of the premises. In an illustrative case, the affidavit upon which the warrant was based read as follows: "Place to be searched: 313 West 27th Street, a dwelling. The apartment of Melvin Lloyd Manley." The defendant objected to the search on the ground that the apartment to be searched was not sufficiently described in the affidavit and warrant.

The court held that the defendant's apartment was sufficiently described for the searching officers to locate it with very little effort:

> It has been generally held that a search warrant directed against a multiple-occupancy structure is invalid if it fails to describe the particular sub-unit to be searched with sufficient definiteness to preclude search of other units located in the larger structure and occupied by innocent persons. But there are exceptions to the general rule. Even though a search warrant against a multiple-occupancy structure fails to describe the particular sub-unit to be searched, it will ordinarily not be held invalid where it adequately specifies the name of the occupant of the sub-unit against which it is directed and provides the searching officers with sufficient information to identify, without confusion or excessive effort, such apartment unit. Manley v. Commonwealth, 211 Va. 146, 151–52, 176 S.E.2d 309, 314 (Supreme Court of Virginia, 1970).

Whenever possible, however, information like room number, apartment number, or floor should be included in the affidavit. If necessary, a diagram showing the location should be made and attached to the affidavit.

Both of the above cases serve to emphasize the importance of including in the affidavit the *name* of the person who owns or occupies the premises to be searched. Under some state statutes, if the owner or occupant of the premises is known to the officer applying for a search warrant, it *must* be included in the description of premises in the affidavit.

In another case involving a multiple-occupancy dwelling, the description in the warrant of the place to be searched (a 4-building apartment complex) gave a wrong street address but correctly stated the apartment number. Since there was was only one apartment with that number in the entire complex, the court held that the description was sufficient:

> [T]he determining factor as to whether a search warrant describes the premises to be searched with sufficient particularity is not whether the description is technically accurate in every detail but rather whether the description is sufficient to enable the executing officer to locate and identify the premises with reasonable effort, and whether there is any reasonable probability that another premises might be mistakenly searched which is not the one intended to be searched under the search warrant. U. S. v. Darensbourg, 520 F.2d 985, 987 (5th Circuit Court of Appeals, 1975).

Although not often so used, it should be remembered that a search warrant may also issue for the search of a person. Again, the standard for determining the validity of a warrant to search an individual's person is whether it describes the individual to be searched with such particularity that he may be identified with reasonable certainty. The cases seem to hold that even though a person's name is unknown or incorrectly stated, the warrant may still be valid if a description of the person is included. U. S. v. Ferrone, 438 F.2d 381 (3rd Circuit Court of Appeals, 1971). Therefore, it is advisable for the law enforcement officer, when applying for a warrant for the search of a person, to state not only the person's name, if known, but also a complete description including weight, height, age, race, clothing, address, and any aliases. State v. Tramantano, 28 Conn.Supp. 325, 260 A.2d 128 (Superior Court of Connecticut, 1969). That way, if the name in the affidavit is incorrect, there is still backup information to enable the person to be identified.

When the search of a person for evidence requires surgery (such as a search for a bullet embedded in the skin) officers may be required to provide additional information in the affidavit to justify the issuance of a warrant. Officers should present medical opinions of more than one doctor that the removal of the evidence will constitute substantially no risk to the patient. Officers should also provide information in the affidavit that the offense is serious, such as murder or armed robbery; that the evidence sought is relevant and material; that there is probable cause that the surgery will produce the evidence; and that the evidence can be obtained in no other way. Some courts require, in addition to the information in the affidavit, an adversary hearing, at which the defendant is represented by counsel, and an opportunity for the defendant to appeal the order directing the surgery. U. S. v. Crowder, 177 U.S.App.D.C. 165, 543 F.2d 312 (District of Columbia Circuit Court of Appeals, 1976).

As a result of the U. S. Supreme Court's decision in the case of Coolidge v. New Hampshire, 403 U.S. 443, 91 S.Ct. 2022, 29 L.Ed.2d 564 (1971) (see Chapter 7 on Search and Seizure of Vehicles Without a Warrant), law enforcement officers will more frequently be required to apply for warrants for the search of vehicles. Again, since vehicles are considered *places* for search and seizure purposes, the affidavit is required to contain a description of the vehicle to be searched sufficiently particular so that it can be located with reasonable certainty. Some courts have held that only the license plate number is necessary to sufficiently describe a motor vehicle for purposes of issuance of a warrant. Bowling v. State, 219 Tenn. 224, 408 S.W.2d 660 (Supreme Court of Tennessee, 1966). License plates, however, can be easily removed or replaced. Therefore, when other information about the vehicle is known, it should be included in the affidavit. Such other information, for instance, would be the make, body style, color, year, location, and owner or operator of the vehicle.

Mail may also be considered a *place* for search and seizure purposes. Courts have ruled that first class domestic mail may not be lawfully opened without a warrant. (Domestic mail is any letter or package travelling wholly within the United States.) Law enforcement officers, therefore, must follow the same procedures to obtain a warrant to search first class mail as to search places, persons, and vehicles.

Particular Description of Things

Besides a particular description of the place to be searched, the sworn affidavit for a search warrant must contain a particular description of the items to be seized. In general, the items to be seized must be described with sufficient particularity so that the officer executing the warrant (1) can identify the items with reasonable certainty, and (2) is left with no discretion as to which property is to be taken.

Therefore, a description of items merely as "stolen goods," "obscene materials," or "other articles of merchandise too numerous to mention," for instance, would be inadequate. Marcus v. Search Warrant, 367 U.S. 717, 81 S.Ct. 1708, 6 L.Ed.2d 1127 (U. S. Supreme Court, 1961). When an item can be described in detail, all available information about it should be included in the affidavit. For example, number, size, color, weight, condition, brand name, and other distinguishing features of items to be seized should be a part of the description where applicable. Also, as mentioned earlier, officers should indicate why the item of property is subject to seizure.

Often, the nature of the property will give some indication as to how detailed a description is necessary. For example, a court upheld the sufficiency of a warrant which authorized a search for:

> "certain items of property, to-wit:
>
> "Various instruments and tools used in performing abortion, which were instrumentalities of such offense * * *."

The court reasoned that because of the unusual nature of the items to be seized, they were described with reasonable particularity in the warrant. A technical identification or description would have required the experience of a trained surgeon. State v. Brown, 205 Kan. 457, 462–63, 470 P.2d 815, 819–20 (Supreme Court of Kansas, 1970).

If it is impossible to describe the items to be seized in detail in the affidavit because of the common nature and nonuniqueness of the items, a general description may suffice. A general description should be accompanied, however, by strong evidence that the items to be seized at a particular place are the actual items that offend against the law, and by evidence that the seizable items cannot be differentiated from similar innocent items. For example, in U. S. v. Scharfman, 448 F.2d 1352 (2d Circuit Court of Appeals, 1971), a shipment containing hundreds of furs had been hijacked. The F.B.I. applied for a warrant to search the defendant's fur store for "fur coats, stoles, jackets and other finished fur products * * *." 448 F.2d at 1353 n.1. The court upheld the general description in the warrant because the affidavit stated that an informant experienced in the fur trade and an employee of the fur shipment's owner had informed the F.B.I. that furs from the shipment were in the defendant's store. The court concluded from these facts that there was a reasonable likelihood that a large collection of similar stolen furs was in the defendant's store.

The primary concern of courts in evaluating descriptions of property in affidavits is to ensure that a person will not be deprived of lawfully possessed property by a seizure made in pursuance of an imprecise search warrant. Even though there is reason to believe that a large collection of similar seizable items are located in a particular place, it may be possible to distinguish the seizable items from similar non-seizable items. An officer applying for a search warrant in this situation must explain in the affidavit the method by which the seizable property can be differentiated from similar innocent property when the warrant is executed. U. S. v. Klein, 565 F.2d 183 (1st Circuit Court of Appeals, 1977). Otherwise, either the warrant will not issue, or it will be declared invalid on appeal.

In a case involving several different items of property, the items to be seized were described in the warrant as follows:

> "one electric heater, one orange colored ice jug, 16 gauge shotgun shells, 22 shells, and so forth" * * *

The court held that this language was specific enough:

> We think, as did the trial judge, that these items were about as particularly described as such commodities can be. Such merchandise is difficult to describe. It may be said that the heater should be described as a "G.E." or a "Westinghouse", it could also be argued there are thousands of Westinghouse heaters. Shotgun shells might be described as Remington, Western, or Winchester or by the name of the manufacturers, still it could be argued there are untold numbers of Winchester, Remington, or "Peters" shotgun shells 12's, 16's and 20's. Poole v. State, 4 Tenn.Cr.App. 41, 54, 467 S.W.2d 826, 832 (Court of Criminal Appeals of Tennessee, 1971).

The description in the above case is probably about as general as it could be without being declared insufficient. If the officer knows the brand names and any other pertinent information, he should include them in the affidavit just to be safe.

Courts will generally allow greater leeway in descriptions of contraband material. Thus, a description merely of "paraphernalia for making coins," "heroin," or "narcotics drugs" will be adequate. The reason for this is that the purpose of the warrant is not to seize specified property but only property of a specified character which by reason of its character is contraband.

Multiple Affidavits

Often a law enforcement officer applying for a search warrant will submit more than one affidavit to the magistrate. The additional or supplemental affidavits may be prepared by the officer or by someone else. The Maine Supreme Judicial Court has said:

> Since the object of the proceedings before the magistrate is to establish probable cause to justify issuance of a search warrant, law enforcement officers should not be hindered in their efforts to describe the basis for probable cause in supporting affidavits. So long as these affidavits are satisfactorily incorporated to all related documents necessary to the application for the warrant * * the reviewing court will be assured of the simultaneous presence of these documents before the magistrate, and the search may be subjected to authoritative judicial review. State v. Gamage, Me., 340 A.2d 1, 7 (1975).

The main concern of the officer applying for a search warrant by means of more than one affidavit is to ensure that all "affidavits are satisfactorily incorporated to all related documents necessary to the application for the warrant." The following procedure is suggested to ensure proper incorporation:

1. Entitle the first or primary affidavit AFFIDAVIT AND REQUEST FOR SEARCH WARRANT.
2. Entitle all additional affidavits SUPPLEMENTAL AFFIDAVIT 1, SUPPLEMENTAL AFFIDAVIT 2, and so forth.
3. Include the following statement in the first or primary affidavit: "This request is also based upon the information in the sworn statements in SUPPLEMENTAL AFFIDAVIT 1, SUPPLEMENTAL AFFIDAVIT 2, * * * which are attached." (The law requires that clear reference be made to all supplemental affidavits.)
4. Securely attach all supplemental affidavits to the primary affidavit. Use a stapler or other semipermanent method of

binding. A paper clip would be unsatisfactory because of its tendency to slip off. By following these simple steps, the officer ensures that the magistrate will be simultaneously presented with all the information upon which probable cause is to be based and that the appellate court will be able to effectively review the magistrate's decision.

Anticipatory Search Warrants

An "anticipatory" search warrant, also called a "prospective" search warrant, is a search warrant issued to search a particular place, container, or person for a particular seizable item which has not yet arrived at the place where the search is to be executed. In recent years law enforcement officers have applied for anticipatory search warrants in increasing numbers, especially in cases involving contraband in the mails and in cases involving informants or undercover officers. A leading case in this area is People v. Glen, 30 N.Y. 2d 252, 331 N.Y.S.2d 656, 282 N.E.2d 614 (Court of Appeals of New York, 1972). In that case law enforcement officers applied for a warrant to search a package allegedly containing narcotics. The affidavit stated that the package was consigned to the defendant, a known drug user, and that it was due to arrive at a Greyhound Bus Depot. The affidavit added that the defendant had called for the package earlier that morning, but it had not yet arrived. The information in the affidavit was based on a tip from an informant whose reliability was adequately demonstrated. The warrant issued and shortly thereafter the officers were advised by a Greyhound clerk that the package had arrived. When the package went uncalled for that day, the officers removed it and examined it, finding marijuana. They returned the package to the depot the next morning. Later that day the defendant accepted delivery of the package and was arrested while leaving the depot.

The defendant contended on appeal that the warrant was invalid because no crime had been committed prior to its issuance and because there was was no present and continuing possession of the contraband at the time of issuance. The court said:

> The ultimate answer to the problem is that as long as the evidence creates substantial probability that the seizable property will be on the premises when searched, the warrant should be sustained. To be sure, where there is no present possession the supporting evidence for the prospective warrant must be strong that the particular possession of particular property will occur and that the elements to bring about that possession are in process and will result in the possession at the time and place specified. Otherwise, the hated general writs of assistance of pre-Revolutionary times would be revived, in effect, despite the constitutional limitations. More-

> over, the issuing Judge should be satisfied that there is no likelihood that the warrant will be executed prematurely. 30 N.Y.2d at 259, 331 N.Y.S.2d at 661, 282 N.E.2d at 617.

Law enforcement officers applying for anticipatory search warrants should take special care to satisfy the requirement that the elements to bring about the possession or presence of particular property at a particular time and place are in process, and they should state these elements in detail in the affidavit. A search warrant was held invalid in State v. Vitale, 23 Ariz.App. 37, 530 P.2d 394 (Court of Appeals of Arizona, 1975), because of failure to satisfy that requirement. In that case, a warrant to search the defendant's pawn shop was issued on the basis that a reliable informant had agreed to sell a stolen television set to the defendant at the pawn shop. The police had the television in their possession at the time they applied for the warrant. After the sale, the warrant was executed and the television was seized.

The defendant contended that the search warrant was invalid. The court agreed, stating that there was no probable cause that a crime had been committed at the time the warrant was issued. The court said:

> The informant had not yet approached appellant regarding the television set at the time the * * * search warrant was issued; also there had not been any recent dealings between the informant and appellant.
>
> * * *
>
> In the instant case, no crime was in progress and it was a matter of speculation whether one would be committed in the future. The course of events strongly suggests that the duty to determine probable cause was improperly shifted from the magistrate to the police. 23 Ariz.App. at 40–41, 530 P.2d at 397–98.

The quoted material suggests that, if there had been some deal or arrangement between the informant and the defendant before the police applied for the warrant, the court might have found the warrant valid on the ground that a crime was in progress or at least was very likely to occur.

In order to ensure that the magistrate is provided with sufficient information to justify the issuance of an anticipatory search warrant, law enforcement officers should present strong evidence in the affidavit that the continuation of a process *already initiated* will result in seizable items arriving at a particular place at a particular time. The affidavit should carefully specify the time when the item to be seized will arrive at the place where the search is to occur and the time thereafter when the execution of the warrant is planned to occur. This information will help to satisfy the magistrate that the warrant will not be executed prematurely.

CONTENTS OF THE WARRANT

If the magistrate is satisfied from the affidavit that there is probable cause to search, he will issue the warrant. Although search warrants differ from state to state, the following characteristics are common to most search warrants, and law enforcement officers should be familiar with them.

1. The warrant must be directed to an officer or class of officers authorized to enforce the laws of the state.

2. The warrant must particularly identify the property to be searched for. The description of the property must set forth meaningful limits for the officer executing the warrant. If the description is either too vague or too broad, the warrant may be declared invalid.

3. The warrant must particularly describe the person or place to be searched. The description of the person or place to be searched must also set meaningful limits for the officer executing the warrant and must not be too vague or too broad.

4. Some states require that the warrant state the grounds of probable cause for its issuance and the names of the persons whose affidavits have been taken in support of it. Usually, the grounds of probable cause do not appear in the body of the warrant itself, but may appear in attached affidavits. The Supreme Judicial Court of Maine has said:

> A basic reason for requiring the grounds of probable cause to appear on the face of the warrant is to provide a reviewing court with a complete record. Clear reference to an attached affidavit setting forth a basis of probable cause serves the same purpose. State v. Hollander, Me., 289 A.2d 419, 421 (Supreme Judicial Court of Maine, 1972).

5. The warrant must command the designated officer to search the person or place named for the property specified.

6. The warrant may specifically direct that it be served only in the daytime, or it may specifically allow a nighttime search, depending on the laws of the particular state.

7. The warrant must designate the judge to whom it shall be returned.

8. The warrant must state the date and time of its issuance.

9. The warrant must be signed by the issuing magistrate.

On page 63 is a form for a typical search warrant, containing spaces for all the elements listed above. It should be noted that the above characteristics need not appear in any particular order.

Form A. O. 93 (Rev. Apr. 1973) **Search Warrant**

United States District Court

FOR THE

UNITED STATES OF AMERICA vs.	Docket No. Case No. **SEARCH WARRANT**

To

Affidavit(s) having been made before me by

that he has reason to believe that { on the person of / on the premises known as }

in the District of

there is now being concealed certain property, namely

here describe property

and as I am satisfied that there is probable cause to believe that the property so described is being concealed on the person or premises above described and that grounds for application for issuance of the search warrant exist as stated in the supporting affidavit(s).

You are hereby commanded to search within a period of ______________________ (not to exceed 10 days) the person or place named for the property specified, serving this warrant and making the search { in the daytime (6:00 a.m. to 10:00 p.m.) / at any time in the day or night* } and if the property be found there to seize it, leaving a copy of this warrant and receipt for the property taken, and prepare a written inventory of the property seized and promptly return this warrant and bring the property before ______________________ as required by law.

Federal judge or magistrate

Dated this day of , 19

______________________________,

Judge (Federal or State Court of Record) or Federal Magistrate.

*The Federal Rules of Criminal Procedure provide: "The warrant shall be served in the daytime, unless the issuing authority, by appropriate provision in the warrant, and for reasonable cause shown, authorizes its execution at times other than daytime." (Rule 41(c)). A statement of grounds for reasonable cause should be made in the affidavit(s) if a search is to be authorized "at any time day or night" pursuant to Rule 41(c).

[B9584]

EXECUTION OF THE WARRANT

The execution of a search warrant is essentially the carrying out of the command or commands appearing on the face of the warrant itself. An officer can therefore determine much of his behavior from simply reading the warrant. However, many of the commands of a search warrant need further clarification and other limitations and duties are imposed by state statutes and various court decisions. The entire subject of execution of search warrants, therefore, will be covered in detail.

Who May Execute

The only person who may execute a search warrant is an officer who is authorized to enforce or assist in enforcing the laws of the state. The warrant will be directed to a particular officer or class of officers. Only the named officer or a member of the named class of officers is authorized to execute the warrant. Of course, if a warrant is directed to a particular officer such as a sheriff, his deputies may execute the warrant and the sheriff himself need not be present. Also, private persons may be enlisted to help in the execution of a warrant, but an officer to whom the warrant is directed must be personally present at the search scene.

Time Considerations

There are three aspects of time which affect a law enforcement officer in the execution of a search warrant. The first of these is the allowable time which an officer may delay between the issuance of the warrant and its execution. In states which have no time limit fixed by statute, court rule, or judicial decision, the law presumes that a reasonable time will be allowed for the warrant to be executed. What is a reasonable time will depend on the facts and circumstances of each case. Several states have statutes which set the outer time limit for the execution of a search warrant. Most require that it be executed and returned within ten days after its date of issuance. Many of these statutes *also* require that the warrant be executed "forthwith." In order to resolve this apparent ambiguity, federal and state courts interpreting these statutes have required that the warrant be executed within a reasonable time after issuance, as long as it is within the statutory period. U. S. v. Harper, 450 F.2d 1032 (5th Circuit Court of Appeals, 1971). *Therefore, even though an officer executes the warrant within the statutory ten (10) day period, the search could still be held unlawful.* The search would be unlawful if there were:

1. *Unnecessary delay* in executing the warrant; and

2. Such delay resulted in some *legal prejudice* to the defendant.

What is an unnecessary delay is determined by the circumstances of each case. One of the chief concerns of courts is that probable cause, existing at the time of issuance of the warrant, continues until the time of its execution. In a case interpreting a statute with both a "ten day" and a "forthwith" provision, a warrant for the seizure of equipment used to manufacture LSD was executed six days after its issuance. The court held that the execution was timely, as the premises were under daily surveillance, and no activity was noted until after the first five days. The court said in that case:

> While it is desirable that police be given reasonable latitude to determine when a warrant should be executed, it is also necessary that search warrants be executed with some promptness in order to lessen the possibility that the facts upon which probable cause was initially based do not become dissipated.
>
> We adopt the reasoning of the Second Circuit in *Dunnings* to the effect that "forthwith" means any time within 10 days after the warrant is issued, provided that the probable cause recited in the affidavit continues until the time of execution, giving consideration to the intervening knowledge of the officers and the passage of time. U. S. v. Nepstead, 424 F.2d 269, 271 (9th Circuit Court of Appeals, 1970).

There are several reasons why an officer would be justified in delaying the execution of a search warrant. For example, weather conditions, distance factors, traffic problems, and similar obstacles may prevent the prompt execution of the warrant. Delays may be necessary to gather sufficient manpower for the search or to protect the safety of the searching officers. Other reasons accepted by the courts for delaying the execution of a search warrant are prevention of destruction of evidence, or prevention of the flight of a suspect. And when the warrant is for the search of both a person and premises, the officers may delay the search until the person is present on the premises. People v. Stansberry, 47 Ill.2d 541, 268 N.E.2d 431 (Illinois Supreme Court, 1971). It is suggested that officers always be prepared to give convincing reasons for any delay in executing a warrant.

The second aspect of time which relates to the execution of a search warrant is the time of day during which it may be executed. Some state laws require that search warrants be executed in the daytime, and the warrants in those states will usually direct the law enforcement officer accordingly. Some of these states may also allow nighttime searches upon a showing of special circumstances by the officer applying for the warrant. Officers, therefore, should take great care in determining when the warrant can be executed. They should not only read the search warrant carefully, but should know their state law regarding the time of day when warrants can be executed.

Courts have differed in their interpretations of when "daytime" and "nighttime" begin and end. This chapter will not go into a discussion of those differences. Probably the safest standard for a law enforcement officer to adopt is that it is "daytime" when there is sufficient natural light to recognize a person's features. Otherwise, it is "nighttime." It is settled law that, even if nighttime searches are prohibited, the execution of a search warrant, begun in the daytime, may be continued into the nighttime as long as it is a reasonable continuation of the search begun earlier. An officer is not required to cut short the reasonable execution of a daytime search warrant just because it becomes dark outside. U. S. v. Joseph, 278 F.2d 504 (3d Circuit Court of Appeals, 1959).

The third aspect of time, as it relates to the execution of a search warrant, is the amount of time allowed for the law enforcement officer to perform the search *once it is initiated.* Since the warrant is a mandate of the court, the officer should be allowed to take as much time as necessary to carry out its purposes. This is particularly so when the items specified are small and easily concealed. State v. Gray, 152 Mont. 145, 447 P.2d 475 (Supreme Court of Montana, 1968). However, if the officer searches a place or person beyond a reasonable time for purposes of harassment or intimidation, it is likely that the search will be declared unlawful.

Gaining Entry

The manner of entry into premises to execute a search warrant must meet constitutional standards of "reasonableness." If the officer does not meet these standards, any subsequent search and seizure may be held illegal and the evidence obtained as a result may therefore be inadmissible in a criminal prosecution.

Statutes ordinarily provide that in order to lawfully gain entry to premises to execute a search warrant, the law enforcement officer must:

1. Knock on the door;
2. Announce his identity as a law enforcement officer;
3. Indicate that he possesses a search warrant; and
4. Announce that it is his purpose to execute the warrant.

If he is then refused entry, he may break open any outer or inner door, any window, or any other part of the house to carry out the command of the warrant.

There are, however, recognized exceptions to this rule requiring that officers first be refused admittance after an announcement of purpose before they are allowed to break in. One exception is for cases involving possible concealment or destruction of evidence or escape of a person to be searched. These situations arise frequently and often involve an officer knocking on a door and announcing his identity. Before he can complete his announcement of authority and purpose, he hears footsteps running from the door, whispers, flushing toilets, or other suspicious sounds. This most often occurs in drug, gambling, and illicit liquor cases. In these cases, where the officer has reason to believe that evidence will be concealed or destroyed, or that a person to be searched will escape, he may enter by force without completing his announcement of authority or purpose and without waiting for a specific refusal of admittance. *The important thing to remember, however, is that the officer must have specific substantial reasons for believing that evidence would be lost or that a person would escape if he did not act immediately. A forced entry without announcement of purpose will not be justified simply by the fact that a case involves narcotics, gambling, liquor, or anything else.* As the Supreme Court of California has said:

> Under the Fourth Amendment, a specific showing must always be made to justify any kind of police action tending to disturb the security of the people in their homes. Unannounced forcible entry is in itself a serious disturbance of that security and cannot be justified on a blanket basis. Otherwise, the constitutional test of reasonableness would turn only on practical expediency, and the amendment's primary safeguard—the requirement of particularity—would be lost. Just as the police must have sufficiently particular reason to enter at all, so must they have some particular reason to enter in the manner chosen. People v. Gastelo, 67 Cal.2d 586, 588–89, 63 Cal.Rptr. 10, 12, 432 P.2d 706, 708 (1967).

It is therefore strongly urged that officers keep a careful record of all the facts and circumstances which led them to believe that there was an immediate danger of loss of evidence or escape. Otherwise, if the officer cannot specifically justify his actions, any evidence he seizes after an unannounced entry may not be admissible in court.

Another exception to the rule requiring announcement of authority and purpose before entry to search is that the announcement is not necessary if the occupants of the premises to be searched already know of the officer's authority and purpose before any announcement. In an illustrative case, officers with a search warrant knocked on the defendant's apartment door and it swung open partially so the officer and occupants were clearly visible to each other. One of the officers was known to the occupants as a narcotics officer. The officers made no announcement of purpose, but waited about twenty seconds and then entered the apartment to conduct the search.

The court held that the unannounced police intrusion here was reasonable. Because the defendant recognized the officers through the partially open door and knew one to be a narcotics officer, the court found that the defendant was reasonably certain of the police purpose before the officers entered his apartment. A formal announcement of authority and purpose in this case would have been a useless gesture. U. S. ex rel. Dyton v. Ellingsworth, 306 F.Supp. 231 (U. S. District Court, D. Delaware 1969).

Again it is strongly urged that the officer keep a careful record of the facts and circumstances which gave him reason to believe that the defendant already knew his authority and purpose, making a formal announcement unnecessary. Also, it is a good idea for the officer to announce that he possesses a warrant, even though he does not announce anything else. This fact may not be as obvious to the occupant of the premises as the officer's authority and purpose may be.

A third exception exists when officers are justified in a belief that there would be a danger to the life or limb of an officer or someone within the premises if an announcement of authority and purpose was given. In a case illustrating this exception, FBI agents believed that a suspect who was a prison escapee with a reputation for always being armed and who was also wanted for murder of a policeman and armed bank robbery was within an apartment. They entered the apartment quietly without making any announcement of their authority or purpose. The court found that the entry to arrest the defendant was lawful on the theory that an announcement would have increased the peril of the agents. Gilbert v. U. S., 366 F.2d 923 (9th Circuit Court of Appeals, 1966). Although this case involved an entry to arrest, the principle applies equally to an entry to search.

Entry When No Response or No One Home

The requirement that an officer must be refused admittance after his announcement of authority and purpose before he may break into premises does not necessarily mean that the refusal must be actually stated. If an occupant of the premises is silent, and fails to call out or open the door after a reasonable opportunity to do so, this may be considered the equivalent of a refusal to admit the officer and the officer may then break in. U. S. v. Poppitt, 227 F.Supp. 73 (U. S. District Court, D. Delaware, 1964). What constitutes a reasonable opportunity to respond depends on the circumstances of each case. It has been held that an officer who yelled, "Police Officer", and then simultaneously kicked down the door, did not comply with standards of reasonableness. People v. Benjamin, 71 Cal.2d 296, 78 Cal.Rptr. 510, 455 P.2d 438 (Supreme Court of California, 1969).

A like rule applies if the residents of the premises are absent. There is no prohibition against executing a search warrant when premises are unoccupied. In fact, if an officer reasonably believes from the circumstances that no one is in the house, he need not make any announcement. As one case stated:

> In this case it would have been an empty gesture for the officers to have announced to an empty house that they were officers and that they were present for the purpose of executing a search warrant. U. S. v. Hawkins, 243 F.Supp. 429 (U.S.District Court, E.D.Tennessee, 1965).

Detention and Search of Persons on the Premises

When a search warrant is issued for the search of a named person or a named person *and* premises, there is no question that officers executing the warrant can detain and search the person named. However, often a person not named in the warrant is on the premises to be searched and the question arises whether that person may be detained or searched. *The general rule is that the search warrant gives a law enforcement officer no authority to search a person who merely happens to be on the premises.* In an illustrative case, police were executing a search warrant for narcotics in the dormitory room of a female university student. She was not present at the time the warrant was served, but the defendant, a male, was seated in the room when police entered. Although the officers did not know the defendant, they immediately searched him, found narcotics on his person, and then searched the room and found more narcotics.

The court held that the evidence found on the defendant was inadmissible in court. The court said that a warrant for a search of premises provides no basis for search of a person who merely happens to be present on the premises and who is not connected in any other way with the premises being searched. State v. Bradbury, 109 N.H. 105, 243 A.2d 302 (Supreme Court of New Hampshire, 1968).

If, however, an officer reasonably believes that a person on the premises poses a threat of physical harm to the officer, he may perform a limited pat-down or frisk of the person for weapons. The officer must be able to point to specific facts and circumstances which led him to believe the person was dangerous. A mere blanket statement that the officer believed the person dangerous will not justify a protective frisk. (See Chapter 10 on Stop and Frisk.)

Of course, if what the officer observes on the premises gives him probable cause for a felony arrest, or an offense is being committed in his presence, he may arrest the person on the premises. The person may then be searched incident to the arrest within the limits established by the *Chimel* case. (See Chapter 4 on Search Incident to Arrest.)

Several states have statutes allowing law enforcement officers to search all persons found on the described premises when executing a search warrant. Courts interpreting the statutes, however, usually require officers to show that the search of persons was reasonable or was based on probable cause. Willis v. State, 122 Ga.App. 455, 177 S.E.2d 487 (Court of Appeals of Georgia, 1970). The Supreme Judicial Court of Massachusetts stated:

> [I]n the overwhelming majority of cases a search based exclusively on the somewhat vague sanction of the language in the "any person present" clause is a clear violation of the proscription against unreasonable searches. An affidavit in support of a warrant which seeks to authorize a search of "any person present" is to be strictly scrutinized. It can only be valid where the underlying circumstances presented to the issuing judge or clerk clearly demonstrate probable cause to search the named premises and to believe that all persons present are involved in the criminal activity afoot. On the latter point, several facts are of particular relevance: the premises or area to be searched are small, confined and private; the nature of the criminal activity is such that the participants (in general) constantly shift or change so that it is, practically, impossible for the police to predict that any specific person or persons will be on the premises at any given time; and the items specifically described in the warrant as the target of the search are of a size or kind which renders them easily and likely to be concealed on the person. Commonwealth v. Smith, 369 Mass. 302, 348 N.E.2d 101, 106–07 (1976).

Intensity of the Search

A search under a search warrant may extend to all parts of the premises described in the warrant. For example, an individual's dwelling place will include his house, garage, and other buildings generally associated with and included within a house or home. State v. Brochu, Me., 237 A. 2d 418 (Supreme Judicial Court of Maine, 1967). It does not follow, however, that the officer executing the warrant may look everywhere within the described premises. He may look only where the items described in the warrant might be concealed. For example, if a search warrant indicated that the items sought were stolen tires, the officer would not be authorized to rummage through desk drawers and other places too small to hold tires. Yet, the officer would have authority to search drawers and small places if the items described in the warrant were coins or pills. The officer should be prepared to justify his looking into any enclosed areas such as drawers and containers by the nature and size of the items he is looking for.

The officer executing a search warrant must be reasonable with regard to the degree of force he uses in conducting the search. An otherwise reasonable search may become unreasonable due to the manner in which it is conducted. Therefore, as we have said, an officer may break into a house or other objects of search if he is denied access to them. Nevertheless, he must exercise a high degree of care to avoid unnecessary damage to the premises or objects. He must conduct the search in a manner designed to do the least damage possible, while still making a thorough examination of the premises. He should carefully replace articles which were necessarily disturbed during the search. Finally, he should avoid any unnecessary injury to the feelings of those present. As the Supreme Judicial Court of Maine has said in an early case:

> Officers must not allow their zeal and beliefs to blind them to the rights of the owners, and occupants of the dwelling house they search. Those rights, as well as the interests of the prosecutor, are to be regarded and protected by officers. * * * However confident the officers were of the guilt of the occupant, the house and its owner were not thereby outlawed. Buckley v. Beaulieu, 104 Me. 56, 61, 71 A. 70, 72 (1908).

Seizure of Items Not Named in the Warrant

Is it proper for a law enforcement officer to seize items *not* named in the warrant when found during the lawful execution of a warrant? By lawful execution of a warrant is meant a search (1) limited in area to the place named in the warrant; and (2) limited in the sense that the police were only looking in places where the items named in the warrant might be concealed. There has been a great deal of differing opinion on this question in the past. Some courts have held that the only items which may be seized pursuant to a search warrant are those named in the warrant, leaving nothing to the discretion of the law enforcement officer. State v. Brochu, Me., 237 A.2d 418 (Supreme Judicial Court of Maine, 1967). Other courts have allowed a seizure of *contraband,* not named in the warrant, which was found in *plain view* during a lawful execution. U. S. v. Zeidman, 444 F.2d 1051 (7th Circuit Court of Appeals, 1971). Still other courts have allowed the seizure of any unlisted evidentiary material observed in plain view as long as the search was not "exploratory," there was probable cause to seize the material, and the material seized had a direct relation to the primary purpose of the search. State v. Quigg, 155 Mont. 119, 467 P.2d 692 (Supreme Court of Montana, 1970).

The U. S. Supreme Court recently dealt with the question of the seizure of items unlisted in the warrant during the execution of a warrant in the case of Cady v. Dombrowski, 413 U.S. 433, 93 S.Ct. 2523, 37 L.Ed.2d 706 (1973). In that case, the police were investigating a possible homicide. The defendant informed them that he believed there was a body lying near his brother's farm. The police found the body and they also found defendant's car at the farm. Through the window of the car, the police observed a pillow case, a backseat, and a briefcase covered with blood. Police then obtained a warrant to search the car. While executing the warrant, police discovered, in "plain view" in the car, a blood-covered sock and a blood-covered floormat. The defendant claimed that the sock and the floormat taken from his car were illegally seized since they were not specifically listed on the application for the search warrant.

The Court held that the seizure of the items was constitutional. Since the warrant was validly issued, and the car was the item designated to be searched, the police were authorized to search the car. Although the sock and floormat were not listed in the warrant, the officers discovered these items in plain view in the car while executing the warrant and therefore could constitutionally seize them without a warrant.

Although the U. S. Supreme Court did not elaborate on its decision, the Cady v. Dombrowski case would appear to authorize seizures of *any item of evidence subject to seizure* which is found in plain view during the execution of a valid search warrant. The officer is cautioned, however, that such a seizure will probably be held illegal if:

1. The seizure was the product of an "exploratory" search; or
2. The items seized had no direct relation to the primary purpose of the search; or
3. The officer did not have probable cause to believe that the items fell within one of the categories of items subject to seizure.

The seizure will also be held illegal if the officer did not meet all the requirements of the plain view doctrine.

The plain view doctrine is discussed in detail in Chapter 6. One of the requirements of the doctrine deserves mention here, however. In the 1971 case of Coolidge v. New Hampshire, the U. S. Supreme Court required that absent exigent circumstances, the discovery of evidence in plain view must be *inadvertent.* This means that if officers are in a position or place where they have a lawful right to be (e. g., in someone's home for purposes of executing a search warrant), they may not seize evidence in plain view *if they knew before they entered the premises that the evidence would be there.* When an officer knows in advance the location of evidence and he intends to seize it, he must obtain a search warrant, or the seizure will be unlawful and the evidence will be inadmissible in court. Coolidge v. New Hampshire, 403 U.S. 443, 470, 91 S.Ct. 2022, 2040, 29 L.Ed.2d 564, 585 (U. S. Supreme Court, 1971). The safest procedure for the law enforcement officer, then, is to carefully list all the items he intends to seize in his affidavit when applying for a search warrant, and not to rely on discovering evidence in plain view during the execution of the warrant.

Duties After Search is Completed

As discussed earlier, a search warrent must be executed and returned either within a reasonable time or within a set time period, usually ten days after its date of issuance. Proper execution of a warrant requires more than merely conducting a search and seizing items described in the warrant. Most state statutes require that an officer who takes property under a warrant must give to the person from whom or from whose premises the property is taken, a copy of the warrant and a receipt for the property taken. If the person is unavailable, the officer must leave a copy of the warrant and a receipt at the place from which the property was taken.

The officer is also required to return the warrant to the judicial officer designated in the warrant promptly after its execution. The warrant must be accompanied by a written inventory or list of all property taken whether the items were described in the warrant or not. A form for making the return and inventory usually appears on the back of the search warrant form. A typical example of a return and inventory form appears on page 74. Some states further require that the inventory be made in the presence of the applicant for the warrant and the person from whose possession or premises the property was taken, if they were present. If they were not present, the inventory must be made in the presence of at least one other credible person. The courts have held that despite statutory provisions regulating the execution and return of search warrants, the giving of a receipt for property taken and the return of the warrant with inventory are ministerial acts. A ministerial act is one which is performed in obedience to the command of a legal authority and which requires no exercise of judgment or discretion by the person performing it. Failure to perform acts of this nature will not void a search warrant or the search conducted under the warrant. People v. Hawthorne, 45 Ill.2d 176, 258 N.E.2d 319 (Supreme Court of Illinois, 1970).

Although the performance of ministerial duties after the search is completed does not affect the validity of the warrant, officers should not take these duties lightly. In the words of the Supreme Judicial Court of Maine:

> Official dereliction in the punctilious observance of Rule 41(d) which has the force of law respecting the steps to be taken in the

RETURN

I received the attached search warrant 19 , and have executed it as follows:

On , 19 at o'clock M, I searched the person or premises described in the warrant and

I left a copy of the warrant with --
name of person searched or owner or "at the place of search"

together with a receipt for the items seized.

The following is an inventory of property taken pursuant to the warrant:

This inventory was made in the presence of

and

I swear that this Inventory is a true and detailed account of all the property taken by me on the warrant.

Subscribed and sworn to and returned before me this day of , 19

---,
Federal Magistrate

FPI LC 12-10-73 100M 7651

> execution of search warrants cannot be overlooked and imposes upon us the instant duty of forewarning all enforcement authorities that we expect full compliance in the future. We are inclined to believe that there exists no such general practice justifying at this time the adoption of an exclusionary rule to compel obedience. State v. Martelle, Me., 252 A.2d 316, 321 (1969).

It is strongly urged, therefore, that officers take pains to carefully comply with the requirements of statutes governing the execution and return of search warrants. Otherwise, the courts may take stronger steps to ensure strict compliance.

ADMINISTRATIVE SEARCH WARRANTS

An administrative search is a routine inspection of a home or business to determine compliance with various statutes and regulations. An administrative search seeks to enforce fire, health, and housing codes, licensing provisions, and the like. It differs from a criminal search in that a criminal search focuses on gathering evidence in order to convict a person of a crime. An administrative search ordinarily does not result in a criminal prosecution.

Before 1967, courts consistently held that administrative searches were not subject to the restrictions of the Fourth Amendment and that a search warrant was not needed to inspect residential or commercial premises for violations of regulatory and licensing provisions. In 1967, in the cases of Camara v. Municipal Court, 387 U.S. 523, 87 S.Ct. 1727, 18 L.Ed.2d 930, and See v. City of Seattle, 387 U.S. 541, 87 S.Ct. 1737, 18 L.Ed.2d 943, the U. S. Supreme Court reversed earlier decisions and held that such administrative inspections were subject to the warrant requirement of the Fourth Amendment. The basis for both the *Camara* and *See* decisions was the Court's belief that a person's right of privacy should not be determined by the nature of the search. In *Camara,* the Court said, "It is surely anomalous to say that the individual and his private property are fully protected by the Fourth Amendment only when the individual is suspected of criminal behavior." 387 U.S. at 530, 87 S.Ct. at 1732, 18 L.Ed.2d at 936. Nevertheless, the Court held that, because administrative searches differ in nature and purpose from criminal searches, the probable cause standard for administrative searches differs in nature and is less stringent than the standard for criminal searches. The Court said:

> The warrant procedure is designed to guarantee that a decision to search private property is justified by a reasonable governmental interest. But reasonableness is still the ultimate standard. If a valid public interest justifies the intrusion contemplated, then there is probable cause to issue a suitably restricted search warrant." 387 U.S. at 539, 87 S.Ct. at 1736, 18 L.Ed.2d at 941.

Despite the less stringent probable cause standard, the U S. Supreme Court and other courts have carved out various exceptions to the warrant requirement for administrative searches. There are exceptions based on emergency, consent, plain view, and open fields. These exceptions are similar to the exceptions to the warrant requirement for criminal searches discussed in Part Two of this book, but the standards are generally less stringent than those required for criminal searches. Another exception, allowing warrantless inspection of certain *licensed and closely regulated enterprises,* has been recognized by the U. S. Supreme Court. In U. S. v. Biswell, 406 U.S. 311, 92 S.Ct. 1593, 32 L.Ed.2d 87 (1972), the Court upheld a warrantless search of a storeroom of a gun dealer licensed under the Gun Control Act of 1968. The Court said:

> [I]f inspection is to be effective and serve as a credible deterrent, unannounced, even frequent, inspections are essential. In this context, the prerequisite of a warrant could easily frustrate inspection; and if the necessary flexibility as to time, scope and frequency is to be preserved, the protections afforded by a warrant would be negligible.
>
> It is also plain that inspections for compliance with the Gun Control Act pose only limited threats to the dealer's justifiable expectations of privacy. When a dealer chooses to engage in this pervasively regulated business and to accept a federal license, he does so with the knowledge that his business records, firearms, and ammunition will be subject to effective inspection. 406 U.S. at 316, 92 S.Ct. at 1596, 32 L.Ed.2d at 92–93.

This exception to the warrant requirement for inspections of licensed and closely regulated businesses has been applied by state and federal courts to a great variety of businesses since the *Biswell* decision.

Administrative searches will not be discussed in further detail because they are seldom conducted by law enforcement officers. Nevertheless, officers should be aware that the line between an administrative and a criminal search can sometimes become blurred. When an administrative search begins to take on the characteristics of a criminal search, the stricter standards applicable to criminal searches come into play. If these stricter standards are not followed, any evidence obtained will be held inadmissible in a criminal prosecution.

An example of an administrative search which took on the characteristics of a criminal search is the case of Michigan v. Tyler, 436 U.S. 499, 98 S.Ct. 1942, 56 L.Ed.2d 486 (U.S. Supreme Court, 1978). That case involved a late night fire in a furniture store leased by the defendant. When the fire was reduced to smoldering embers, the fire chief, while investigating the cause of the fire, discovered two plastic containers of flammable liquid. The chief summoned a police detective to investigate possible arson. The detective took several pictures but, because visibility was hindered by darkness, steam, and smoke, the investigators departed the scene at 4 a. m. and returned shortly after daylight to continue the investigation. More evidence of arson was found and seized at this time. About a month later, a state police arson investigator made several visits to the fire scene and obtained evidence which was used at trial in convicting the defendant. At no time was any warrant or consent to search obtained.

The Court held that the investigative activity on the day of the fire was legal, but that the evidence-gathering activity a month after the fire was an illegal search and seizure.

> [W]e hold that an entry to fight a fire requires no warrant, and that once in the building, officials may remain there for a reasonable time to investigate the cause of the blaze. Thereafter, additional entries to investigate the cause of the fire must be made pursuant to the warrant procedures governing administrative searches. * * * Evidence of arson discovered in the course of such investigations is admissible at trial, but if the investigating officials find probable cause to believe that arson has occurred and require further access to gather evidence for a possible prosecution, they may obtain a warrant only upon a traditional showing of probable cause applicable to searches for evidence of crime. 436 U.S. at 511–12, 98 S.Ct. at 1951, 56 L.Ed.2d at 500.

The important thing for the law enforcement officer to remember is that once a search is directed toward gathering evidence for a criminal prosecution, the officer must obtain a criminal search warrant as described in this chapter. The officer cannot avoid this requirement by using other governmental officials to conduct searches under the guise of an administrative or regulatory inspection.

EFFECT OF ILLEGAL SEARCH AND SEIZURE

For purposes of this discussion an illegal search and seizure is a search and seizure which is conducted without a valid search warrant and which does not fall within any of the exceptions to the search warrant requirement discussed in Part Two of this book. The most important effect of an illegal search and seizure is the exclusion of seized evidence in court from use against the person from whom it was taken. The so-called exclusionary rule, as it relates to search and seizure, states that evidence obtained by law enforcement officers in violation of an accused person's Fourth Amendment rights cannot be used in evidence against him, either in a federal or state criminal prosecution. The exclusionary rule for federal prosecutions was established by the U. S. Supreme Court in 1914 in the case of Weeks v. U. S., 232 U.S. 383, 34 S.Ct. 341, 58 L.Ed. 652. The rule was not applied to state prosecutions until the 1961 landmark U. S. Supreme Court decision in Mapp v. Ohio, 367 U.S. 643, 81 S.Ct. 1684, 6 L.Ed. 2d 1081. The *Mapp* case held that, as a matter of due process of law under the Fourteenth Amendment, the Fourth Amendment is applicable to the states. To enforce the Fourth Amendment guarantees, the court held that evidence obtained by an illegal search and seizure is inadmissible in state courts, the same as it is in federal courts.

Although courts and commentators have proposed many arguments and rationales both in favor of and against the exclusionary rule, it is generally agreed today that the primary purpose of the rule is to deter police conduct that violates citizens' constitutional rights. This purpose was well stated by the United States Supreme Court in the 1968 case of Terry v. Ohio:

> Ever since its inception, the rule excluding evidence seized in violation of the Fourth Amendment has been recognized as a principal mode of discouraging lawless police conduct * * *. Thus its major thrust is a deterrent one, * * * and experience has taught that it is the only effective deterrent to police misconduct in the criminal context, and that without it the constitutional guarantee against unreasonable searches and seizures would be a mere "form of words." 392 U.S. 1, 12, 88 S.Ct. 1868, 1875, 20 L.Ed.2d 889, 900–01.

The exclusionary rule is broad and far-reaching in scope and does more than simply bar the admission in court of the items of evidence seized. The rule also bars the admission of any oral testimony regarding what was found, seen, or heard during the conduct of an illegal search and seizure. Likewise, the rule bars the admission during trial of testimony of an accused at the pretrial hearing on his motion to suppress the evidence taken from him. Furthermore, fruits of an illegal search and seizure cannot be used against the victim of the illegal activity. This is known as the "fruit of the poisonous tree doctrine." A fruit of an illegal search and seizure is any evidence obtained indirectly as a result of it. Examples of fruits of an illegal search and seizure are information or leads derived from it; other physical evidence obtained as a result of it; the testimony of witnesses discovered as a result of it; statements or admissions made or overheard during it; and confessions prompted by confronting persons with evidence obtained during it.

Not all fruits of an illegal search and seizure will be held inadmissible—only those fruits which are obtained by *exploitation* of the primary illegality. The leading case establishing this principle is Wong Sun v. U. S., 371 U.S. 471, 83 S.Ct. 407, 9 L.Ed.2d 441 (U. S. Supreme Court, 1963). In that case narcotics agents illegally broke into Toy's laundry and followed him into his living quarters where he was arrested and handcuffed. Almost immediately thereafter, Toy told the agents that Yee had been selling narcotics. The agents subsequently seized heroin from Yee, who told them that it had been brought to him by Toy and Wong Sun. Wong Sun was illegally arrested, arraigned, and released on his own recognizance. Several days later, Wong Sun voluntarily made an oral confession to a narcotics agent during interrogation.

Toy argued that his statement and the heroin later seized from Yee were fruits of the illegal entry into his dwelling and his illegal arrest. The Court agreed and held both inadmissible. Wong Sun claimed that his statement was the fruit of his illegal arrest. The Court disagreed:

> We have no occasion to disagree with the finding of the Court of Appeals that his arrest, also, was without probable cause or reasonable grounds. At all events no evidentiary consequences turn upon that question. For Wong Sun's unsigned confession was not the fruit of that arrest, and was therefore properly admitted at trial. On the evidence that Wong Sun had been released on his own recognizance after a lawful arraignment, and had returned voluntarily several days later to make the statement, we hold that the connection between the arrest and the statement had "become so attenuated as to dissipate the taint." 371 U.S. at 491, 83 S.Ct. at 419, 9 L.Ed.2d at 457.

Therefore, if evidence is obtained by means sufficiently distinguishable to be purged of the taint of primary illegality, the primary illegality has not been exploited and the evidence will be admissible.

In determining the admissibility of fruits of an illegal search and seizure courts talk in terms of the "attenuation" or "dissipation" of the taint. In the words of the Supreme Court of California:

> That degree of "attenuation" which suffices to remove the taint from evidence obtained directly as a result of unlawful police conduct requires at least an intervening independent act by the defendant or a third party which breaks the causal chain linking the illegality and evidence in such a way that the evidence is not in fact obtained "by exploitation of that illegality". People v. Superior Court (Casebeer) 71 Cal.2d 265, 271–72, 78 Cal.Rptr. 210, 215, 455 P.2d 146, 151 (1969).

It should be noted that the United States Supreme Court has held that, because of the cost to the truth-finding process of disqualifying knowledgeable witnesses, the exclusionary rule should be invoked with much greater reluctance when the fruit of the poisonous tree is the testimony of a live witness rather than an inanimate object. U. S. v. Ceccolini, 435 U.S. 268, 98 S.Ct. 1054, 55 L.Ed.2d 268 (1978). Therefore, courts will not exclude the testimony of a witness discovered as the result of a Fourth Amendment violation, unless the court finds a more direct link between the discovery and the violation than is required to exclude physical evidence. Also, the court must find that the Fourth Amendment violation is the type that will be deterred by application of the exclusionary rule.

When evidence is obtained from sources independent of an illegal search and seizure and not by exploitation of it, the evidence is not "fruit of the poisonous tree" and is admissible. As stated by the U. S. Supreme Court in Silverthorne Lumber Co. v. U. S., 251 U.S. 385, 40 S.Ct. 182, 64 L.Ed. 319 (1920):

> The essence of a provision forbidding the acquisition of evidence in a certain way is that not merely evidence so acquired shall not be used before the court but that it shall not be used at all. Of course this does not mean that the facts thus obtained become sacred and inaccessible. If knowledge of them is gained from an independent source they may be proved like any others, but the knowledge gained by the government's own wrong cannot be used in the way proposed. 251 U.S. at 392, 40 S.Ct. at 183, 64 L.Ed. at 321.

The discussion of "attenuation" or "dissipation" and "independent source" serves to highlight an important feature of the exclusionary rule. The exclusionary rule does *not* necessarily bar or stop a prosecution. At most, the rule will cause the suppression of evidence obtained during or fruits of an illegal search and seizure. If that evidence or those fruits are essential to the prosecution's case against an accused, the prosecution may decide not to prosecute. If, however, the prosecution has sufficient other evidence from sources independent of the illegal search and seizure, or evidence from which the taint of the illegal search and seizure has dissipated or attenuated, the prosecution may go forward despite the illegal police conduct.

Also, the exclusionary rule does not bar the use of evidence obtained by exploitation of an illegal search and seizure to attack or impeach the defendant's credibility as a witness. In so holding the U. S. Supreme Court said:

> It is one thing to say that the Government cannot make an affirmative use of evidence unlawfully obtained. It is quite another to say that the defendant can turn the illegal method by which evidence in the Government's possession was obtained to his own advantage, and provide himself with a shield against contradiction of

his untruths. Walder v. U. S., 347 U.S. 62, 65, 74 S.Ct. 354, 356, 98 L.Ed. 503, 507 (1954).

In some instances, evidence obtained during an illegal search and seizure may be used in strictly *civil* cases, i. e., cases instituted to enforce or protect private rights or to redress or prevent private wrongs. For example, the U. S. Supreme Court recently held that evidence seized unconstitutionally but in good faith by a state law enforcement officer may be used in a federal civil proceeding. The Court reasoned that the exclusionary rule's primary purpose of deterring unlawful police conduct would not be served by applying it to exclude from the civil proceeding of one sovereign evidence seized unconstitutionally but in good faith by a criminal law enforcement agent of another sovereign. U. S. v. Janis, 428 U.S. 433, 96 S.Ct. 3021, 49 L.Ed.2d 1046 (1976).

Other possible effects of an illegal search and seizure are civil and criminal liability of the officer conducting the search and seizure. As with an illegal arrest, the consequences for the officer depend upon the circumstances of each case including the officer's good faith, the degree of care used, the degree of force used, and the seriousness of the situation.

It should be obvious from this discussion that the effects of an illegal search and seizure are far-reaching and potentially devastating to the prosecution of a criminal case or to the furtherance of the law enforcement officer's career. It is vitally important for law enforcement officers not only to learn and apply the information in this chapter and in Part Two, but to keep abreast of continually changing developments in the law of search and seizure.

SUMMARY

The general rule is that all searches and seizures conducted without a warrant are unreasonable and in violation of the Fourth Amendment to the U. S. Constitution. Although there are many well-defined exceptions to this rule (discussed in Part Two), searches made under the authority of a warrant are not only greatly preferred by the courts, but also give the law enforcement officer greater protection from liability.

The material presented in this chapter has been designed to give the law enforcement officer the basic information he needs to properly obtain and execute a search warrant. The discussion has necessarily been general, because the specifics of the law of search warrants differ from state to state. Every law enforcement officer must learn for himself the peculiarities of his own state's search warrant law. The treatment of probable cause in this chapter has also been general. It will be discussed in detail in Chapter 3.

All law enforcement officers are again reminded that because of recent U. S. Supreme Court limitations on warrantless searches, there are now more situations in which law enforcement officers are required to obtain search warrants before conducting searches and seizures. It is, therefore, essential for officers to be thoroughly familiar with the information presented in this chapter and to implement this knowledge in their daily operations.

3

PROBABLE CAUSE

Probable cause has already been discussed to a limited extent as an integral part of the preceding chapters on Arrest and Search Warrants. Every law enforcement officer, therefore, should be generally familiar with the term. Nevertheless, because probable cause is so basic to criminal procedure, it is important that all officers have as complete an understanding of it as possible. This chapter will attempt to explain in detail all aspects of probable cause as it concerns the law enforcement officer. The material presented here should not be read in isolation but is designed to be read in conjunction with the previous chapters.

DEFINITION

A good place to begin a discussion of probable cause is with a definition. Two different but similar definitions of probable cause will be quoted, one for search and one for arrest, because different types of information are required to establish probable cause in each case. The most quoted definition of probable cause to *search* is that found in Carroll v. U. S., 267 U.S. 132, 45 S.Ct. 280, 69 L.Ed. 543 (U. S. Supreme Court, 1925). In that case, the Court said that probable cause exists when:

> * * * the facts and circumstances within their (the officers') knowledge and of which they had reasonably trustworthy information (are) sufficient in themselves to warrant a man of reasonable caution in the belief that (seizable property would be found in a particular place or on a particular person). (parenthetical material supplied) 267 U.S. at 162, 45 S.Ct. at 288, 69 L.Ed. at 555.

Paraphrasing the *Carroll* case, the U. S. Supreme Court in Draper v. U. S., 358 U.S. 307, 79 S.Ct. 329, 3 L.Ed.2d 327 (1959), said that probable cause for *arrest* exists when:

> "the facts and circumstances within their [the arresting officers'] knowledge and of which they had reasonably trustworthy information [are] sufficient in themselves to warrant a man of reasonable caution in the belief that" an offense has been or is being committed. 358 U.S. at 313, 79 S.Ct. at 333, 3 L.Ed.2d at 332.

These definitions differ only in that the facts and circumstances which would justify an arrest may be different from those that would justify a search. This chapter will be concerned with that part of the definition of probable cause which is common to both arrests and searches, namely, the nature, quality, and amount of information necessary to establish probable cause. We will concentrate on facts and circumstances which the law enforcement officer must have within his knowledge before he can arrest or search, with or without a warrant. Of course, it is impossible to say exactly what combination of facts will provide probable cause in any given situation, because every situation is different in some way. Nevertheless, an attempt will be made to indicate the types of information which a judge or magistrate will consider in deciding whether probable cause exists, whether in an application for an arrest or search warrant, at a motion to suppress hearing, or at a trial.

Sources of Information

Information about possible criminal activity can come to a law enforcement officer's attention in two possible ways: (1) The officer may himself perceive the activity; or (2) someone else may perceive the activity and relay the information to the officer. These two types of information sources are treated differently by the courts in determining whether there is probable cause for a warrantless arrest or search or for the issuance of an arrest or search warrant. Because of these differences in treatment, the two types of information sources will be discussed separately.

INFORMATION OBTAINED THROUGH THE OFFICER'S OWN SENSES

When applying for an arrest or search warrant, the law enforcement officer should state, *in writing,* in the complaint or affidavit the underlying facts upon which probable cause for the issuance of the warrant is to be based. The laws of some states allow law enforcement officers to supplement their affidavits for warrants with oral testimony. Nevertheless, as stated in Chapter 2, the better and safer practice for all officers is to include *all* the information from which probable cause is to be determined in the affidavit itself. Then, if the validity of the warrant is later challenged, the court hearing the challenge would have a complete record before it. The officer need not state all he knows about a particular case as long as he states sufficient facts to support a finding of probable cause. However, because judges and magistrates differ, and because probable cause is such an elusive concept, the officer takes a chance if he does not state all the facts within his knowledge in the complaint or affidavit.

The officer must have the same considerations in mind when he decides to arrest or search without a warrant. Even though he does not have to write down the facts to support a finding of probable cause in warrantless situations, he must be prepared to justify his arrest or search if it is later challenged at trial or at a motion to suppress hearing. Therefore, whether he goes the warrant route or not, the officer must have sufficient information for probable cause in his mind *before* he conducts any arrest or search.

One type of information which an officer will use to support his finding of probable cause is information which comes to him through his own senses. This would include not only what the officer might have seen, but also what he might have heard, smelled, touched, or tasted. Furthermore, an officer's perceptions may be given additional weight because of his experience or expertise in a particular area. As one court has said:

> Among the pertinent circumstances to be considered is the qualification and function of the person making the arrest. An officer of a narcotics detail may find probable cause in activities of a suspect and in the appearance of paraphernalia or physical characteristics which to the eye of a layman could be without significance. His action should not, therefore, be measured by what might not be probable cause to an untrained civilian passerby, but by a standard appropriate for a reasonable, cautious, and prudent narcotics officer under the circumstances of the moment. State v. Poe, 74 Wash. 2d 425, 428–29, 445 P.2d 196, 199 (Supreme Court of Washington, 1968).

Indications of Criminal Activity Which May Contribute to Probable Cause

When criminal activity is committed in an officer's presence, and is perceived by the officer through one or more of his senses, these perceptions are clearly information which would be sufficient for probable cause to support either the issuance of a warrant or, in the proper circumstances, an arrest or search without a warrant. Most information which comes to an officer's attention, however, is seldom as clearcut as an offense being committed in his presence. Usually the officer has to develop probable cause from a series of facts which do not add up to a crime being committed in his presence. The following is a list of the types of facts and circumstances which may be used by a law enforcement officer in developing probable cause along with a discussion of the relative importance each is likely to be accorded by a judge or magistrate.

Flight

The flight of a suspect when approached by a law enforcement officer is one factor to be considered in determining whether there is probable cause. An example of this is a case in which officers in a patrol car had received information by radio about illegal activities involving non-tax-paid whiskey. They had been given a description of a car and of its occupants who were said to be involved in this illegal activity. When the officers spotted the car, they pulled up to it and called out the nickname of the defendant, whom they recognized. Defendant then threw his car into reverse and sped away. The officers overtook him after a short chase and approached his car. As they approached, they smelled the odor of moonshine whiskey and observed tin cans and plastic jugs in the back seat of the vehicle. They then arrested the defendant.

The court held that the arrest was valid and supported by probable cause. For purposes of this discussion, it is important that the court specifically held that the flight of the defendant was one factor *among others* to be considered in determining whether there was probable cause. U. S. v. Brock, 408 F.2d 322 (5th Circuit Court of Appeals, 1969).

Flight by itself, however, will not support a finding of probable cause. This point is illustrated by the U. S. Supreme Court case of Wong Sun v. U. S., 371 U.S. 471, 83 S.Ct. 407, 9 L.Ed.2d 441 (1963). In that case, federal officers arrested a man named Hom Way at two o'clock in the morning and found narcotics in his possession. Hom Way told the officers that he had purchased an ounce of heroin from a person named "Blackie Toy." At six o'clock that same morning, the officers went to a laundry operated by James Wah Toy. When Toy answered the door, one officer identified himself, whereupon Toy slammed the door and ran to his living quarters at the rear of the building. The officers broke in, followed Toy to his bedroom, and arrested him there.

The U. S. Supreme Court held that the arrest was made without probable cause. First, the officers had no basis in experience for confidence in the reliability of Hom Way's information. (More will be said about reliability of informants later.) Second, the mere fact of Toy's flight did not provide a justification for a warrantless arrest without further information. On this point, the Court said:

> Toy's refusal to admit the officers and his flight down the hallway thus signified a guilty knowledge no more clearly than it did a natural desire to repel an apparently unauthorized intrusion. * * *
>
> A contrary holding here would mean that a vague suspicion could be transformed into probable cause for arrest by reason of ambiguous conduct which the arresting officers themselves have provoked. 371 U.S. at 483–84, 83 S.Ct. at 415, 9 L.Ed.2d at 452–53.

Real or Physical Evidence

Another way in which officers may establish probable cause is by the observation and evaluation of real or physical evidence. A good example is a case in which officers were summoned at 2:00 A.M. to a store which had been recently burglarized. The officers discovered two sets of footprints in fresh-fallen snow leading from the store to the tire tracks of an automobile. Two persons apparently had entered the automobile. Since the automobile tire tracks were identifiable by a distinctive tread, the officers followed them. After a short distance, the officers met another officer who had found a checkbook belonging to the store owner in the road. Further down the road the officers found a bag containing electrical parts. They then came upon a car parked in the middle of the road with its lights off. The only other vehicle the officers had seen since leaving the scene of the crime was driven by a person known to the officers. As the patrol car approached the parked car, the parked car turned on its lights and drove off. The officers stopped the car, arrested its two occupants for breaking and entering, and searched them incident to the arrest.

The court found that the items of real evidence found and the reasonable inferences drawn from the evidence, together with the highly suspicious circumstances, provided probable cause to arrest the defendants. The court added:

> Although the possibility of mistake existed, as it invariably does in a probable cause situation, they would have been remiss in their duty if they had not arrested the defendants promptly. State v. Heald, Me., 314 A.2d 820, 825 (Supreme Judicial Court of Maine, 1973).

Furtive Conduct

Law enforcement officers are frequently confronted with suspicious circumstances, secretive movements, or other furtive conduct, which give them reason to believe either that criminal activity is afoot or that the person or persons observed are attempting to hide contraband, instrumentalities, or other evidence of crime. Usually, such circumstances or conduct will at least justify an officer's further investigation to determine whether a crime is being or is about to be committed. (See Chapter 10 on Stop and Frisk.)

Furtive conduct by itself, however, will usually not be enough to establish probable cause to arrest or search. The reason for this is that a person may be making a totally innocent gesture, asserting a constitutional right, or reacting in fear to an officer's approach. Also, a person's nervous state in the presence of a law enforcement officer will not alone amount to probable cause. The Supreme Court of Colorado has stated that "[i]t is normal for law-abiding persons, as well as persons guilty of criminal activity, to be nervous when stopped by a policeman for a traffic offense." People v. Goessl, 186 Colo. 208, 211, 526 P.2d 664, 665 (1974). Such actions may often be mistaken for guilty behavior by a law enforcement officer investigating a possible crime. An individual should not be subject to arrest or search on such uncertain information.

A typical case illustrating this point involved a police officer who had spotted a car parked illegally with the defendant sitting in it. The officer pulled up next to the vehicle in order to advise the defendant it was illegally parked. As the officer approached, he noticed the defendant lean forward in the driver's seat. The officer directed defendant to get out of the car, patted him down, and searched under the seat of the car. Marijuana was found and seized.

The court held the search and seizure illegal. In order to constitute probable cause for a search, there must be something more than a furtive gesture such as a motorist bending over in the front seat. The gesture must have some guilty significance arising either from specific information known to the officer or from additional suspicious circumstances observed by him. In this case, there were no such additional factors, and the search was not justified. Gallik v. People, 5 Cal.3d 855, 97 Cal.Rptr. 693, 489 P.2d 573 (Supreme Court of California, 1971).

When there are such additional circumstances, however, furtive action may provide one of the factors upon which probable cause may be based. In one such case, officers entered the home of one Bracamonte to execute a search warrant. As they entered, they spotted defendant standing in the living room. The officers recognized defendant because they had been told by informants that defendant was a narcotics dealer, and they had observed him in the company of narcotics suppliers on several occasions. The officers noticed that defendant's right hand was clenched in a fist behind his right leg and they asked him what he was concealing. Defendant made a further gesture to conceal his hand from view and then raised it in an upward motion toward his mouth. One officer grabbed his hand and opened his fist finding a balloon which contained what was later determined to be heroin. Defendant was placed under arrest.

The court held that the officers had probable cause to arrest defendant and to search him incident to the arrest. The court said that defendant's presence in a place suspected of narcotics activity, his past dealings in narcotics, combined with his furtive movements supplied the necessary probable cause. With respect to furtive movements, the court said:

> [T]o add to the highly suspicious circumstances, appellant not only attempted to hide something behind his leg in a clenched fist, but when the officer inquired as to what he was hiding, appellant moved his clenched fist rapidly toward his mouth. Swallowing narcotics is a popular method of avoiding detection, and movements of the hand toward the mouth have consistently been held to be the type of furtive movement that may be assessed in the probable cause equation. People v. Rodriquez, 274 Cal.App.2d 770, 775, 79 Cal.Rptr. 240, 243–44 (California Court of Appeal, 1969).

Perceptions of Narcotics Usage

An officer's perceptions of narcotics usage may be considered in determining the existence of probable cause. This is similar to perceptions of furtive conduct except that furtive conduct is usually voluntary whereas indications of narcotics usage are usually involuntary. The indicators of narcotics usage that are considered by courts in determining whether there is probable cause are abnormal contraction of pupils, discolored tissue on arms, fresh needle marks on arms, slurred speech, difficulty in balancing, nervousness, sweating, and heavy eyelids. Observation of one or two of these factors, standing alone, is probably not sufficient information to establish probable cause. When many such factors are present, however, or when there are other suspicious circumstances, chances are greater that the information available will support a finding of probable cause.

An example of perceptions of narcotics use providing probable cause is a case in which officers were investigating a report of suspicious activity of a person who had boarded a bus. The officers checked the bus and asked the suspicious person to dismount. While talking to him, they noticed that he was extremely nervous, sweating profusely, and the pupils of his eyes were extremely constricted despite poor lighting. The officers shined a flashlight in his eyes and noticed no apparent reaction to the light. Questions had to be repeated to him as though he were in a daze. The officers, being experienced narcotics officers, formed the opinion that the defendant was under the influence of a narcotic and arrested him. The court held that the observations of the officers were sufficient to establish probable cause to arrest. People v. Gregg, 267 Cal.App.2d 567, 73 Cal. Rptr. 362 (Court of Appeal of California, 1968).

Admissions

A defendant's admission of criminal conduct to a law enforcement officer can often provide probable cause for an arrest. In fact, this is often all that is needed because an admission provides such direct evidence of the defendant's guilt that the officer need look no further. An example is a case in which officers observed a vehicle driven by defendant fail to stop for a traffic light, and they followed it into a gas station. The officers intended only to issue a traffic citation. As the vehicle stopped, the defendant and two passengers stepped from the vehicle and advanced toward the officers. The officers patted them down to protect themselves and one officer thought he felt capsules in defendant's pocket. He asked him if he had any pills in his pocket and the defendant responded, "They're reds. They belong to my mother." The officer then asked the defendant to take out the pills. When he did, the officer seized them. Later chemical analysis indicated they were seconal.

The court found that the usage of the term "reds" to describe seconal was so common that they could take judicial notice of it. The admission by the defendant was held to be sufficient in itself to provide probable cause and the arrest and seizure were both upheld. People v. Hubbard, 9 Cal.App.3d 827, 88 Cal.Rptr. 411 (California Court of Appeal, 1970).

It is worthy of note that in the preceding case, the court discussed at length whether the defendant should have been given *Miranda* warnings before the officer asked him about the pills. It was held that defendant was not in custody for purposes of *Miranda* because there was no "compelling atmosphere" and he was only subject to a "transitory" restraint. The important thing for the law enforcement officer to remember, however, is that whenever a defendant's admission or confession becomes part of a case, the requirements of *Miranda* must be satisfied, if they apply. Otherwise the admission or confession itself and any evidence seized as a result of it will be inadmissible in court. Guidelines for the law enforcement officer with respect to *Miranda* can be found in Chapter 9.

Failure to Explain or Evasiveness

When a suspect, confronted by a law enforcement officer, fails to explain or provides unsatisfactory explanations for his suspicious conduct or presence near the scene of a crime, his behavior may contribute to probable cause for an arrest. Common examples of this type of behavior are failing to produce identification, giving a false identification or alias, and giving false information about other matters. Usually, failure to explain or evasiveness standing alone will not be enough to provide probable cause.

In one case, State Police had been notified that rental trucks were being used to transport stolen goods in a certain area of the state. An officer patrolling in this area stopped a rental truck for a routine check for registration, driver's license, and rental papers. Noticing that the truck was heavily loaded, the officer asked the defendant what he was carrying. The defendant claimed that his truck was empty. A subsequent search revealed a cargo of stolen cigarettes.

The court held that probable cause to search was provided by the officer's knowledge that rental trucks were being used in the area to transport stolen goods combined with the defendant's obvious lie. A search warrant was not needed in this situation because the truck was a movable vehicle and could be searched under the *Carroll* doctrine once there was probable cause to search. U. S. v. Gomori, 437 F.2d 312 (4th Circuit Court of Appeals, 1971). For a complete discussion of Search and Seizure of Vehicles Without a Warrant, see Chapter 7.

High Crime Area

Another factor which may contribute to a finding of probable cause is a suspect's unusual behavior in or near a high crime area. In a case illustrating this point, officers at 3:30 a. m. spotted a parked car with its headlights on in an area in which drug offenses were frequently committed. They noticed a man in a second car across the street receiving something from a white paper sack held by the driver of the first car. The officers approached the second car and observed a broken left window vent and the defendant in the back seat stuffing something behind the seat cushion. They ordered all four occupants out of the car and, as they emerged, a sack fell to the ground and broke, disgorging numerous pills and capsules resembling dangerous drugs. The occupants of the car were then arrested.

The court held that the combination of circumstances—the high-crime neighborhood, the hour, the apparent transfer of something, the suspicious conduct of some of the men, the broken vent window, and finally the broken bag full of pills and capsules—was sufficient to give the officers probable cause to arrest the occupants of the car. People v. Nieto, 267 Cal.App.2d 1, 72 Cal.Rptr. 764 (Court of Appeal of California, 1968).

It should be noted that the mere observation of a suspect acting in an innocent manner in a high crime area will not be enough for probable cause. There must be other facts indicative of possible criminal activity before there can be justification for an arrest or search.

Presence at the Scene

Closely related to the observation of a suspect in a high crime area is the observation of a suspect and his conduct near the scene of recent criminal activity. Again, this standing alone will not support probable cause for an arrest or search, but combined with other factors, it may be sufficient.

In a case illustrating the point, an officer received a radio report that a break was in progress at a certain building. When the officer got to the building, he discovered that the rear window had been broken and metal bars over the window spread to permit the entrance of a person. He observed no suspects at the scene but heard voices coming from the second floor porch of an adjoining building. He entered this building and went up to the roof where he found defendants, lightly clad on a cold night, attempting to conceal themselves. He arrested them, frisked them for weapons, and found coins which were later admitted into evidence.

The court found that the radio warning that a break was in progress, the observations of the officer at the scene, the presence of the defendants near the scene of the crime, lightly clad on a cold winter night, and their attempt to conceal themselves were sufficient to give the officer probable cause to arrest the defendants. State v. Mimmovich, Me., 284 A.2d 282 (Supreme Judicial Court of Maine, 1971).

Reputation of Premises

The mere fact that a person is on premises where officers have reason to believe there is criminal activity will not alone justify either an arrest or a search of the person. Such a fact, however, may be considered with others in assessing probable cause for an arrest. We have already seen in People v. Rodriquez, discussed above under *Furtive Conduct,* how defendant's presence in a place suspected of narcotics activity combined with the other facts in the case contributed to the court's finding probable cause for an arrest.

Association With Other Known Felons

Association of a suspect with other known felons is considered in much the same way as presence on ill-reputed premises for purposes of determining probable cause. It will not be sufficient alone to provide probable cause to arrest or search, but is one factor to be considered along with other indications of criminality.

In an illustrative case, police had arrested two associates of the defendant and her companion in connection with a bank robbery and had found part of the stolen money on these associates. The police knew that the defendant and her companion and the alleged robbers had been staying at the same motel when the alleged robbers were arrested only two days after the robbery. The police also knew that they had recovered only a portion of the money from the bank. The additional fact that defendant and her companion had moved from the motel where they were staying immediately after their associates were arrested and registered under an assumed name at another motel convinced the court that officers had probable cause to arrest the defendant. U. S. v. Whitney, 425 F.2d 169 (8th Circuit Court of Appeals, 1970).

Past Criminal Conduct

The mere fact that a suspect has a known criminal record will not alone provide probable cause for an arrest. As the U. S. Supreme Court said in the 1964 case of Beck v. Ohio:

> We do not hold that the officer's knowledge of the petitioner's physical appearance and previous record was either inadmissible or entirely irrelevant upon the issue of probable cause * * * But to hold that knowledge of either or both of these facts constituted probable cause would be to hold that anyone with a previous criminal record could be arrested at will. 379 U.S. 89, 97, 85 S.Ct. 223, 228, 13 L.Ed.2d 142, 148 (1964).

As the court implies, however, the prior criminal activity of the suspect is a factor to be considered among others in the determination of probable cause. In an illustrative case, an officer observed in plain view in the back of a truck, coils of copper wire, which were of a type and amount that was not readily available to the ordinary citizen, nor would the ordinary citizen ever have use for that type and amount. The officer knew this because he had considerable experience investigating copper wire thefts. Furthermore, the officer knew the defendant to be a copper wire thief and had arrested him on several felony charges before.

Based on this information the court found probable cause to seize the wire in the truck. The court emphasized, however, that the officer could not have seized the wire unless he had a reasonable foundation for the belief that it was stolen. The large amount and unusual nature of the copper wire observed in the back of the defendant's truck provided this reasonable foundation. These observations plus the knowledge of defendant's prior criminal activity provided probable cause to seize the wire. Defendant's prior criminal activity alone would not have been enough. State v. Temple, 7 Or. 91, 488 P. 2d 1380 (Court of Appeals of Oregon, 1971).

Unusual Hour

The time of day can also be a factor in determining whether there is probable cause to arrest or search. Of course, a person will not be subject to search merely because he happens to be acting in an innocent manner at an early hour of the morning. If other factors are present, however, such as furtive conduct in a high crime area, the hour of the day may be a relevant factor in determining whether an arrest or search is justified. The case of People v. Nieto appearing above under High Crime Area is a good example of how the time of day enters into the probable cause equation.

Suspect Resembles Description

A law enforcement officer may have obtained a physical description of a suspect or seen a mug shot from a police bulletin or wanted poster. If he spots someone who closely resembles such a description, an arrest of that person will be valid as based on probable cause. In fact, it has been held that the arrest would be justified even if the person arrested was the wrong person.

An example is a case in which an officer had received a photograph of a murder suspect at an early morning briefing session. He studied the photograph and later, while cruising in his patrol car, observed defendant, who closely resembled the suspect in the photograph, driving the other way. The officer pulled defendant's car over, arrested defendant for murder, and found evidence of another crime as a result of a search incident to arrest. It turned out that defendant was not the person portrayed in the police photograph.

The court, however, held that the arrest was valid because probable cause could be found where the defendant bore a striking resemblance to a picture of a murder suspect in a police bulletin. And even though defendant was not the murder suspect, the court said that once the police have reasonable cause to arrest one party, and when they reasonably mistake a second party for the first party, the arrest of the second party is a valid arrest. The evidence seized incident to the arrest was therefore found to be admissible. People v. Prather, 268 Cal.App.2d 748, 74 Cal.Rptr. 82 (California Court of Appeal, 1969).

Facts Arising During Investigation or Temporary Detention

It is very important for the law enforcement officer to realize that probable cause to arrest or search may arise during investigation or questioning of a suspect or in the typical "stop and frisk" situation. In these situations, the officer may initially only be seeking information or merely investigating suspicious circumstances. Yet during the temporary detention other facts may come to the officer's attention either from the words or actions of the detained person or from other sources. For example, the person may give evasive answers, attempt to flee, act in a furtive manner, or the officer may perceive any of the other indications of possible criminal activity discussed above. If these facts and circumstances are sufficient to establish probable cause to arrest or search, then the officer may act accordingly.

The most important case in this area is the U. S. Supreme Court case of Terry v. Ohio, 392 U.S. 1, 88 S.Ct. 1868, 20 L.Ed.2d 889 (1968). This case and the entire subject of Stop and Frisk are discussed in Chapter 10. Several of the cases summarized in that chapter deal with the manner in which probable cause to arrest or search may arise from the stop and frisk situation. Officers are encouraged to read Chapter 10 and study the examples given.

Summary

The law enforcement officer should look for the types of information discussed above when he is on the beat and should know what relative importance a judge or magistrate is likely to place on each type of information in determining whether there is probable cause. Most importantly, however, the officer should make sure that he has sufficient information *before* he acts. Thus, if he decides to make an arrest or search without a warrant, he should be prepared *at that time* to justify his action with specific facts and circumstances sufficient for probable cause. Likewise, if the officer decides to apply for a warrant, he must state *in writing*, in the complaint or affidavit, the specific facts and circumstances which he feels give him probable cause to arrest or search. Of course, because probable cause is such an indefinite concept and because some judges and magistrates have stricter standards than others, the court may still find a lack of probable cause despite the officer's painstaking efforts. Nevertheless, a careful and systematic approach by the officer is likely to result in more solidly based cases, less waste of time and effort, and fewer violations of individual rights.

INFORMATION OBTAINED BY THE OFFICER THROUGH INFORMANTS

While a law enforcement officer's perceptions are an important source of information for probable cause, it is not possible for a law enforcement officer to be present at the scene to observe every crime that happens. In fact, the majority of crimes are committed out of the presence of law enforcement officers, and yet there is still an obvious need to make arrests and searches in these types of crime. More importantly, arrests and searches made in connection with crimes committed out of the presence of law enforcement officers must conform to the same constitutional standards as those made in connection with observed crimes.

The difficulty for the law enforcement officer lies in obtaining the authority to arrest or search when he has not personally observed any facts or circumstances upon which probable cause may be based. The only solution, of course, is that his information must come from third persons, or informants, who have themselves personally observed such facts and circumstances. The difficulty does not stop there, however. The officer is still faced with the task of convincing a magistrate that the information supplied to him by the informant is reliable and worthy of being acted upon. The following discussion will be devoted to setting forth the procedures to be followed by law enforcement officers in establishing probable cause to arrest or search, with or without a warrant, when the information comes from persons other than the officer himself.

For purposes of discussion, we will concentrate on the situation in which the officer is applying for a search warrant based upon information from third persons. We do this to make the presentation more easily understandable and to emphasize again that the officer should *write down,* in the complaint or affidavit, all the information upon which probable cause is to be based. The same probable cause considerations, however, are involved in arrest warrants and in warrantless arrests and searches, except of course, that the information need not be written down in the warrantless situation. The term *informant* will be used throughout the discussion to refer to any third person from whom a law enforcement officer obtains information on criminal activity.

The method of establishing probable cause through the use of an informant's information is sometimes referred to as the *hearsay* method of establishing probable cause, as opposed to the direct observation method discussed above. The hearsay method has been developed in recent years through decisions of the U. S. Supreme Court and various state courts. These decisions have set out definite requirements for law enforcement officers using information received from third persons in preparing complaints or affidavits for warrants, although there are many areas that still need to be clarified. The purpose of these requirements is to ensure that there is a substantial basis for the magistrate to credit the hearsay information. Jones v. U. S., 362 U.S. 257, 80 S.Ct. 725, 4 L.Ed.2d 697 (U. S. Supreme Court, 1960). If the officer does not carefully follow these requirements, either he will be unable to obtain a warrant; or, as is more frequently the case, the magistrate will issue a warrant but it will be declared invalid later; or, in the case of a warrantless arrest or search, his arrest or search will later be declared unlawful and any evidence seized will be inadmissible in court.

The Aguilar Case

The leading case setting out the standards for establishing probable cause under the hearsay method is the U. S. Supreme Court case of Aguilar v. Texas, 378 U.S. 108, 84 S.Ct. 1509, 12 L.Ed.2d 723 (1964). The *Aguilar* case sets out a *two-pronged test* for determining probable cause when the information in the affidavit is either entirely or partially obtained from an informant.

1. The affidavit must describe underlying circumstances from which a neutral and detached magistrate may determine that the informant had a sufficient basis for his knowledge and that his information was not the result of mere rumor or suspicion.

2. The affidavit must describe underlying circumstances from which the magistrate may determine that the informant was credible or his information reliable.

Both prongs of the *Aguilar* test must be satisfied in order to establish probable cause. Each prong of the *Aguilar* test will be discussed separately here, emphasizing the duties of the law enforcement officer in each case.

Prong 1: Informant's Basis of Knowledge

The law enforcement officer must demonstrate to the magistrate in the affidavit underlying circumstances enabling the magistrate to independently evaluate the accuracy of an informant's conclusion. This is usually done by showing how the informant knows the information he has furnished. To satisfy this requirement, the affidavit must show either:

1. That the informant himself saw or perceived first hand the information he related to the officer; or
2. That the informant's information came from another source, but there is good reason to believe it.

Informant's Information is First Hand

If the informant came upon his information by personal observation, the law enforcement officer should have few problems in satisfying the first prong of the *Aguilar* test. The officer merely has to state, in the affidavit, *how, when,* and *where* the informant obtained the information which he has furnished. A perfect example is a case in which the officer stated in the affidavit:

> * * * For approximately the past two months I have received information from an informant whose information has recently resulted in narcotic arrests and convictions that a Gregory Daniels who resides at 929 Logan N, (down) has been selling marijuana, hashish and heroin. My informant further states that he has seen Daniels sell drugs, namely: heroin and further that he has seen Daniels with heroin on his person. The informant has seen heroin on the premises of 929 Logan N, (down) within the past 48 hours. * * * State v. Daniels, 294 Minn. 323, 325, 200 N.W.2d 403, 404 (Supreme Court of Minnesota, 1972).

The court said, with regard to this affidavit:

> There seems to be no dispute that such personal observation satisfies that part of the *Aguilar* test which requires that the affidavit contain facts to enable the magistrate to judge whether the informant obtained his knowledge in a reliable manner. 294 Minn. at 328–29, 200 N.W.2d at 406.

It is very important that the officer state in the affidavit the *time* when the informant obtained his information. This is especially true in affidavits used to apply for search warrants because probable cause to search can become stale with time. In one case, a law enforcement officer stated in his affidavit that his informant had told him that he had sold certain (stolen) property to the defendant. But the officer did not state when the sale took place. The court said that the affidavit was deficient because it failed to show that the information received from the informant was fresh as opposed to being remote. Windsor v. State, 48 Ala.App. 474, 265 So.2d 916 (Court of Criminal Appeals of Alabama, 1972).

Sometimes, no matter how carefully an officer establishes an informant's method of obtaining his information, unavoidable errors in that information result in a serious injustice to a defendant. Courts will refuse to find probable cause to support the officer's actions in these situations. An example is a case in which officers picked up the defendant for hitchhiking and sent his name through the computer at the National Crime Information Center (N.C.I.C.), a national clearinghouse for law enforcement agencies administered by the F.B.I. The computer reported that the defendant was wanted in another city for a parole violation. The officers booked the defendant and subsequently found a gun in his possession. The defendant was eventually charged for the possession of the gun. The N.C.I.C. report was later found to be false. The defendant had satisfied the parole violation five months earlier. The court ordered the suppression of all evidence resulting from the defendant's arrest. The court said:

> [A] computer inaccuracy of this nature and duration, even if unintended, amounted to a capricious disregard for the rights of the defendant as a citizen of the United States. The evidence compels a finding that the government's action was equivalent to an arbitrary arrest, and that an arrest on this basis deprived defendant of his liberty without due process of law. U. S. v. Mackey, 387 F.Supp. 1121, 1125 (U. S. District Court for Nevada, 1975).

In this case, then, although the officers acted properly in all respects, evidence was ruled inadmissible through no fault of their own. It should be noted that a computer, as an informant, is usually assumed to have accurate information and officers should feel free to act on such information.

Informant's Information is Hearsay

If the informant's information comes from a third person, that person and his information must satisfy both prongs of the *Aguilar* test. The officer preparing the affidavit must, therefore, show how the third person knows the information he furnished to the informant, as described in the previous section. For example, if the third person saw criminal activity taking place, a statement in the affidavit to that effect would be sufficient to satisfy the first prong of the *Aguilar* test. The officer must also, however, satisfy prong 2 of the *Aguilar* test with respect to *both* the informant *and* the third person. Prong 2 of *Aguilar* will be discussed later in this chapter.

Detailing Informant's Information

Courts recognize one other method of satisfying the first prong of the *Aguilar* test besides stating how, when, and where the informant came by the information which he provided. In the U. S. Supreme Court case of Spinelli v. U. S., 393 U.S. 410, 89 S.Ct. 584, 21 L.Ed.2d 637 (1969), the Court said:

> In the absence of a statement detailing the manner in which the information was gathered, it is especially important that the tip describe the accused's criminal activity in sufficient detail that the magistrate may know that he is relying on something more substantial than a casual rumor circulating in the underworld or an accusation based merely on an individual's general reputation. 393 U.S. at 416, 89 S.Ct. at 589, 21 L.Ed.2d at 644.

The *Spinelli* case cited another U. S. Supreme Court case, Draper v. U. S., 358 U.S. 307, 79 S.Ct. 329, 3 L.Ed.2d 327 (1954), as an example of sufficient use of detail to satisfy the first prong of the

Aguilar test. In the *Draper* case, the informant did not state the way in which he had obtained his information. The informant did, however, report that the defendant had gone to Chicago the day before by train and that he would return to Denver by train with three ounces of heroin on one of two specified mornings. In addition, the informant went on to describe, with minute particularity, the clothes that the defendant would be wearing and the bag he would be carrying upon his arrival at the Denver station. The Supreme Court said:

> A magistrate, when confronted with such detail, could reasonably infer that the informant had gained his information in a reliable way. 393 U.S. at 417, 89 S.Ct. at 589, 21 L.Ed.2d at 644.

In Soles v. State, 16 Md.App. 656, 299 A.2d 502 (Maryland Court of Special Appeals, 1973), probable cause to conduct a warrantless search of an automobile was found even though the officer was unable to tell how, when, or where the informant obtained his information. The court held that the information given by the informant was sufficiently detailed to indicate that he had gained his information in a reliable way. Relevant parts of the officer's testimony at the motion to suppress hearing are quoted below, because the testimony indicates the type of detail that courts require to show that an informant spoke from personal knowledge:

> The informant described the appellant in the following detail:
>
> "A. The source described Mr. Soles. He gave—told me that the name of the subject was Soles. He didn't know any other name. Just Soles. He described Mr. Soles as being approximately five foot eight inches in height, approximately 160 pounds, as being a Negro male, approximately in his early 30's. I believe one age was 35 years of age. He said he had a receding hairline slightly, a small bush cut. He said his hair wasn't a big bush. He said it was short. He said he had a goatee and he was light skinned."
>
> The informant described the appellant's automobile in the following detail:
>
> "A. It was a late model blue convertible with a white top bearing New York tags, I believe WQ 9579, something like that; WX 9579. My recollection isn't real good on that."
>
> The informant described the operation generally and the cocaine specifically in the following detail:
>
> "THE WITNESS: The source called me at home and related to me that he had information about a male subject from New York who was a major distributor of cocaine to several known narcotics dealers in Washington. He related to me that this source was named Soles. He also indicated to me that he had given the tag number of Soles' car to my partner, Officer Rob-

> ert Polzin, earlier that week, and in the conversation with this source he related to me that Soles had in excess of an eighth of a kilo of cocaine in his trunk of his car inside a briefcase. He said this cocaine would be inside a glass jar. He stated that Soles had several thousand dollars in cash on him, which were the assets from the sale of part of the cocaine he brought down from New York. He stated he was armed with a pistol, and stated that he would be leaving Washington for New York before three o'clock that evening."
>
> The trial judge, "when confronted with such detail, could reasonably infer that the informant had gained his information in a reliable way," * * * that is, via first-hand observation. Upon our independent review, we draw such an inference. 16 Md.App. at 663–66, 299 A.2d at 507–08.

The important thing for the law enforcement officer to remember is that if he does not know the manner in which his informant obtained his information, he can still satisfy the first prong of the *Aguilar* test by obtaining as much detail as possible from the informant and stating *all* of it in the complaint or affidavit.

Prong 2: Informant's Veracity

In addition to demonstrating how the informant obtained his information, the officer must demonstrate to the magistrate in the affidavit underlying circumstances to convince the magistrate of the informant's veracity, i. e., whether he is credible or his information is reliable. Since there are few, if any, cases dealing with the reliability of the informant's information, this discussion will be limited to methods for establishing the credibility of the informant. The amount and type of information the officer must provide to establish credibility of the informant depends partially upon whether the informant's identity is disclosed or undisclosed.

Disclosure of Informant's Identity

Whether the informant's identity is disclosed or not is an important consideration in establishing the credibility of an informant. If a law enforcement officer identifies his informant by name in the affidavit, a magistrate is more likely to accept the credibility of the informant because he can have the disclosed informant appear before him if he feels further facts are necessary. Therefore, usually, if the informant's name and address is provided in the affidavit, the officer does not need to do anything further to establish his credibility. People v. Glaubman, 175 Colo. 41, 485 P.2d 711 (Supreme Court of Colorado, 1971).

The court in the *Glaubman* case stated:

> She made her information known to the police, and the police verified the information which was available. She was identified by name and is not on the same footing as the common informant who seeks to remain nameless and hidden and barters and sells information to the police. The nature of informants, which are a necessary part of police work, is such that the common informant is hidden behind a cloak of anonymity. A special privilege has been granted to the police to insure that the identity of the informant is not disclosed, except under circumstances that would promote or cause a failure of justice if identity of the informer was withheld from the defendant. * * * More often than not, the informant is paid or provides information in exchange for immunity from prosecution for his own misdeeds.
>
> Our view, which is supported by a number of decisions, is that the citizen-informer, adviser, or reporter who acts openly to see that our laws are enforced should be encouraged, and his information should not be subjected to the same tests as are applied to the information of an ordinary informer. * * *
>
> When citizens are involved, it cannot be expected that they would have had past transactions or dealings with the police. * * *
>
> * * *
>
> We now announce that henceforth, Colorado will follow the citizen-informer rule and will recognize that a citizen who is identified by name and address and was a witness to criminal activity cannot be considered on the same basis as the ordinary informant. We believe, and hold, that the constitutional safeguards afforded under the Fourth and Fourteenth Amendments to the United States Constitution * * * are met when the affidavit supporting an arrest warrant or search warrant contains the name and address of the citizen-informant who was a witness to criminal activity and includes a statement of the underlying circumstances. * * * 175 Colo. at 50–52, 485 P.2d at 716–717.

When the informant's identity is undisclosed, however, the magistrate has no way of determining for himself whether the informant is credible. The magistrate must depend entirely on the information supplied to him by the law enforcement officer in the affidavit. Therefore, the magistrate requires detailed factual information from the officer on the informant's credibility when his identity is undisclosed. The remainder of this chapter is devoted to a discussion of the nature of this information.

To aid in determining credibility, courts make a further distinction between the *ordinary citizen informant* and the *criminal informant.* The amount and quality of information needed to establish an informant's credibility depends on this distinction.

Ordinary Citizen Informant

Some courts have said that an undisclosed ordinary citizen informant is presumed credible and no further evidence of his credibility need be stated in the affidavit. One court has stated:

> One cannot approach the problem of informants whose information may or may not be sufficient to create "probable cause" as if there was only two classes: reliable informants whose information has previously been tested by the police and "all others." A multitude of cases * * * attest to the fact that information from a citizen who purports to be the victim of or to have witnessed a crime may, under certain circumstances, provide a sufficient basis for an arrest. People v. Griffin, 250 Cal.App.2d 545, 550–51, 58 Cal.Rptr. 707, 711 (California Court of Appeals, 1967).

As the above quote indicates, the ordinary citizen who is either a victim of crime or eyewitness to crime is considered to be a credible informant even though his credibility has not been previously tested. U. S. v. Mahler, 442 F.2d 1172 (9th Circuit Court of Appeals, 1971). The reason behind this rule has been stated by the Supreme Court of Wisconsin:

> [A]n ordinary citizen who reports a crime which has been committed in his presence, or that a crime is being or will be committed, stands on much different ground than a police informer. He is a witness to criminal activity who acts with an intent to aid the police in law enforcement because of his concern for society or for his own safety. He does not expect any gain or concession for his information. An informer of this type usually would not have more than one opportunity to supply information to the police, thereby precluding proof of his reliability by pointing to previous accurate information which he has supplied. State v. Paszek, 50 Wis.2d 619, 184 N.W.2d 836, 843 (1971).

In addition, the credibility of a citizen informant is accepted because, in contrast to the underworld informant, the citizen informant would be likely to fear the consequences of committing perjury. Also, an ordinary citizen would not want to risk a civil suit which might require him to pay damages if he were vindictive in his report. People v. Hicks, 38 N.Y.2d 90, 378 N.Y.S.2d 660, 341 N.E.2d 227 (Court of Appeals of New York, 1975). Fellow law enforcement officers are also considered to be credible informants without having their credibility established. Brooks v. U. S., 416 F.2d 1044 (5th Circuit Court of Appeals, 1969).

Some courts have suggested that more information about an undisclosed ordinary citizen informant is required to establish his credibility. The Arkansas Supreme Court held that there was no probable cause to arrest when the only information officers had was an anonymous telephone tip that a certain car was occupied by two armed men. The court said:

> [I]f this arrest must be upheld on the basis of sufficient probable cause, any officer may arrest anyone at any time and justify his action by attributing it to an anonymous telephone call. The protection of the Bill of Rights is not to be so readily circumvented. Conor v. State, 260 Ark. 172, 175, 538 S.W.2d 304, 305 (1976).

The court indicated that the officers should have either obtained more information about the informant or more facts pointing to the commission of an offense before the court would find probable cause to arrest. The Supreme Court of Virginia, however, found the informant credible in a case where the affidavit stated that, while the informant had not previously furnished information to the police concerning violations of the narcotics laws, he was steadily employed, was a registered voter, enjoyed a good reputation in his neighborhood and had expressed concern for young people involved with narcotics. Brown v. Commonwealth, 212 Va. 672, 187 S.E.2d 160 (1972).

In another Virginia case, an officer applying for a search warrant stated in the affidavit that he had known the ordinary citizen informant and his family for many years and that the informant was known to be credible. The court said:

> Although more extensive background information would be highly desirable, "a common sense and realistic" interpretation of the affidavit * * * leads us to the conclusion that it contains information reported by a first time citizen informer whose name was withheld by the affiant.
>
> Public-spirited citizens should be encouraged to furnish to the police information of crimes. Accordingly, we will not apply to citizen informers the same standard of reliability as is applicable when police act on tips from professional informers or those who seek immunity for themselves, whether such citizens are named * * * or, as here, unnamed. Guzewicz v. Commonwealth, 212 Va. 730, 735–36, 187 S.E.2d 144, 148 (Supreme Court of Virginia, 1972).

It is apparent, then, that there is some disagreement on how much backup information needs to be stated in the affidavit to establish the credibility of the undisclosed ordinary citizen informant. Since the issue has not been settled, it is strongly recommended that the law enforcement officer make every effort to provide in the affidavit additional information, if available, relating to the citizen informant's credibility as was done in the two Virginia cases cited above.

Criminal Informant

Unlike the ordinary citizen, whose credibility may sometimes be presumed, the criminal informant's credibility must be established by a statement of underlying facts and circumstances establishing credibility. A criminal informant may be a professional police informant, a person with a criminal record, an accomplice in a crime, or a person seeking immunity for himself. Usually, the criminal informant will not want his identity disclosed in the affidavit, but even if it is disclosed, the law enforcement officer should state in the affidavit the reasons why he believes a criminal informant to be a credible person. The following facts will be considered relevant by a magistrate toward establishing the credibility of a criminal informant:

1. Informant has given accurate information in the past. The usual method of establishing the credibility of a criminal informant is by showing that the informant has given accurate information in the past which has led to arrests, convictions, recovery of stolen property, or some like accomplishment. This is sometimes referred to as establishing the informant's "track record."

Courts will usually not read affidavits attempting to establish the credibility of informants with undue technicality. U. S. v. Ventresca, 380 U.S. 102, 85 S.Ct. 741, 13 L.Ed.2d 684 (U. S. Supreme Court, 1965). Nevertheless, a law enforcement officer may not simply state by way of conclusion that the informant is credible because he has proved his credibility in the past. He must give a factual statement citing other cases or incidents in which the informant has given accurate information in the past.

It should be noted that the important factor in establishing the credibility of an informant by this method is *accuracy* of the information supplied by the informant in the past. In one case, a defendant argued that the credibility of an informant against him had not been established because there was no proof that his prior tips had resulted in convictions. The court found the informant credible despite the failure of any of his tips to result in convictions. The language of the court in emphasizing the importance of the *accuracy* of the tips, rather than their resulting in convictions, is worthy of quotation:

> Convictions, while corroborative of an informer's reliability, are not essential in establishing his reliability. Arrests, standing alone, do not establish reliability, but information that has been proved accurate does. Arrestees may not be prosecuted; if prosecuted they may not be indicted; if indicted they may not be tried; if tried, they may not be convicted. If a case is tried, the informer may never testify; his credibility may never be passed upon in court. The true test of his reliability is the accuracy of his information. People v. Lawrence, 133 Ill.App.2d 542, 544, 273 N.E.2d 637, 639 (Appellate Court of Illinois, 1971).

It is worthwhile to give some examples of the kinds of statements in affidavits that have been found to be satisfactory to establish the credibility of a criminal informant. In one case, the court found sufficient a statement that the informant had "furnished reliable and accurate information on approximately 20 occasions over the past four years." U. S. v. Dunnings, 425 F.2d 836, 839 (2nd Circuit Court of Appeals, 1969). In another case, the court held that the credibility of the informant was sufficiently shown where the affidavit stated that the informant's information "has recently resulted in narcotic arrests and convictions." State v. Daniels, 294 Minn. 323, 329, 200 N.W.2d 403, 406–07 (Supreme Court of Minnesota, 1972). A third more detailed affidavit, which was found to be sufficient, specified that on one occasion within the last two weeks a search warrant had been issued pursuant to information from the informant and narcotics were seized, and within the last month the informant introduced the officer to an individual who he said was a dealer and heroin was purchased by the officer from that person. U. S. v. Smith, 462 F.2d 456 (8th Circuit Court of Appeals, 1972).

It is strongly suggested that, where possible, the officer follow the example of the third case cited and give as much detail as to the informant's credibility as possible. In the other two cases, even though the court found the informant credible, the information in the affidavits came very close to being mere conclusions of the affiant, and the affidavits were, therefore, very close to being insufficient. Officers should tell the magistrate in the affidavit when previous information was furnished; whether evidence was found which the informant said would be found; whether an informant's information was the major basis for an arrest or conviction or only a minor factor; whether the informant always provided correct information; and any other information that will help the magistrate make an informed judgment about an anonymous informant's truthfulness. In addition, the officer could describe for the magistrate such things as "the informer's general background, employment, personal attributes that enable him to observe and relate accurately, position in the community, reputation with others, personal connection with the suspect, any circumstances which suggest the probable absence of any motivation to falsify, the apparent motivation for supplying the information, the presence or absence of a criminal record or association with known criminals, and the like." U. S. v. Harris, 403 U.S. 573, 600, 91 S.Ct. 2075, 2090, 29 L.Ed.2d 723, 743 (U. S. Supreme Court, 1971) (dissenting opinion). Officers should realize that no special words will automatically convince a magistrate of an informant's credibility. Therefore, the officer should recite in the affidavit all he knows about an informant without revealing the informant's identity.

If an officer has no *personal* knowledge of circumstances demonstrating that an informant is credible, he may state in the affidavit information about the informant's credibility received from other law enforcement officers. State v. Lambert, Me., 363 A.2d 707 (Supreme Judicial Court of Maine, 1976). The officer should state the names of other law enforcement officers and he should state in detail how those officers acquired personal knowledge of the informant's credibility.

A dog trained to react to controlled substances may also be considered an informant. The dog's credibility can also be established by presenting the "track record" of the dog and its handler. In U. S. v. Race, 529 F.2d 12 (1st Circuit Court of Appeals, 1976), a dog reacted positively to two wooden crates in an airline warehouse containing some 300 crates. The dog's reaction provided the basis for probable cause to arrest the defendant. The court said:

> We do not, of course, suggest that any dog's excited behavior could, by itself, be adequate proof that a controlled substance was present, but here the Government laid a strong foundation of canine reliability and handler expertise. Murphy [the dog's handler] testified that the dog had undergone intensive training in detecting drugs in 1971, that he had at least four hours a week of follow-up training since then, as well as work experience, and that the strong reaction he had to the crates was one that in the past had invariably indicated the presence of marijuana, hashish, heroin or cocaine. 529 F.2d at 14.

2. Informant made admissions or turned over evidence against his own penal interest. The U. S. Supreme Court has held in the case of U. S. v. Harris, 403 U.S. 573, 91 S.Ct. 2075, 29 L.Ed.2d 723 (1971), that an admission made by an informant against his own penal interest is sufficient information to establish the credibility of the informant. The informant admitted that over a long period and currently he had been buying illicit liquor at a certain place. The Court said:

> People do not lightly admit a crime and place critical evidence in the hands of the police in the form of their own admissions. Admissions of crime, like admissions against proprietary interests, carry their own indicia of credibility—sufficient at least to support a finding of probable cause to search. That the informant may be paid or promised a "break" does not eliminate the residual risk and opprobrium of having admitted criminal conduct. 403 U.S. at 583–84, 91 S.Ct. at 2082, 29 L.Ed.2d at 734.

The Supreme Judicial Court of Maine has extended the U. S. Supreme Court's decision to include the turning over of self-incriminating evidence as worthy of consideration toward establishing an informant's credibility. In the case of State v. Appleton, Me., 297 A.2d 363 (1972), an informant had purchased certain drugs at the defendant's apartment and the same day brought those drugs into the police to be tested. A law enforcement officer applied for a warrant to search the apartment, stating both that the defendant had purchased the drugs and that he had delivered them to the police.

The court held that these actions of the informant justified a belief in the credibility of his story. The court said that "[a]n informant is not likely to turn over to the police such criminal evidence unless he is certain in his own mind that his story implicating the persons occupying the premises where the sale took place will withstand police scrutiny." 297 A.2d at 369.

Therefore, a law enforcement officer may establish the credibility of an informant if the informant has made admissions or turned over evidence against his own penal interest. The officer need only state in the affidavit the underlying facts of the admission or the turnover of evidence. Officers should note, however, that some state courts will not find an informant credible merely because the information he provides is against his penal interest. In Wilson v. State, 314 A.2d 905 (1973), the Delaware Supreme Court held that the mere admission by the informant of complicity in the alleged robbery of a doctor's office was not enough to establish her credibility. The court held that the officer had to provide corroborative evidence of credibility in the affidavit in addition to the admission against interest.

3. Informant has served as such over a period of time. It has been held that the credibility of an informant can be established by a law enforcement officer even though he does not demonstrate the informant's "track record" or his admission or his turning over of evidence against his penal interest. In the case of U. S. v. Stallings, 413 F.2d 200 (7th Circuit Court of Appeals, 1969), the officer, applying for a search warrant, merely stated in the affidavit that his informant had been an informant of the local police department and the Federal Bureau of Narcotics during a two-month period, and that the informant had been purchasing unlawful drugs from the defendant during this period. The court held that the informant's credibility, while not expressly stated could be inferred from the statement made by the officer.

It should be noted that this method of establishing credibility is only to be used in emergencies or where it is impossible to use other methods. Also, some courts may not accept this method of establishing the credibility of the informant.

4. Informant conducted investigation under supervision of law enforcement officer. The Maine Supreme Judicial Court has approved another method of establishing the credibility of an informant. If an officer can show the magistrate that an informant worked under the close supervision of the officer in gathering evidence of criminal activity, the magistrate can consider such supervision as an indication of the informant's credibility. The Maine court said:

> We think that where an informer works in tandem with a law officer, the law officer continually coaching and observing the in-

> former, the reports of the informer may be deemed credible even where certain material aspects of the informer's activities are without the officer's personal knowledge or observation. We think the law officer's physical proximity and active participation in the informant's intrigue is sufficient corroboration at least to provide, in part, a factual basis for the magistrate's conclusion that the informant is credible or his information reliable. State v. Gamage, Me., 340 A.2d 1, 16 (1975).

The officer preparing the affidavit in support of a request for a search warrant should state the details of his observations and transactions with the informant. A mere statement that the officer supervised the informant will probably not suffice. Officers should note that some courts may not accept this method of establishing the credibility of the informant.

* * *

This concludes our discussion of the two-pronged *Aguilar* test for establishing probable cause when the information is obtained by the officer through informants. The law enforcement officer should keep in mind when applying for an arrest or search warrant, that his main purpose is to show in the affidavit or complaint that there is a substantial basis for crediting the information supplied. This means that the officer must convince the magistrate that the affidavit is not merely based upon casual rumor overheard at a bar or on the street, nor is it an accusation based merely on an individual's reputation. This is the reason for the requirement of stating underlying facts to establish the informant's basis of knowledge and his veracity. If the officer, in his complaint or affidavit, can satisfy both of these prongs of the test, and the informant's information is sufficient to establish probable cause, the magistrate will very likely issue the arrest or search warrant. If, however, the officer is unable to satisfy the second *Aguilar* prong on the informant's veracity *or* if the informant's information is not sufficient to establish probable cause, even though both prongs of *Aguilar* are satisfied, there is still the possibility that the information in the affidavit may be *corroborated* by other information to establish probable cause. We turn now to a discussion of how corroboration may work to cure an otherwise insufficient affidavit.

CORROBORATION

When a law enforcement officer attempts to obtain an arrest or search warrant based on information from an informant, he will often be unable to satisfy one or both of the *Aguilar* standards in his complaint or affidavit. He may not have sufficient information to establish the informant's credibility or he may not be able to show how the informant came upon the information or obtain sufficient detail on criminal activity from the informant to convince a magistrate that the information was obtained in a dependable manner.

Despite this initial failure to satisfy the *Aguilar* requirements, however, the officer still has one method by which he may cure the deficiencies of the affidavit. This is by *corroboration* of the information in the affidavit from independent investigation by himself or other law enforcement officers. *Corroboration* simply means strengthening or making more certain the information supplied by the informant by stating in the affidavit backup or supporting information obtained by law enforcement officials.

Corroboration is a very useful tool of the law enforcement officer in establishing probable cause. Most cases involve many pieces of information which are neither purely a result of the direct observation of a law enforcement officer nor purely the observations of an informant. There is usually a mixture of these two types of information. For instance, an officer may receive a tip from a third person about criminal activity, and through surveillance or independent investigation, the officer may himself perceive certain indications of criminal activity. By writing this corroborating information in the affidavit in addition to establishing the credibility of the informant and the basis of knowledge of his information, the officer enables the magistrate to consider all facts which may bear upon probable cause, no matter what the source of the information is. Therefore, the magistrate is not limited to considering only the informant's information, but he may also consider other information provided by the law enforcement officer in support of the informant's information. This additional information can very often mean the difference between a magistrate's issuing or not issuing a warrant.

Effect of Corroborative Information on Probable Cause

The corroborative information provided by the law enforcement officer in the affidavit may work in three possible ways:

1. The information may result from direct perception of crime or perception of such strong indications of criminal activity that the information may *itself* provide the basis for probable cause to search or arrest, independent of the informant's information. (See above under *Indications of Criminal Activity Which May Contribute to Probable Cause*). Corroborative information of this nature will provide probable cause to search even if neither Prong 1 nor Prong 2 of the *Aguilar* test is met.
2. The officer's information may support or verify the hearsay information provided by the informant. For example, if an officer has not been able to satisfy the requirements of Prong 2 of the *Aguilar* test, his independent supporting information may provide the necessary verification of the informant's report. In other words, if some of the significant

details of the informant's information are shown to be true by independent observation of the law enforcement officer, then the magistrate is encouraged to believe that all of the story is probably true and that the informant is credible.

3. The officer's information may be added to hearsay information which meets *Aguilar* standards. Although neither are sufficient unto themselves to establish probable cause, when combined they may provide enough incriminating information to establish probable cause. It must be strongly emphasized here that the officer's perceptions will serve to corroborate the hearsay information in the affidavit *only* if these perceptions are presented to the magistrate. As stated earlier, the preferred method of presenting information on probable cause to the magistrate is by writing it in the complaint or affidavit. Therefore, the officer is strongly advised to *write down* in the affidavit in addition to the information supplied to satisfy the *Aguilar* test: (1) All of *his* perceptions which relate to the criminal activity for which the search warrant is being sought; and (2) All of *his* perceptions relating to the information provided by the informant.

Rather than discuss further the ways in which corroboration works and how the law enforcement officer should use corroborative information to obtain a search warrant, we turn now to a detailed discussion of two cases which illustrate the use of corroboration. The cases have been chosen because their fact situations are similar, their results are different, and they both contain an extensive discussion of corroboration. This method of presentation has been chosen because corroboration does not easily lend itself to a setting out of specific guidelines. More importantly, the law in this area is still somewhat unsettled and any hard and fast rules would not be meaningful.

Spinelli v. U. S.

The first case to be discussed is the U. S. Supreme Court decision in Spinelli v. U. S., 393 U.S. 410, 89 S.Ct. 584, 21 L.Ed.2d 637 (1969). This is the leading case on corroboration and should therefore be familiar to all law enforcement officers.

In this case, the defendant was convicted of traveling to St. Louis, Missouri, from a nearby Illinois suburb with the intention of conducting gambling activities prohibited by Missouri law. On appeal, the defendant challenged the validity of a search warrant which was used to obtain incriminating evidence against him. The affidavit in support of the search warrant contained the following allegations:

1. The F.B.I. had kept track of defendant's movements on five days during August 1965. On four of these occasions, de-

fendant was seen crossing a bridge from Illinois to St. Louis between 11 a. m. and 12:15 p. m. On four of the five days, defendant was seen parking his car in a lot used by residents of a certain apartment house between 3:30 p. m. and 4:45 p. m. On one day, defendant was followed further and seen to enter a particular apartment in the building.

2. An F.B.I. check with the telephone company revealed that this apartment contained two telephones listed under the name of Grace Hagen and carried two different numbers.
3. Defendant was known to the affiant and to federal law enforcement agents and local law enforcement agents as a "bookmaker, an associate of bookmakers, a gambler, and an associate of gamblers." 393 U.S. at 414, 89 S.Ct. at 588, 21 L.Ed.2d at 642.
4. The F.B.I. had been informed by a confidential reliable informant that defendant was operating a handbook and accepting wagers and disseminating wagering information by means of telephones which have been assigned the same numbers as the phones in the above-mentioned apartment.

The Court first discussed in detail, allegation number 4, the information obtained from the informant. The Court said:

> The informer's report must first be measured against *Aguilar's* standards so that its probative value can be assessed. If the tip is found inadequate under *Aguilar*, the other allegations which corroborate the information contained in the hearsay report should then be considered. 393 U.S. at 415, 89 S.Ct. at 588, 21 L.Ed.2d at 643.

The Court found the informant's tip inadequate under *Aguilar*. Prong 2 was not satisfied because the affiant merely stated that he had been informed by a "confidential reliable informant." This was a mere conclusion or opinion of the officer-affiant because no *underlying circumstances* were stated to show the magistrate that the informant was credible.

For similar reasons, Prong 1 was not satisfied either. The affidavit did not state sufficient *underlying circumstances* from which the informant concluded that defendant was running a bookmaking operation. There was no statement as to how, when or where the informant received his information—whether he personally observed the defendant at work or whether he ever placed a bet with him. Furthermore, if the informant came by his information from third persons, there was no explanation of why these sources were credible or how they obtained their information.

Finally, the affidavit did not describe the defendant's alleged criminal activity in sufficient detail to convince a magistrate that the information was more than mere rumor or suspicion. The only facts supplied were that the defendant was using two specified telephones and that these phones were being used in gambling operations. As the Court said, this meager report could easily have been obtained from an offhand remark at a neighborhood bar.

The Court then turned to a consideration of the other information supplied in the affidavit—allegations 1 and 2 above—to see if they provided sufficient corroboration of the informant's information or provided probable cause in themselves. The Court found that these two items reflected only innocent-seeming activity and data. Defendant's travels to and from the apartment building and his entry into a particular apartment could not be taken as indicative of gambling activity. And there was certainly nothing unusual about an apartment containing two separate telephones. The Court, therefore, concluded:

> At most, these allegations indicated that Spinelli could have used the telephones specified by the informant for some purpose. This cannot by itself be said to support both the inference that the informer was generally trustworthy and that he had made his charge against Spinelli on the basis of information obtained in a reliable way. 393 U.S. at 417, 89 S.Ct. at 589, 21 L.Ed.2d at 644.

Finally, the Court considered allegation 3—that defendant was "known" to the F.B.I. and others as a gambler. The Court called this a bald and unilluminating assertion of police suspicion and said that it may not be used to give additional weight to allegations that would otherwise be insufficient.

It is important to note that since the decision in the *Spinelli* case, the U. S. Supreme Court has decided that the alleged criminal reputation of a suspect *may* be considered by a magistrate in evaluating an affidavit for a search warrant. U. S. v. Harris, 403 U.S. 573, 91 S. Ct. 2075, 29 L.Ed.2d 723 (1971). In the *Harris* case, the Court said that the reason why criminal reputation couldn't be used in *Spinelli* was because *Spinelli* contained no factual indication of past criminal activities on the defendant's part to back up the assertion. The affiant officer in the *Harris* case had stated in the affidavit that the defendant had a reputation for four years as a trafficker of non-tax-paid distilled spirits, that the officer had received information from all types of persons as to the defendant's activities, and that during this period, a sizeable stash of illicit whiskey had been found in an abandoned house under defendant's control. The Court held that when a criminal reputation is supported by such factual statements indicating prior criminal conduct, the reputation can be considered along with the other allegations. Criminal reputation will be considered again below in the discussion of the case of Dawson v. State. The important thing for the law enforcement officer to remember is that if he wishes to use a suspect's criminal reputation in an affidavit in support of a warrant, he should provide *underlying facts* indicating prior criminal conduct.

The *Spinelli* case is valuable to the law enforcement officer in that it traces through all the *Aguilar* requirements for establishing probable cause using an informant's information and gives reasons why each test was not met by the affidavit in that case. It then considers other information in the affidavit as corroboration of the informant's information and gives specific reasons why the corroborative information is inadequate. Officers should read the case in its entirety to clear up any questions not answered in this chapter.

We turn now to a consideration of Dawson v. State, 11 Md.App. 694, 276 A.2d 680 (Court of Special Appeals of Maryland, 1971), a case also involving gambling. The case is very similar to the *Spinelli* case, except that the search warrant in *Dawson* was found to be valid. Our discussion will center on the differences between the two cases which caused the court in the *Dawson* case to reach a different conclusion.

Dawson v. State

In the *Dawson* case, the defendant was convicted of unlawfully maintaining premises for the purpose of selling lottery tickets and of unlawfully betting, wagering, or gambling on the results of horse races. He appealed, claiming among other things that the search warrant for his home was illegal because adequate probable cause had not been shown. The affidavit for the warrant contained nine paragraphs. The first paragraph listed the investigative experience of the affiant and ended with his conclusion that gambling activities were at that time being conducted at defendant's premises. The third through ninth paragraphs contained the direct observations of the affiant officer. These paragraphs will be considered later. The second paragraph dealt with hearsay information and is quoted below:

> That on Thursday April 17, 1969 your affiant interviewed a confidential source of information who has given reliable information in the past relating to illegal gambling activities which has resulted in the arrest and conviction of persons arrested for illegal gambling activities and that the source is personally known to your affiant. That this source related that there was illegal gambling activities taking place at 8103 Legation Road, Hyattsville Prince George's County, Maryland by a one Donald Lee Dawson. That the source further related that the source would call telephone #577–5197 and place horse and number bets with Donald Lee Dawson. 11 Md.App. at 704–05, 276 A.2d at 685.

The court analyzed this paragraph in terms of the two-pronged *Aguilar test.* Considering the informant's basis of knowledge first, the court found that *Aguilar* was satisfied. The affidavit stated that the informant had personally called the phone number 577-5197 and had placed horse and number bets with the defendant. This is in contrast with the *Spinelli* case, where nothing was said about how the informant obtained his information.

As to the credibility of the informant, the court felt that the information furnished was close to borderline. In that the affidavit stated that both arrests and convictions had resulted from the informant's information in the past, it was more than a mere conclusion or opinion of the officer-affiant. Also the circumstances stated went further to establish the informant's credibility than those in *Spinelli* where the informant was merely described as a "confidential reliable informant." The court implied that more specific information on the informant's credibility would have been desirable but said:

> It may well be that the facts here recited are enough to establish the credibility of the informant. In view of the strong independent verification hereinafter to be discussed, however, it is unnecessary for the State to rely exclusively on such recitation. 11 Md.App. at 706–07, 276 A.2d at 686.

The court, then, assumed for purposes of discussion that the credibility of the informant had *not* been adequately established and it went on to discuss *corroboration.*

In its discussion of corroboration, the court made a concerted effort to compare the affidavit in this case with that in *Spinelli.* We turn now to a discussion of the information in paragraphs three through nine of the affidavit in *Dawson* to see how it corroborates the informant's information.

In these paragraphs, the affiant stated that a surveillance of the defendant's activities had been conducted over a six day period in April of 1969. The following things were observed or otherwise learned during this period and stated in the affidavit:

—Defendant was observed to be engaged in no apparent legitimate employment during the period.

—Defendant had two telephones in his residence with two separate lines, both of which had silent listings.

—One of defendant's silent listings had been picked up in the course of a raid on a lottery operation three years earlier in another town.

—On each day of observation, the defendant was observed to purchase an Armstrong Scratch Sheet, which gives information about horses running at various tracks that day.

—On each morning of observation, defendant was observed to leave his house between 9:02 and 10:20 a. m., to return to his house between 11:20 a. m. and 12:06 p. m. and to remain in his house until after 6:00 p. m. The affiant, who was experienced and expert in gambling investigations, stated that the hours between noon and 6:00 p. m. are those when horse and number bets can be placed and when the results of betting become available.

—On each day of observation, defendant was observed during his morning rounds, to stop at a number of places, including liquor stores and restaurants, for very short periods of time. He never purchased anything from any of the stores nor did he eat or drink at the restaurants. The affiant stated that such brief regular stops are classic characteristics of the pick-up man phase of a gambling operation:

> He picks up the "action" (money and/or list of bets) from the previous day or evening from prearranged locations—"drops." At the same time, he delivers cash to the appropriate locations for the payoff of yesterday's successful players. 11 Md.App. at 711, 276 A.2d at 689.

—On one of the days, defendant was observed in close association all day with another person who was known to have been arrested for alleged gambling violations three years before.

—Finally, it was ascertained that defendant himself had been arrested and convicted of gambling violations about three years before.

The court considered each one of these allegations in detail. It found that each allegation, taken separately, could admittedly have been consistent with innocent conduct on the defendant's part. The court, however, refused to consider each allegation separately. Instead, the court said:

> * * * [P]robable cause emerges not from any single constituent activity but, rather, from the overall pattern of activities. Each fragment of conduct may communicate nothing of significance, but the broad mosaic portrays a great deal. The whole may, indeed, be greater than the sum of its parts. 11 Md.App. at 707–08, 276 A. 2d at 687.

Furthermore, the court placed great weight on the investigating officer's experience in investigating gambling activities and the interpretations he was able to place on the defendant's conduct.

The court, therefore, concluded:

> In reviewing the observations, the ultimate question for the magistrate must be What is revealed by the whole pattern of activity? In the case at bar, the various strands of observation, insubstantial unto themselves, together weave a strong web of probable guilt. 11 Md.App. at 712, 276 A.2d at 689.

The court then went on to compare this case with the *Spinelli* case and to explain why the affidavit here was sufficient to provide probable cause where the one in *Spinelli* was not. The court pointed out several differences between this case and the *Spinelli* case: (1)

In *Spinelli,* there were no observations of the "pick-up man" type of activity, whatsoever. (2) In *Spinelli,* there was no observed association with a previously arrested gambler. (3) In *Spinelli,* there was no daily purchase of an Armstrong Scratch Sheet to evidence some daily interest in horseraces. (4) In *Spinelli,* neither Spinelli's nor Grace Hagen's phone number had been previously picked up in a raided gambling headquarters. (5) In *Spinelli,* Spinelli was not a convicted gambler. (6) Finally, and perhaps most importantly, the confidential hearsay information in *Spinelli* was so inadequate under *Aguilar* as to lend *no* additional light or interpretation to the direct observations. In contrast, in the *Dawson* case, the confidential hearsay information was very substantial and would significantly enhance the direct observations, if it were so needed. This is important to the law enforcement officer because it emphasizes the point that the courts will look to the totality of the information provided in the affidavit rather than attempt to mechanically determine the existence of probable cause through a rigid formula. As the court in the *Dawson* case stated:

> The hearsay information may, of course, reinforce the direct observation just as the direct observation may reinforce the hearsay information. There is no one-way street from direct observation to hearsay information. Rather, each may simultaneously cross-fertilize and enrich the other. 11 Md.App. at 713, 276 A.2d at 690.

It is therefore again strongly urged that the law enforcement officer, when applying for a search warrant *write down* in the affidavit, *all* the information he has relating to a suspect's criminal activity, whether it be direct observation or hearsay. Then, if either the hearsay or direct observation information, taken separately, is insufficient to establish probable cause, the court still has the opportunity to consider the two types of information in corroboration of each other, and perhaps find enough for probable cause in this manner. NOTE: This is *not* to say that a law enforcement officer should just state all his information in a haphazard manner in the affidavit and hope the magistrate can somehow put it all together and find probable cause. Where an informant's information is involved, the officer should carefully set out the required information to satisfy both prongs of the *Aguilar* test. He should also, however, state in an *orderly* manner, any corroborative information, in order to give the magistrate the chance to consider that information on its own merits and also to consider it in conjunction with the informant's information.

SUMMARY

This concludes the discussion of probable cause. It is perhaps worthwhile to briefly review some of the major points of advice that have been presented. On pages 83–95 we attempted to define probable cause and we discussed some of the various indications of criminal activity which a magistrate will consider in determining the existence of probable cause. The main advice for the law enforcement officer presented here was that there are many different types of information which can contribute to probable cause and that the officer should keep *all* of his senses tuned to these various indications of criminal activity. More importantly, *before* an officer acts, either to apply for a warrant, or to conduct a warrantless arrest or search (under the proper circumstances), he should make sure that he has sufficient information upon which to base his actions and that he can support his actions before a magistrate or judge.

On pages 96–109, we attempted to present guidelines for establishing probable cause when the information about criminal activity comes from an informant. The main point of advice for the law enforcement officer was that he must satisfy the two-pronged test of the *Aguilar* case before the hearsay information can be considered toward establishing probable cause. The purpose of these requirements is to ensure that the magistrate has a substantial basis for crediting the information supplied and that the information is not based on mere rumor or suspicion. It should again be emphasized that when applying for an arrest or search warrant, the officer should avoid stating conclusions or opinions in the complaint or affidavit without also stating *underlying facts and circumstances* to back up those conclusions.

In the remaining pages, we discussed how an officer can cure the defects in an affidavit which does not satisfy the *Aguilar* requirements by corroborating the information in the affidavit with information obtained through his own perceptions. Again, emphasis was placed on the desirability of *writing* in an *orderly* manner, in the affidavit, *all* the relevant information in the officer's possession. This is the best way to ensure that the magistrate will consider *all* the available information in determining whether there is probable cause for the issuance of a warrant.

By keeping these items of advice in mind and carefully following the guidelines presented in this chapter, the law enforcement officer should have little trouble justifying any lawful arrest or search, whether conducted with or without a warrant.

PART TWO

EXCEPTIONS TO THE SEARCH WARRANT REQUIREMENT

4

SEARCH INCIDENT TO ARREST

The preceding three chapters have dwelt heavily on the procedures and requirements for obtaining and executing arrest and search warrants. The main reason for this early emphasis is to impress upon law enforcement officers the importance of obtaining a warrant whenever possible. From the time of the adoption of the U. S. Constitution, the law has preferred warrants based upon probable cause as the chief means of balancing the need for efficient and effective law enforcement against the need to protect the rights of individual citizens to be secure against unreasonable searches and seizures. In Aguilar v. Texas, 378 U.S. 108, 84 S.Ct. 1509, 12 L.Ed.2d 723 (1964), the U. S. Supreme Court stated that the preference for warrants is so strong that less persuasive evidence will justify the issuance of a warrant than would justify a warrantless search or warrantless arrest. The Court said:

> [W]hen a search is based upon a magistrate's, rather than a police officer's determination of probable cause, the reviewing courts will accept evidence of a less "judicially competent or persuasive character than would have justified an officer in acting on his own without a warrant," * * * and will sustain the judicial determination so long as "there was a substantial basis for [the magistrate] to conclude that [seizable evidence was] probably present * * *." 378 U.S. at 111, 84 S.Ct. at 1512, 12 L.Ed.2d at 726.

The warrant procedure is preferred because it places responsibility for deciding the delicate question of probable cause with a neutral and detached judicial officer. Thereby, law enforcement is served, because law enforcement officers are enabled to search certain persons or places and to seize certain persons or things, when the officers can show reasonable grounds that the person, place, or thing is significantly connected with criminal activity. The Fourth Amendment rights of citizens are also served by the warrant procedure, because the decision to allow a search and seizure is removed from the sometimes hurried and overzealous judgment of law enforcement officers engaged in the competitive enterprise of investigating crime.

Nevertheless, in practice, situations often arise in which the time and effort needed to obtain a warrant would unjustifiably frustrate enforcement of the laws. In order to ensure that the delicate balance between individual rights and law enforcement is maintained, courts have carved out various exceptions to the warrant requirement and have allowed warrantless searches in certain situations. One of the most important of these situations is a search made incident to a lawful arrest. We begin our coverage of the exceptions to the search warrant requirement, therefore, with a discussion of Chimel v. California, 395 U.S. 752, 89 S.Ct. 2034, 23 L.Ed.2d 685 (U. S. Supreme Court, 1969) the leading case on search incident to arrest.

CHIMEL v. CALIFORNIA

It is important for every law enforcement officer to realize that since June 23, 1969, the law of search incident to arrest has been controlled by the U. S. Supreme Court case of Chimel v. California. This case, like *Miranda, Wade-Gilbert-Stovall,* and *Terry,* which will be discussed later, is considered a landmark case and should be very familiar to all law enforcement officers.

In the *Chimel* case, law enforcement officers arrived at the defendant's home with a warrant for his arrest for the burglary of a coin shop. The defendant was not at home, but his wife let the officers in to wait for him. When the defendant arrived, the officers handed him the warrant and asked if they could look around. He objected, but the officers searched the entire house anyway on the basis of the lawful arrest. The officers found coins and other items which were later used in court to obtain a conviction against the defendant.

The U. S. Supreme Court found the search of the entire house unreasonable. The following quotation from the case summarizes the court's reasoning:

> When an arrest is made, it is reasonable for the arresting officer to search the person arrested in order to remove any weapons that the latter might seek to use in order to resist arrest or effect his escape. Otherwise, the officer's safety might well be endangered, and the arrest itself frustrated. In addition, it is entirely reasonable for the arresting officer to search for and seize any evidence on the arrestee's person in order to prevent its concealment or de-

> struction. And the area into which an arrestee might reach in order to grab a weapon or evidentiary items must, of course, be governed by a like rule. A gun on a table or in a drawer in front of one who is arrested can be as dangerous to the arresting officer as one concealed in the clothing of the person arrested. There is ample justification, therefore, for a search of the arrestee's person and the area "within his immediate control"—construing that phrase to mean the area from within which he might gain possession of a weapon or destructible evidence. 395 U.S. 752, 762–63, 89 S.Ct. 2034, 2040, 23 L.Ed.2d 685, 694.

This case is considered a landmark because it drastically changed the allowable area of search incident to arrest from that allowed under previous law. Under pre-*Chimel* law, an officer was allowed to search incident to arrest the area considered to be in the "possession" or under the "control" of the arrested person. These vague standards were interpreted by the courts to include areas that were not necessarily under the defendant's "physical control" but were within his "constructive possession." This interpretation allowed law enforcement officers to search an entire residence incident to an arrest made therein and gave police almost free reign in deciding what would be searched. Furthermore, because neither a written application for a warrant nor proof of probable cause before a magistrate was required, the search incident to arrest was administratively more convenient and was heavily relied on by law enforcement officers.

The *Chimel* case has changed all this. Although a warrant or probable cause is still not needed, *Chimel* has made it much more difficult for officers to obtain admissible evidence as a result of a search incident to arrest. The remainder of this chapter will be devoted to discussing the impact of the *Chimel* case and the various other aspects of the law of search incident to arrest.

Allowable Purposes of a Search Incident to Arrest

Under the rule of the *Chimel* case, there are only two legitimate purposes for which a law enforcement officer may search a person incident to his arrest. The officer may:

1. Search for and remove weapons which the arrestee might use to resist arrest or effect an escape; and
2. Search for and seize evidence on the arrestee's person in order to prevent its concealment or destruction.

Law enforcement officers should always keep these allowable purposes in mind because all the other rules regarding the scope, intensity, and allowable objects of a search incident to arrest relate to the purpose for which the search is made. A search made incident to arrest for any reason other than these allowable purposes will be held unreasonable by a court and any evidence seized will be inadmissible in court.

SCOPE OF SEARCH INCIDENT TO ARREST

Types of Evidence Which May Be Seized

In general, the types of evidence which a law enforcement officer may search for and seize incident to an arrest are the same as they are for any search and seizure, whether under warrant or not. The range of seizable objects therefore includes:

1. *Weapons* which the prisoner may use to injure the officer or others or effect his escape;
2. *Fruits of the crime* for which the arrest is made;
3. *Instrumentalities* used to commit the crime;
4. *Contraband*, the possession of which constitutes a crime; and
5. *Evidence* of the crime or evidence that the person arrested committed it. People v. Lewis, 26 N.Y.2d 547, 552, 311 N. Y.S.2d 905, 909, 260 N.E.2d 538, 541 (Court of Appeals of N. Y., 1970).

Furthermore, in connection with a search incident to arrest, an officer may seize not only evidence tending to establish the crime for which the arrest is made but also evidence of other crimes. In a case illustrating this point, the defendant was arrested under a warrant for possessing and transporting explosives. During a search incident to the arrest, the arresting officer found a third person's Selective Service Certificate and Classification Card. Defendant was convicted of knowingly and unlawfully having in his possession a Selective Service Certificate and Classification Card issued to another. The court held that the certificate and card were admissible in court, despite the fact that they did not relate to the offense of possessing explosives:

> The general rule is that incident to a lawful arrest, a search without a warrant may be made of portable personal effects in the immediate possession of the person arrested. The discovery during a search of a totally unrelated object which provides grounds for prosecution of a crime different than that which the accused was arrested for does not render the search invalid. U. S. v. Simpson, 453 F.2d 1028, 1031 (10th Circuit Court of Appeals, 1972).

Relationship Between Scope of Search and Offense Arrested For

There is controversy among the courts with regard to whether or not a law enforcement officer may conduct a full-scale search of the person incident to *every* arrest. Prior to 1973, the generally accepted rule was that an officer conducting a search incident to arrest had to have a definite object or class of objects in mind, and the search could not go beyond the reasonable limits within which that object or class of objects was likely to be found. Also, the object searched for had to be related to the offense which prompted the arrest. In 1973, the U. S. Supreme Court decided two cases which greatly expanded the allowable scope of a search incident to arrest—U. S. v. Robinson, 414 U.S. 218, 94 S.Ct. 467, 38 L.Ed.2d 427 (1973) and Gustafson v. Florida, 414 U.S. 260, 94 S.Ct. 488, 38 L.Ed.2d 456 (1973).

Both the *Robinson* and *Gustafson* cases involved full-scale searches conducted incident to lawful arrests for minor traffic violations, and in both cases the Court found that it was reasonable for the officer to inspect the contents of a cigarette package found on the arrestee's person. (Illegal drugs were found in both cases.)

In the *Robinson* case, the Court said:

> It is the fact of the lawful arrest which establishes the authority to search, and we hold that in the case of a lawful custodial arrest a full search of the person is not only an exception to the warrant requirement of the Fourth Amendment, but is also a "reasonable" search under that Amendment. 414 U.S. at 235, 94 S.Ct. at 477, 38 L.Ed.2d 441.

This language was quoted with approval in the *Gustafson* decision, 414 U.S. at 263–64, 94 S.Ct. at 491, 38 L.Ed.2d at 460. Therefore, under the *Robinson* and *Gustafson* decisions, whenever an officer makes a lawful custodial arrest, he is entitled to make a full-scale search of the arrestee's person incident to the arrest.

It is worthwhile to clarify a few matters relating to the meaning and impact of these two decisions. First of all, when conducting a search incident to arrest, the officer need not have a specific object or class of objects in mind to search for. Even if the arrest is for an offense which could produce no evidence, such as loitering or many minor traffic offenses, the officer is still allowed to conduct a full-scale search of the arrestee's person. The fact of the lawful arrest justifies the search.

Also, the court in the *Robinson* and *Gustafson* decisions authorized a full-scale search of the person incident only to a lawful *custodial* arrest. The reason why the word custodial is important is that in many states, the term arrest is applied to situations in which an officer stops a person and issues a ticket, citation, or notice to appear in court, instead of taking the person into custody. A full-scale search would not be authorized in situations in which the officer merely issues a ticket, citation, or notice to appear. In other words, the officer must take the arrested person into custody in order to justify a full-scale search.

Finally, it should be noted that the *Robinson* and *Gustafson* decisions dealt only with a search of the *person* incident to arrest, and said nothing about the search of the *area* within the arrestee's immediate control. Therefore, in order to be certain that a search conducted in connection with an arrest is lawful, officers should obtain a warrant before searching any area beyond the arrestee's person, especially in situations involving arrests for motor vehicle violations.

The controversy over allowing full searches incident to all lawful custodial arrests comes about because some state courts have refused to follow the rule of the *Robinson* and *Gustafson* decisions. These state courts, based on interpretations of their *state* constitutions, have held that a warrantless search of a person incident to his lawful custodial arrest must be limited despite the *Robinson* and *Gustafson* decisions. The Supreme Court of Hawaii, for example, has limited the warrantless search of an arrestee's person incident to his lawful custodial arrest, (1) to disarming the arrested person when there is reason to believe from the facts and circumstances that he may be armed; and (2) to discovering evidence related to the crime *for which the person was arrested.* State v. Kaluna, 55 Hawaii 361, 372, 520 P.2d 51, 60 (Supreme Court of Hawaii, 1974). Under this more restrictive rule, an officer would not be allowed to search for *evidence* incident to offenses which would not produce evidence (such as loitering and minor traffic offenses), and he would not be allowed to search for weapons unless he could point to specific facts and circumstances indicating the likelihood that the arrested person was armed and dangerous. It is recommended, as the safest procedure, that officers follow this more restrictive rule, unless they are certain that their state courts have adopted the rule of the *Robinson* and *Gustafson* cases or a different rule.

The California Supreme Court has also refused to go along with the U. S. Supreme Court's decisions in the *Robinson* and *Gustafson* cases. In California, an officer may not conduct a full body search of an arrested person when the arrest will be disposed of by a mere citation or the suspect will be transported in a law enforcement vehicle to a police facility where he will be given the opportunity to post bond. Officers may, however, conduct a pat down frisk for weapons before placing an arrested person in a law enforcement vehicle for transportation to the station house. The court recognized the increased danger to law enforcement officers in this situation. People v. Longwill, 14 Cal.3d 943, 123 Cal.Rptr. 297, 538 P.2d 753 (1975).

The remainder of this chapter will proceed on the assumption that the courts in the officer's state have refused to accept the broad holding of the *Robinson* and *Gustafson* decisions and have adopted the more restrictive rule stated above in the *Kaluna* case. It should be noted, however, that if the courts in the officers' state have adopted the holding of the *Robinson* and *Gustafson* cases, the officer is entitled to conduct a full-scale search of the arrestee's body for weapons or evidence incident to every lawful custodial arrest.

SEARCH OF ARRESTEE'S BODY

A search incident to arrest of the arrestee's body may include:

1. A search of the arrestee's body and a seizure of items of evidence on or in the arrestee's body. Items seized during such a search might include hair samples, fingernail clippings, blood, and drugs hidden within the body. Of course, officers must use reasonable and painless procedures in obtaining such evidence. An example is the case of Commonwealth v. Tarver, 369 Mass. 302, 345 N.E.2d 671 (Supreme Judicial Court of Massachusetts, 1975), in which the court upheld a seizure of hair samples from the head, chest, and pubic area of a person incident to the arrest of that person for murder and sexual abuse of a child.

2. A seizure of items of evidence or weapons immediately associated with the arrestee's body. Items which might be seized would include clothing, billfolds, jewelry, wristwatches, and weapons strapped or carried on the person. An example is the case of State v. Smith, 295 Minn. 65, 203 N.W.2d 348 (Supreme Court of Minnesota, 1972), in which the court held that the seizure of the defendant's boots at the time of booking was a valid search and seizure incident to arrest.

3. A search of items of evidence or weapons immediately associated with the arrestee's body which have been seized under number 2 above. Such a search would include going through the pockets of clothing, examining clothing for bloodstains, hair, dirt, or other such evidence, and examining weapons for bloodstains, fingerprints, or serial numbers. An example is the case of Parker v. State, Tex.Crim. App., 544 S.W.2d 149 (Court of Criminal Appeals of Texas, 1976), in which officers, while on surveillance, stopped the defendant and another man as they emerged from an apartment which was suspected of containing illegal drugs. While the officers were attempting to obtain information about the apartment, they discovered a weapon on the defendant and a bag containing a white powder nearby. They arrested the defendant, searched him, and seized his billfold. In the

billfold were found packets of a white powder which was later determined to be cocaine. The court held that the officers had probable cause to arrest the defendant. The full search of the defendant and the seizure and search of his billfold incident to the lawful custodial arrest were held reasonable under the Fourth Amendment.

4. A seizure of other personal property not immediately associated with the arrestee's body, but which the arrestee is carrying or otherwise has under his immediate control. Property which might be seized would include luggage, attache cases, bundles, or packages. Before June 21, 1977, many courts held that law enforcement officers could not only *seize* incident to arrest personal property carried by or under the immediate control of the arrestee, but could also *search* that property for weapons or evidence. For example, in U. S. v. Mehciz, 437 F.2d 145 (9th Circuit Court of Appeals, 1971), the defendant was lawfully arrested on a drug possession charge while carrying a small overnight suitcase. The arresting officers took the suitcase and handcuffed the defendant so there was no danger he could get to the suitcase. An officer then opened the suitcase and found drugs inside. The court upheld the search of the suitcase as a valid search incident to arrest.

On June 21, 1977, however, the U. S. Supreme Court, in U. S. v. Chadwick, 433 U.S. 1, 97 S.Ct. 2476, 53 L.Ed.2d 538, severely limited the *search* of luggage and other personal property after it has been seized incident to arrest. In the *Chadwick* case, the defendants arrived in Boston from San Diego by train and loaded a large double-locked footlocker, which they had transported with them, into the trunk of their waiting car. Federal narcotics agents, who had probable cause to arrest and to search the footlocker, but no warrants, arrested the defendants. The agents took exclusive control over the footlocker and took it and the defendants to the federal building in Boston. An hour and a half later, the agents, without the defendants' consent and without a search warrant, opened the footlocker and found large amounts of marijuana.

The U. S. Supreme Court held that the search of the footlocker was illegal and that the seized marijuana was inadmissible evidence. Because the *Chadwick* case is so important and because lower court interpretations of the case are conflicting and, as yet, few in number, an extensive quotation of the Supreme Court's reasoning in the case is presented here:

> The potential dangers lurking in all custodial arrests make warrantless searches of items within the "immediate control" area reasonable without requiring the arresting officer to calculate the probability that weapons or destructible evidence may be involved. [citing U. S. v. Robinson and Terry v. Ohio] However, warrantless

searches of luggage or other property seized at the time of an arrest cannot be justified as incident to that arrest either if the "search is remote in time or place from the arrest," * * * or no exigency exists. Once law enforcement officers have reduced luggage or other personal property not immediately associated with the person of the arrestee to their exclusive control, and there is no longer any danger that the arrestee might gain access to the property to seize a weapon or destroy evidence, a search of that property is no longer an incident of the arrest.

Here the search was conducted more than an hour after federal agents had gained exclusive control of the footlocker and long after respondents were securely in custody; the search therefore cannot be viewed as incidental to the arrest or as justified by any other exigency. Even though on this record the issuance of a warrant by a judicial officer was reasonably predictable, a line must be drawn. In our view, when no exigency is shown to support the need for an immediate search, the Warrant Clause places the line at the point where the property to be searched comes under the exclusive dominion of police authority. Respondents were therefore entitled to the protection of the Warrant Clause with the evaluation of a neutral magistrate, before their privacy interests in the contents of the footlocker were invaded. 433 U.S. at 15–16, 97 S.Ct., at 2485–86, 53 L.Ed.2d at 550–51.

Footnotes to the *Chadwick* opinion indicate that the Court's decision was based in large part on its belief that the defendants' legitimate privacy interests were violated. In footnote 10 the Court said:

Unlike searches of the person, United States v. Robinson, 414 U.S. 218 (1973); United States v. Edwards, 415 U.S. 800 (1974), searches of possessions within an arrestee's immediate control cannot be justified by any reduced expectations of privacy caused by the arrest. Respondents' privacy interest in the contents of the footlocker was not eliminated simply because they were under arrest. 433 U.S. at 16 n. 10, 97 S.Ct. at 2486 n. 10, 53 L.Ed.2d at 551 n. 10.

In footnote 8 the Court said:

Respondents' principal privacy interest in the footlocker was of course not in the container itself, which was exposed to public view, but in its contents. A search of the interior was therefore a far greater intrusion into Fourth Amendment values than the impoundment of the footlocker. Though surely a substantial infringement with respondents' use and possession, the seizure did not diminish respondents' legitimate expectation that the footlocker's contents would remain private. 433 U.S. at 13–14 n. 8, 97 S.Ct. at 2485 n. 8, 53 L.Ed.2d at 550 n. 8.

In one of the few cases to discuss the *Chadwick* case in detail at this writing, the 7th Circuit Court of Appeals expanded upon the Supreme Court's brief mention of privacy interests:

> The Court appears to be distinguishing—for purposes of whether a warrant is required to search property in police custody that was seized from a suspect at the time of arrest—between searches of an arrestee's clothing, as in *Edwards*, or items that were in his pockets, as in *Robinson*, from searches of other possessions, such as luggage, that were within his immediate control. Warrantless searches of the former items after they come in police custody can be characterized as searches of the arrestee's person because they do not involve any greater reduction in the arrestee's expectations of privacy than that caused by the arrest itself. Warrantless searches of the latter items, however, affect privacy interests other than those reduced by the arrest itself and thus can be conducted only as long as the danger exists that the arrestee might gain access to the property to seize a weapon or destroy evidence. U. S. v. Berry, 560 F.2d 861, 864 (U. S. Court of Appeals, Seventh Circuit, 1977).

To summarize, law enforcement officers may *seize* incident to arrest luggage and other personal property not immediately associated with the arrestee's body if it is within the arrestee's immediate control. Once officers have such property under their immediate control and there is no further danger that the arrestee might gain access to the property to seize a weapon or destroy evidence, officers may *not search* the property without a warrant or consent. Of course, if officers believe that the property contains some immediately dangerous instrumentality, such as explosives, they may search the property and disarm the weapon or otherwise end the danger. They may do so even if the property is under their exclusive control.

Use of Force

When making a search of a person incident to arrest, a law enforcement officer may use the degree of force necessary to protect himself, prevent escape, and prevent the destruction or concealment of evidence. Because the courts will review the use of force strictly, an officer should use as little force as is necessary to accomplish his legitimate purpose.

Courts have upheld seizures of drugs when the arrested person attempted to swallow them and an officer put a "choke hold" on the defendant, forcing him to spit out the drugs. Salas v. State, Fla.App., 246 So.2d 621 (District Court of Appeal of Florida, 1971).

A search incident to arrest to prevent the concealment of evidence may even extend to pumping the stomach or probing body cavities. However, the following conditions should be met before such a search is conducted:

1. There must be good reason to believe that the person has within his body evidence which should be removed. In a recent case, officers actually observed the defendant thrust drug capsules into his mouth and quickly swallow them. People v. Jones, 20 Cal.App.3rd 201, 97 Cal.Rptr. 492 (Court of Appeal of California, 1971).
2. The search must be made by a doctor working under sanitary conditions and in a medically approved way.
3. Force may be used only to the extent necessary to make the person submit to the examination. Blackford v. U. S., 247 F.2d 745 (9th Circuit Court of Appeals, 1957).

SEARCH OF AREA WITHIN ARRESTEE'S IMMEDIATE CONTROL

A good way to begin the discussion of search of the area within the arrestee's immediate control is by repeating the second part of the quote from the *Chimel* case which appeared at the beginning of this chapter:

> And the area into which an arrestee might reach in order to grab a weapon or evidentiary items must, of course, be governed by a like rule. A gun on a table or in a drawer in front of one who is arrested can be as dangerous to the arresting officer as one concealed in the clothing of the person arrested. There is ample justification, therefore, for a search of the arrestee's person and the area "within his immediate control"—construing that phrase to mean the area from within which he might gain possession of a weapon or destructible evidence. 395 U.S. at 763, 89 S.Ct. at 2040, 23 L.Ed.2d at 694.

It is not possible to derive from this quote definite guidelines as to how large an area around an arrestee is "within his immediate control" and is therefore subject to search by an officer. This determination depends on several factors such as the size and shape of the room, the size and agility of the arrestee, whether the arrestee was handcuffed or otherwise subdued, the size and type of evidence being sought, the number of people arrested, and the number of officers present. The following case summaries should give some idea of how courts have recently treated the question of permissible area of search incident to arrest.

In a case dealing with the question of the area within a defendant's reach, officers went to the defendant's trailer home to arrest him as a participant in an armed robbery. They found him lying in bed. One officer immediately searched under the blankets for a gun as other officers attempted to subdue the defendant, who was resisting. Two revolvers were found in a box at the foot of the bed. The court held that this was within the area of defendant's reach and that the revolvers were admissible in evidence. People v. Spencer, 22 Cal.App.3rd 786, 99 Cal.Rptr. 681 (Court of Appeal of California, 1972).

It is clear that if a person is arrested out of doors, a search of that person's home or apartment cannot be justified as incident to the arrest. Thus, in a case where the defendant was arrested in his back yard and the arresting officers then went up to his apartment and searched it, the evidence found in the apartment was inadmissible. The court held that such a search as incident to arrest was unreasonable as extending beyond the arrestee's reach. Frazier v. State, Okl. Cr.App., 488 P.2d 613 (Court of Criminal Appeals of Oklahoma, 1971).

However, if it is necessary for an arrested person to go into a different area of the premises from that in which he was arrested, the officer, for his own protection, may accompany him and search if necessary. A case illustrating this point involved an arrest under warrant for conspiracy to commit extortion. The arrest took place early in the morning and the arrested person was in his bedclothes. One of the officers suggested that the defendant change into street clothes before leaving for the station. The defendant agreed and went to his bedroom followed by the officers. As the defendant went to a chest of drawers to obtain clothing, one of the officers searched the drawer and found a blackjack and several other weapons. The defendant was convicted of illegal possession of a blackjack.

The court held the search was lawful:

> Certainly, if immediately after a lawful arrest, the arrestee reads the arrest warrant and without coercion consents to go to his bedroom to change into more appropriate clothing, the arresting officers—incident to that arrest—may search the areas upon which the arrestee focuses his attention and are within his reach to gain access to a weapon or to destroy evidence. Giacalone v. Lucas, 445 F.2d 1238, 1247 (6th Circuit Court of Appeals, 1971).

Search of Persons Other Than the Arrestee

Often, when an arrest is made, there are other persons in the vicinity besides the arrested person. If a potential accomplice of the arrested person is located on the premises where the arrest was made, it has been held that police may search the area within the accomplice's immediate control. In such a case, two defendants were arrrested in their apartment. The arresting officers then noticed two men lying on two couches in the living room. A gun and ammunition had already been found on the premises and the officers did not know the identity of the other two men. One officer directed the two men to stand and another officer searched two end tables near the men. The officer found obscene materials.

The court held that the search was reasonable for the protection and safety of the officers. Not only had weapons already been found in the apartment but it was reasonable to assume that the two men were accomplices of the arrested persons:

> Both men had apparently been sleeping in the Portela apartment and were likely relatives or intimate friends of the Portelas. Since they were both in full view of Portela, who had already been placed under arrest, it would be reasonable for the agents to assume that if Portela had signalled the two unidentified men, they would have been able to reach over and draw a weapon out of the end tables. U. S. v. Manarite, 314 F.Supp. 607, 615 (U. S. District Court, Southern District of N. Y., 1970).

In U. S. v. Vigo, 487 F.2d 295 (2nd Circuit Court of Appeals, 1973), the court upheld the search of the purse of the defendant's female companion incident to the arrest of the defendant. The court said that a woman's purse is a reasonable place to conceal a weapon.

SEARCH OF OTHER AREAS OF THE PREMISES

Under the rule of the *Chimel* case, an officer is not allowed to search any other areas of the premises except the limited area within the arrestee's immediate control. There may, however, be circumstances justifying an officer's going into other areas to merely look around. For example, an officer, for his own protection, may look into other rooms, to see if other persons are around. Also, he may have to go through other rooms in leaving the premises. These movements of the law enforcement officer are not considered searches because the officer is not looking for weapons or incriminating evidence. Nevertheless, if an officer observes such evidence lying open to view, he may seize it, and it will be admissible in court under the "plain view" doctrine. (See Plain View, Chapter 6)

In a bank robbery case, the defendant was arrested in his girl friend's apartment. At the time of his arrest, the apartment was dark and the defendant was nude. One of the officers went to get clothing for the defendant and found two jackets of the type that had been described as having been worn by the bank robbers. On the way out of the apartment, one of the officers turned on the kitchen light so he could see his way. On the floor was revealed money from the robbery.

The court held that both the jackets and the money were admissible in evidence. Finding no violation of the *Chimel* rule, the court said:

> Since they were bound to find some clothing for Titus rather than take him nude to FBI headquarters on a December night, the fatigue jackets were properly seized under the "plain view" doctrine. Welch was entitled to turn on the kitchen lights, both to assist his own exit and to see whether the other robber might be about; when he saw the stolen money, he was permitted to seize it. Everything the agents took was in their "plain view" while they were where they had a right to be; there was no general rummaging of the apartment * * * U. S. v. Titus, 445 F.2d 577, 579 (2nd Circuit Court of Appeals, 1971).

In another case, officers arrested the defendant in a dentist's office for robbery of a liquor store. They went into other rooms of the dentist's suite to look for possibly dangerous persons and found a stolen bottle of whiskey in plain view in the dentist's laboratory.

The court held that the bottle of whiskey was admissible in evidence. The officers had no way of knowing who else might be on the premises. They were justified in conducting a search of the suite to assure themselves that no hostile and possibly dangerous persons were hiding in other rooms. The bottle of whiskey was in plain view in the dentist's laboratory and there was no evidence that the officers engaged in any general search of the premises beyond that necessary to find any other persons that might have been present. U. S. v. Miller, 145 U.S.App.D.C. 312, 449 F.2d 974 (District of Columbia Court of Appeals, 1971).

OTHER REQUIREMENTS FOR A VALID SEARCH INCIDENT TO ARREST

Arrest Must Be Lawful

In our discussion up to this point, whenever we have spoken of search incident to arrest, it has been assumed that the arrest was a *lawful* arrest. This point deserves to be emphasized because, if the arrest is not lawful, the search incident to that arrest will automatically be held unlawful by the court, even if all proper procedures are followed in conducting the search. It therefore becomes very important for the law enforcement officer to both know and carefully comply with the law of arrest. A detailed discussion of the law of arrest can be found in Chapter 1.

Search Must be Contemporaneous With Arrest

The general rule is that a search made incident to arrest is not reasonable unless it is made contemporaneously with the arrest. To be contemporaneous, a search must be conducted as close in time to the arrest as is practically possible. In a case illustrating this point, the defendant, a suspected possessor of narcotics, was lawfully arrested on a downtown street corner. The officers then took him to his home some distance away and there conducted an intensive search which yielded narcotics. On the basis of this evidence, defendant was convicted of narcotics possession.

The Court held the search of the house was unreasonable:

> In the circumstances of this case, however, the subsequent search of the petitioner's home cannot be regarded as incident to his arrest on a street corner more than two blocks away. A search "can be incident to an arrest only if it is substantially contemporaneous with the arrest and is confined to the immediate vicinity of the arrest." James v. Louisiana, 382 U.S. 36, 37, 86 S.Ct. 151, 151, 15 L.Ed.2d 30, 31 (U. S. Supreme Court, 1965).

The reason for this rule is that the law gives an officer the right to search an arrested person only (1) to protect himself, (2) to prevent escape, and (3) to prevent the destruction or concealment of evidence. If an officer delays a search, it indicates that he was not concerned about any of those three possibilities, but that he conducted the search for another reason, thereby making the search illegal.

Sometimes, however, it is not feasible for an officer to search immediately upon making an arrest. This would be true if the officer intended to make a search of the arrestee's body cavities for drugs, if the arrestee was a person of the opposite sex, or if other circumstances make a search inadvisable. In these situations, the officer should remove the arrested person from the scene and conduct the search as soon as favorable circumstances prevail. For example, in one case, an arrest for an armed bank robbery took place in a crowded hotel lobby, which was lit only by candles because of a power failure. The court held that under these circumstances it was proper for officers to make only a cursory search for weapons at the hotel and to make a more thorough search later at the station. U. S. v. Miles, 413 F.2d 34 (3rd Circuit Court of Appeals, 1969).

Sometimes, even though it is feasible to search an arrested person at the time of arrest, under certain circumstances courts will allow a delay between the arrest and search for a good reason. The U. S. Supreme Court made such an exception to the general rule in the case of U. S. v. Edwards, 415 U.S. 800, 94 S.Ct. 1234, 39 L.Ed.2d 771 (1974). In that case the defendant was arrested shortly after 11 P. M. for attempting to break into a building. The defendant was taken to jail. Law enforcement officials had probable cause to believe that the defendant's clothing contained paint chips from the crime scene. Since the police had no substitute clothing for the defendant, they waited until the next morning to seize his clothing without a warrant. Paint chips matching those at the break scene were found on the clothing.

The Court held that, despite the delay, the clothing was lawfully seized incident to the defendant's arrest. The administrative process and the mechanics of arrest had not yet come to a halt the next morning. The police had custody of the defendant and the clothing and could have seized the clothing at the time of arrest. It was reasonable to delay the seizure until substitute clothing was available. It is worthwhile to repeat here the Court's language which was quoted earlier in Chapter 1 on Arrest:

> [O]nce the accused is lawfully arrested and is in custody, the effects in his possession at the place of detention that were subject to search at the time and place of his arrest may lawfully be searched and seized without a warrant even though a substantial period of time has elapsed between the arrest and subsequent administrative processing, on the one hand, and the taking of the property for use as evidence on the other. 415 U.S. at 807, 94 S.Ct. at 1239, 39 L.Ed.2d at 778.

Officers should note that the *Edwards* case does *not* say that a law enforcement officer may delay a search incident to the arrest of a person for as long as he wishes. Nor does the case sanction *all* delays in searching and seizing evidence incident to arrest. The officer must be able to provide good reasons for delaying a search incident to arrest and the duration of the delay must relate to those reasons. Otherwise the search and seizure may be declared illegal.

It should also be noted that the *Edwards* case involved the search of an item closely associated to the arrestee's person, namely his clothing. Under the ruling of U. S. v. Chadwick (discussed earlier under SEARCH OF ARRESTEE'S BODY) officers would not be justified in delaying a search incident to arrest of luggage, briefcases, and other portable effects.

Therefore, officers may delay a search incident to arrest only under the following conditions:

1. There is a good reason for the delay;
2. The duration of the delay is reasonable under the circumstances; and
3. The item or items searched were closely related to the arrestee's person, e. g. clothing and pocket items, when they were seized.

The requirement that the search be substantially contemporaneous with the arrest does not necessarily mean that the arrest must precede the search. Although this will almost always be the case, under certain circumstances the search may precede the arrest and still be a valid search incident to arrest. In order for this to be true, the following requirements must be present:

1. There must be probable cause for arrest before either the search or the arrest is carried out; and
2. Both the arrest and search must be integral parts of a single incident.

Usually the search will occur before the arrest when there is a dangerous situation or an emergency. This, however, is not necessary in order for the search to be valid. An example is a case in which a law enforcement officer had probable cause to arrest the defendant based upon another officer's tip, his own observations, and other information. The officer encountered the defendant outside his house, immediately searched him finding heroin, and then arrested him. The court upheld the search on the ground that the fruits of the search were in no way necessary to establish probable cause for the arrest which immediately followed. Also, the search was substantially contemporaneous with the arrest and confined to the immediate vicinity of the arrest. U. S. v. Thomas, 432 F.2d 120 (9th Circuit Court of Appeals, 1970).

Arrest Must Not Be a Pretext to Justify Search

A law enforcement officer may not use an arrest as a pretext to search for evidence. If the arrest even though technically valid, is actually a mere pretext by which the officer attempts to justify an otherwise illegitimate search, the search will be held unreasonable. The standard by which a law enforcement officer will be judged has been stated by the U. S. Court of Appeals for the 9th Circuit:

> Whether or not an arrest is a mere pretext to search is a question of the motivation or primary purpose of the arresting officer. Improper motivation has been found where the arrest is for a minor offense which serves as a mere 'sham' or 'front' for a search for evidence of another unrelated offense for which there is no probable cause to arrest or search * * * It has also been found where the arresting officer deliberately delays making the arrest in order to allow the arrestee to enter the premises which the officer desires to search. Williams v. U. S., 418 F.2d 159, 161 (9th Circuit Court of Appeals, 1969).

Who May Conduct the Search

If practical, the law enforcement officer making the arrest should conduct the search incident to the arrest. As mentioned earlier, this search should be made at substantially the same time as the arrest. If an officer makes an arrest and does not search the arrested person right away, but some time later allows another officer to search him, the later search may be held unlawful. It would not meet the requirement of spontaneousness nor would it indicate a concern for the protection of the officer or the prevention of the destruction or concealment of evidence.

Nevertheless, if the arresting officer transfers an arrested person to the custody of another officer, the second officer may again search the arrested person. This second search is allowed because the second officer is entitled to protect himself and is not required to rely on the assumption that the arrestee has been thoroughly searched for weapons by the arresting officer. U. S. v. Dyson, 277 A.2d 658 (District of Columbia Court of Appeals, 1971).

SEARCH INCIDENT TO DETENTION

The U. S. Supreme Court in the 1973 decision of Cupp v. Murphy, 412 U.S. 291, 93 S.Ct. 2000, 36 L.Ed.2d 900 (1973) has decided that a law enforcement officer may conduct a limited warrantless search of a person merely *detained* for investigation. The Cupp v. Murphy case does not technically belong in an article on search incident to arrest because there was no arrest in the case. Nevertheless, the Court relied heavily on the *Chimel* case in its opinion, and therefore, because of its importance, Cupp v. Murphy will be discussed here separately from the materials on search incident to arrest.

In Cupp v. Murphy, the defendant having been notified of his wife's strangulation, voluntarily came to police headquarters and met his attorney there. Police noticed a dark spot on defendant's finger and asked if they could take a scraping from his fingernails. Defendant refused. Under defendant's protest and without a warrant, police proceeded to take the samples, which turned out to include particles of skin and blood of defendant's wife and fabric from her clothing. The evidence was admitted at trial and defendant was convicted of second degree murder. In habeas corpus proceedings (to be explained in Chapter XIII), defendant claimed that the fingernail scrapings were a product of an unconstitutional search.

The Court held that the momentary seizing of the defendant to get the fingernail scrapings constituted a seizure governed by the Fourth Amendment. The Court, citing the *Chimel* case, also recognized that under prescribed conditions, warrantless searches incident to an arrest are constitutionally valid. In this case, however, no formal arrest was made, nor was there a search warrant. Without a formal arrest or search warrant, a full *Chimel* search, extending to the defendant's person and the area into which he could have reached, would not have been permissible.

The Court found that *probable cause* to arrest the defendant did exist, however. Furthermore, after the police requested the scrapings, the defendant began rubbing his hands behind his back, perhaps attempting to destroy the evidence. Stressing the limited nature of the search, i. e., only taking fingernail scrapings, and the easily destructible nature of the evidence, the Court allowed the search under a limited application of the *Chimel* case.

Certain aspects of this decision shoud be emphasized to clear up any possible misunderstanding about the permissible extent of the search of a detained person by law enforcement officers. First of all, the Court clearly held that even though the defendant was not arrested, his detention against his will constituted a seizure of his person and was governed by the Fourth Amendment. Since the police in this case did not have a search warrant, nor could they satisfy any of the exceptions to the warrant requirement, the Supreme Court had to justify the search incident to the detention on the basis of the unique facts of the case. These facts were:

1. Defendant was not arrested but was detained only long enough to take the fingernail scrapings.
2. The search was very limited in extent. (The Court was careful to point out that a full *Chimel* search would not have been justified without an arrest. The officers therefore could not have searched the defendant's entire person and the area into which he could reach.)
3. The evidence—blood on the fingernails—was readily destructible.
4. The defendant made attempts to destroy the evidence.
5. There was probable cause to arrest the defendant, even though he was not actually arrested.

All of these considerations were essential to the Court's decision. Therefore, a law enforcement officer should make sure all five factors are present when he conducts a warrantless search of a detained person. If they are not all present, the officer should take the safer route and apply for a search warrant.

SUMMARY

The *Chimel* case has significantly narrowed the scope of a search authorized incident to a lawful arrest. Only for purposes of protection of the officer, prevention of escape, and prevention of concealment or destruction of evidence may an officer make such a search. Furthermore, the search is limited to the person of the individual arrested and the area into which he might reach to grab a weapon or destroy evidence. The resulting effect of these limitations is to take away from the law enforcement officer his previous right to search the entire premises incident to an arrest. Now, under *Chimel,* if the officer has probable cause to search for fruits, instrumentalities, contraband, or other evidence in the place where he plans to make an arrest, he must first obtain a valid search warrant. If the officer does not have probable cause, then he must limit his search incident to arrest according to the guidelines discussed in this chapter or justify it on the basis of some other exception to the search warrant requirement. The result in many cases will be that the officer will have to simply refrain from searching or else take the risk that the evidence he seizes will be held inadmissible in court. Where possible, then, it is always advisable for an officer to obtain a search warrant.

The U. S. Supreme Court decision in the 1973 case of Cupp v. Murphy now allows law enforcement officers to conduct a limited search of a person merely detained for investigation. The scope of such a search is more limited than that under the *Chimel* rule, and there are several other conditions, outlined in this chapter, which must be satisfied before such a search will be legal. Again, unless a law enforcement officer is sure all the conditions are satisfied, the safer procedure is to obtain a search warrant.

5

CONSENT SEARCHES

Another well-established exception to the search warrant requirement is the "consent search." A consent search occurs when an individual allows a law enforcement officer to search his person, premises, or belongings. The officer requests consent to search when he has neither a warrant nor justification for the search under any of the other exceptions to the warrant requirement. The consenting individual thereby relinquishes any right he has to object to the search on constitutional grounds, and any evidence seized as a result of the search will be admissible in court despite the fact that there was no warrant and no probable cause to search. A consent search may also provide a benefit to the consenting party who is innocent of any wrongdoing.

> If the search is conducted and proves fruitless, that in itself may convince the police that an arrest with its possible stigma and embarassment is unnecessary, or that a far more extensive search pursuant to a warrant is not justfied. In short, a search pursuant to consent may result in considerably less inconvenience for the subject of the search, and, properly conducted, is a constitutionally permissible and wholly legitimate aspect of effective police activity. Schneckloth v. Bustamonte, 412 U.S. 218, 228, 93 S.Ct. 2041, 2048, 36 L.Ed.2d 854, 863 (U. S. Supreme Court, 1973).

It is not surprising, then, that the consent search is frequently relied upon by law enforcement officers, because it is faster than warrant procedures and it does not require the often difficult determination of whether there is probable cause, either to search or to arrest. However, because of this comparative lack of effort required to obtain a consent to search, there are many opportunities for abuse of an individual's Fourth Amendment rights by law enforcement officers. In order to protect those rights, courts will look closely at the circumstances surrounding every consent search to determine if the consent was truly voluntary. The U. S. Supreme Court stated its views on this subject in the following language from its 1973 decision in the case of Schneckloth v. Bustamonte:

> [T]he Fourth and Fourteenth Amendments require that consent not be coerced, by explicit or implicit means, by implied threat or covert force. For, no matter how subtly the coercion were applied, the resulting "consent" would be no more than a pretext for the unjustified police intrusion against which the Fourth Amendment is directed. * * *
>
> The problem of reconciling the recognized legitimacy of consent searches with the requirement that they be free from any aspect of official coercion cannot be resolved by any infallible touchstone. To approve such searches without the most careful scrutiny would sanction the possibility of official coercion; to place artificial restrictions upon such searches would jeopardize their basic validity. Just as was true with confessions, the requirement of "voluntary" consent reflects a fair accommodation of the constitutional requirements involved. In examining all the surrounding circumstances to determine if in fact the consent to search was coerced, account must be taken of subtly coercive police questions, as well as the possibly vulnerable subjective state of the person who consents. Those searches that are the product of police coercion can thus be filtered out without undermining the continuing validity of consent searches. In sum, there is no reason for us to depart in the area of consent searches, from the traditional definition of "voluntariness." Schneckloth v. Bustamonte, 412 U.S. 218, 229, 93 S.Ct. 2041, 2048–49, 36 L.Ed.2d 854, 864 (1973).

When the prosecuting attorney attempts to introduce into court evidence obtained as a result of a consent search, the court will require him to prove by "clear and convincing evidence" that the consent was in fact voluntarily given, and not the result of duress or coercion, express or implied. The prosecutor's proof will consist almost entirely of the law enforcement officer's testimony about his actions in obtaining the consent and conducting the search. The remainder of this chapter will therefore be devoted to explaining in detail the meaning of the voluntariness requirement and providing guidelines for the law enforcement officer in conducting consent searches.

REQUIREMENT THAT THE CONSENT BE VOLUNTARY

As the U. S. Supreme Court in Schneckloth v. Bustamonte has said, there are no set rules for determining whether or not a consent to search has been voluntarily and freely given. Courts will look to all the circumstances surrounding the giving of the consent in making this decision. The following examples should give some helpful guidelines to law enforcement officers in determining what circumstances the courts consider important in deciding the question of voluntariness of consent.

Force or Threat of Force

The most obvious situation in which courts will find a lack of voluntariness of consent is a law enforcement officer's use of force or threat of force in obtaining the consent. Thus, in a case where a defendant was confronted by police with drawn guns and a riot pistol, and was told they would get a warrant if necessary, the court held that the defendant did not give free and voluntary consent to search the vehicle when he gave the officers the keys to his car in an atmosphere of "dramatic excitement." Weed v. U. S., 340 F.2d 827 (10th Circuit Court of Appeals, 1965). Also, in a case where a defendant permitted entry into his apartment only after officers threatened to kick down his door, the court held that the consent was obviously not free and voluntary. People v. Loria, 10 N.Y.2d 368, 373, 223 N.Y.S. 2d 462, 466–67, 179 N.E.2d 478, 482 (Court of Appeals, of New York, 1961). Any such blatant display of force will always cause a consent to be held invalid because it was involuntary.

Sometimes, in order to protect themselves and others, officers must utilize force or the threat of force in their initial confrontation with a suspect. Despite the coercive nature of an initial confrontation, officers may still be able to obtain a valid consent to search. Officers must, however, do everything in their power to ensure that the consent is voluntary. In People v. Parker, 45 Cal.App.3rd 24, 119 Cal.Rptr. 49 (California Court of Appeal, 1975) officers, believing a suspect to be armed, entered his hotel room with guns drawn. After they ascertained that the room's occupant was unarmed, the officers holstered their guns. They then obtained consent to search after indicating to the occupant that he could deny permission to search. The court found that the consent to search was voluntary under the totality of the circumstances.

Submission to Authority

The show of force or coercion by law enforcement officers need not be of such intensity as in the above cases for a court to hold that a consent to search was not voluntary. It has been held that even an implied or suggested assertion of authority by law enforcement officers may be enough to cause a resulting consent to search to be considered involuntary. The rationale behind this is that a person's submission to such a show of authority may not be an expression of his free will but may be nothing more than a show of respect for the supremacy of the law. Therefore the mere acquiescence or submission of a defendant to an assertion of authority by a law enforcement officer will usually not support a finding of voluntary consent.

An example is a case in which officers arrested the defendant for driving the wrong way on a one-way street. As the defendant was standing between his car and the police car, one of the officers went to the passenger side of his car and attempted to open the door in order to look for "anything in violation of the law." Finding it locked, the officer requested that defendant open it, and defendant complied. When the door opened, a shaving kit fell to the ground. The kit was later found to contain marijuana.

The court held that the defendant did not voluntarily consent to the search of his car:

> Mere acquiescence in the orders, suggestions, or requests of the police can never be equated with consent. * * * Thus, a finding of voluntary consent can never rest solely on the fact that an accused did some consensual act or gave permission to the police to search, but is a question of fact which must be decided in light of the circumstances attending the alleged consent. * * *
>
> Among the factors to be considered are the setting in which the consent was obtained; what was said and done by the parties present; the age, intelligence, and educational background of the person consenting. * * * Commonwealth v. Burgos, 223 Pa. Super. 325, 329, 330, 299 A.2d 34, 37 (Superior Court of Pennsylvania, 1972).

The court noted that the officer had already attempted to enter the car when he asked defendant to open the door. Consent under such circumstances could hardly be voluntary, because it is unlikely that a suspect would assert opposition to a search which appeared inevitable. Furthermore, defendant here was under arrest and did not speak English very well. It is likely then that he might have understood the request as an order, and thus merely acquiesced rather than voluntarily consented to the request.

Failure to Object to Search

Another example shows that a person's mere failure to object to a search will not in itself constitute the full and unqualified voluntary consent required by the law. An officer investigating the ringing of a burglar alarm in an office building saw defendant in one of the offices. Defendant let the officer into the office and satisfactorily explained his presence as the owner of the office. As defendant walked away, he picked up a large envelope and placed it in his pocket. The officer than asked him "What did you put in your pocket? Let me see it." Defendant then handed over the package, saying that it contained marijuana and that he had a permit for it. The officer arrested him for felonious possession of a narcotic drug.

The court found that the defendant's handing over of the package at the policeman's direction was the equivalent of a search and seizure:

> This was not a voluntary act, a consent to waive the constitutional right to be free from unreasonable searches and seizures, but rather a submission to authority. No inference of consent may be drawn from the mere failure of a person to argue or object to a demand of an officer. Our courts "indulge every reasonable presumption against waiver" of fundamental constitutional rights. * * * People v. Abramson, 40 Misc. 723, 724, 243 N.Y.S.2d 819, 821 (Supreme Court of New York, 1963).

Nevertheless, although failure to object, by itself, will not establish a valid consent, it is still *some evidence* of consent, and when it is accompanied by other factors such as defendant's active cooperation with the officers in conducting the search, it may satisfy the requirement of free and voluntary consent on his part. Thus, there was voluntary consent in a case where the defendant directed the route to his apartment, pointed out the closet where his clothing was, and made no objection to the examination of bloodstained clothing or the taking and retention of it by the police. It is to be noted that there was nothing in this case to suggest violence, threats of violence, intimidation, or overawing of the defendant by the police. State v. Hannah, 150 Conn. 457, 191 A.2d 124 (Supreme Court of Connecticut, 1963).

Misrepresentation, Deception, and Stealth

The courts look with disfavor upon any consent to search which is obtained by misleading or deceiving the person giving the consent as to the authority of the officer conducting the search. In the often cited case of Bumper v. North Carolina, officers went to the home of a rape suspect to look for evidence. The home was owned and occupied by defendant's grandmother. The officers told the grandmother that they had a search warrant and she let them in. During the course of their search, a rifle was found.

At the hearing on the motion to suppress the rifle as evidence, the prosecutor did not rely on the warrant to support the legality of the search but relied on the grandmother's consent. (In fact, no warrant was ever returned nor was there any information about the conditions under which it was issued.)

The U. S. Supreme Court held that a search cannot be justified on the basis of consent when that consent has been give only after the officer conducting the search has asserted that he possesses a warrant:

> When a prosecutor seeks to rely upon consent to justify the lawfulness of a search, he has the burden of proving that the consent was, in fact, *freely and voluntarily given.* This burden cannot be discharged by showing no more than acquiescence to a claim of lawful authority. A search conducted in reliance upon a warrant cannot later be justified on the basis of consent if it turns out that the warrant was invalid. The results can be no different when it turns out that the State does not even attempt to rely upon the validity of the warrant, or fails to show that there was, in fact, any warrant at all.
>
> When a law enforcement officer claims authority to search a home under a warrant, he announces in effect that the occupant has no right to resist the search. The situation is instinct with coercion—albeit colorably lawful coercion. Where there is coercion there cannot be consent. Bumper v. North Carolina, 391 U.S. 543, 548–50, 88 S.Ct. 1788, 1792, 20 L.Ed.2d 797, 802–03 (1968).

In another case, involving a different type of official misrepresentation, officers had arrested the defendant for robbery and murder and questioned him at police headquarters. He made no incriminating statements at that time. The next day, officers, without a search warrant, went to defendant's home to conduct a search. They falsely told defendant's wife that he had admitted the crime and had sent the police for the "stuff." The frightened and upset wife admitted the officers to the apartment and led them to money evidence from the robbery.

The court held that the consent given by the wife was not voluntary:

> [I]t is well established that the consent may not be gained through stealth, deceit, or misrepresentation, and that if such exists this is tantamount to implied coercion * * * Commonwealth v. Wright, 411 Pa. 81, 85, 190 A.2d 709, 711 (Supreme Court of Pennsylvania, 1963).

Custody or Arrest

In U. S. v. Watson, 423 U.S. 411, 96 S.Ct. 820, 46 L.Ed.2d 598 (1976), the U. S. Supreme Court held that a consent to search will not be held involuntary solely because the person giving the consent is under arrest or is otherwise in custody. Nevertheless, the fact that a person is deprived of his freedom of action by law enforcement officers or is under arrest is important in determining voluntariness of consent. Although *every* case in which a person giving consent is under such constraint will *not necessarily* result in a determination of involuntariness, the courts tend to examine very carefully any consent given under these circumstances. It is generally felt that a person who has been taken into custody or arrested is "more susceptible to duress or coercion from the custodial officers." U. S. v. Richardson, 388 F.2d 842, 845 (6th Circuit Court of Appeals, 1968). Some courts have gone so far as to require counsel for a person in custody before police may obtain a valid consent to search. The Indiana Supreme Court held that because of the inherently coercive nature of in-custody interrogation, a person in custody of the police is entitled to the presence and advice of counsel prior to deciding whether to give consent to search. Pirtle v. State, 263 Ind. 16, 323 N.E.2d 634 (1975). Therefore, when the validity of the search is tested in court, a heavier burden is placed on the prosecutor to prove the consent was freely and voluntarily given when the consenter was in custody than when he was not.

The law enforcement officer must be especially careful in ensuring that consent is voluntary when the person giving the consent is in custody or under arrest. He can do this by carefully noting indications of the person's willingness to allow the search, and by not doing anything himself which would tend to influence or coerce the person to consent. For example, if a person in custody gives his consent to search and actively cooperates with the officer, or expresses a belief that no incriminating evidence will be found, courts will usually find these factors indicative of voluntariness. Also, if a person has been informed of his right to refuse to allow the search by the custodial officer, a subsequent consent is usually considered to be voluntarily given.

On the other hand, if the person in custody is subjected to additional coercive action by the law enforcement officer such as handcuffing, display of weapons, or incarceration, courts are likely to consider a resulting consent to search involuntary. The same would be true if an officer conducted an interrogation of a person in custody without giving *Miranda* warnings, or attempted to deceive or mislead him. Furthermore, evasive or uncooperative conduct on the part of the person in custody is considered to be an indication that the consent is not voluntary.

It must be reemphasized here that none of the above mentioned factors will determine by itself whether a consent is voluntary or involuntary. Courts will look to *all* the surrounding facts and circumstances, and it is nearly impossible to predict how a court will decide in any given situation. About all that can definitely be said in this context is that it will be harder to prove a consent was voluntary when the person giving the consent was in custody than if he was not. Law enforcement officers should be aware of all the variables which the courts consider so they can control the situation as much as possible or at least make a rational decision on whether to conduct a search based on consent or to get a warrant.

NOTE: The foregoing principles apply when the defendant's arrest or detention is legal. However, when the arrest or detention is illegal, courts will generally hold that any consent given is "fruit of the poisonous tree" and necessarily involuntary. As one court recently stated:

> At the time of the initial arrest, appellant consented to the search of his automobile. Generally where a person has consented to a search this removes a later objection that it was conducted without a warrant. However, where the consent and search are accompanied by an illegal arrest, the events are so intertwined, one with the other, that the consent does not expunge the taint of the illegal arrest. State v. Barwick, 94 Idaho 139, 142, 483 P.2d 670, 673 (Supreme Court of Idaho, 1971).

It is very important, therefore, when a consent to search is obtained from a person under arrest, that the arrest be carried out in compliance with the requirements set out in Chapter 1. Otherwise the consent will be involuntary and the search illegal. When possible, officers should obtain consent to search from a person before the person is arrested or otherwise restrained. As a general rule, the sooner consent is sought, the fewer factors tending to show involuntariness will be present.

Knowledge of Right to Refuse Consent

Another factor which the courts consider in determining the voluntariness of consent is whether or not the consenting person knew of his right to refuse to consent. Prior to the U. S. Supreme Court decision in Schneckloth v. Bustamonte, discussed above, some courts ruled that the state had to prove that the person from whom a consent search was sought knew he had the right to refuse consent, or none of the evidence seized would be admissible in court. Other courts ruled that the knowledge of the right to refuse consent was only one of the factors to be considered in determining voluntariness. The U. S. Supreme Court settled the matter with respect to non-custodial searches in Schneckloth v. Bustamonte, agreeing with the latter view:

> Voluntariness is a question of fact to be determined from all the circumstances, and while the subject's knowledge of a right to refuse is a factor to be taken into consideration, the prosecution is not required to demonstrate such knowledge as a prerequisite to establishing a voluntary consent. * * * 412 U.S. at 248–49, 93 S.Ct. at 2059, 36 L.Ed.2d at 875.

Therefore, a law enforcement officer, in order to obtain a valid consent to search from a person not in custody, does not have to ensure that the person knows of his right to refuse consent. This means that the officer does *not* have to give any warnings before conducting a non-custodial consent search.

Nevertheless, even though formal warnings are not required for non-custodial consent searches, the courts still consider a person's knowledge of his right to consent as *one* of the factors in determining voluntariness. An officer who wants to make sure he is obtaining a valid consent to search, *may* give a person formal warnings of his rights. Furthermore, since the courts have not yet decided whether knowledge of the right to refuse consent is necessary for a valid consent when the consenting person is *in custody,* it would be a good idea for the officer to give such warnings when a person is under arrest or otherwise in custody. The following suggested simple warnings should adequately inform a person of his right to refuse consent:

> I am a law enforcement officer. I would like to request permission from you to search your premises (person, belongings).
>
> You have an absolute right to refuse to grant permission for me to search unless I have a search warrant.
>
> If you do grant permission to search, anything found can be used against you in a court of law. If you refuse, I will not make a search at this time.

A consent to search given by a person after receiving warnings such as these, is likely to be considered voluntary by a court, assuming there has been no coercion by the officer.

Of course, if an officer has clear indications that the person consenting already knows that he can insist on a search warrant if he so desires, there would be no need for the officer to give any warnings. An example is a case in which the defendant, when asked by an officer to sign a Consent Search form said, "If I don't sign this, you are going to get a search warrant." The court in that case said that this statement demonstrated defendant's awareness of his right to resist the officer's search in the absence of a warrant. His subsequent signature on the form was therefore a relinquishment of a *known* right. U. S. v. Curiale, 414 F.2d 744 (2nd Circuit Court of Appeals, 1969). It is very important for an officer in situations like the above, to make careful notes of any indications that the person knows of his right to refuse consent. Such information can greatly help the court in determining voluntariness of consent.

Some state courts have refused to follow the Schneckloth v. Bustamonte "totality of the circumstances" test and have required that the consenting person be aware of his right to refuse consent in addi-

CONSENT TO SEARCH

____
Date

____
Location

I, ______________________, having been informed of my constitutional right not to have a search made of my person or the premises hereinafter mentioned without a search warrant and of my right to refuse to consent to such a search, and knowing that if I consent to such a search, anything found can be used against me in court, hereby authorize __________________ and __________________,
(names of officers or agents)

____
(titles of officers or agents and name of agency)

to conduct a complete search of (my person) my premises located at ______________________________________.
These (officers or agents) are authorized by me to take from my (person) premises any letters, papers, materials or other property which they may desire.

This written permission is being given by me to the above-named persons voluntarily and without threats or promises of any kind.

____
(signed)

Witnesses: ______________________

____

[B9603]

tion to his consent being otherwise voluntary. The New Jersey Supreme Court held that the state constitution demands that "the validity of a consent to search, even in a noncustodial situation, must be measured in terms of waiver; i. e., where the state seeks to justify a search on the basis of consent it has the burden of showing that the consent was voluntary, an essential element of which is knowledge of the right to refuse consent." State v. Johnson, 68 N.J. 349, 353–54, 346 A.2d 66, 68 (1975). Likewise, the court in Case v. State, Okl.Cr. App., 519 P.2d 523 (Court of Criminal Appeals of Oklahoma, 1974), held that officers must give *Miranda* warnings prior to obtaining consent. Officers should determine whether courts in their state interpret their state constitution to require that the consenting person be aware of his rights before a consent search is conducted.

Clearness and Explicitness of Consent

Another factor to be considered in determining the voluntariness of consent is whether the expression of consent is clear, explicit, and unequivocal. Hesitation or ambiguity in the expression of consent could be one indication that the consent is not voluntary.

It is immaterial whether a person's consent to search is written or verbal. Both are equally effective in waiving the person's right to later object to the search. A signed and witnessed writing, however, provides the best proof of a clear, voluntary, waiver of a known right. A suggested form for obtaining a written consent to search appears on page 150.

Consent need not be expressed in words but may be implied by a person's acts or conduct. An example of this is a case in which police were investigating the death of an infant and went to the home of the defendant. The officers asked the defendant's husband if they could go into the room containing the infant's crib. The husband handed the officers the keys, saying that he did not want to go in there himself. Incriminating evidence against the defendant was found in the room.

The court held that a valid consent to search had been given by the husband although he did not express it verbally or in writing. The fact that he handed the officers the keys, knowing their intent to search the room, was a clear and unequivocal expression of his consent. People v. Crews, 38 Ill. 331, 231 N.E.2d 451 (Supreme Court of Illinois, 1967).

Officers should describe in their reports any statements made or conduct engaged in by the consenting person. Even statements or conduct which seem unimportant at the time of the search may prove meaningful later to a judge or an attorney.

Physical and Mental Condition

Officers should carefully note physical or mental deficiencies of persons from whom they obtain consent to search. A person giving consent may claim later in court that he lacked mental capacity to consent because of insanity, use of alcohol or drugs, or physical disability. Officers can negate such claims by testifying about their observations at the time consent was given. Also, some courts determine the voluntariness of the consent on the basis of facts as they objectively appeared to the officer at the time of consent. People v. Gurley, 23 Cal.App.3d 536, 100 Cal.Rptr. 407 (California Court of Appeal, 1972).

The emotional state of the consenting person may also be important. If an officer can testify that the consenting party was calm and cooperative, a court is more likely to find voluntary consent.

Notification of Counsel

If a defendant has retained counsel in connection with a criminal charge, officers should notify the defendant's counsel before obtaining a consent to search. In Tidwell v. Superior Court, 17 Cal.App.3d 780, 95 Cal.Rptr. 213 (California Court of Appeal, 1971), a law enforcement officer obtained from the defendant, who was being held in the county jail, consent to search the defendant's automobile. At the time, the defendant was represented by appointed counsel on a separate charge, but the officer did not notify counsel before obtaining consent. The court suppressed the evidence holding that once counsel is appointed the police may not obtain consent to search without notifying counsel.

Experience and Background

The experience and background of a person consenting to a search can be important factors in determining the voluntariness of consent. A person who is knowledgeable about investigative and legal proceedings is less likely to be coerced or intimidated by law enforcement authorities than a person ignorant in these areas. On the other hand, it may be more difficult to establish voluntary consent by an illiterate person or one who cannot speak or understand English. Officers should tell the court what they know about the experience and background of consenting persons to assist the court in determining the voluntariness of consent.

SCOPE OF CONSENT SEARCHES

There are several limitations to the scope or extent to which a law enforcement officer can conduct a search by consent. One of the most obvious of these limitations is that, although there may be a valid consent in all respects to an officer's request, it may not be a consent to *search* at all. The best example of this is the situation in which an officer is permitted to *enter* someone's home in compliance with the officer's request for an interview. This does *not* automatically give the officer a right to search the place. There is a vital distinction between the granting of admission to one's home for the purposes of conversation and the granting of permission to thoroughly search the place.

In a case illustrating this principle, officers investigating a murder knocked on defendant's hotel room door and were invited in by the defendant. The defendant was not advised that they were police officers nor was any request made by them to search his room. Nevertheless, a search was conducted and incriminating evidence found.

The court held that the invitation to enter his room, extended by the defendant to the person who knocked on the door, did not constitute a consent to search his room. Quoting from another case, the court said:

> "* * * To justify the introduction of evidence seized by a police officer within a private residence on the ground that the officer's entry was made by invitation, permission, or consent, there must be evidence of a statement or some overt act by the occupant of such residence sufficient to indicate his intent to waive his rights to the security and privacy of his home and freedom from unwarranted intrusions therein. An open door is not a waiver of such rights. * * *" Duncan v. State, 278 Ala. 145, 159, 176 So.2d 840, 853 (Supreme Court of Alabama, 1965).

Throughout the rest of this discussion of the scope of consent searches, officers should keep in mind that they must first carefully determine the scope of consent given by the consenting person, and then they must be careful not to exceed those limits. When a consent search is challenged in court or at a hearing on a motion to suppress the prosecution must establish that the scope of the search did not exceed the scope of the consent.

"Plain View" Doctrine

Although an invitation to enter premises is not the equivalent of a consent to search the premises, this does not mean that an officer must ignore contraband or other criminal evidence lying in plain view. Under the "plain view" doctrine, as long as an officer is in a place or position in which he has a legal right to be as the result of a prior valid intrusion into a constitutionally protected area, he may seize any criminal evidence which is lying open to view.

In a case illustrating this point, officers were investigating a robbery, and preliminary information led them to suspect a man named Albert. The officers went to Albert's apartment, knocked on the door, identified themselves, and were invited into the apartment by Albert, who opened the door and walked back into the room. The defendant was present in the apartment as a guest of Albert. While talking to the two men, the officers noticed various objects fitting the description of items stolen in the robbery lying in plain view. They arrested the two men and seized the evidence observed.

The court held that the evidence seized was admissible against the defendant (Albert's guest). Because the officers were rightfully in the room by Albert's invitation, they were also rightfully there with respect to defendant. Seeing what was patently and obviously open to view was therefore not a search, and seizing the evidence was not a violation of defendant's rights. Robbins v. MacKenzie, 364 F. 2d 45 (1st Circuit Court of Appeals, 1966).

Area of Search

Assuming, however, that an officer is able to obtain a valid consent not just to *enter* premises, but consent to actually *search* those premises, there may still be limitations on the scope or extent of the search. One such limitation relates to the bounds of the area to be searched. Although it is impossible to give operational guidelines as to how large an area a law enforcement officer may search after obtaining a person's consent, in general it can be said that it depends on the words or actions used by the person giving the consent. It should be noted that the area allowed to be searched is different for consent searches, for searches incident to arrest, and for searches made under warrant.

In a case in which an officer had received permission to "look around" an apartment, the court held that this did not authorize the officer to open and search boxes and suitcases which he had been informed were the property of persons other than the person giving consent. In other words, an officer can only search those parts of premises over which the person giving consent has some possessory right or control, and not personal property which he knows belongs to some other person. People v. Cruz, 61 Cal.2d 861, 40 Cal.Rptr. 841, 395 P.2d 889 (Supreme Court of California, 1964). In another case, where a valid consent was given to officers to search the trunk of a car, the court held that this consent did not extend to a search of the passenger area of the car and that evidence found in the passenger area was inadmissible in court. State v. Johnson, 71 Wash.2d 239, 427 P.2d 705 (Supreme Court of Washington, 1967).

Furthermore, the limitation on the area of search allowed by consent applies equally to searches of the person as to premises. For example, in a case in which an individual consented to a search of his person for *weapons*, it was held that this did not constitute a consent to conduct a general exploratory search of his person. Incriminating evidence seized was held inadmissible in court. People v. Rice, 259 Cal.App.2d 399, 66 Cal.Rptr. 246 (Court of Appeal of California, 1968).

In a particularly interesting case involving both a non-verbal consent and a limitation on the area of the person allowed to be searched by consent, a police officer, while questioning the defendant with regard to narcotics, asked him whether he was still using or carrying narcotics. When defendant replied that he was not, the officer asked him if he minded if he checked him for needle marks. Defendant said nothing but put his arms out sideways. The officer did not check defendant's arms but instead patted down defendant's coat and found marijuana cigarettes.

The court held that the search went beyond the area to which the defendant had consented to allow a search:

> Bowens' putting out his arms sideways in response to a query whether he minded allowing the officer to check "if he had any marks on him" could hardly be said to be naturally indicative or persuasive of the giving of an intended consent to have the officer switch instead to a general search of his pockets—in which he had two marijuana cigarettes. Oliver v. Bowens, 386 F.2d 688, 691 (9th Circuit Court of Appeals, 1967).

It would seem then, as a general rule, that if an officer asks for and obtains a consent to search a specific area, whether in a place or on a person, the officer is limited to that specific area. If he searches beyond it, any evidence he seizes is likely to be held inadmissible in court.

Time

Another limitation on the scope of a search by consent relates to the length of time over which the consent is valid. In a case illustrating this limitation, officers were investigating the death of defendant's wife and they obtained a valid consent from the defendant to search his home. The officers conducted a search and found nothing. At this point in time, defendant had not been accused of anything. However, later in the day, police received information giving them probable cause to arrest the defendant for his wife's murder and to obtain a search warrant for his premises. Defendant was arrested that evening but the search warrant could not be executed at that time because it ran only in the daytime. Therefore, officers went back the next day with the search warrant and found certain incriminating evidence.

Since there was some question as to the validity of the warrant, the state attempted to justify this second search on the basis that the defendant's earlier consent continued in effect, after his arrest, to the next day. The court rejected this contention with the following reasoning:

> The officers entered the defendant's home on the 5th under the protection of his consent. By nightfall, however, the defendant had ceased to be the husband assisting in the solution of his wife's death and had become the man accused of his wife's murder by poison (and) held under arrest for hearing.
>
> When the defendant became the accused, the protective cloak of the Constitution became more closely wrapped around him. * * *
>
> The consent of December 5 in our view should be measured on the morning of the 6th by the status of the defendant as the accused. There is no evidence whatsoever that the consent of the 5th was ever discussed with the defendant at or after his arrest, or that he was informed of the State's intent to enter and search his home on the 6th on the strength of a continuing consent. We conclude, therefore, that consent of the defendant had ended by December 6, and accordingly the officers were not protected thereby on the successful search of the 6th. State v. Brochu, Me., 237 A.2d 418, 421 (Supreme Judicial Court of Maine, 1967).

It is recommended then, that once an officer conducts a consent search and stops it for whatever reason, if he desires to conduct a search of the same place or person the next day or later the same day, he should obtain a new consent from the person involved. This would be especially true in cases where intervening events, such as the arrest of the consenting person, suggest that a second consent might not be given so readily as the original consent.

Object of Search

The scope of the search may also be limited by the object for which the consenting person allows the officer to search. In People v. Superior Court (Arketa), 10 Cal.App.3d 122, 89 Cal.Rptr. 316 (California Court of Appeal, 1970), a person gave officers consent to search his premises for a possible suspect of a crime. The officers conducted a thorough search of the house and its closets for a crowbar without advising the person that they wanted to look for a crowbar. The court invalidated the search because it went beyond the scope of the consent granted. Therefore, officers should not look in areas where the object for which they have consent to search could not be located because of its size or character.

Revocation of Consent

Although there is some disagreement on the question, the prevailing view appears to be that consent, once given, may be revoked or withdrawn at any time after the search has been partially completed. A case illustrating this principle involved a police officer who was investigating a defendant parked at a late hour in a high arrest area of town. The defendant consented to let the officer look around inside his vehicle. After doing so, the officer asked to look into defendant's trunk. Defendant also initially consented to this. However, after the officer had spent some time looking in the trunk, the defendant felt he was being harassed and he told the officer to stop. The officer did not stop at this time and later found contraband in the trunk.

The court held that the defendant had withdrawn his consent and that the evidence found after the withdrawal was inadmissible in court:

> Neither do we find any reason to hold that a consent, once given, may not be withdrawn. It is true that the contrary view has been expressed. * * * We do not believe that this is the present law, particularly in view of the explicit statement in the *Miranda* case that a defendant consenting to answer police questioning without a lawyer may withdraw such waiver at any time. We see no reason, in this respect, to distinguish between withdrawal of waiver of legal representation during investigation and withdrawal of consent to search once given. People v. Martinez, 259 Cal.App.2d 943, 945–46, 65 Cal.Rptr. 920, 922 (Appellate Department, California Superior Court, 1968).

WHO MAY GIVE CONSENT

In general, the only person who is able to give a valid consent to a search is the person whose constitutional protection against unreasonable searches and seizures would be invaded by the search if it were conducted without consent. This means, for example, that when the search of an individual's body or clothing is contemplated, the only person who can consent to such a search is the individual himself. The same rule applies to searches of premises except that when several people have varying degrees of interest in the same premises, more than one person may be qualified to give consent to search.

In certain situations, the law recognizes authority in a third person to consent to a search of property even though he is not the person against whose interests the search is being conducted. In U. S. v. Matlock, 415 U.S. 164, 94 S.Ct. 988, 39 L.Ed.2d 242 (1974), the U. S. Supreme Court stated the test for determining whether a third person could consent to a search of premises or effects:

> [W]hen the prosecution seeks to justify a warrantless search by proof of voluntary consent, it is not limited to proof that consent was given by the defendant, but may show that permission to search was obtained from a third party who possessed *common authority over or other sufficient relationship to the premises or effects sought to be inspected.* 415 U.S. at 171, 94 S.Ct. at 993, 39 L.Ed.2d at 249–50 (emphasis supplied).

The Court then defined "common authority":

> Common authority is, of course, not to be implied from the mere interest a third party has in the property. The authority which justifies the third-party consent does not rest upon the law of property, with its attendant historical and legal refinements, * * * but rests rather on mutual use of the property by persons generally having joint access or control for most purposes, so that it is reasonable to recognize that any of the co-inhabitants has the right to permit the inspection in his own right and that the others have assumed the risk that one of their number might permit the common area to be searched. 415 U.S. at 171 n. 7, 94 S.Ct. at 993 n. 7, 39 L.Ed.2d at 250 n. 7.

Since questions of who may give valid consent are often confusing and complicated, and since courts tend to carefully scrutinize any waiver of a person's constitutional rights, it is worthwhile to examine some examples of consent search situations where the person giving consent is not the person against whose interests the search is being conducted. The officer should keep in mind, throughout the discussion of third party consent situations, that he must make the necessary inquiries to determine if the party from whom consent is sought is a proper party to authorize the search in question.

Persons Having Equal Rights or Interests in Property

It is well settled that when two or more persons have substantially equal rights of ownership, occupancy, or other possessory interest in premises to be searched or property to be seized, any one of such persons may legally authorize a search and seizure thereof, and thereby bind the others and waive their right to object. An example is a case in which police obtained a valid consent to search a defendant's apartment from a co-defendant in a case involving a break into a bank. The co-defendant who gave the consent was living with the defendant at the time and evidence showed that he had a right to use and occupy the premises. The police found evidence incriminating the defendant in the apartment.

The court held that the co-defendant, being a joint tenant or resident of the apartment could consent to the entry and search of the apartment:

> This court and other courts have held that where there are multiple lawful residents of a premises, any one of such persons may give permission to enter and that if incriminating evidence is found, it may be used against all. Wright v. U. S., 389 F.2d 996, 998 (8th Circuit Court of Appeals, 1968).

In determining whether a person is a joint occupant of premises, courts will look to such factors as whether he paid rent, how long he stayed, whether the person left his belongings on the premises, whether the person possessed a key, and whether there was any written or oral agreement among other parties as to the person's right to use and occupy the premises.

Another case which illustrates the same principle, only applied to personal property, is the U. S. Supreme Court case of Frazier v. Cupp. In that case, the defendant, at his murder trial, objected to the introduction into evidence of clothing seized from his duffel bag. At the time of the seizure, the duffel bag was being used jointly by the defendant, and his cousin and had been left in the cousin's home. When police arrested the cousin, they asked him if they could have his clothing. The cousin directed them to the duffel bag and both the cousin and his mother consented to its search. During the search, the officers came upon defendant's clothing in the bag and it was seized as well.

The Court upheld the legality of the search over defendant's objections:

> Since Rawls [the cousin] was a joint owner of the bag, he clearly had authority to consent to its search. The officers therefore found evidence against the petitioner while in the course of an otherwise lawful search. [*plain view doctrine*] * * * Petitioner argues that Rawls only had actual permission to use one compartment of the bag and that he had no authority to consent to a search of the other compartments. We will not, however, engage in such metaphysical subtleties in judging the efficacy of Rawls' consent. Petitioner, in allowing Rawls to use the bag and in leaving it in his house, must be taken to have assumed the risk that Rawls would allow someone else to look inside. We find no valid search and seizure claim in this case. Frazier v. Cupp, 394 U.S. 731, 740, 89 S.Ct. 1420, 1425, 22 L.Ed.2d 684, 693–94 (1969).

Officers should note that a third party may give consent to search if he has common authority to use the premises to be searched, even though he is not *actually* using the premises at the time of the search. In U. S. v. Cook, 530 F.2d 145 (7th Circuit Court of Appeals, 1976), the defendant's landlady consented to a search of a poultry house on her property. The poultry house consisted of a large room in which the landlady had segregated an area with wire fence for her exclusive use. She gave the defendant permission to use the remaining space, but she retained the right to use the space if necessary. The defendant claimed that, since neither the landlady nor her family *actually* used the defendant's area, there was no common authority. The court upheld the search, however, ruling that the defendant had assumed the risk that the landlandy would permit others to inspect the premises.

A third party cannot consent to a search of more than that over which he has common authority. In U. S. v. Bussey, 507 F.2d 1096 (9th Circuit Court of Appeals, 1974), the court held that a participant with the defendant in a bank robbery had authority to consent to a search of the motel room which she and the defendant occupied with others. She did not, however, have authority to consent to a search of the defendant's personal luggage.

Landlord—Tenant

A landlord has *no* implied authority to consent to a search of a tenant's premises or a seizure of his property during the period of the tenancy. This rule holds true even though the landlord has the authority to enter the tenant's premises for the limited purposes of inspection or for performance of repairs or housekeeping services. Chapman v. U. S., 365 U.S. 610, 81 S.Ct. 776, 5 L.Ed.2d 828 (U. S. Supreme Court, 1961). However, once the tenancy has terminated, and the landlord has the primary right to occupation and control of the premises, the landlord may consent to a search of the premises. Furthermore, the landlord's consent will be valid after the termination of the tenancy even though the former tenant has left personal belongings on the premises. People v. Urfer, 274 Cal.App.2d 307, 79 Cal.Rptr. 60 (California Court of Appeal, 1969).

Hotel Employee—Hotel Guest

The U. S. Supreme Court has held that the principles governing a landlord's consent to a search of tenant's premises apply with equal force to consent searches of hotel (and motel) rooms allowed by hotel employees. In the case of Stoner v. California, police were investigating a robbery and they went to the defendant's hotel. The defendant was not in his room and police obtained permission from the hotel clerk to search the room. Items of evidence incriminating the defendant in the robbery were found in the room.

The Court held that the search was illegal and that the items seized could not be used against the defendant in court. The defendant's constitutional right was at stake here—not the clerk's or the hotel's. Therefore, only the defendant, either directly or through an agent, could waive that right. There was no evidence that the police had any basis whatsoever to believe that the night clerk had been authorized by the defendant to permit the police to search his room:

> It is true * * * that when a person engages a hotel room he undoubtedly gives "implied or express permission" to "such persons as maids, janitors or repairmen" to enter his room "in the performance of their duties." * * * But the conduct of the night clerk and the police in the present case was of an entirely different order. * * *
>
> No less than a tenant of a house * * * a guest in a hotel room is entitled to constitutional protection against unreasonable searches and seizures. * * * That protection would disappear if it were left to depend upon the unfettered discretion of an employee of the hotel. Stoner v. California, 376 U.S. 483, 489–90, 84 S.Ct. 889, 893, 11 L.Ed.2d 356, 361 (1964).

Host—Guest

A different situation is presented when the person against whom a search for evidence is directed is merely a guest on the premises of his host and the host consents to a search of the premises. Here, courts have generally held that the host or primary occupant of the premises may give a valid consent to a search of the premises and any evidence found would be admissible against the guest. An example is a case in which a lady householder had "taken in," without payment of rent, her grandnephew and another young man. While she was tidying up her home, she found a loaded pistol and other items which caused her to be alarmed. She called the police and gave them permission to search the premises. The incriminating evidence found by the police as a result of this consent search was held admissible in court over the objections of the guests. Woodard v. U. S., 254 F.2d 313 (District of Columbia Court of Appeals, 1958).

However, if the person against whom the search for evidence is directed is a long-term guest and has a section of the premises set aside exclusively for his own use, the consent of the host may not be effective to authorize a search. Reeves v. Warden, 346 F.2d 915 (4th Circuit Court of Appeals, 1965). The question whether a host may consent to a search of the guest's area of the premises turns then on such factors as the length of time of the guest's stay, the exclusiveness of his control of a particular area of the premises, and his reasonable expectation of privacy in that area of the premises.

Employer—Employee

In general, an employer may consent to a search of any part of the employer's premises that is used by an employee. Thus, it has been held that a search of an employee's locker in his employer's plant was legal upon the consent of the employer. The court in that case considered the fact that the employer owned the property, and under the terms of the contract between the employer and the employee's union, the employer retained a master key to all employee lockers. State v. Robinson, 86 N.J.Super. 308, 206 A.2d 779 (Superior Court of New Jersey, 1965).

However, when the employer does not retain such control over the premises, he may not effectively consent to a search of an area used by an employee. For example, a leading case in this area held that the official superior of a government employee who was assigned a desk for her exclusive use could not validly consent to the search of the employee's desk. The court's reasoning was as follows:

> In the absence of a valid regulation to the contrary, appellee was entitled to, and did keep private property of a personal sort in her desk. Her superiors could not reasonably search the desk for her purse, her personal letters, or anything else that did not belong to the government and had no connection with the work of the office. Their consent did not make such a search by the police reasonable. U. S. v. Blok, 188 F.2d 1019, 1021 (District of Columbia Circuit Court of Appeals, 1951).

Courts have generally held that the reverse situation—whether an employee can consent to the search of his employer's premises—depends upon the scope of the employee's authority. Generally, the average employee, such as a clerk, janitor, handyman, driver, or other person temporarily in charge, may not give such consent. U. S. v. Block, 202 F.Supp. 705 (U. S. District Court, Southern District of New York, 1962). However, if the employee is a manager or other person of considerable authority who is left in complete charge for a substantial period of time, then it is likely that he would be able to effectively consent to a search of his employer's premises. U. S. v. Antonelli Fireworks Co., 155 F.2d 631 (2nd Circuit Court of Appeals, 1946). In People v. Litwin, 44 A.D.2d 492, 355 N.Y.S.2d 646 (New York Supreme Court, Appellate Division, 1974), the court held that a baby-sitter has insufficient interest in the premises of his or here employer to give a valid consent to search the premises.

School Official—Student

Situations often arise in which a high school or college administrative official consents to a search of student lockers or rooms by law enforcement authorities. The high school situation usually involves the search of lockers and the college situation, the search of dormitory rooms. Courts have treated these two situations differently.

Courts have held that the search of a high school student's locker, when authorized by a school official, is valid because of the relationship between the school authorities and the students. The school authorities are held to have an obligation to maintain discipline over students and usually they retain partial access to the students' lockers so that neither has an exclusive right to use and possession of the lockers. Thus, in a case where the locker of a student suspected of burglary was opened by police with the consent of school authorities and incriminating evidence found, the court said:

> Although a student may have control of his school locker as against fellow students, his possession is not exclusive against the school and its officials. A school does not supply its students with lockers for illicit use in harboring pilfered property or harmful substances. We deem it a proper function of school authorities to inspect the lockers under their control and to prevent their use in illicit ways or for illegal purposes. We believe this right of inspection is inherent in the authority vested in school administrators and that the same must be retained and exercised in the management of our schools if their educational functions are to be maintained and the welfare of the student bodies preserved. State v. Stein, 203 Kan. 638, 640, 456 P.2d 1, 3 (Supreme Court of Kansas, 1969).

The courts have arrived at a different conclusion when college dormitory rooms are the subject of the search. In these cases, the courts have stressed that a search cannot be based on the college's authority to maintain discipline over young students. People v. Cohen, 57 Misc. 366, 292 N.Y.S.2d 706 (District Court of New York, 1968). Also, even though a college may reserve the right to enter the rooms of students for inspection purposes, such a regulation cannot be applied so as to give consent to a search for evidence for the primary purpose of criminal prosecution. Piazzola v. Watkins, 442 F.2d 284 (5th Circuit Court of Appeals, 1971). Therefore, in a case in which police, aided by the Dean of Men, searched the defendant's room at a university and found marijuana, the evidence was held to be inadmissible in court. Even though the university had the right to check the room for damages, wear, and unauthorized appliances, this did *not* mean that the defendant "was not entitled to have a 'reasonable expectation of freedom from governmental intrusion', or that he gave consent to the police search, or gave the University authority to consent to such search." Commonwealth v. McCloskey, 217 Pa.Super. 432, 435–36, 272 A.2d 271, 273 (Superior Court of Pennsylvania, 1970).

Attorney—Client

Consent given by a defendant's attorney, when duly authorized to do so by the defendant, makes an ensuing search of the defendant's premises lawful. Thus, in a case where a calf and a cow were seized from defendant's property, and evidence relating thereto introduced against him in court, it was held that the search and seizure were legal because consent to search had been given by defendant's attorney after consulting with defendant. Brown v. State, 81 Nev. 397, 404 P.2d 428 (Supreme Court of Nevada, 1965).

Husband—Wife

Although there is some disagreement on the issue, it is generally held that one spouse may consent to a search of family premises on the basis that husband and wife are joint occupants with equal rights in the premises. An example of this is a case where officers were investigating a murder and questioned a suspected defendant's wife in regard to it. The wife volunteered information that the defendant had fired a pistol into the ceiling of their home some time ago. She later validly consented to officers searching for and seizing the bullet in the ceiling, which was used as evidence in convicting the defendant.

The court sustained the search on the basis that the consent was voluntary, the place of the search was the home of the defendant's wife, and the premises were under the immediate and complete control of the wife at the time of the search. Furthermore, the bullet could not be considered a personal effect of the husband, over which the wife would have no power to consent to search.

It is important to note the underlying rationale of the court's decision that the wife could consent to a search of the family premises:

> It is not a question of agency, for a wife should not be held to have authority to waive her husband's constitutional rights. This is a question of the wife's own rights to authorize entry into premises where she lives and of which she had control. Roberts v. U. S., 332 F.2d 892, 896–97 (8th Circuit Court of Appeals, 1964).

A similar situation was presented in the U. S. Supreme Court case of Coolidge v. New Hampshire, 403 U.S. 443, 91 S.Ct. 2022, 29 L.Ed.2d 564 (1971). In that case, two officers went to the defendant's home, while he was at the police station under investigation for murder, in order to check out his story with his wife. While there, the officers asked the wife if defendant owned any guns, and she replied, "Yes, I will get them in the bedroom." She then took four guns out of a closet and gave them to the officers. The officers then asked her what her husband had been wearing on the night in question, and she produced several pairs of trousers and a hunting jacket. The police seized all this evidence, and it was used against the defendant in court.

The Court found no objection to the introduction of the above described evidence in court. In fact the Court found that the actions of the police did not even amount to a search and seizure. Because the Court discussed in detail the significance of the actions of the police, and because of the importance of the issue, it is worthwhile here to quote the Court's opinion at length:

> [I]t cannot be said that the police should have obtained a warrant for the guns and clothing before they set out to visit Mrs. Coolidge, since they had no intention of rummaging around among Coolidge's effects or of dispossessing him of any of his property. Nor can it be said that they should have obtained Coolidge's permission for a seizure they did not intend to make. There was nothing to compel them to announce to the suspect that they intended to question his wife about his movements on the night of the disappearance or about the theft from his employer. Once Mrs. Coolidge had admitted them, the policemen were surely acting normally and properly when they asked her, as they had asked those questioned earlier in the investigation, including Coolidge himself, about any guns there might be in the house. The question concerning the clothes Coolidge had been wearing on the night of the disappearance was logical and in no way coercive. Indeed, one might doubt the competence of the officers involved had they not asked exactly the questions they did ask. And surely when Mrs. Coolidge of her own accord produced the guns and clothes for inspection, rather than simply describing them, it was not incumbent on the police to stop her or avert their eyes.
>
> * * *
>
> In assessing the claim that this course of conduct amounted to a search and seizure, it is well to keep in mind that Mrs. Coolidge described her own motive as that of clearing her husband, and that she believed that she had nothing to hide. She had seen her husband himself produce his guns for two other policemen earlier in the week, and there is nothing to indicate that she realized that he had offered only three of them for inspection on that occasion. The two officers who questioned her behaved, as her own testimony shows, with perfect courtesy. There is not the slightest implication of an attempt to coerce or dominate her, or for that matter, to direct her actions by the more subtle techniques of suggestion that are avail-

> able to officials in circumstances like these. To hold that the conduct of the police here was a search and seizure would be to hold, in effect, that a criminal suspect has constitutional protection against the adverse consequences of a spontaneous, good-faith effort by his wife to clear him of suspicion. 403 U.S. at 488–90, 91 S.Ct. at 2049–50, 29 L.Ed.2d at 596.

Parent—Child

A parent's consent to search premises owned by the parent will be effective against a child who lives on those premises. In this context, one court has said:

> Hardy's father gave his permission to the officers to enter and search the house and the premises *which he owned* and in which his son lived with him. Under the circumstances presented here the voluntary consent of Hardy's father to search *his own* premises is binding on Hardy and precludes his claim of violation of constitutional rights. Commonwealth v. Hardy, 423 Pa. 208, 216, 223 A.2d 719, 723 (Supreme Court of Pennsylvania, 1966).

A parent may not consent to a search of an area of the parent's home occupied by the child, however, if the child uses the room exclusively, has sectioned it off, has furnished it with his own furniture, pays rent, or otherwise establishes an expectation of privacy. State v. Peterson, Mo.App., 525 S.W.2d 599 (Missouri Court of Appeals, 1975). Furthermore, parents may not consent to a search of a child's room in their home if the child has already refused to grant such consent. People v. Mortimer, 46 A.D.2d 275, 361 N.Y.S.2d 955 (New York Supreme Court, Appellate Division, 1974). The court in that case said, "Constitutional rights may not be defeated by the expedient of soliciting several persons successively until the sought-after consent is obtained." 46 A.D.2d at 277, 361 N.Y.S.2d at 958.

As a general rule, a minor living in his parents' home does not have sufficient authority to consent to a search of the home in the absence of his parents. May v. State, Miss., 199 So.2d 635 (Supreme Court of Mississippi, 1967).

Bailor—Bailee

A bailee of personal property may consent to its search if he has full possession and control of the property. (A bailee is a person in rightful possession of personal property by permission of the owner or bailor). One example of this situation is the case of Frazier v. Cupp discussed earlier. Another example involved a defendant who loaned his car to a friend for his personal use. Police, who were investigating a theft, asked the friend for permission to search the trunk of the car. The friend opened the trunk and the police found incriminating evidence against the defendant.

The court held that the search was legal and that the evidence found was admissible against the defendant. The friend had been given rightful possession and control over the automobile and could do with it whatever was reasonable under the circumstances. The defendant had reserved no exclusive right to the trunk when he gave his friend the key. The friend's opening of the trunk for the police, then, was a reasonable exercise of his control over the car for the period during which he was permitted to use it. U. S. v. Eldridge, 302 F.2d 463 (4th Circuit Court of Appeals, 1962).

However, if the person giving consent has only limited custody over the property, such as for shipment or storage purposes, evidence found by law enforcement officers would not be admissible in court against the owner of the property. Thus an airline could not consent to the search of a package which defendant had wrapped and tied and delivered to the airline solely for transportation purposes. Corngold v. U. S., 367 F.2d 1 (9th Circuit Court of Appeals, 1966). Nor could the owner of a boat who had agreed to store certain of defendant's items on his boat give a valid consent to police to search and seize the items. Commonwealth v. Storck, 442 Pa. 197, 275 A.2d 362 (Supreme Court of Pennsylvania, 1971).

Reasonable Expectation of Privacy

Since the U. S. Supreme Court decision in Katz v. U. S., 389 U.S. 347, 88 S.Ct. 507, 19 L.Ed.2d 576 (1967), courts have considered a person's reasonable expectation of privacy as one factor in determining whether consent to search his property could be given by a third person. In U. S. v. Novello, 519 F.2d 1078 (5th Circuit Court of Appeals, 1975) the defendant rented an enclosed storage area and was informed that the area was accessible only to the rental agent and to those working with him. The defendant's truck, which contained marijuana, was stored in the area. Law enforcement officers acting on an informant's tip, obtained consent to enter the enclosed area from one of the persons having access. The officers discovered marijuana in the truck. The court held that the defendant had no reasonable expectation of privacy in the storage area and upheld the search. The court said, "One who knows that others have of right general and untrammeled access to an area, a right as extensive as his own, can scarcely have much expectation of secrecy in it or confidence about whom they may let inspect it." 519 F.2d at 1080.

The Oregon Court of Appeals relied upon a defendant's reasonable expectation of privacy to invalidate the search of a bedroom in a private residence which the defendant occupied under a rental agreement. A Mr. Larson and his two daughters leased and occupied the residence along with the defendant. The defendant was the only occupant of a private room under an agreement with Larson. One of Larson's daughters gave consent to search defendant's room where incriminating evidence was found. The court held that Larson's daughter could not consent to a search of the defendant's room. The defendant had a reasonable expectation of privacy in the room because he rented the room, was the sole occupant of the room, and had never given anyone permission to enter it. State v. Fitzgerald, 19 Or.App. 860, 530 P.2d 553 (Court of Appeals of Oregon, 1974).

Officers must determine whether a person has exhibited a reasonable expectation of privacy before they may search his premises pursuant to consent given by a third person. Officers should find out whether the consenting person had common authority over the premises or the object to be searched. Also, officers should look for indicators that the occupant or owner intended to keep the premises or object private. These indicators might be written or verbal agreements, locks, or partitions. If an officer cannot give good reasons for believing that a consent to search given by a third party does not violate another person's reasonable expectation of privacy, the search is likely to be declared invalid.

SUMMARY

Consent to search may often be obtained by law enforcement officers with little effort. Courts therefore tend to look very closely at the circumstances surrounding the giving of consent. The courts exercise a strong presumption against consents to search and they place a heavy burden on prosecutors to prove that a consent to search was given voluntarily. Evidence seized as a result of a consent to search which was not voluntary will be inadmissible in court. The following factors are considered in determining voluntariness of consent:

1. Force or threat of force by officers.
2. Indications of consenting person's submission to authority.
3. Indications that a person merely failed to object to a search rather than actively consented.
4. Misrepresentation, deception, or stealth of officers.
5. Consenting person was under arrest or otherwise in custody.
6. Consenting person's awareness of his right to refuse consent to search.
7. Clearness and explicitness of the expression of consent.

The scope of a consent search may be limited in both area and time. These limitations are usually determined by the intent of the consenting person as indicated by his words or actions. An officer should carefully determine the extent of his authority to search before beginning. Moreover, consent to search may be revoked by the person giving it at any time.

The constitutional right to refuse to consent to a search is a personal right of the individual against whom the search is directed. A person other than the person against whose interests the search is being conducted cannot effectively consent to a search of property unless (1) he has been specifically authorized to do so, or (2) he possesses common authority over or has other sufficient relationship to the premises or effects sought to be inspected.

*

6

PLAIN VIEW

Observation by law enforcement officers of items of evidence lying in plain view has for some time been one of the most important methods of gathering evidence of crime. Mere observation is seldom thought of as a means of gathering evidence, perhaps because on the surface, this method is so simple and seemingly self-evident. Also, observations of evidence in plain view usually occur as a byproduct of other activities which a law enforcement officer is performing, and the observations are therefore often unintentional. Nevertheless, the plain view doctrine enables alert and observant law enforcement officers to obtain admissible evidence against offenders of the law who are careless or unwary enough to leave such evidence in open view. Furthermore, the observation and seizure of such evidence may, in most cases, be made without probable cause or the necessity of going through complex warrant procedures. In this sense, the plain view doctrine can be considered another exception to the search warrant requirement.

Of course, the apparent simplicity of the plain view doctrine does not convert it into a license to conduct general exploratory searches anywhere, anytime, and in any manner. The doctrine has its carefully prescribed limitations which have been set out in court decisions over the years. This chapter will attempt to define the plain view doctrine and illustrate its various aspects through the use of recent court decisions from various jurisdictions. Whenever possible, suggested procedures for law enforcement officers will be set out.

DEFINITION

The plain view doctrine has been stated simply and concisely in the U. S. Supreme Court decision in Harris v. U. S.:

> It has long been settled that objects falling in the plain view of an officer who has a right to be in a position to have that view may be introduced in evidence. * * * 390 U.S. 234, 236, 88 S.Ct. 992, 993, 19 L.Ed.2d 1067, 1069, (1968).

It is worthwhile to note at the outset that the observation by a law enforcement officer of evidence in plain view is *not* considered to be a *search*. A search can be defined as a prying quest for something concealed from observation. If an item is lying in the open, unconcealed, it follows that an officer's merely looking at the item does not constitute a search. Furthermore, because such an observation does not constitute a search, it is not governed by the Fourth Amendment, and the officer, in most cases, need not obtain a warrant to seize the evidence. As one court has said:

> "Where no search is required, the constitutional guarantee is not applicable. The guaranty applies only in those instances where the seizure is assisted by a necessary search. It does not prohibit a seizure without a warrant where there is no need of a search, and where the contraband subject matter is freely disclosed and open to the eye and hand." * * * State v. Mosher, Me., 270 A.2d 451, 453 (Supreme Judicial Court of Maine, 1970).

ELEMENTS OF THE PLAIN VIEW DOCTRINE

For purposes of discussion, the plain view doctrine can be broken into six separate elements or requirements, all of which must be satisfied by a law enforcement officer before a seizure of an item of evidence under the doctrine can be legally justified. These requirements are:

1. The officer, as a result of a prior valid intrusion into a constitutionally protected area, must be in a position in which he has a legal right to be;
2. The officer must not unreasonably intrude on any person's reasonable expectation of privacy;
3. The officer must actually observe the item of evidence;
4. The item of evidence must be lying in the open;
5. It must be immediately apparent to the officer that the item observed is evidence "subject to seizure";
6. The discovery of the item of evidence by the officer must be inadvertent.

The remainder of this chapter will be devoted to an elaboration on and explanation of these requirements.

1. The officer, as the result of a prior valid intrusion into a constitutionally protected area, must be in a position in which he has a legal right to be

The first requirement is the most important element of the plain view doctrine and also the one which causes the most problems. It would be impossible to list all the situations in which a law enforcement officer would be in a position in which he has a legal right to be as the result of a prior valid intrusion into a constitutionally protected area. The U. S. Supreme Court, however, listed some of these situations in its 1971 decision in the case of Coolidge v. New Hampshire:

> What the "plain view" cases have in common is that the police officer in each of them had a prior justification for an intrusion in the course of which he came inadvertently across a piece of evidence incriminating the accused. The doctrine serves to supplement the prior justification—whether it be a warrant for another object, hot pursuit, search incident to lawful arrest, or some other legitimate reason for being present unconnected with a search directed against the accused—and permits the warrantless seizure. * * * 403 U. S. at 466, 91 S.Ct. at 2038, 29 L.Ed.2d at 583.

The following is a discussion of cases illustrating the first element of the plain view doctrine.

Effecting an Arrest or Search Incident to Arrest

A law enforcement officer may lawfully seize an object that comes into view during a lawfully executed arrest or a search incident to arrest. There is a possibility of confusion here between the plain view doctrine and the law of search incident to arrest. The law of search incident to arrest was discussed in detail in Chapter 4. There it was stated that under the rule of Chimel v. California, 395 U.S. 752, 89 S.Ct. 2034, 23 L.Ed.2d 685 (U. S. Supreme Court, 1969), a law enforcement officer may search an arrested person only for weapons or to prevent the destruction or concealment of evidence. The extent of such a search is limited to the arrestee's person and the area within his immediate control, "construing that phrase to mean the area from within which he might gain possession of a weapon or destructible evidence." 395 U.S. at 763, 89 S.Ct. at 2040, 23 L.Ed.2d at 694.

The plain view doctrine does *not* extend the permissible area of search incident to arrest. The Court in the *Chimel* case specifically said:

> There is no comparable justification, however, for routinely searching any room other than that in which an arrest occurs—or for that matter, for searching through all the desk drawers or other closed or concealed areas in that room itself. Such searches, in the absence of well-recognized exceptions, may be made only under the authority of a search warrant. 395 U.S. at 763, 89 S.Ct. at 2040, 23 L.Ed.2d at 694.

Nevertheless, when the arresting officer inadvertently observes a piece of evidence, unconcealed, but outside the area under the immediate control of the arrestee, the officer may seize it, so long as the plain view was obtained in the course of a lawful arrest or an appropriately limited search incident to arrest.

Executing a Search Warrant

In the case of Cady v. Dombrowski, 413 U.S. 433, 93 S.Ct. 2523, 37 L.Ed.2d 706 (1973), the U. S. Supreme Court held that an officer executing a valid search warrant could legally seize items of evidence lying in plain view even though they were not particularly described in the warrant. For purposes of this discussion then, a law enforcement officer executing a valid search warrant is in a position in which he has a legal right to be.

The Cady v. Dombrowski case is discussed in detail in Chapter 2. A part of that discussion, however, should be reemphasized here. Although an officer executing a search warrant is authorized to seize items not named in the search warrant lying in plain view, his authority is limited. A seizure of unnamed items will probably be held illegal if:

1. The seizure was the product of an "exploratory search"; or
2. The items seized had no direct relation to the primary purpose of the search; or
3. The officer did not have probable cause to believe that the items fell within one of the categories of items subject to seizure.

If any of these conditions exist, the officer should obtain another search warrant for items unnamed in the original warrant.

If an officer does not have a warrant to search premises, he may not enter the premises to secure them while a search warrant is being obtained, unless there are exigent circumstances. It follows that any evidence observed open to view after such an illegal entry will not be admissible under the plain view doctrine, because the officer was not in a position in which he had a legal right to be. U. S. v. Griffin, 502 F.2d 959 (6th Circuit Court of Appeals, 1974).

Hot Pursuit

A law enforcement officer who is lawfully on premises in hot pursuit of a dangerous person may seize items of evidence which fall within his plain view. In the 1967 U. S. Supreme Court case of Warden v. Hayden, the police were informed that an armed robbery had taken place and that a suspect, wearing a light cap and dark jacket had entered a certain house less than five minutes before they reached it. Several officers entered the house and began to search for the described suspect and for weapons which he had used in the robbery and might use against them. One officer, while searching the cellar, found in a washing machine, clothing of the type that the fleeing man was said to have worn. The Court held that the seizure of the clothing was lawful:

> [T]he seizures occurred prior to or immediately contemporaneous with Hayden's arrest, as part of an effort to find a suspected felon, armed, within the house into which he had run only minutes before the police arrived. The permissible scope of search must, therefore, at the least, be as broad as may reasonably be necessary to prevent the dangers that the suspect at large in the house may resist or escape. 387 U.S. at 299, 87 S.Ct. at 1646, 18 L.Ed.2d at 787.

If, however, the felon had already been taken into custody when the officer looked into the washing machine, the seizure of the clothing would have been unlawful. There no longer would have been any danger of the fleeing felon using a weapon against the officers, and therefore, no reason to look for weapons in the washing machine.

To summarize then, an officer who enters a constitutionally protected area in hot pursuit of a fleeing felon is in a position in which he has a legal right to be and may seize items of evidence in plain view in the course of his pursuit and in protecting himself from harm.

It should be noted that hot pursuit does not necessarily involve a violent crime or a dangerous person. The U. S. Supreme Court held that there was a hot pursuit when officers chased the defendant, whom they had probable cause to believe had just purchased illegal drugs, from her doorway into her house. U. S. v. Santana, 427 U.S. 38, 96 S.Ct. 2406, 49 L.Ed.2d 300 (U. S. Supreme Court, 1976).

Responding to an Emergency

Related to the hot pursuit situation is the situation in which an officer responds to an emergency and observes items of evidence in plain view. An example is a case in which two police officers responded to a report by citizens that a woman was screaming for help in a certain house. The officers went to the house. A man answered the door, said "Wait a minute," and then closed the door again. One officer heard shuffling inside the apartment and the other officer observed a man attempting to escape out a back window. After identifying himself and demanding admittance (which was not granted), the officer at the entrance to the house kicked in the door. While investigating the situation inside, he observed marijuana in plain view on a table.

The court found that the combination of circumstances presented to the officer justified his forced entry:

> The probability that a woman within the apartment was the unwilling victim of some criminal act was increased rather than lessened by the conduct of those within the apartment after the police presented themselves at the door; that conduct can only have had the effect of heightening the sense of emergency.
>
> * * *
>
> Having entered reasonably in an emergency "they did not have to blind themselves to what was in plain sight simply because it was disconnected with the purpose for which they entered." * * * People v. Clark, 262 Cal.App.2d 471, 476–77, 68 Cal.Rptr. 713, 717 (California Court of Appeal, 1968).

An emergency will often justify a "protective search" of premises by law enforcement officers during which evidence may be observed in plain view. In People v. Sturgis, 76 Misc.2d 1053, 352 N.Y.S.2d 942 (Supreme Court of New York, 1973), law enforcement officers engaged in a gun battle with several suspects who were inside a home. The officers then entered the home and arrested several persons. To protect themselves, officers looked throughout the home for other persons. Narcotics were discovered lying open to view and were seized. The court held that the protective search by the officers was proper because of exigent circumstances, and that the seizure of the narcotics was lawful under the plain view doctrine.

The Supreme Court of California has summarized the reasoning of many courts in cases involving "protective searches."

> "During a lawful search of premises for persons believed to be in hiding, police officers may seize contraband evidence 'in plain sight.' * * * Under such circumstances there is, in fact, no search for evidence. * * *" People v. Block, 6 Cal.3d 239, 243, 103 Cal.Rptr. 281, 283, 499 P.2d 961, 963 (1971).

There is a temptation for law enforcement officers to attempt to justify otherwise illegal searches by resorting to this combination of the plain view doctrine and response to an emergency. It should be noted that the courts will look carefully at these types of cases and will rule the search illegal if a genuine emergency does not exist or if a search goes beyond what is necessary to respond to the emergency. On this issue the U. S. Supreme Court stated that "a warrantless search must be 'strictly circumscribed by the exigencies which justify its initiation,' * * *." Mincey v. Arizona, 437 U.S. 385, 393, 98 S.Ct. 2408, 2414, 57 L.Ed.2d 290, 300 (1978). Again, when there is a question about the legality of a search or seizure, the officer should apply for a warrant.

The important thing to remember in all these cases, however, is that the officer must have a legal justification for his intrusion into a constitutionally protected area. If he has such legal justification and is in a position in which he has a right to be, he may seize, without violating the Fourth Amendment, any items of evidence that he observes lying open to view.

2. The officer must not unreasonably intrude on any person's reasonable expectation of privacy

There are limits to the general rule that any observation made by a law enforcement officer after he has made a valid intrusion into a constitutionally protected area will not be a violation of the Fourth Amendment. In a recent California case, a law enforcement officer observed the defendant and another man go into the men's room of a city park and not come out for about five minutes. The officer then entered the plumbing access area of the rest room and observed the men performing illegal sexual acts. The officer had observed no other suspicious acts by the defendant before the defendant entered the men's room.

The court held that this was not a plain view observation by the officer but an illegal search. The language of the court in this case is worthy of quotation:

> The People here urge us to hold that clandestine observation of doorless stalls in public rest rooms is not a "search" and hence is not subject to the Fourth Amendment's prohibition of unreasonable searches. This would permit the police to make it a routine practice to observe from hidden vantage points the rest room conduct of the public whenever such activities do not occur within fully enclosed toilet stalls and would permit spying on the "innocent and guilty alike." Most persons using public rest rooms have no reason to suspect that a hidden agent of the state will observe them. The expectation of privacy a person has when he enters a rest room is reasonable and is not diminished or destroyed because the toilet stall being used lacks a door.
>
> Reference to expectations of privacy as a Fourth Amendment touchstone received the endorsement of the United States Supreme

> Court in Katz v. United States (1968) 389 U.S. 347, 88 S.Ct. 507, 19 L.Ed.2d 576. Viewed in the light of Katz, the standard for determining what is an illegal search is whether defendant's "reasonable expectation of privacy was violated by unreasonable governmental intrusion." * * * People v. Triggs, 8 Cal.3d 884, 891, 106 Cal.Rptr. 408, 412–13, 506 P.2d 232, 236–37 (Supreme Court of California, 1973).

Therefore, what might seem on the surface to be a mere plain view observation becomes a *search* when it unreasonably intrudes upon a person's reasonable expectation of privacy. As a search, the officer's observations must be based on probable cause, at the minimum, in order to be reasonable. In this case, the officer's only suspicion was the defendant's prolonged stay in the rest room, which could have been consistent with innocent activity. This suspicion was not sufficient to provide probable cause. The officer's clandestine observations were, therefore, prompted only by a general curiosity to determine what, if anything, was going on within the rest room. As such, the observations were an illegal exploratory search under the Fourth Amendment.

This case and others following the *Katz* decision present problems for law enforcement officers with regard to the plain view doctrine. The officer must not only determine whether his intrusion into a constitutionally protected area is lawful, but he must also make sure that he is not intruding upon someone's reasonable expectation of privacy. The latter determination can be a difficult one and there are few guidelines as yet to aid the officer.

3. The officer must observe the item of evidence

The law enforcement officer must actually *see* the item of evidence lying in the open in order to lawfully seize it under the plain view doctrine. At first this seems to be merely stating the obvious. A California case, however, has held that officers, who merely *smelled* fresh marijuana but did *not actually see* it lying in the open, could not legally search for the marijuana and seize it without a warrant. In that case, officers had made a legal entry of an apartment to arrest some suspects. They had therefore made a valid intrusion into a constitutionally protected area. They did not find any of the suspects in the apartment, but distinctly smelled fresh marijuana. They traced the smell to a closed bag inside a carton in the closet. The officers opened the bag, seized the marijuana, and arrested the defendant several hours later when he arrived back at the apartment.

The court held the seizure of the marijuana illegal. The court said that if the evidence had been in plain *sight*, the officers could have seized it, because the officers were rightfully on the premises looking for persons believed to be in hiding. In this case, however, the marijuana was *not* in plain sight. It was in cellophane bags inside a closed brown paper bag that was in an open box in an open closet. The officers, in smelling the marijuana and tracing it to the bag, had *probable cause* to believe that marijuana was in the bag. They could, therefore, have obtained a *search warrant* for the marijuana based on probable cause. They could *not,* however, legally go into the bag and seize the marijuana because the marijuana itself was not in plain view. In this case, there were no exigent circumstances to justify an immediate seizure of the marijuana.

The language of the Supreme Court of California is valuable here to try to clear up a point on probable cause which confuses many law enforcement officers:

> However strongly convinced officers may be that a search will reveal contraband, their belief, whether based on the sense of smell or other sources, does not justify a search without a warrant. The point of the Fourth Amendment, which often is not grasped by zealous officers, is not that it denies law enforcement the support of the usual inferences which reasonable men draw from evidence. Its protection consists in requiring that those inferences be drawn by a neutral and detached magistrate instead of being judged by the officer engaged in the often competitive enterprise of ferreting out crime. Any assumption that evidence sufficient to support a magistrate's disinterested determination to issue a search warrant will justify the officers in making a search without a warrant would reduce the Amendment to a nullity and leave the people's homes secure only in the discretion of police officers. * * * People v. Marshall, 69 Cal.2d 51, 57, 69 Cal.Rptr. 585, 588–89, 442 P.2d 665, 668–69 (Supreme Court of California, 1968).

In a word, then, if an officer has made a valid intrusion into a constitutionally protected area and has probable cause to believe that an item of evidence is in a certain place, but he does not *see* the item lying in his plain view, the officer must obtain a search warrant before he can legally seize the item unless there are truly exigent circumstances.

4. The item of evidence must be lying in the open

The requirement of the plain view doctrine that the evidence must be lying in the open has been expressed in several ways. Among the terms used by different courts are "in plain view," "in plain sight," "in open view," "open to view," and "in the open." All of these mean substantially the same thing, but do not give much help to the law enforcement officer in determining what items he may and may not seize. The best way to determine the meaning of these terms is to examine the cases interpreting them.

First of all, it is well settled that a law enforcement officer may use mechanical or electrical aids to assist him in observing items of evidence, as long as he is in a position in which he has a legal right to be and is not intruding upon someone's reasonable expectation of privacy. In one case, a law enforcement officer was told, when he arrived at a drive-in restaurant, that a car had been parked in the parking lot for an hour with its lights on and with a person lying in the back seat. The officer went over to the car to see if anything was wrong. He shined a flashlight into the car and observed defendant lying in the back with a sawed-off shotgun resting on the floorboard between his feet. He then arrested the defendant and seized the shotgun.

The court held that the observation of the shotgun by the officer was not a search. The officer was in a position in which he had a legal right to be, and his use of the flashlight did not, in itself, make his observations unlawful:

> When the circumstances of a particular case are such that the police officer's observation would not have constituted a search had it occurred in daylight, then the fact that the officer used a flashlight to pierce the nighttime darkness does not transform his observation into a search. Regardless of the time of day or night, the plain view rule must be upheld where the viewer is rightfully positioned, seeing through eyes that are neither accusatory nor criminally investigatory. The plain view rule does not go into hibernation at sunset. Marshall v. U. S., 422 F.2d 185, 189 (5th Circuit Court of Appeals, 1970).

In another case, an officer stationed himself in a field about fifty yards from the defendant's house and with the aid of binoculars, watched the activities of the defendant, a known liquor violator. The officer observed the defendant placing two large cardboard boxes (each of which contained six gallons of untaxed whiskey) into a 1961 Buick. The liquor was later found in the car while it was being operated on a public street by another person. The court held that the officer's use of binoculars to observe defendant's activities did not constitute an illegal search. U. S. v. Grimes, 426 F.2d 706 (5th Circuit Court of Appeals, 1970).

Another question which arises in connection with whether an object is open to view is how far an officer may go in examining an item more closely before the examination constitutes a search rather than a mere plain view observation. In a case dealing with this question, police were lawfully in the defendant's apartment for the purpose of arresting him. While they were looking for him, one officer observed a pair of shoes believed to have been worn by the defendant at the time of a murder. The officer picked up the shoes and examined the heels. After obtaining a search warrant, he returned and seized the shoes. The shoes were introduced in evidence against the defendant.

The court held that the examination of the heels of the shoes was not an illegal search:

> Detective Shelby was lawfully in defendant's apartment. He reasonably believed defendant to be hiding in the apartment and had every right, supported by probable cause, to search for the suspected killer. Shelby's discovery of the shoes was not the result of a general search for evidence. Rather, the pair of shoes was seen during the course of the search for Eddington. In our view, Shelby's subsequent action in lifting the shoes and examining their heels involved no more than "legitimate and restrained investigative conduct undertaken on the basis of ample factual justification" * * * People v. Eddington, 387 Mich. 551, 564–65, 198 N.W.2d 297, 302 (Supreme Court of Michigan, 1972).

In another case involving closer examination of items, officers had valid warrants to arrest defendant and to search his store for intoxicating liquors and apparatus used for manufacturing intoxicating liquors. Upon arrival at the store, the officers immediately arrested defendant and seized a small quantity of beer. One officer then went to the upstairs residential area to search, and noticed two rifles leaning against a wall in a closet. The officer removed the rifles, took them downstairs to copy down their serial numbers, and returned them to the closet. The officers later learned that the rifles had been stolen, and they went back to the store and seized them under a second warrant.

The court held that the officer's removing the rifles from the closet and copying down their serial numbers was an illegal search. Although the search warrant for liquor and apparatus gave the officers a valid prior justification for their intrusion, the court held that the removal and examination of the rifles could be justified only if it was immediately apparent that the rifles were evidence of crime:

> Here, Officer Brodt inadvertently discovered the rifles in the upstairs clothes closet while searching for alcoholic beverages but it was not "immediately apparent" that the rifles were "evidence incriminating the accused." The rifles were not contraband; there was no nexus between the rifles and the crimes of selling or possessing intoxicating liquor without a license; nor did the officers at that time have any knowledge that the rifles were evidence of any other crimes. U. S. v. Gray, 484 F.2d 352, 355 (Sixth Circuit Court of Appeals, 1973).

It was only *after* the officer had copied down the serial numbers of the rifles and had checked them with the National Crime Information Center that he learned that they were stolen and therefore incriminating. (The requirement that it be immediately apparent to the law enforcement officer that he has incriminating evidence before him is discussed under element 5. of the plain view doctrine.)

For reasons similar to those in the previous case, an officer is not allowed to open a closed container lying in plain view in order to determine if there is incriminating evidence inside it, unless there is a genuine emergency. An example is a case in which officers were conducting a narcotics raid on an apartment, and they observed defendant's purse lying on a table. One of the officers opened the purse and found a small bag of marijuana. When the defendant admitted that the purse was hers, she was arrested for possession of marijuana.

The court held that the seizure of the marijuana was illegal. Even though the purse was in plain view, the marijuana itself was not. The officer had to break into the purse to find the marijuana. This was an illegal search because the officer had no warrant, nor could he justify the search under any of the exceptions to the warrant requirement. State v. Keller, 255 La. 367, 231 So.2d 354 (Supreme Court of Louisiana, 1970).

As these cases indicate, it may not always be clear to the officer whether he is allowed to examine an item more closely without it being considered a search. When in doubt, the officer should obtain a search warrant, unless the situation presents an immediate danger of loss or destruction of evidence.

5. It must be immediately apparent to the officer that the item observed is evidence "subject to seizure"

The requirement that it be immediately apparent to the officer that the item observed is evidence "subject to seizure" simply means that he must have probable cause to believe that the item comes within one of the categories of property which are allowed to be seized under state statute. These categories of property have been listed and discussed in Chapter 2. They are:

1. Property stolen or embezzled; or
2. Property designed or intended for use or which is or has been used as a means of committing a criminal offense (instrumentalities); or
3. Property, the possession of which is unlawful (contraband); or
4. Property consisting of nontestimonial evidence which will aid in a particular apprehension or conviction ("mere evidence").

In a case illustrating this requirement of the plain view doctrine, a Massachusetts police officer arrested defendant and two companions for trespassing. They had parked their car on private property. While waiting for assistance, the officer observed articles of clothing wrapped in cellophane lying inside the car. Later, after the car had been removed to the police station, the officer learned through police channels that similar clothing had been recently stolen in Maine. He obtained a search warrant and seized the clothing.

The court found the search warrant defective but upheld the seizure because the items of clothing were in the officer's plain view. The court said:

> Even where * * * no search is necessary, the accompanying seizure must be accompanied by probable cause or reasonable grounds to believe that the property falls within a category which warrants the seizure. * * * State v. Mosher, Me., 270 A.2d 451, 453 (Supreme Judicial Court of Maine, 1970).

In this case, the officer had reasonable grounds to believe that the articles of clothing were *stolen* (category 1 above), based on the report that similar articles had been stolen in Maine.

The important consideration for the law enforcement officer for purposes of this article is that before he seizes any property under the plain view doctrine, he must have probable cause to believe that it falls within one of the categories of property allowed to be seized by statute. Otherwise, the seizure will be illegal. For example, if the Massachusetts officer in the *Mosher* case had seized the articles of clothing when he first observed them, the seizure would have been illegal. At that time, he had no reason to believe they were stolen or that they came under any other category of seizable property. It was only after he received the report that similar clothing had been stolen in Maine that he had probable cause to believe the property was seizable.

In Shipman v. State, 291 Ala. 484, 282 So.2d 700 (Alabama Supreme Court, 1973), law enforcement officers detained several persons on a storeowner's complaint that they were acting in an unruly manner. As one of the persons (the defendant) was being confronted by an officer, the officer observed him transfer an object from one part of his person to the top of his boot. The object, though clearly not a weapon, was seized and was later determined to be heroin. The court held that even though the object was in plain view its seizure was illegal, because the officer did not have probable cause to believe it was contraband. The court said:

> The reason for this rule is apparent. If the rule were otherwise, an officer acting on mere groundless suspicion, could seize anything and everything belonging to an individual which happened to be in plain view on the prospect that on further investigation some of it might prove to have been stolen or to be contraband. It would open the door to unreasonable confiscation of a person's property while a minute examination of it is made in an

> effort to find something criminal. Such a practice would amount to the "general exploratory search from one object to another until something incriminating at last emerges" which was condemned in Coolidge v. New Hampshire * * *. Ex post facto justification of a seizure made on mere groundless suspicion, is totally contrary to the basic tenets of the Fourth Amendment.
>
> * * *
>
> For an item in plain view to be validly seized, the officer must possess some judgment at the time that the object to be seized is contraband and that judgment must be grounded upon probable cause. 291 Ala. at 488, 282 So.2d at 704.

6. The discovery of the item of evidence by the officer must be inadvertent

The so-called "inadvertency" requirement of the plain view doctrine is best illustrated by the 1971 U. S. Supreme Court case of Coolidge v. New Hampshire, 403 U.S. 443, 91 S.Ct. 2022, 29 L.Ed.2d 564 (1971). In that case, police went to the defendant's house to arrest him for murder. They also had a warrant to search his Pontiac car for evidence of the murder. They seized the car, which was parked and plainly visible in the driveway, and brought it back to the station where it was searched. Vacuum sweepings from the car were used as evidence at the defendant's trial, and he was convicted.

The search warrant was later found to be invalid and the prosecution attempted to justify the seizure of the automobile on the theory that, since the car was an "instrumentality of the crime," and was seized while lying in plain view, no warrant was needed. The Court said that the plain view doctrine could not be used to justify the seizure in this case because the discovery of the evidence was not inadvertent:

> [T]he discovery of evidence in plain view must be inadvertent. The rationale of the exception to the warrant requirement, as just stated, is that a plain-view seizure will not turn an initially valid (and therefore limited) search into a "general" one, while the inconvenience of procuring a warrant to cover an inadvertent discovery is great. *But where the discovery is anticipated, where the police know in advance the location of the evidence and intend to seize it, the situation is altogether different. The requirement of a warrant to seize imposes no inconvenience whatever, or at least none which is constitutionally cognizable in a legal system that regards warrantless searches as "per se unreasonable" in the absence of "exigent circumstances."* (emphasis supplied). 403 U.S. at 470–71, 91 S.Ct. at 2040, 29 L.Ed.2d at 585–86.

The significance of the inadvertency requirement for the law enforcement officer is that it reemphasizes the importance of obtaining a search warrant in situations where the officer (1) expects to discover certain evidence, (2) knows its location in advance, and (3) intends to seize it. Unless there are "exigent circumstances", or an emergency, a warrantless seizure in such circumstances will *not* be justified under the plain view doctrine.

It is worthwhile to include here an example of a case in which the court found sufficient "exigent circumstances" to justify the use of the plain view doctrine to support the warrantless seizure of items whose location law enforcement officers already knew. Law enforcement agents on several occasions observed the defendant purchase laboratory equipment and chemicals used in the manufacture of amphetamine and carry them into his home. On one occasion, the agents entered the apartment with defendant's consent on the pretense of making an emergency phone call. They observed the laboratory equipment on a kitchen counter. The agents, stationed at a nearby apartment, also observed someone working in the laboratory, and they detected a smell of ether, which is employed in manufacturing amphetamine. Late one night, the agents observed defendant dismantling the laboratory equipment. Believing that defendant was attempting to flee, they called their superiors, who said they would attempt to obtain a search warrant. In the meantime, the agents at the scene went to "secure" the defendant's apartment while waiting for the delivery of the warrant. When they arrived at the apartment, they immediately arrested the defendant and seized the laboratory equipment, which was in plain view.

Defendant claimed that the seized equipment should not have been admitted into evidence because although it was in plain view, the agents knew beforehand that the equipment was in the apartment. Defendant cited the case of Coolidge v. New Hampshire, which held, as we have seen, that the "plain view" doctrine applies only when the discovery of the evidence is inadvertent, not where the discovery is anticipated, where the police know in advance the location of the evidence, and intend to seize it.

The court held that the warrantless seizure in this case was valid. The agents made efforts to obtain a search warrant—a warrantless seizure was not planned. When the agents saw the equipment being dismantled, however, they reasonably concluded that defendant's flight was imminent and that incriminating evidence was about to be carried away. The situation having become acute, immediate action by the agents was required:

> Coolidge does not require suppression of evidence seized in plain view during an arrest where the circumstances have become ex-

> igent merely because prior knowledge of the evidence was acquired shortly before the seizure. U. S. v. Lisznyai, 470 F.2d 707, 710 (2d Circuit Court of Appeals, 1972).

This case indicates again the strong preference of the courts for warrants. It is likely that the court would have held the search illegal in this case, had not the agents already begun the process of obtaining a search warrant when the emergency plain view search was made. Here, however, the attempt to obtain a warrant clearly showed that a warrantless seizure of the evidence in plain view was *not* planned, but was in response to an emergency.

In Ludlow v. State, 262 Ind. 266, 314 N.E.2d 750 (Supreme Court of Indiana, 1974), the court invalidated a warrantless seizure of narcotics because the seizure was anticipated. In that case law enforcement officers received information that certain narcotics were in a home in which there were five persons. When the officers discovered that they had arrest warrants for two of the five persons, they went to the home. The officers entered the home, discovered the narcotics lying open to view, and seized them. The court held that the discovery of the narcotics was not inadvertent because the entry to execute the arrest warrants was merely a pretext to search for the narcotics. Because the seizure of the narcotics was anticipated, the plain view doctrine did not apply and the seizure was unlawful.

* * *

This concludes our discussion of the six basic requirements of the plain view doctrine. It is important for the officer to realize that in order to justify a warrantless seizure of an item of evidence under the plain view doctrine, all six of these requirements must be met. If any one of them is not met, and the officer cannot justify the seizure under any of the exceptions to the warrant requirement, the courts will consider the warrantless seizure illegal, and anything seized will be inadmissible in court.

7

SEARCH AND SEIZURE OF VEHICLES WITHOUT A WARRANT

Basically the same rules apply to the search of vehicles as to the search of fixed premises. For instance, it is well settled law that an automobile is a personal "effect" within the meaning of the Fourth Amendment and as such is clearly protected against unreasonable searches and seizures. Therefore, law enforcement officers should obtain a warrant whenever they want to search a motor vehicle unless the situation falls within one of the exceptions to the warrant requirement discussed in this chapter or in other chapters of this book. Guidelines for obtaining a warrant can be found in Chapters 2 and 3.

Courts have created exceptions to the warrant requirement for motor vehicles because of the unique nature of motor vehicles. Some of their unique characteristics are their mobility, their use as transportation to and from scenes of crimes, and their employment in transporting dangerous weapons, stolen goods, contraband, and implements of crime. Also, a person has a lesser expectation of privacy in a motor vehicle because it travels public thoroughfares where its occupants and contents are open to view; it seldom serves as a residence or permanent place for personal effects; it is required to be registered and its occupant is required to be licensed; it is extensively regulated with respect to the condition and manner in which it is operated on public streets and highways; it periodically undergoes an offical inspection; and it is often taken into police custody in the interests of public safety.

This chapter will discuss the exceptions to the warrant requirement for searches and seizures of motor vehicles and will present guidelines for the law enforcement officer to give him a better understanding of his rights and limitations in this area.

THE CARROLL DOCTRINE

The capacity of a motor vehicle to be moved quickly to an unknown location or beyond the jurisdictional reach of a law enforcement officer often makes it impossible to obtain a warrant to search a vehicle. In many cases, if the officer takes the time to obtain a search warrant, he takes the risk that contraband, fruits of a crime, instrumentalities of a crime, or other criminal evidence will be destroyed, removed, or concealed in the meantime. Courts have responded to this problem by allowing warrantless searches of vehicles when the officer has probable cause to believe that the vehicle contains items subject to seizure and exigent circumstances prevent the officer from obtaining a warrant. Carroll v. U. S., 267 U.S. 132, 45 S.Ct. 280, 69 L.Ed.2d 543 (U. S. Supreme Court, 1925). The *Carroll* doctrine, as this ruling is called, has proved over the years to be an important tool of law enforcement. Officers have resorted to this doctrine to justify vehicle searches in situations when (1) it is impossible to obtain a warrant, (2) there are no grounds for an arrest and thus no justification for a search incident to arrest, and (3) consent to search cannot be obtained.

Probable Cause Requirement

The controlling consideration in the search of a vehicle without a warrant is probable cause to believe that the vehicle contains items which are connected with criminal activity and thus are subject to seizure. Probable cause, again, is cause based upon grounds which would satisfy the mind of an ordinary, prudent, and cautious person that the vehicle contains these items. Certainty is not required, but more than mere suspicion is necessary. Probable cause is discussed in detail in Chapter 3.

As in all search and seizure cases, probable cause depends on the particular circumstances of each situation, and the law enforcement officer must be able to explain the factors which contributed to his arriving at probable cause. Courts will be quick to suppress evidence seized which was not the product of probable cause.

Exigent Circumstances Requirement

Of equal importance to the probable cause requirement in searches of vehicles without a warrant is the requirement that such searches be allowed only in exigent circumstances, i. e., when obtaining a warrant is not possible or practicable. In general, it may be said that the practicability of obtaining a warrant depends on whether or not a vehicle is in a mobile or movable condition. If the vehicle is in running order and there is a possibility that a delay to obtain a warrant will result in removal of the car to an unknown location, resulting in the concealment or destruction of evidence, then an immediate search, based on probable cause, may be conducted. However, once the possibility of removal of the vehicle no longer exists, the right to proceed without a warrant terminates.

Officers should note that exigent circumstances justifying a warrantless search of a vehicle may arise at any time after a law enforcement officer has probable cause to search a vehicle. An officer is not precluded from conducting a warrantless search of a vehicle under the *Carroll* doctrine merely because he fails to obtain a search warrant at the first practicable moment after he has probable cause. The U. S. Supreme Court has said:

> Exigent circumstances with regard to vehicles are not limited to situations where probable cause is unforeseeable and arises only at the time of arrest. * * * The exigency may arise at any time, and the fact that the police might have obtained a warrant earlier does not negate the possibility of a current situation's necessitating prompt police action. Cardwell v. Lewis, 417 U.S. 583, 595–96, 94 S.Ct. 2464, 2472, 41 L.Ed.2d 325, 338 (1974).

The determination of whether a vehicle loses its movable character depends upon the circumstances of each case. Certain guidelines for this determination have been set out by the courts. It is now well settled that a vehicle which is placed in a police storage lot after the occupants have been jailed and the keys removed from their possession is no longer in a movable condition. Welch v. U. S., 411 F.2d 66 (10th Circuit Court of Appeals, 1969); Preston v. U. S., 376 U.S. 364, 84 S.Ct. 881, 11 L.Ed.2d 777 (U. S. Supreme Court, 1964). On the other hand, a vehicle does not lose its movable character merely because it has been brought to a temporary halt or has been momentarily left unattended. The possibility of removal of the vehicle is present whether the vehicle is parked or in transit on the open road. Armada v. U. S., 319 F.2d 793 (5th Circuit Court of Appeals, 1963).

A United States Supreme Court case, Chambers v. Maroney, 399 U.S. 42, 90 S.Ct. 1975, 26 L.Ed.2d 419 (1970), has enlarged the scope of search and seizure of vehicles without a warrant. In that case, the police had information that armed robbers, carrying the fruits of the crime, had fled the robbery scene in a light blue compact stationwagon. The car was said to be carrying four men, one wearing a green sweater and another wearing a trench coat.

The Court held that the officers had probable cause to arrest the occupants of such a stationwagon, which they had stopped, and probable cause to search the car for guns and stolen money.

In addition to probable cause, the court also examined whether the car was in movable condition, thus satisfying the requirement of exigent circumstances. The arrest of the four men had taken place in a dark parking lot, and to facilitate the search, the car was brought to the police station and the search thereby delayed for a short period. Despite this delay and despite the fact that all four occupants of the car were under arrest, the court allowed the search. There is no question that exigent circumstances existed at the time of the arrest at the parking lot. The Court apparently felt that since a search would have been justified at this time, there was little difference between a search on the open highway and a later search at the station:

> The probable-cause factor still obtained at the station house and so did the mobility of the car unless the Fourth Amendment permits a warrantless seizure of the car and the denial of its use to anyone until a warrant is secured. In that event there is little to choose in terms of practical consequences between an immediate search without a warrant and the car's immobilization until a warrant is obtained. 399 U.S. at 52, 90 S.Ct. at 1981, 26 L.Ed.2d at 429.

The Court also noted that a careful search at the dark parking lot was impractical and perhaps not safe for the officers.

In recent years, the U. S. Supreme Court has indicated that the "exigent circumstances" requirement of the *Carroll* doctrine will be satisfied if there is even a slight possibility that evidence in a vehicle will be removed or destroyed. In Cardwell v. Lewis, 417 U.S. 583, 94 S.Ct. 2464, 41 L.Ed.2d 325 (1974), the Court found exigent circumstances justifying the warrantless seizure of the defendant's automobile from a commercial parking lot where he had left it prior to his appearance at the police station, where he was arrested. The defendant had been fully aware that he was under investigation for several months and he had told his attorney to see that his wife and family got the car. The Court was concerned that the attorney or a family member might remove evidence from the car if the police delayed seizing it. In Texas v. White, 423 U.S. 67, 96 S.Ct. 304, 46 L.Ed.2d 209 (U. S. Supreme Court, 1975), the Court upheld the mid-afternoon search of the defendant's vehicle at the station house after the defendant had been arrested in the vehicle while attempting to pass bad checks at a bank drive-in window. Although the Court found probable cause to search, the Court assumed "exigent circumstances" without discussing it. Furthermore, the Court allowed the officers to remove the automobile from the bank to the station house without discussing the justification for the removal on the basis of safety or practicality.

Despite the U. S. Supreme Court's allowance of searches of vehicles under the *Carroll* doctrine with only minimal requirements for exigent circumstances, state courts may interpret their own constitutions to require stricter standards of law enforcement officers. Therefore, officers should always be able to justify the existence of exigent circumstances. Also officers should be able to justify removing a vehicle from the scene of the stop to the station house to search it.

Operation of the Carroll Doctrine—Examples

1. Suspicious Circumstances

Probable cause to search a vehicle may be established by a combination of suspicious circumstances. An example is a case in which officers observed a vehicle pull from a parking lot, squeal its tires, and leave the scene at a high rate of speed. The vehicle had no license plate light. The officers stopped the vehicle for the traffic offenses, and while talking to the driver (defendant), one officer noticed the other occupants of the vehicle make "furtive gestures" as if they were trying to hide something on the floorboard. The officer also noticed a pile of money lying loose on the middle of the front seat. Shortly before, the officers had heard a robbery broadcast, including a description of one suspect which fit the defendant. The defendant told the officers that he had never been in trouble before, but after checking with headquarters, they determined that he had been arrested many times for robbery, assault, and carrying a pistol. After weighing these factors, the officers searched the car and found a gun, a stocking mask, and a bag of coins. The court found that the furtive gestures, combined with the information about the defendant's criminal record and the radio broadcast constituted probable cause to search. The search was therefore lawful. Trusley v. State, Tex.Cr. App., 505 S.W.2d 861 (Court of Criminal Appeals of Texas, 1974).

However, in a case in which the defendant merely behaved nervously after being stopped for having one missing license plate, the court suppressed the heroin seized in a warrantless search of defendant's vehicle. The defendant's nervousness alone did not give the police probable cause to believe that seizable evidence was in the car and the warrantless search of the car was unjustified. People v. Reed, 37 Ill.2d 91, 227 N.E.2d 69 (Supreme Court of Illinois, 1967).

2. Prior Information

Chambers v. Maroney (above) is an example of a case in which police had prior information that a robbery had been committed as well as descriptions of the getaway car and the suspects upon which to base their probable cause to search.

But in a case where the defendant was arrested for a minor traffic offense and the police had no knowledge of a robbery having been committed or of any other suspicious circumstances except the observance of a rubberized cord hanging from the closed trunk lid of defendant's car, there was no probable cause to search the vehicle. The court did not consider the rubber cord a particularly suspicious circumstance, certainly not enough to provide probable cause to search, without other information. A search on probable cause is only valid if the officer has specific property in mind to search for as a result of the information he has received. The officer may *not* conduct a general exploratory search to find evidence of guilt without prior probable cause to believe the vehicle contains items legally subject to seizure. People v. Erickson, 31 Ill.2d 230, 201 N.E.2d 422 (Supreme Court of Illinois, 1964).

3. Vehicle not movable

In the 1971 case of Coolidge v. New Hampshire, 403 U.S. 443, 91 S.Ct. 2022, 29 L.Ed.2d 564 (1971), the U. S. Supreme Court indicated that the exigent circumstances requirement would not be satisfied if there were no real possibility that someone would remove the car and conceal or destroy evidence within it. In the *Coolidge* case, the police had known for some time of the probable role of defendant's automobile in a crime. The police went to defendant's home, arrested him inside his house, and escorted his wife and children to another town to spend the night. There were no other adult occupants of the house. The vehicle was unoccupied and in defendant's driveway. Police towed the vehicle to the station house and searched it there without a warrant.

The Court held that the search of the automobile could not be justified under the Carroll doctrine because the car was not movable, nor were there any other "exigent" circumstances to justify the search:

> [S]urely there is nothing in this case to invoke the meaning and purpose of the rule of Carroll v. U. S.—no alerted criminal bent on flight, no fleeting opportunity on an open highway after a hazardous chase, no contraband or stolen goods or weapons, no confederates waiting to move the evidence, not even the inconvenience of a special police detail to guard the immobilized automobile. In short, by no possible stretch of the legal imagination can this be made into a case where "it is not practicable to secure a warrant," * * * and the "automobile exception," despite its label, is simply irrelevant. 403 U.S. at 462, 91 S.Ct. at 2035–36, 29 L.Ed.2d at 580.

4. Movable Vehicle Following Fixed Habitual Pattern

In some situations even a completely movable vehicle cannot be searched on probable cause alone. An example is a case in which police surveillance of a gambling suspect revealed that the suspect followed an almost fixed, habitual pattern of time, place, and movement and his use of an automobile was merely incidental to this pattern. A warrantless search of the vehicle and the suspect revealed incriminating evidence. The court held the search illegal, finding no exigent circumstances to indicate that the delay necessary to obtain a warrant would have resulted in the removal of the vehicle or its contents. Clay v. U. S., 239 F.2d 196 (5th Circuit Court of Appeals, 1956).

The *Clay* case highlights the key question a law enforcement officer must ask regarding the "exigent circumstances" requirement—is it practicable to obtain a search warrant? That is to say, do the circumstances allow sufficient opportunity to secure and execute a warrant without unduly risking the loss of evidence believed to be contained in the car. If it is practicable to obtain a warrant, then a search of the vehicle is not permissible without a warrant, and evidence seized will not be admissible in court.

5. Entry Upon Private Premises

Courts have held that when law enforcement officers, acting on probable cause and following closely behind a vehicle, would have been authorized to stop and search the vehicle while on a public street, they may properly follow the vehicle onto private property and conduct the search there.

An example is a case in which an informant's tip and careful surveillance gave police officers probable cause to believe that a certain automobile contained contraband. The officers followed the auto until the defendant parked it in his garage. The subsequent warrantless search of the car in the garage was held valid by the Court:

> [I]t seems plain enough that just before he entered the garage the following officers properly could have stopped petitioner's car, [and] made search * * *
>
> Passage of the car into the open garage closely followed by the observing officer did not destroy this right. * * * Scher v. U. S., 305 U.S. 251, 255, 59 S.Ct. 174, 176, 83 L.Ed. 151, 154 (U. S. Supreme Court, 1938).

6. Probable Cause to Search Automobile Trunk

The trunk of an automobile may be treated differently from the rest of the automobile for purposes of the probable cause requirement of the *Carroll* doctrine. In Wimberly v. Superior Court, 16 Cal.3rd 557, 128 Cal.Rptr. 641, 547 P.2d 417 (1976), the California Supreme Court held that a person has a greater reasonable expectation of privacy in a closed area such as an automobile trunk than in an open area like a passenger compartment.

In the *Wimberly* case, law enforcement officers observed a car at approximately 2:30 A.M. speeding and weaving between lanes. The officers stopped the car. One officer, with the aid of a flashlight, observed what appeared to be marijuana seeds near a smoking pipe on the floor of the car. The officer requested that the car's occupant hand him the pipe. The officer smelled burnt marijuana in the pipe and noticed the burnt residue of seeds and stems in the pipe. The two occupants were ordered out of the car and the officers noticed a slight odor of burnt marijuana coming from inside the car. A plastic bag containing a small quantity of marijuana was found in the pocket of a jacket lying on the floor. The officers then opened the trunk with a key and found several pounds of marijuana.

The court found exigent circumstances and probable cause to search the passenger area of the car. The court, however, found no probable cause to search the trunk. The officers' observations indicated only that the suspects were "casual users" of marijuana and not "dealers." Therefore, it was not reasonable to conclude that there was additional contraband in the trunk.

Under the ruling in the *Wimberly* case, officers must make a separate determination of probable cause to search a trunk under the *Carroll* doctrine, even though they have probable cause to search the passenger area. Of course, in many cases, officers will have probable cause to search both the trunk and the passenger area.

7. Exigent Circumstances Despite Immovability

A law enforcement officer may have sufficient exigent circumstances under the *Carroll* doctrine even though the vehicle to be searched is not in a movable condition. In U. S. v. Robinson, 533 F. 2d 578 (District of Columbia Circuit Court of Appeals, 1976), officers had probable cause to believe that an unoccupied, parked, locked automobile had been recently used as a getaway car. The police surrounded the automobile with a substantial number of officers, thereby eliminating any possibility of movability. The automobile was then searched and incriminating evidence was found.

The court held that even though the movability requirement was not satisfied, the search was valid under the *Carroll* doctrine. Time was of the essence and it was not practicable to obtain a warrant.

> There was need to proceed as quickly as possible to apprehend the robbers who had used this as the getaway car in an armed bank robbery consummated about an hour prior to the search. There was strong probable cause to believe this was the getaway car. Bank robbers known to have been armed were at large, posing current dangers to the police and other citizens. An immediate search of the car could well produce the information needed to speedily apprehend the culprits. Delay to obtain a warrant would have impeded a promising police investigation and conceivably provided the added time needed by the bank robbers to avoid capture altogether. * * *
>
> We therefore hold that this getaway car case entails exigent circumstances that justify a warrantless search of the car for clues as to identity or location of suspects. 533 F.2d at 583.

The *Robinson* case indicates that law enforcement officers may, under limited conditions, search a vehicle without warrant, even though the vehicle is immobilized. The following conditions should exist, however, before such a search is undertaken: (1) a serious offense; (2) a clear showing of probable cause; (3) reasonable belief that the suspects are armed; (4) a likelihood that the suspects will escape if not speedily apprehended; and (5) a peaceable entry into the vehicle.

Also, if a vehicle or its contents present a potential danger to the pubic safety if not searched immediately, the "exigent circumstances" requirement of the *Carroll* doctrine may be satisfied, even though the car is not movable. In U. S. v. Cepulonis, 530 F.2d 238 (1st Circuit Court of Appeals, 1976), a law enforcement officer observed, through the window of an automobile, a sawed-off shotgun protruding from beneath the front seat. The court upheld the immediate warrantless seizure of the shotgun, finding probable cause and also finding that someone other than the car's owner (who was in custody) could have moved the car. The court went on to say:

> Moreover, a legitimate concern for public safety counselled against leaving the car, with a loaded shotgun visible through the window, unguarded in the Motel parking lot and "vulnerable to intrusion by vandals." * * * Under the circumstances the agents were faced with a choice whether to seize and hold the car while securing a warrant or to carry out an immediate warrantless search. 530 F.2d at 243.

8. Warrantless Search of Movable Containers

Several courts have held that the *Carroll* doctrine applies not only to motor vehicles but to all movable containers. These courts reason that a box, suitcase, or other container is readily movable. In some cases these containers are even more movable than an automobile. Also such containers might contain items which an officer could have probable cause to seize. Therefore, the "probable cause" and "exigent circumstances" requirements of the *Carroll* doctrine could both be applied to the search of such containers.

The Supreme Court of California considered whether the *Carroll* doctrine should be limited to searches of automobiles and similar self-propelled vehicles such as trucks, trains, boats, or airplanes, or extended to other non-self-propelled containers. The court said:

> Is a box or trunk assigned to a common carrier for shipment to a remote destination a "thing readily moved" or a "fixed piece of property"? The answer, self-evidently, is the former. To be sure, such a box has neither wheels nor motive power; but these features of an automobile are legally relevant only insofar as they make it movable despite its dimensions. A box, which is a fraction of the size and weight of an automobile, is movable without such appurtenances. * * *
>
> What is true of a box or trunk is true of all goods or chattels consigned to a common carrier for shipment. As they are no less movable than an automobile, the reasons for the rule permitting a warrantless search of a vehicle upon probable cause are equally applicable to the search of such chattel. People v. McKinnon, 7 Cal.3d 899, 909, 103 Cal.Rptr. 897, 904, 500 P.2d 1097, 1104 (1972).

In the *McKinnon* case, officers had probable cause to believe that five cartons contained contraband. The cartons were about to be shipped on a common carrier from San Diego to Seattle, thus providing exigent circumstances.

In U. S. v. Johnson, 467 F.2d 630 (2nd Circuit Court of Appeals, 1972), three bank robbers had been arrested. Officers had trustworthy information that two suitcases, one of which contained a shotgun, could be found outside the rear door of a certain apartment building. The court upheld the warrantless search and seizure of the suitcases on the basis of the *Carroll* doctrine. The court reasoned that because the suitcases could have been removed from their position outside the apartment building at any moment, they were similar to movable automobiles.

The U. S. Supreme Court has recently called into question the reasoning of those courts which have likened movable objects to motor vehicles under the *Carroll* doctrine. In U. S. v. Chadwick, 433 U.S. 1, 97 S.Ct. 2476, 53 L.Ed.2d 538 (1977), the Court invalidated a warrantless search of a large double-locked footlocker, which federal drug agents had legally seized after arresting the persons who had just loaded it into a car, and which the agents searched at a federal building an hour and a half after the arrests. One basis for the decision was the lack of movability of the footlocker. Once the footlocker had been seized and taken into custody, there was not the slightest danger that it or its contents could have been removed before a search warrant could have been obtained.

The other basis for the decision was the difference between a footlocker and an automobile with respect to a person's expectation of privacy. The Court said:

> The factors which diminish the privacy aspects of an automobile do not apply to respondents' footlocker. Luggage contents are not open to public view, except as a condition to a border entry or common carrier travels; nor is luggage subject to regular inspections and official scrutiny on a continuing basis. Unlike an automobile, whose primary function is transportation, luggage is intended as a repository of personal effects. In sum, a person's expectations of privacy in personal luggage are substantially greater than in an automobile. 433 U.S. at 13, 97 S.Ct. at 2484, 53 L. Ed.2d at 549.

It is not clear from the Court's opinion whether the Court intended to exclude only large, cumbersome containers like footlockers from warrantless searches under the *Carroll* doctrine or whether all movable objects other than motor vehicles are to be excluded. Because of this lack of clarity and the conflicting reasoning of other courts, law enforcement officers should not conduct warrantless searches of movable containers under the *Carroll* doctrine unless absolutely necessary. Nevertheless, when officers have a strong showing of probable cause, when evidence is almost certain to be lost or destroyed unless a search is made immediately, and when there is insufficient time to obtain a warrant, officers should search a highly movable container rather than lose the evidence.

EXAMINATION OF AN IMPOUNDED VEHICLE

Impoundment

It is common practice among some police departments for the arresting officer to take possession of a vehicle whenever the driver or person in control is taken into custody and to remove the vehicle to the nearest garage or police lot. In some jurisdictions, the officer may even have a duty to impound the vehicle in order to insure its adequate safekeeping during the period of the arrestee's confinement. This is especially true when there is no friend or relative of the vehicle's owner available to take responsibility for it. If the car is not impounded for safekeeping, the owner might later make unfounded claims of theft or loss of property.

However, the right or duty to impound does not automatically follow as an incident of the arrest or taking into custody. Absent circumstances justifying the impounding of the vehicle, there is some question about the legality of impoundment where the arrestee desires to leave the vehicle in the custody of another party who can remove it to safety. In a case in which both occupants of the car were intoxicated, and there was no one to drive or take charge of it, the court favored impoundment over leaving the car unattended on the street. People v. Havenstein, 4 Cal.App.3d 710, 84 Cal.Rptr. 528 (California Court of Appeal, 1970).

In another case involving a defendant arrested for driving under the influence, the defendant made arrangements to have his brother and mother take care of his car. The arresting officer, however, refused to relinquish the car and impounded it. The contents were later inventoried and LSD tablets were found. The court held that the impoundment of the car, and therefore the inventory search of it, was illegal. The court said:

> We hold that where police assumed custody of defendant's automobile for no legitimate state purpose other than safekeeping, and where defendant had arranged for alternate means, not shown to be unreasonable, for the safeguarding of his property, impoundment of defendant's automobile was unreasonable and, therefore, the concomitant inventory was an unreasonable search under the Fourth Amendment. State v. Goodrich, —— Minn. ——, 256 N.W.2d 506, 507 (Supreme Court of Minnesota, 1977).

The removal of an unoccupied parked vehicle is clearly justified when the vehicle constitutes a traffic hazard or otherwise violates local parking ordinances. The U. S. Supreme Court specifically authorized impoundment of vehicles under such circumstances:

> In the interests of public safety and as part of what the Court has called "community caretaking functions," * * * automobiles are frequently taken into police custody. Vehicle accidents present one such occasion. To permit the uninterrupted flow of traffic and in some circumstances to preserve evidence, disabled or damaged vehicles will often be removed from the highways or streets at the behest of police engaged solely in caretaking and traffic control activities. Police will also frequently remove and impound automobiles which violate parking ordinances and which thereby jeopardize both the public safety and the efficient movement of vehicular traffic. The authority of police to seize and remove from the streets vehicles impeding traffic or threatening public safety and convenience is beyond challenge. South Dakota v. Opperman, 428 U.S. 364, 368–69, 96 S.Ct. 3092, 3096, 49 L.Ed.2d 1000, 1005 (1976).

Examination and Inventory

Assuming that the vehicle has been lawfully impounded, the question then arises as to whether or not a valid search for incriminating evidence can be made without a warrant. Since the possibility of removal or detruction of the evidence terminates when the vehicle is placed in storage, even though probable cause exists, the warrantless search of an impounded vehicle after the occupant's arrest is illegal. Westover v. U. S., 342 F.2d 68 (9th Circuit Court of Appeals, 1965). The type of impoundment situation discussed here must be clearly distinguished from the situation in which the vehicle is forfeited to the state under a statute (see Cooper v. California, 386 U.S. 58, 87 S.Ct. 788, 17 L.Ed.2d 730 (U. S. Supreme Court, 1967)), or is seized as the fruit or instrumentality of a crime (see Abrams v. State, 223 Ga. 216, 154 S.E.2d 443 (Supreme Court of Georgia, 1967)). Under these separate procedures, the automobile is seized in its entirety and no further trespass is involved by its later examination. (These situations will be discussed later.) The general police authority to impound, which we are discussing here, however, is much more limited. The authority to impound does not carry with it the right to assume complete control or dominion over the property and everything contained therein, but is restricted solely to those measures which are reasonably necessary to insure the safe custody of the owner's property, to protect the police against claims or disputes over lost or stolen property, and to protect the police from potential danger. South Dakota v. Opperman, 428 U.S. 364, 96 S.Ct. 3092, 49 L. Ed.2d 1000 (U. S. Supreme Court, 1976).

In order to accomplish these purposes, the officer may examine the vehicle and take an inventory of the property in the car so that it may be returned to the owner later on. This procedure will also prevent false charges of theft or loss during the period of the owner's confinement. This type of examination is not considered a search, but is viewed rather as a simple administrative-custodial procedure. As such, however, this procedure cannot be used as a pretext to rummage around for incriminating materials to circumvent the warrant requirement. Harris v. U. S., 370 F.2d 477 (District of Columbia Circuit Court of Appeals, 1966).

Accordingly, the scope of the examination and inventory must be restricted solely to those areas of the vehicle where a person would ordinarily be expected to store his belongings. The examination, therefore, would usually include an unlocked glove compartment, an unlocked trunk, the sun visors, the front and rear seat areas, and other places in which property is ordinarily kept, but would not include hidden areas. People v. Andrews, 6 Cal.App.3d 428, 85 Cal.Rptr. 908 (California Court of Appeal, 1970). As a part of the inventory, a notation should be made of the vehicle identification number, the motor number, and the make, model, and license plate number of the car in order that it may be readily identified later. Cotton v. U.

S., 371 F.2d 385 (9th Circuit Court of Appeals, 1967). Officers should not open locked glove compartments or locked trunks to make inventories of their contents, because the protection of the property, themselves, and others would not ordinarily require it. Also such an inventory may violate the owner's reasonable expectation of privacy. State v. Boster, 217 Kan. 618, 539 P.2d 294 (Kansas Supreme Court, 1975). But when an officer reasonably believes that the contents of an automobile or the contents of a locked compartment in an automobile present a danger to himself or others, he may make a search to remedy the danger.

The intensity of the examination and inventory must also be limited according to its purpose. Thus, if the officer dismantles the vehicle, looks behind the upholstery, or in any other manner indicates that his purpose is other than to protect the arrestee's property, the courts will consider the examination to be a pretext for a search designed to uncover evidentiary materials. In that event the inventory will be considered an illegal search and the fruits of the search will be inadmissible in court.

Likewise, if police delay making an inventory of the contents of an impounded vehicle for an unreasonable period of time, the inventory may be ruled an illegal search. An unreasonably delayed inventory indicates that police were not really concerned about safeguarding the owner's property or protecting themselves against claims or from danger, but were primarily interested in looking for evidence. A vehicle inventory should be conducted as soon as possible after the impoundment, taking into consideration the police agency's manpower, facilities, workload, and other circumstances. If the inventory is delayed for more than a day or two without good reason, it is likely to be declared illegal.

It is important that each law enforcement agency have standard procedures for inventorying impounded vehicles, or such inventories may be declared illegal. The U. S. Supreme Court, in upholding the validity of an inventory of an impounded car in South Dakota v. Opperman, emphasized that the police in that case were using a standard inventory form pursuant to standard police procedures. The Court said, "The decisions of this Court point unmistakably to the conclusion reached by both federal and state courts that inventories pursuant to standard police procedures are reasonable." 428 U. S. at 372, 96 S.Ct. at 3098, 49 L.Ed.2d at 1007. The 9th Circuit Court of Appeals invalidated an inventory search of a legally impounded automobile because the local police department did not have a standard procedure regarding the inventorying of an impounded vehicle's contents. The court said:

> [E]ven if an investigatory motive was not shown, our decision would be the same because the inventorying of impounded cars was

> not shown to be a routine practice and policy of *this* police department, as was the case in *Opperman* * * *. It is the inventorying practice and not the impounding practice that, if routinely followed and supported by proper noninvestigatory purposes, could render the inventory a reasonable search under *Opperman*. The fact that other police departments routinely follow such a practice may give support to the proposition that such a practice, if locally followed, is reasonable. It does not, however, render reasonable a search where the inventorying practice is not locally followed and the search, thus, is a departure from local practice. U. S. v. Hellman, 556 F.2d 442, 444 (1977).

Plain View Doctrine

While it cannot be the officer's purpose to look for evidence of crime while conducting a bona fide inventory, if he unexpectedly discovers contraband or other items subject to seizure, these items may properly be seized and are admissible in evidence. Since he is lawfully conducting an inventory in the vehicle and there has been no search in the legal sense, the situation is governed by the "plain view" doctrine discussed in Chapter 6.

In a case illustrating the application of the plain view doctrine to the inventory situation, local officers stopped a vehicle which was being operated without license plates. Neither of the occupants claimed to be the owner of the automobile nor did they know to whom it belonged, Furthermore, the driver's statement that he had borrowed the vehicle from a used car dealer was not consistent with information disclosed on the registration sticker. On the basis of these facts, the officers arrested the two men on a charge of auto theft. After the arrest, as a normal procedure before impounding the vehicle, the officers began an inventory of all personal property found therein. One of the officers picked up a jacket on the front seat where defendant had been sitting and noticed in plain sight a burned cigarette. Since it appeared to him to be marijuana, the officer searched the jacket and found another such cigarette in the left-hand pocket. The defendant later admitted that he had purchased the cigarettes approximately one week earlier.

On appeal of the defendant's conviction for illegal possession of marijuana, the court held that the marijuana cigarette was legally obtained by the officer:

> In the course of making the inventory of the contents of the car, the officer merely removed the jacket from the front seat revealing in plain sight the narcotic. How it got there could not be determined but it is clear that when the officer picked up the jacket the cigarette was there for all to see. Actually, the officer's ob-

servation of the cigarette was not the result of a search, for it appeared in plain sight in the normal course of the reasonable and valid activity of the officer in making the inventory incidental to impounding the car. People v. Nebbitt, 183 Cal.App.2d 452, 460, 7 Cal.Rptr. 8, 13 (California Court of Appeal, 1960).

In another case illustrating the application of the plain view doctrine to an automobile inventory, officers came upon a closed satchel during an inventory of the contents of a lawfully impounded vehicle. They opened the satchel and found marijuana. The court held that the contents of the closed satchel did not come within the plain view doctrine and were inadmissible as evidence of a crime. Although the satchel itself was in plain view of the officer as he inventoried the contents of the vehicle, the contents of the satchel were not in his plain view. State v. Gwinn, Del., 301 A.2d 291 (Delaware Supreme Court, 1972). Officers should obtain a search warrant before opening any closed container found during an inventory of the contents of a vehicle.

IMPOUNDMENT OF VEHICLE UNDER FORFEITURE STATUTES

Another ground for allowing a warrantless search of a vehicle by law enforcement officers is the seizure and impoundment of the vehicle under a specific state forfeiture statute. In the case of Cooper v. California, 386 U.S. 58, 87 S.Ct. 788, 17 L.Ed.2d 730 (U. S. Supreme Court, 1967), the defendant was arrested for selling heroin wrapped in brown paper to a police informer. At the time of the arrest, the defendant's car was seized and impounded pursuant to a state forfeiture statute. The statute required that any officer making an arrest for a narcotics offense involving the use of a vehicle must seize and hold such vehicle as evidence pending a judicial declaration of forfeiture or release. Evidence showed that the defendant used his vehicle in connection with his possession and transportation of narcotics. One week after the seizure, police searched the car and discovered a piece of brown paper in the glove compartment. The brown paper was later introduced at trial. The state had not acquired title to the car at the time of the search.

This search could not be justified under the *Carroll* doctrine because there were no exigent circumstances. The car had been in police custody for a week, during which time the police could easily have obtained a warrant. Nevertheless, the Court held the search legal. The Court said that the car was lawfully held by the police in connection with criminal activity under the state forfeiture statute. Since the car was to be held for a considerable period of time, and since the police could deny possession of the car to its owner, the police had possessory rights of their own for the limited purpose of searching the vehicle.

The *Cooper* case allows law enforcement officers to conduct a warrantless search of a vehicle, in the absence of exigent circumstances, when all the following conditions are met:

1. A state statute requires law enforcement officers to seize vehicles involved in certain offenses and hold them pending forfeiture proceedings.
2. A vehicle is seized by the officer in connection with an offense named in the state forfeiture statute, and impounded.
3. The search of the car is closely related to the reason the defendant was arrested, the reason his vehicle was impounded, and the reason it is being retained.
4. The officer expects that the car will be in police custody for a considerable time.
5. The officer can legally deny possession of the car to the owner.

The *Cooper* decision does not require that officers have probable cause to search a car impounded under a forfeiture statute. Nevertheless, if the officer does have probable cause to search, he should obtain a search warrant.

INSTRUMENTALITY OF A CRIME

The motor vehicle is unique in that, besides its obvious use as a transporter of people and goods related to crime, it can itself be an instrumentality of crime. Some courts have taken the view that for certain types of crimes, the entire automobile may be seized as an instrumentality of the crime, much like the seizure of any other weapon. Then, the argument continues, a vehicle could be examined and tested, much like a weapon, for hair, bloodstains, soil, fingerprints, and other physical evidence. Weaver v. Lane, 382 F.2d 251 (7th Circuit Court of Appeals, 1967). This theory would be particularly useful in cases of rape, robbery, and other violent crimes where the automobile itself is the scene of the crime or an integral part of it. Some courts have shown an inclination toward this theory. For example, in the case of State v. Poulin, Me., 268 A.2d 475 (Supreme Judicial Court of Maine, 1970), the court gave as one of the reasons for justifying the seizure of an automobile, that the automobile was an instrumentality of a probable crime. However, this is still a very unsettled area of the law, and the law enforcement officer should proceed on the basis of established principles and obtain a warrant rather than attempt to justify a warrantless seizure of a vehicle on the theory that it is an instrumentality of a crime.

EXPECTATION OF PRIVACY

In recent years, the U. S. Supreme Court and other courts have begun to analyze warrantless searches and seizures of vehicles in terms of whether they intrude upon a person's reasonable expectation of privacy. In Cardwell v. Lewis, 417 U.S. 583, 94 S.Ct. 2464, 41 L. Ed.2d 325 (1974), the U. S. Supreme Court held that, where probable cause exists, a warrantless examination of the exterior of a car is not unreasonable under the Fourth and Fourteenth Amendments. The Court said:

> One has a lesser expectation of privacy in a motor vehicle because its function is transportation and it seldom serves as one's residence or as the repository of personal effects. A car has little capacity for escaping public scrutiny. It travels public thoroughfares where both its occupants and its contents are in plain view. * * * This is not to say that no part of the interior of an automobile has Fourth Amendment protection; the exercise of a desire to be mobile does not, of course, waive one's right to be free of unreasonable governmental intrusion. But insofar as Fourth Amendment protection extends to a motor vehicle, it is the right to privacy that is the touchstone of our inquiry. 417 U.S. at 590–91, 94 S.Ct. at 2469–70, 41 L.Ed.2d at 335.

In South Dakota v. Opperman, 428 U.S. 364, 96 S.Ct. 3092, 49 L. Ed.2d 1000 (1976), the U. S. Supreme Court approved the warrantless inventory of an automobile impounded for parking violations. The Court said:

> Besides the elements of mobility, less rigorous warrant requirements govern because the expectation of privacy with respect to one's automobile is significantly less than that relating to one's home or office. In discharging their varied responsibilities for ensuring the public safety, law enforcement officials are necessarily brought into frequent contact with automobiles. Most of this contact is distinctly noncriminal in nature. * * * Automobiles, unlike homes, are subjected to pervasive and continuing governmental regulation and controls, including periodic inspection and licensing requirements. As an everyday occurrence, police stop and examine vehicles when license plates or inspection stickers have expired, or if other violations, such as exhaust fumes or excessive noise, are noted, or if headlights or other safety equipment are not in proper working order. 428 U.S. at 367–68, 96 S.Ct. at 3096, 49 L.Ed.2d at 1004.

The quoted passages indicate that the courts are imposing fewer restrictions on law enforcement officers with regard to warrantless searches of vehicles. Nevertheless, even though the reasonable expectation of privacy in one's vehicle is less than that in his person, home, or office, officers must not violate that expectation when conducting searches or inventories of vehicles.

Electronic Beepers

An electronic "beeper" is a small radio transmitter that broadcasts only a signal. A beeper neither records nor transmits any sounds other than its signal, but the signal can be monitored by directional finders, enabling law enforcement officers to determine the beeper's location. The attachment of an electronic beeper to a vehicle without previously obtaining a warrant was held to violate the vehicle owner's reasonable expectation of privacy in U. S. v. Holmes, 521 F.2d 859 (5th Circuit Court of Appeals, 1975). In that case, government agents planted an electronic "beeper" on a van parked in a public lot, while the owner was completing a marijuana sale to a state undercover agent. The "beeper" enabled the agents to follow the van to the headquarters of a drug ring. All evidence obtained as a result of following the van was declared illegally seized by the court. The court said:

> We are unwilling to hold that Holmes, and every other citizen, runs the risk that the government will plant a bug in his car in order to track his movements, merely because he drives his car in areas accessible to the public. The presence or absence of a physical intrusion into the interior of the car does not affect this conclusion.
>
> * * *
>
> No rational basis occurs to us for distinguishing the violation of the expectation of privacy involved in the installation of a "beeper" on a car, in order to trace its movement, from placing of a tap on the outside of a telephone booth in order to overhear and record conversations [citing Katz v. U. S., 389 U.S. 347, 88 S.Ct. 507, 19 L.Ed.2d 576 (U. S. Supreme Court, 1967)]. In addition, of course, the "beeper" installation was accomplished by an actual trespass. 521 F.2d at 865.

Other courts have upheld the warrantless monitoring of beepers placed on cars on the ground that a person has no reasonable expectation of privacy while driving on the public roads. In U. S. v. Hufford, 539 F.2d 32 (9th Circuit Court of Appeals, 1976), government agents suspected the defendant of engaging in illicit drug activity. The agents learned that the defendant had placed an order for two large drums of caffeine, which is used in the manufacture of amphetamines, from a chemical company. With the consent of the company, the agents installed an electronic beeper in one of the drums. When the defendant picked up the drums, the agents, relying on visual observation and primarily on signals from the beeper, followed his truck to a rental garage. At the rental garage, the agents obtained evidence which eventually led to the defendant's conviction.

With respect to the agents' use of the beeper, the court said:

> We hold that while the installation of the beeper in the drum was a probing, exploratory quest for evidence, the defendants did not have a reasonable expectation of privacy. Katz v. United States, 389 U.S. 347, 88 S.Ct. 507, 19 L.Ed.2d 576 (1967). Therefore, the defendants are not entitled to Fourth Amendment protection.
>
> Hufford did not have a reasonable expectation of privacy as he drove along the public road. While he hoped that his travel would go unmonitored, his movements were knowingly exposed to the public, and therefore are not a subject of Fourth Amendment protection. * * *
>
> The lower court concluded that agents could not have determined the location of the rental garage but for the beeper. But the device only augments that which can be done by visual surveillance alone; with more agents and more automobiles or planes, Hufford's movements could have easily been followed without the use of a beeper. We see no distinction between visual surveillance and use of an electronic beeper to aid the agents in following the movements of an automobile along public roads provided no Fourth Amendment violation occurred when the beeper was attached. 539 F.2d at 33–34.

There are few specific guidelines to help the officer determine when a person has a reasonable expectation of privacy in an automobile. Officers should follow the advice presented in this chapter and use their common sense. When an officer believes that a warrantless search or trace of a vehicle may violate a person's reasonable expectation of privacy, he should apply for a warrant.

Searches by Dogs

In U. S. v. Solis, 536 F.2d 880 (9th Circuit Court of Appeals, 1976), the court held that the use of specially trained dogs to detect the smell of marijuana in a vehicle did not violate the reasonable expectation of privacy of the vehicle's owner. In that case, a drug agent suspected that marijuana was hidden in the floor of a certain semi-trailer parked at the rear of a gas station. The agent went to the gas station and found the semi-trailer with what appeared to be white talcum powder on its doors. The officer knew from his training and experience that marijuana was often smuggled in semi-trailer floors and that talcum powder was often used to conceal marijuana's odor. The agent notified the Customs office which sent two Customs officers with specially trained marijuana sniffing dogs.

The dogs, who were determined to be extremely reliable, reacted positively to marijuana in the semi-trailer. A search warrant was obtained and the marijuana was seized.

The court held that the use of the dogs to help the officers establish probable cause to search was reasonable and did not violate the defendant's reasonable expectation of privacy. The court said:

> The dogs' intrusion such as it was into the air space open to the public in the vicinity of the trailer appears to us reasonably tolerable in our society. There was no invasion of the "curtilage"—the trailer. No sophisticated mechanical or electronic devices were used. The investigation was not indiscriminate, but solely directed to the particular contraband. There was an expectation that the odor would emanate from the trailer. Efforts made to mask it were visible. The method used by the officers was inoffensive. There was no embarrassment to or search of the person. The target was a physical fact indicative of possible crime, not protected communications. We hold that the use of the dogs was not unreasonable under the circumstances and therefore was not a prohibited search under the fourth amendment. 536 F.2d at 882–83.

Courts are in disagreement over the search and seizure implications of the use of drug-detecting dogs. The safest procedure for law enforcement officers is to make sure drug-detecting dogs are reliable and to obtain a warrant before conducting a search based on a dog's reactions.

SUMMARY

The vehicle exception to the search warrant requirement is embodied in the so-called *Carroll* doctrine. The *Carroll* doctrine states that a warrant must be obtained to search any vehicle unless:

1. There is probable cause to believe that the vehicle contains items subject to seizure; *and*
2. It is not practicable to secure a warrant because of "exigent circumstances." "Exigent circumstances" usually means that the vehicle is in a movable condition and any delay to obtain a warrant would likely result in the removal of the vehicle to an unknown location with a resulting destruction or concealment of evidence.

The examination and inventory of a lawfully impounded vehicle may also be conducted without a warrant. This procedure, however, is not considered to be a search but a mere administrative procedure to protect the property of the owner of the vehicle. The examination and inventory of a vehicle must be limited in scope and intensity by the purpose for which it is allowed. Nevertheless, evidence found in "plain view" during such an examination and inventory will be admissible in court.

Seizure and impoundment of a vehicle under a state forfeiture statute and seizure of a vehicle as an instrumentality of a crime may also provide legal justification for a warrantless search of the vehicle. All these vehicle exceptions to the warrant requirement, however, involve possible intrusions on Fourth Amendment rights. Courts will look very closely at any warrantless evidence-gathering activities in vehicles by law enforcement officers in vehicles. It is recommended that law enforcement officers follow warrant procedures with regard to vehicle searches, unless there is a genuine emergency or a strictly legitimate impoundment and inventory situation. Officers should also be careful not to violate anyone's reasonable expectation of privacy when searching vehicles.

8

OPEN FIELDS AND ABANDONED PROPERTY

To open the discussion of the "open fields" and "abandoned property" exceptions to the search warrant requirement, we must again refer to the Fourth Amendment to the U. S. Constitution. The Fourth Amendment guarantees "the right of the people to be secure in their persons, *houses*, papers, and effects, against unreasonable *searches* and seizures * * * " (emphasis supplied) U.S.C.A.Const. Amend. IV. The word "houses" and the word "searches" are italicized because the meaning of open fields depends upon court interpretation of the word "houses," and the meaning of abandoned property depends upon court interpretations of the word "searches." To introduce the legal meanings of these terms and their interrelationships, we will begin with a summary of Hester v. U. S., 265 U.S. 57, 44 S. Ct. 445, 68 L.Ed. 898 (U. S. Supreme Court, 1924). This case established the concepts of open fields and abandonment in the law of search and seizure.

HESTER v. U. S.

In the case of Hester v. U. S., revenue officers, acting on information, went to the house of Hester's father. As they approached, they saw one Henderson drive up to the house. The officers concealed themselves and observed Hester come out of the house and hand Henderson a quart bottle. An alarm was given. Hester went to a nearby car and removed a gallon jug, and he and Henderson fled across an open field. One of the officers pursued, firing his pistol. Henderson threw away his bottle, and Hester dropped his jug, which broke, keeping about one quart of its contents. A broken jar, still containing some of its contents, was found outside the house. The officers examined the jug, the jar, and the bottle and determined that they contained illicitly distilled whiskey. The officers had neither a search warrant nor an arrest warrant.

The defendant was convicted of concealing distilled spirits, and contended on appeal that the testimony of the two officers was inadmissible because their actions constituted an illegal search and seizure. The Court said:

> It is obvious that even if there had been a trespass, the above testimony was not obtained by an illegal search or seizure. The defendant's own acts, and those of his associates, disclosed the jug, the jar and the bottle—and there was no seizure in the sense of the law when the officers examined the contents of each after it had been *abandoned* * * *
>
> The only shadow of a ground for bringing up the case is drawn from the hypothesis that the examination of the vessels took place upon Hester's father's land. As to that, it is enough to say that, apart from the justification, the special protection accorded by the Fourth Amendment to the people in their "persons, houses, papers and effects," is not extended to the *open fields*. The distinction between the latter and the house is as old as the common law. (emphasis supplied) 265 U.S. at 58–59, 44 S.Ct. at 446, 68 L.Ed. at 900.

The *Hester* decision has been heavily criticized, but has been applied and interpreted by many courts, and remains in effect today. The *Hester* case itself is not very helpful to the law enforcement officer, but the decisions of other courts following it have expanded upon and clarified its holdings. The remainder of this chapter will be devoted to setting out guidelines for the law enforcement officer on the search and seizure of open fields and abandoned property.

OPEN FIELDS

The open fields doctrine has been simply and clearly stated by the U. S. Supreme Court in the *Hester* case:

> [T]he special protection accorded by the Fourth Amendment to the people in their "persons, houses, papers and effects," is not extended to the open fields. 265 U.S. at 59, 44 S.Ct. at 446, 68 L.Ed. at 900.

The open fields doctrine is very important to the law enforcement officer because it allows him to search for and seize evidence in the open fields without a warrant, probable cause, or any other legal justification. Even if the officer trespasses on the land of another while searching the open fields, the evidence he seizes will not be inadmissible for that reason. Furthermore, the officer himself will not be held liable for trespass in a civil suit if the trespass was required in the performance of his duties. Giacona v. U. S., 257 F.2d 450 (5th Circuit Court of Appeals, 1958). The Supreme Court of Wisconsin has even allowed use of a backhoe and scraper in the open fields to dig for a body. Conrad v. State, 63 Wis.2d 616, 218 N.W.2d 252 (1974).

The problem for the law enforcement officer lies in determining where the area protected by the Fourth Amendment ends and the open fields begin. In order to make this determination, the officer must look to the meaning given by the courts to the word "houses" in the Fourth Amendment.

The word "houses" in the Fourth Amendment has been given a very broad meaning by the courts. Courts have held that the Fourth Amendment protects people in their homes, whether owned, rented, or leased. The term "houses" has also been held to include any quarters in which a person is staying or living, whether permanently or temporarily. Examples of other protected living quarters are hotel and motel rooms, apartments, rooming and boarding house rooms, and even hospital rooms. Furthermore, the protection of the Fourth Amendment is not restricted to places of residence, but extends to places of business also. U. S. v. Botsch, 364 F.2d 542, 547 (2nd Circuit Court of Appeals, 1966). The protection extended to places of business is limited, however, to those areas or sections which are not open to the public. As one court has said:

> [A] private business whose doors are open to the general public is also to be considered open to entry by the police for any proper purpose not violative of the owner's constitutional rights—e. g., patronizing the place or surveying it to promote law and order or to suppress a breach of the peace. State v. La Duca, 89 N.J.Super. 159, 165, 214 A.2d 423, 426 (New Jersey Superior Court, 1965).

For purposes of convenience, the word "house" will be used in the remainder of this chapter to refer to either residential or commercial premises covered by the Fourth Amendment.

Courts have also extended the meaning of "houses" under the Fourth Amendment to include the "ground and buildings immediately surrounding a dwelling." Rosencranz v. U. S., 356 F.2d 310, 313 (1st Circuit Court of Appeals, 1966). This area is commonly known as the "curtilage." The concept of curtilage is vital to the open fields doctrine because the open fields are considered to be all the space that is not contained within the curtilage. There are no clear cut rules to assist the law enforcement officer in determining the extent of the curtilage. Each case is decided by the courts on its own particular facts and circumstances. We turn now to a discussion of the facts and circumstances which courts rely on in determining the extent of the curtilage.

Determination of Curtilage

In order to determine whether property to be searched falls within the curtilage of a house (as house is defined under the Fourth Amendment), the law enforcement officer must consider many factors. As one court has said:

> Whether the place to be searched is within the curtilage is to be determined from the facts, including its proximity or annexation to the dwelling, its inclusion within the general enclosure surrounding the dwelling, and its use and enjoyment as an adjunct to the domestic economy of the family. Care v. U. S., 231 F.2d 22, 25 (10th Circuit Court of Appeals, 1956).

We will consider a variety of court decisions to clarify the meaning of this quote and to provide more specific guidelines for the law enforcement officer.

Residential Yard

Courts differ in opinion as to whether the residential yard is within the curtilage. In one case, law enforcement officers investigating a robbery obtained a search warrant to search defendant's premises. The officers searched the residence and an outbuilding and finally found a shotgun in the front yard, eight to ten feet from the street. The warrant was later held to be invalid. The court held that the front yard was within the curtilage of defendant's house and was subject to the same constitutional protection as the house itself. Since the officers' only justification for being on the premises was an invalid search warrant, the search was illegal. State v. Buchanan, Mo., 432 S.W.2d 342 (Supreme Court of Missouri, 1968).

In another case, however, the court held that entry into a residential yard, even if a trespass, and the observation of that which is open to view is not prohibited by the Fourth Amendment. An officer had received information that defendant was growing marijuana under a fig tree outside his residence. The officer went to defendant's residence to investigate. The premises were described by the court as a house that faced the street with a driveway that ran along the east of the house and terminated in a garage at the rear and east of the house. Defendant's residence was attached to the rear of the garage. The fig tree was about twenty feet from the defendant's door. The officer observed marijuana plants growing in a keg near the base of the tree, partially covered by the leaves and limbs of the tree.

In finding the seizure of the plants legal, the court said:

> [T]hey were located a scant 20 feet from defendant's door to which presumably delivery men and others came, and the front house, as well as defendant's house, apparently had access to the yard. Under the circumstances it does not appear that defendant exhibited a subjective expectation of privacy as to the plants. Furthermore, any such expectation would have been unreasonable. * * * People v. Bradley, 1 Cal.3d 80, 85, 81 Cal.Rptr. 457, 459, 460 P.2d 129, 131 (Supreme Court of California, 1969).

The main difference between these two cases appears to be that the defendant's yard in the *Bradley* case was semi-public in nature, because residents of the front house, delivery men, and others had access to it. Apparently, the defendant's yard in the *Buchanan* case did not allow such access. Judging by the different approaches taken by the courts in these two cases, it would be difficult to definitely say whether the residential yard is or is not to be considered part of the curtilage. The safest procedure for the law enforcement officer is to treat the residential yard of a house as part of the curtilage unless there are clear indications that the person residing in the house had no reasonable expectation of privacy in the yard. More importantly, since there will always be considerable doubt as to whether the residential yard falls within the curtilage, the officer should obtain a warrant for searches of this area when possible.

Fences

If the area immediately surrounding the house is enclosed by a fence, the area within the fence is usually defined as the curtilage. In a case illustrating this point, law enforcement officers investigating a murder learned that the defendant had been seen target shooting in a field outside his farm some time before the murder. The officers obtained a search warrant (which was later held invalid), went to the farm, and found spent bullets and shell casings outside a fence and about 250 feet from the dwelling house. The bullets and casings were used as evidence in convicting the defendant.

The court held that the search and seizure without a valid warrant was legal because it was conducted in the open fields, outside the curtilage. The court said:

> The evidence discloses that the area around the dwelling and outbuildings habitually used and necessary and convenient for family purposes was enclosed by a substantial fence. When such fence is erected it ordinarily defines the curtilage, particularly in a rural area. Patler v. Commonwealth, 211 Va. 448, 451, 177 S.E.2d 618, 620 (Supreme Court of Appeals of Virginia, 1970).

Family Use

Another factor which officers should consider in determining the extent of the curtilage is the area's use for family purposes in connection with the dwelling. As one court has said, "curtilage has been held to include * * * such place as is necessary and convenient to a dwelling, and is habitually used for family purposes * * *." U. S. v. Potts, 297 F.2d 68, 69 (6th Circuit Court of Appeals, 1961).

In the *Patler* case, discussed above under *Fences*, the defendant claimed that the field outside the fence was part of the curtilage because it was used for family picnics, was regularly mowed, and the children played there. The court found that the family picnics were infrequent and that one would expect a non-grazing field to be regularly mowed. The evidence was therefore "insufficient to establish the necessity, convenience and habitual use for family purposes which would be required in order to extend the curtilage to include the field." 211 Va. at 451, 177 S.E.2d at 621.

Of course, it is often impossible for an officer to know if, and to what extent, a part of a person's premises are used for family purposes. Nevertheless, the officer can sometimes obtain this information by observation or by asking questions. Again, when there is doubt in the officer's mind whether the place to be searched is in the open fields, he should obtain a warrant.

Multiple Occupancy Dwellings

Multiple occupancy dwellings are treated somewhat differently from single occupancy dwellings for purposes of determining the extent of curtilage. Some courts have held that the shared areas of multiple occupancy buildings such as common corridors, passageways, and yards, are not entitled to the protection of the Fourth Amendment, because many people have access to them. Nevertheless, there are many different types of multiple occupancy dwellings, and courts will look to all the facts and circumstances in defining the curtilage. In an illustrative case, two law enforcement officers who had information that narcotics were being sold on defendant's premises were observing defendant's behavior at his residence in a four-unit apartment building. Over a 45-minute period, the officers observed several people enter defendant's apartment, and each time defendant would go into his backyard and remove a shaving kit from beneath some rubbish under a tree. One of the officers then went into the backyard and seized the shaving kit while the other officer arrested defendant. Chemical analysis revealed that the shaving kit contained heroin.

The government argued that the defendant's backyard was an area common to or shared with other tenants and should not be entitled to the protection usually afforded the curtilage of a purely private residence. The court held, however, that the backyard was a protected area and that the seizure and search of the shaving kit was illegal:

> The backyard of Fixel's home was not a common passageway normally used by the building's tenants for gaining access to the apartments. * * * Nor is the backyard an area open as a corridor to salesmen or other businessmen who might approach the tenants in the course of their trade. * * * This apartment was Fixel's home, he lived there and the backyard of the building was completely removed from the street and surrounded by a chain link fence. * * * While the enjoyment of his backyard is not as exclusive as the backyard of a purely private residence, this area is not as public or shared as the corridors, yards or other common areas of a large apartment complex or motel. Contemporary concepts of living such as multi-unit dwellings must not dilute Fixel's right to privacy any more than is absolutely required. We believe that the backyard area of Fixel's home is sufficiently removed and private in character that he could reasonably expect privacy. Fixel v. Wainwright, 492 F.2d 480, 484 (Fifth Circuit Court of Apeals, 1974).

Courts have also held that porches and fire escapes outside a person's apartment or unit in a multiple occupancy dwelling fall within the curtilage of the apartment or unit. As one court reasoned:

> Unlike public halls or stairs which are public areas used in common by tenants and their guests or others lawfully on the property, a fire escape in a non-fireproof building is required outside of each apartment as a secondary means of egress for the ocupants of that apartment. While it is true that in the event of fire others might have occasion to lawfully pass over the fire escape of another, this would be the only time that one might be lawfully on the fire escape of another. People v. Terrell, 53 Misc. 32, 38–39, 277 N.Y.S.2d 926, 933 (Supreme Court of New York, 1967).

Garages

Garages are usually held to be part of the curtilage, especially if they are near or attached to the dwelling house and used in connection with it. Therefore, in a case in which a garage and a house were surrounded on three sides by a fence and the garage was close to the house, 50 to 75 feet from the street, the garage was held to be within the curtilage. Commonwealth v. Murphy, 353 Mass. 458, 233 N.E.2d 5 (Supreme Judicial Court of Massachusetts, 1968). A garage not used by its owner in connection with his residence, however, was held to be not within the curtilage. People v. Swanberg, 22 A.D.2d 902, 255 N.Y.S.2d 267 (Supreme Court of New York, 1964).

Also a garage used in connection with a multi-unit dwelling was held not to be within the curtilage, because it was used in common by many tenants of the dwelling. People v. Terry, 70 Cal.2d 410, 77 Cal.Rptr. 460, 454 P.2d 36 (Supreme Court of California, 1969).

Other Outbuildings

In determining whether the outbuildings are part of the curtilage, the courts consider such factors as distance from the dwelling house, presence or absence of a fence, and family use of the building. A barn was held to be within the curtilage where there was a driveway between the dwelling and the barn, tracks of vehicles and footprints were visible in the snow leading to both house and barn, and there were no separating barriers. Rosencranz v. U. S., 356 F.2d 310 (1st Circuit Court of Appeals, 1966). In another case, a barn was held to be within the curtilage even though it was surrounded by a fence and separated from the house by a private driveway. The barn was 70 to 80 yards from the house, and there was a gap in the fence allowing entrance into the barnyard from the private driveway in front of the house. Walker v. U. S., 225 F.2d 447 (5th Circuit Court of Appeals, 1955). A whiskey still located 250 yards from the back of a house on open land was held to be in the open fields, however. Atwell v. U. S., 414 F.2d 136 (5th Circuit Court of Appeals, 1969). And a concrete outbuilding, which was located only 150 to 180 feet from the nearest residence, was held to be outside the curtilage of the residence, because it was separated by a fence and a gate. Brock v. U. S., 256 F.2d 55 (5th Circuit Court of Appeals, 1958).

Other outbuildings such as sheds, chicken houses, and smokehouses have been held to be within the curtilage depending on various factors. Very few definite guidelines for the law enforcement officer can be obtained from the cases in this area. It is strongly suggested that, if the officer has any doubt whether an outbuilding is within the curtilage or in the open fields, he should obtain a warrant before searching the building.

Unoccupied Tracts

An unoccupied, uncultivated, remote tract of land is almost always held to be outside the curtilage and in the open fields. An example is a case in which police investigating a shooting incident obtained admissions from the defendant that he had left two guns in a vacant wooded area which he owned. The area was about one half mile from the scene of the shooting incident and was remote from human habitation. The police searched the area without a warrant and found the guns. The court held that the search was not constitutionally unreasonable because the area was an open field. People v. La

Rosa, 25 A.D.2d 587, 267 N.Y.S.2d 235 (Supreme Court of New York, 1966).

A harder question is presented when the area searched is not completely vacant but is being used as a building lot. Law enforcement officers had received a complaint that lumber, sacks of cement, and a cart had been stolen. Investigation led the officers to suspect the defendant. They went to defendant's property, where he was laying the foundation for a house, searched it without a warrant, and found some of the stolen items.

The court held that the area searched came within the category of open fields, even though a house was in the process of construction on it:

> If the lot had been left completely untouched, there could be no doubt that it would fall within the ruling of the *Hester* case. That a large quantity of building material has been brought upon the lot and a foundation for a house dug out, or even completely laid, does not change the nature of the place. Not even the broad policy of protection against "invasion of 'the sanctity of a man's home and the privacies of life'," * * * is infringed by what took place here. Defendant's constitutional rights were not violated. People v. Grundeis, 413 Ill. 145, 152, 108 N.E.2d 483, 487 (Supreme Court of Illinois, 1952).

Reasonable Expectation of Privacy

In determining the legality of the search in many of the cases discussed above, courts have considered whether the person owning the premises had a reasonable expectation of privacy in the area searched. In this sense, reasonable expectation of privacy could be considered just another one of the facts and circumstances used to determine the extent of the curtilage. Since the U. S. Supreme Court decision in Katz v. U. S., 389 U.S. 347, 88 S.Ct. 507, 19 L.Ed.2d 576 (1967), however, a person's reasonable expectation of privacy has taken on a whole new meaning and importance in the law of search and seizure. In the *Katz* case, a landmark opinion involving electronic eavesdropping, the U. S. Supreme Court stated that "the Fourth Amendment protects people, not places." 389 U.S. at 351, 88 S.Ct. at 511, 19 L.Ed.2d at 582. A later court decision said that *Katz*

> shifts the focus of the Fourth Amendment from "protected areas" to the individual's expectations of privacy. Whether the government's activity is considered a "search" depends upon whether the individual's reasonable expectations of privacy are disturbed. Davis v. U. S., 413 F.2d 1226, 1232 (5th Circuit Court of Appeals, 1969).

Although not all courts have taken the view that expectation of privacy is the primary factor to be considered in search and seizure cases, there appears to be a trend in that direction. The trend is particularly evident, for example, in cases in which the concepts of curtilage and open fields are difficult to apply. An example is a case in which law enforcement officers of the Forest Service were investigating the unauthorized cutting and removal of Christmas trees from Government lands. In connection with the investigation, the officers cut off the top portion of some stumps on the Government lands and attempted to match them with some trees stockpiled behind a motel. The stockpile was located about 20 to 35 feet from the motel and about 5 feet from a parking area used by personnel and patrons of the motel. The defendant operated and lived at the motel. The officers made several matches of stump cuts with trees, and the defendant was convicted of stealing the trees.

On appeal, the court held that the search and seizure was illegal because the officers had no warrant and the stockpile of trees was located within the curtilage of defendant's abode. The court applied the traditional tests for curtilage based upon proximity to the dwelling and inclusion within the general enclosure surrounding the dwelling.

The court went on, however, to further discuss the concepts of curtilage and privacy. Because the court's language indicates a growing trend in the law, it is quoted at length here:

> We wish to add, however, that it seems to us a more appropriate test in determining if a search and seizure adjacent to a house is constitutionally forbidden is whether it constitutes an intrusion upon what the resident seeks to preserve as private even in an area which, although adjacent to his home, is accessible to the public. * * *
>
> The "curtilage" test is predicated upon a common law concept which has no historical relevancy to the Fourth Amendment guaranty. In Jones v. U. S., 362 U.S. 257, 266, 80 S.Ct. 725, 733, 4 L.Ed.2d 697, the Supreme Court warned, in connection with another search and seizure problem that:
>
>> "[I]t is unnecessary and ill-advised to import into the law surrounding the constitutional right to be free from unreasonable searches and seizures subtle distinctions, developed and refined by the common law in evolving the body of private property law * * *."
>
> If the determination of such questions is made to turn upon the degree of privacy a resident is seeking to preserve as shown by the facts of the particular case, rather than upon a resort to the ancient concept of curtilage, attention will be more effectively focused on the basic interest which the Fourth Amendment

was designed to protect. As the Supreme Court recently said in Camara v. Municipal Court of City and County of San Francisco, 387 U.S. 523, 528, 87 S.Ct. 1727, 1730, 18 L.Ed.2d 930:

> "The basic purpose of this Amendment, as recognized in countless decisions of this Court, is to safeguard the privacy and security of individuals against arbitrary invasions by governmental officials."

Wattenburg v. U. S., 388 F.2d 853, 857–58 (9th Circuit Court of Appeals, 1968).

The court also found the search and seizure of the Christmas trees illegal under the "reasonable expectation of privacy" test.

The "reasonable expectation of privacy" test may be difficult for the law enforcement officer to apply, because it involves determining a person's state of mind. It is suggested that in order to determine whether a place may be legally searched without a warrant, the law enforcement officer apply the traditional tests for determining the extent of the curtilage discussed above. In addition, however, the officer should put himself in the position of a person owning property, and ask himself if he would reasonably expect to be free from governmental intrusion in the particular area of the property to be searched. If the officer has any doubt whether or not a person is seeking to preserve his privacy in the area to be searched, the officer should obtain a warrant.

Open Fields, Plain View, and Observations into Constitutionally Protected Areas

The open fields and plain view doctrines are often confused by law enforcement officers. The "plain view doctrine" states that if a law enforcement officer, as the result of a prior valid intrusion into a constitutionally protected area, is in a position in which he has a legal right to be, he may lawfully seize items of evidence lying in his plain view. (See Chapter 6.) The open fields doctrine differs from the plain view doctrine in that, under the open fields doctrine, a law enforcement officer does not have to concern himself with the validity of his prior intrusion into a constitutionally protected area. If the officer is outside the curtilage of a house, in the open fields, he is not in a constitutionally protected area. In the open fields, therefore, the officer may not only seize items which are open to his view, but he may search for items hidden from his view and seize them. Furthermore, the officer, from a vantage point in the open fields, may make observations into constitutionally protected areas to detect criminal activity or criminal evidence. Such observations may be used as a basis for probable cause to make an arrest or to obtain a search warrant. An example is a case in which law enforcement officers obtained a search warrant on the basis of observations of illicit whiskey containers from a vantage point in the open fields. The court in that case said:

> [I]t is of no significance that the object of the agents' observations was within the curtilage, so long as the observations were made from without the curtilage. The protection of the Fourth Amendment extends only to the curtilage, and observations made from without the curtilage thus do not violate the Amendment whether made from an open field belonging to the defendant or from the public street. U. S. v. Sims, 202 F.Supp. 65, 67 (U. S. District Court, Eastern District of Tennessee, 1962).

In this type of situation, however, the officer may *not enter* into the constitutionally protected area to make a warrantless seizure of the items he has observed, or to conduct a warrantless search for other items, unless the situation falls within the *Carroll* doctrine. (See Chapter 7 on Search and Seizure of Vehicles Without a Warrant.)

In recent cases involving observations into constitutionally protected areas, courts have begun emphasizing the reasonable expectation of privacy of the person whose premises or activities are being observed by law enforcement officers. An example is a case in which a narcotics officer was investigating a tip about heroin dealing. He went to the place where the dealing was said to be taking place. It was a single family dwelling, 70 feet from the sidewalk, with access from the west. There were no doorways or defined pathways on the east side of the house, and a strip of land covered with grass and dirt separated the east side of the house from the driveway of the apartment next door. The officer went to the east side of the house, peeked through a two-inch gap under the partially drawn shade of a closed window, and observed indications of criminal activity.

The court held that the officer's observations constituted an illegal search. The court initially analyzed the problem in terms of whether the officer was standing upon a part of the property surrounding the house that had been opened, expressly or impliedly, to public use. Under the facts, the officer was found to have made his observations from a position in which he had no right to be. Since neither a warrant nor one of the established exceptions to the warrant requirement justified the intrusion, it was unlawful.

The court went on, however, to discuss the officer's actions at length, in terms of the defendant's reasonable expectation of privacy:

> [T]he generic *Katz* rule permits the resident of a house to rely justifiably upon the privacy of the surrounding areas as a protection from the peering of the officer unless such residence is "exposed" to that intrusion by the existence of public pathways or other invitations to the public to enter upon the property. This justifiable reliance on the privacy of the property

surrounding one's residence thus leads to the *particular* rule that searches conducted without a warrant from such parts of the property *always* are unconstitutional unless an exception to the warrant requirement applies. * * *

Pursuant to the principles of *Katz,* therefore, we do not rest our analysis exclusively upon such abstractions as "trespass" or "constitutionally protected areas" or upon the physical differences between a telephone booth and the land surrounding a residence; we do, however, look to the conduct of people in regard to these elements. Taking into account the nature of the area surrounding a private residence, we ask whether that area has been opened to public use; if so, the occupant cannot claim he expected privacy from all observations of the officer who stands upon that ground; if not, the occupant does deserve that privacy. Since the eavesdropping officer in the case before us stood upon private property and since such property exhibited no invitation to public use, we find that the officer violated petitioner Lorenzana's expectations of privacy, and hence, his constitutional rights. Lorenzana v. Superior Court of Los Angeles County, 9 Cal.3d 626, 638, 108 Cal.Rptr. 585, 594, 511 P.2d 33, 42 (Supreme Court of California, 1973).

It is difficult to formulate rules to guide law enforcement officers in determining when they are violating a person's reasonable expectation of privacy. Common sense will often aid the officer in making that determination. Nevertheless, broad principles can be stated to help the officer balance the need to investigate crime with the need to respect the reasonable expectation of privacy of all persons.

In general, if an officer gathers information while situated in a public place or in a place where an ordinary citizen with legitimate business might be expected to be, the officer will not be invading anyone's reasonable expectation of privacy. Therefore, an officer's observations from an ordinary means of access to a dwelling, such as a front porch or side door, will not ordinarily violate a person's reasonable expectation of privacy. People v. Willard, 238 Cal.App.2d 292, 47 Cal.Rptr. 734 (California District Court of Appeal, First District, 1966).

Once an officer is in a place where he has a legitimate right to be, he may look around and peer through windows or other openings. The Supreme Court of California has stated:

"Peering through a window or a crack in the door or a keyhole is not, in the abstract, genteel behavior, but the Fourth Amendment does not protect against all conduct unworthy of a good neighbor. * * *

[I]t is the duty of a policeman to investigate, and *we cannot say that . . . the Fourth Amendment itself draws the blinds the*

> *occupant could have drawn and did not."* * * * People v. Berutko, 71 Cal.2d 84, 93, 77 Cal.Rptr. 217, 222, 453 P.2d 721, 726 (Supreme Court of California, 1969).

Also, so long as the officer is where he has a right to be, he may listen at doors or gather evidence with his other senses. In U. S. v. Perry, 339 F.Supp. 209 (U. S. District Court, Southern District of California, 1972), the court said:

> The general rule is that information obtained by an officer using his natural senses, where the officer has a right to be where he is, is admissible evidence. The fact that the information is in the form of conversations emanating from a private space, such as a hotel room, is not a bar to its admissibility. 339 F.Supp. at 213.

A great number of cases illustrating these basic principles have been decided throughout the country. It would serve no purpose to present further examples of these cases, because courts in every jurisdiction differ in their interpretations of the meaning of "reasonable expectation of privacy." Officers investigating crime should become very sensitive to the reasonable expectations of privacy of all persons. When in doubt about the legality of any kind of intrusion, officers should obtain a search warrant.

Open Fields—Summary

A law enforcement officer may search for and seize items of evidence lying in the open fields without probable cause, search warrant, or other legal justification, and not violate a person's Fourth Amendment rights. An officer may also legally make observations into constitutionally protected areas in order to detect criminal activity or evidence, from a vantage point in the open fields. The open fields are the portions of a person's premises lying outside the curtilage of his home or business. Whether or not a piece of land or building falls within the curtilage can be determined by consideration of the following factors:

1. Inclusion within the residential yard;
2. Enclosure by a fence;
3. Use in connection with the dwelling for family purposes;
4. Distance or remoteness from main dwelling; and
5. Use or invitation to use by the public.

Since the 1967 U. S. Supreme Court decision in Katz v. U. S., which held that "the Fourth Amendment protects people, not places," courts have increasingly analyzed the legality of warrantless searches in terms of the defendant's reasonable expectation of privacy, in addition to the concepts of curtilage and open fields. Law enforcement officers, therefore, must be careful to avoid warrantless intrusions not only into the curtilage of a person's house, but also into any area which the person reasonably seeks to preserve as private.

ABANDONED PROPERTY

As stated earlier, the meaning of the term abandoned property depends upon the interpretation given to the word "searches" in the Fourth Amendment. Courts have held that no search occurs when a law enforcement officer observes property voluntarily discarded by a person. And it is not an illegal seizure to pick up such property and use it as evidence against the person in court. The Fourth Amendment's protection does not extend to such property because when one abandons property, he brings his right to privacy in it to an end. A person cannot complain about the seizure of property no longer in his possession and its use as evidence in court.

Abandoned property is treated by the courts similarly to seizable property found lying in plain view. Since no search under the Fourth Amendment is involved, officers may lawfully seize such property without a warrant or probable cause. The main difference between the abandonment doctrine and the plain view doctrine centers around the nature of the place from which the officer seizes an object. Under the plain view doctrine, if a law enforcement officer, as the result of a prior *valid* intrusion into a constitutionally protected area, is in a position in which he has a legal right to be, he may lawfully seize items of evidence lying open to view. The plain view doctrine is only applicable *after* the law enforcement officer has lawfully entered into a *constitutionally protected area.* If a law enforcement officer, acting lawfully, seizes objects that have been discarded on the street, in a public park, or in some other place *not* protected by the Fourth Amendment to the Constitution, the seizure is legal under the abandonment doctrine. The abandonment doctrine, unlike the plain view doctrine, involves *no intrusion into a constitutionally protected area.* It is important for the law enforcement officer to learn this distinction, because in order to lawfully seize items that have been discarded within a constitutionally protected area, the officer must be lawfully present in the constitutionally protected area. Otherwise, the plain view doctrine is not satisfied, and any item of evidence seized will be inadmissible in court.

When a law enforcement officer attempts to justify a seizure of property on the ground that it was abandoned, he must be prepared to prove it. Abandonment is never presumed by the courts but must be established by the prosecution. It is very important, therefore, for law enforcement officers to take careful notes on all the circumstances surrounding the seizure of property on the basis of abandonment. The officer may have to justify the seizure later at a trial or hearing.

In order to properly testify, the officer needs to know what factors the courts consider important in determining whether property has been abandoned. The remainder of this chapter will be devoted to a discussion of specific facts and circumstances bearing upon the issue of abandonment, as illustrated by decisions of courts throughout the country.

Factors Determining Abandonment

The factors which the courts consider in determining whether property has been abandoned can be classified into four broad categories:

1. Nature of the place where the property was left;
2. Indications of intent to abandon property;
3. Lawfulness of police behavior; and
4. Reasonable expectation of privacy in the property.

Most cases dealing with the issue of abandonment will involve circumstances falling into more than one of the four categories. For example, the nature of the place where an object is left is usually a strong indication of a person's intent to abandon the property and also of his expectation of privacy in it. Nevertheless, there are usually one or two circumstances in each case which provide the primary basis for a court's decision on the issue of abandonment. These are the circumstances which will be emphasized in the cases discussed under each category.

Nature of Place Where Property Left

The nature of the place where property is left is an important determinant of whether the property has been abandoned or not. In the case of Hester v. U. S., summarized above, the U. S. Supreme Court held that it was proper for law enforcement officers to retrieve property discarded by the defendant in an open field. The Court said that the protection of the Fourth Amendment did not extend to the open fields. Although it is not clear whether the primary basis for the Court's decision in *Hester* was abandonment or the "open fields" doctrine, it is clear that the place of discard had a bearing on the Court's determination of abandonment. The Court specifically noted that the evidence was not obtained by entry into the house.

It follows logically that if an object discarded in the open fields of a person's private property is considered abandoned, an object discarded in a public place will also be considered abandoned. An example is a case in which law enforcement officers had defendant under surveillance for violation of federal narcotic laws. As the defendant disembarked from an airplane at a public airport, he apparently recognized one of the officers, and he discarded contraband narcotics. The officers retrieved the narcotics and immediately arrested the defendant. The court held that the discarded narcotics were admissible in court. There had been no illegal search because the narcotics were abandoned. Vincent v. U. S., 337 F.2d 891 (8th Circuit Court of Appeals, 1964).

In another case, the defendant threw a package of heroin into the courtyard of a six-story apartment building. The defendant's only rights in the courtyard were to use it in common with other tenants and with members of the public who had business there. The court held that the warrantless seizure of the abandoned package from the courtyard was legal. U. S. v. Lewis, 227 F.Supp. 433 (U. S. District Court, Southern District of New York, 1964).

When, however, an object is discarded in response to illegal police activity, and falls within the curtilage of a person's home or business, a warrantless seizure of the object will be illegal. In an illustrative case, officers went to a woman's residence to arrest her without a warrant for a narcotics violation. Her husband, the defendant, came to the door but retreated without opening it. Defendant's wife then came to the door, clad only in a slip, and asked the officer to wait until she dressed. Meanwhile, the defendant ran upstairs and threw a package out of the window into an enclosed backyard. The officers then broke into the house, allegedly to arrest the defendant's wife, and without knowing the contents of the thrown package. The package was seized by another officer stationed outside and was found to contain heroin. The court held that the seizure of the package was illegal, stating that the enclosed backyard in which the thrown package landed was part of the curtilage of the defendant's home and was entitled to the same protection as the home itself. It should be noted that a major reason for the court's holding the seizure illegal was the court's finding that the officers entered the residence illegally. If the police had entered legally, the seizure of the package would probably have been upheld under the plain view doctrine. Hobson v. U. S., 226 F.2d 890 (8th Circuit Court of Appeals, 1955).

It therefore appears that if an object is voluntarily discarded outside the curtilage of a house, it will be considered abandoned; if discarded inside the curtilage, the legality of its seizure will be governed by the plain view doctrine.

Under certain circumstances, however, a law enforcement officer may search for and seize objects inside a house, without a warrant or probable cause and without satisfying any of the exceptions to the warrant requirement. When a person has abandoned or vacated premises, it is not unlawful for officers to search for and seize items of evidence or any other items left on the premises. The leading case on this point is the U. S. Supreme Court case of Abel v. U. S., 362 U. S. 217, 80 S.Ct. 683, 4 L.Ed.2d 668 (1960). In the *Abel* case, officers of the Immigration and Naturalization Service arrested defendant in his hotel room, under an administrative arrest warrant, and charged him with being illegally in this country. Before he was escorted out of his room, defendant was permitted to pack his personal belongings. He packed nearly everything in the room except for a few things which he left on a window sill and put in a wastebasket. He then checked out of the hotel, turned in his keys, and paid his bill. Shortly thereafter, an F.B.I. agent, with the permission of the hotel management, searched the defendant's room without a warrant. In the wastebasket, the F.B.I. agent found a hollow pencil containing microfilm and a block of wood containing a "cipher pad."

The Court held that the search for and seizure of the pencil and block of wood was legal:

> These two items were found by an agent of the F.B.I. in the course of a search he undertook of petitioner's hotel room, immediately after petitioner had paid his bill and vacated the room. They were found in the room's wastepaper basket, where petitioner had put them while packing his belongings and preparing to leave. No pretense is made that this search by the F.B.I. was for any purpose other than to gather evidence of crime, that is, evidence of petitioner's espionage. As such, however, it was entirely lawful, although undertaken without a warrant. This is so for the reason that at the time of the search petitioner had vacated the room. The hotel then had the exclusive right to its possession, and the hotel management freely gave its consent that the search be made. Nor was it unlawful to seize the entire contents of the wastepaper basket, even though some of its contents had no connection with crime. So far as the record shows, petitioner had abandoned these articles. He had thrown them away. So far as he was concerned, they were bona vacantia. There can be nothing unlawful in the Government's appropriation of such abandoned property * * * The two items which were eventually introduced in evidence were assertedly means for the commission of espionage, and were themselves seizable as such. These two items having been lawfully seized by the Government in connection with an investigation of crime, we encounter no basis for discussing further their admissibility as evidence. 362 U.S. at 241, 80 S.Ct. at 698, 4 L.Ed. at 687–88.

It is important to note that if the defendant in the *Abel* case had not vacated his room, the hotel management could not have given consent to search the room. (See Chapter 5 on Consent Searches.) The key question, then, for the law enforcement officer who wants to search a house without a warrant, probable cause, or other justification, is whether the person residing there intended to abandon it. Various indications of intent to abandon, relied upon by the courts, are discussed in the next section.

Indications of Intent to Abandon Property

One of the main circumstances relied upon by courts in determining whether property has been abandoned is the *intent* of the person vacating or discarding property to relinquish all title, possession, or claim to it. Sometimes intent to abandon is fairly easy to establish, as when a person voluntarily throws an object away, without any inducement by the police. There are many situations, however, in which a person's intent to abandon property is not so easily established. In these situations, the law enforcement officer must carefully note all indications of intent to abandon in case the search or seizure is later challenged at a trial or hearing. The following discussion will highlight the various indications of intent relied upon by the courts in determining abandonment. The discussion will be divided into three parts—premises, objects, and motor vehicles—because intent to abandon is determined in different ways for each kind of property.

Premises

In the case of Abel v. U. S., summarized above, the Court found that a hotel room had been abandoned when the person moved his personal belongings out of the room, paid his bill, checked out, and turned in his key. In another case involving a hotel room, a court found that the defendant had abandoned a room which he had rented on March 23, when he failed to pay his bill on March 28, and did not return to or communicate with the hotel prior to his arrest on April 8. At the time he rented the room, the defendant said he intended to stay only one night. A search of the defendant's baggage left in the room was therefore held not to violate his property rights. U. S. v. Cowan, 396 F.2d 83 (2nd Circuit Court of Appeals, 1968).

In a case involving abandonment of an *apartment*, law enforcement officers were allowed to search defendant's apartment without a warrant, even though the defendant had three days to go on his lease period. The court said:

> What were the circumstances showing abandonment? Baggett quit his job, received pay for one day's work, told several people

> that he was going to New Orleans to get a job, paid all bills that he owed except one, told his friends in Little Rock good-bye on the 11th, turned the apartment keys over to the owner, and took all personal belongings to New Orleans with him. Of course, had he returned within the two days before his rent came due, he could not have gone into his apartment for Ballard [the landlord] had the keys. The fact that the rent was paid up for three days after Baggett left does not mean that the apartment had not been abandoned. Baggett v. State, 254 Ark. 553, 554, 494 S.W.2d 717, 719 (Supreme Court of Arkansas, 1973).

The following quote from a case involving a warrantless search of a house illustrates other indications of intent to abandon:

> [I]t was clearly established that even though the Mannings had rented the * * * house for thirty days, they departed after the first day leaving no personal belongings. The door was unlocked, food was on the table, and dishwater was in the sink. Thirty days later the same condition prevailed. Moreover, the decayed food created a stench, the grass was uncut, and the weeds had grown high.
>
> These circumstances strongly indicate that the Mannings had abandoned the house * * *. U. S. v. Manning, 440 F.2d 1105, 1111 (5th Circuit Court of Appeals, 1971).

We have seen that the non-public areas of a business office come within the Fourth Amendment's protection against unreasonable searches and seizures. If the office is abandoned by its occupant, however, it no longer has this protection. The indications of intent to abandon an office are similar to those for a room or house. An example is a case in which U. S. postal inspectors, without a warrant, searched for and seized business records from an office which had previously been rented by the defendant. The defendant claimed that the search and seizure was illegal, because he did not intend to abandon the office and the records kept there. The court found that the facts indicated an intent to abandon. The search and seizure were made on June 12, 1972. Defendant had rented the office from May 1, 1971 through October 31, 1971, but had left the state in August 1971. No rent had been paid for the office beginning November 1, 1971, nor did defendant, his wife, or any business associate or employee visit the office after November 1, 1971. Finally, the office had been padlocked by the U. S. District Attorney during February 1972. Mullins v. U. S., 487 F.2d 581 (8th Circuit Court of Appeals, 1973).

It should be noted that the mere absence of a person from premises does not make the premises abandoned, unless the person had an *intent* to abandon the premises. Therefore, in a case where the defendant's absence from his apartment was involuntary because of his arrest and incarceration, the court held that the prosecution should bear an especially heavy burden of showing that he intended to abandon it. The prosecution did not satisfy this burden by merely showing defendant's absence without showing any other indications of intent to abandon. U. S. v. Robinson, 430 F.2d 1141 (6th Circuit Court of Appeals, 1970).

Objects

Some of the indications of intent to abandon premises are also applicable to objects. Objects, however, can be moved from place to place, and many can be carried on the person. Therefore, courts consider different factors in determining intent to abandon objects.

A strong indication of a person's intent to abandon property is leaving the property unattended and unclaimed for a long period of time. An example is a case in which two men left a U-Haul trailer at a service station, asking permission to leave it there for two or three days. The men stated that "everything we own is in the trailer." Ten days later, the men not having returned, the service station attendant called law enforcement authorities. The trailer was searched without a warrant and stolen whiskey was found. The court held that the search was legal because the property had been abandoned. U. S. v. Gulledge, 469 F.2d 713 (5th Circuit Court of Appeals, 1972).

In other cases involving warrantless searches and seizures of objects, the object is often picked up by a law enforcement officer immediately after it is dropped, thrown away, or otherwise discarded by a person. In these cases, courts cannot rely on the length of time the object has been left alone to determine whether it has been abandoned. Courts must look to other circumstances such as the conduct of the defendant and the manner of disposal of the object. In an illustrative case, a police officer approached the defendant without probable cause to make an arrest, and the defendant dropped a tin box to the ground. The officer immediately picked up the box, opened it and found heroin. The court held that the evidence was insufficient to constitute an abandonment:

> There is no proof that the defendant threw it away or attempted to dispose of it in any manner which might have manifested the requisite intention to abandon. Moreover, the police officer's testimony reveals that he picked up the box so soon after it had been dropped that it is impossible to determine whether or not the defendant, if given the opportunity, would have picked up the box himself. Absent any such proof, the seizure of the tin box under the circumstances of this case cannot be sustained. People v. Anderson, 24 N.Y.2d 12, 14, 298 N.Y.S.2d 698, 699, 246 N.E.2d 508, 509 (Court of Appeals of New York, 1969).

However, when the manner of disposal indicates that the defendant intended to permanently relinquish possession of the property because of consciousness of guilt or fear of potential apprehension, the courts usually find abandonment. One example is a case in which officers were lawfully at the residence of one Hammond, waiting to arrest her under a warrant. The defendant came to the residence at the invitation of Hammond's husband. When the defendant recognized one of the officers he began to run toward the front of the house, discarding several packets into a pantry. The packets were seized and were found to contain narcotics. The court held that the defendant's voluntary act of throwing the packets into the pantry was an abandonment of the packets. U. S. v. Martin, 386 F.2d 213 (3rd Circuit Court of Appeals, 1967). (Although the court spoke in terms of abandonment in this case, the seizure of the packets could also have been justified under the plain view doctrine.)

Another example of disposal of objects out of consciousness of guilt or fear of apprehension is a case in which defendant threw packages out of an automobile he was driving when he noticed he was being pursued by a car with flashing lights and a siren. Law enforcement officers were lawfully chasing defendant's auto because they had seen it pick up a man whom the officers had probable cause to arrest. The packages were recovered and were found to be stolen goods. The court found the seizure legal and allowed the introduction of the packages in evidence against the defendant. Stack v. U. S., 368 F.2d 788 (1st Circuit Court of Appeals, 1966). It should be carefully noted that there was no illegal activity on the part of law enforcement officers in either of the above cases.

When there is evidence that an object was intentionally concealed, courts will usually find there was no intent to abandon the object and therefore no abandonment. In an illustrative case, officers seized a bottle in a barrel located in a garage under the main house where the owner dwelt. The prosecution claimed the bottle had been abandoned. The court disagreed saying that "[t]he position of the bottle well down in the barrel and covered with trash and paper strongly suggests that it was intentionally hidden and concealed there." State v. Chapman, Me., 250 A.2d 203, 212 (Supreme Judicial Court of Maine, 1969).

Sometimes courts find an intent to abandon property when the defendant fails to object or take any other affirmative action, but merely allows evidence to be seized in the ordinary course of events. Defendant was in jail, having been arrested for bank robbery. He was given a haricut pursuant to routine jail procedures, and the hair clippings were turned over to the F.B.I., at their request, and used as evidence. In response to defendant's claim of an illegal search and seizure, the court said:

> At no time has defendant objected to the legality of the prison procedures under which he received his haircut. He has never claimed that the haircut was illegally or improperly given. The thrust of his contention is rather that a warrant should have been obtained before the shorn locks were appropriated by the state officer for analysis. Cox, however, never indicated any desire or intention to retain possession of the hair after it had been scissored from his head. Clippings such as those preserved in the instant case are ordinarily abandoned after being cut. Cox in fact left his hair and has never claimed otherwise. The deputy sheriff was not obliged to inform him that, if abandoned, his hair would be taken and analyzed. Having voluntarily abandoned his property, in this case his hair, Cox may not object to its appropriation by the government. * * * U. S. v. Cox, 428 F.2d 683, 687–88 (Seventh Circuit Court of Appeals, 1970).

Before seizing a discarded object without a warrant then, law enforcement officers should attempt to determine whether the discarding person intended to abandon the property. Courts usually find an intent to abandon when an object as been left unattended and unclaimed for an unreasonable length of time, or when the object was discarded out of consciousness of guilt or fear of apprehension. However, when the facts indicate that the person accidentally dropped or intentionally concealed an object, courts will usually not find an intent to abandon. No particular affirmative action by a person is required to indicate an intent to abandon, and such an intent may be found when a person merely fails to object to the seizure of his property in the ordinary course of events.

Motor Vehicles

Motor vehicles are unique for purposes of abandonment in that they are treated both as premises and as objects. In a case in which the defendant, who was tampering with a cigarette machine, left his car in the street and fled on foot to avoid apprehension by an officer, the court said:

> Sometimes an automobile takes on the characteristics of a man's castle. Other times an automobile takes on the characteristic of an overcoat—that is, it is movable and can be discarded by the possessor at will. If appellant in his endeavors to avoid the clutches of the law had discarded his overcoat to make his flight more speedy, no one would think that an officer was unreasonably invading his privacy or security in picking up the overcoat and searching it thoroughly. In that situation most people would agree that the fleeing suspect had abandoned his coat as a matter of ex-

> pediency as well as any rights relative to its search and seizure. What difference can there be when a fleeing burglar abandons his automobile to escape the clutches of the law? We can see no distinction and consequently hold that when property is abandoned officers in making a search thereof do not violate any rights or security of a citizen guaranteed under the Fourth Amendment. Thom v. State, 248 Ark. 180, 182, 450 S.W.2d 550, 552 (Supreme Court of Arkansas, 1970).

It follows, then, that in order to determine whether an automobile is abandoned, law enforcement officers should apply the same considerations as those discussed above under *Premises* and *Objects.* It should be noted, however, that if an officer has probable cause to search a vehicle and the vehicle is movable or there are other exigent circumstances, he may conduct a warrantless search of it under the *Carroll* doctrine, whether or not it is abandoned. (See Chapter 7 on Search and Seizure of Vehicles Without a Warrant.)

Lawfulness of Police Behavior

In many of the cases discussed above, property was left or discarded in response to either the presence or the activities of law enforcement officers. In determining whether such property is abandoned, courts examine very closely the lawfulness of the law enforcement officer's role in each incident. It can be safely stated that if a person discards evidence as a direct result of the unlawful presence or activity of a law enforcement officer, the courts will not consider his act a voluntary abandonment, but rather a forced response to the unlawful police behavior.

There are numerous examples of cases in which a person discarded an object in response to the lawful activities of the police, and courts have considered the object abandoned, and therefore seizable without a warrant or other justification. Examples include the following situations:

1. Officers arrested defendant on authority of a warrant and, while escorting him to the police car, defendant threw away a marijuana cigarette. Oliver v. State, 85 Nev. 10, 449 P.2d 252 (Supreme Court of Nevada, 1969).
2. An officer with probable cause to arrest defendant was pursuing defendant's car and contraband was thrown from the car. Capitoli v. Wainwright, 426 F.2d 868 (5th Circuit Court of Appeals, 1970).
3. Officers were lawfully approaching defendant for questioning, and defendant dropped a bundle of marijuana cigarettes. People v. Blackmon, 276 Cal.App.2d 346, 80 Cal.Rptr. 862 (Court of Appeal of California, 1969).

4. Officers, attempting to execute a valid search warrant, temporarily detained defendant at the scene of the search, and defendant discarded a package containing incriminating evidence. State v. Romeo, 45 N.J. 188, 203 A.2d 23 (Supreme Court of New Jersey, 1964).

Examples should also be given of cases in which unlawful police activity caused the court to rule that a discarded object was not voluntarily abandoned. In a case involving an arrest and search, a law enforcement officer received an anonymous phone call informing him that defendant could be apprehended at a given place and time with narcotics in his possession. Officers went to the designated place and observed the defendant in his car. The officers told him he was under arrest and to get out of his car and place his hands on top of it. As defendant did this, he flipped into the street a plastic vial containing narcotics, which the officers retrieved.

The court held that the arrest was unlawful for lack of probable cause. The court also refused to find that the plastic vial was abandoned, because it was thrown away as a result of a *threat* of an illegal search:

> Had the appellant here thrown the item away before the search had been threatened the argument of abandonment might well be persuasive. Here however he threw the vial away only after being told to turn and place his hands atop his vehicle, the position commonly known to be employed by police in searching a suspect for weapons. The vial, as evidenced by the record, was not seen by the officers until it was thrown by appellant. Had it been seen before the threat of an illegal search had been made, even in appellant's hand, the plain view doctrine *may* have applied. But that is not this case. The vial was seen and secured only as a result of the threat of a search, an illegal search. Clearly it was the fruit of illegal activity by the police and ought to have been excluded. Bowles v. State, 256 Ind. 27, 31–32, 267 N.E.2d 56, 59 (Supreme Court of Indiana, 1971).

In another case, an officer was investigating a window smashing incident at a hotel. He spotted at another hotel, a car believed to have been involved in the incident, and he went to the room occupied by its owner, in order to interview the owner. The officer had neither a warrant nor probable cause to arrest, and he did not intend to make an arrest. After knocking twice and receiving no response, the officer kicked in the door only to find that the defendants had escaped through a window. They were apprehended shortly. Stolen jewelry was found beneath the window where it had been thrown when the officer began kicking down the door.

The court held that there was no voluntary abandonment of the jewelry:

> [S]ince the initial entry was improper and the items were thrown out of the window as a direct result of that illegality, the police were not entitled to the fruits and the admission of the jewelry in evidence was reversible error. * * * Fletcher v. Wainwright, 399 F.2d 62, 64–65 (5th Circuit Court of Appeals, 1968).

In a third case involving illegal police activity, the defendant was walking down the street when he observed police officers in an unmarked car. Defendant quickened his pace, and one of the officers got out of the car and began to pursue him. Defendant then began to run, and the officer while giving chase, observed defendant throw a cigarette pack under a parked automobile. Defendant was apprehended, and the cigarette pack was recovered and found to contain heroin.

The court held that the officers had no jurisdiction to arrest the defendant or to seize him under the *Terry* rule (discussed in Chapter 10). The only conduct of the defendant observed by the police was his quickening pace when he observed the officers. This alone could not provide probable cause to arrest nor would it justify a stop of the defendant, because it was not sufficient to give rise to a reasonable belief that criminal activity was afoot. Since the discarding of the cigarette pack was a direct result of the unlawful and coercive action of the police in chasing the defendant, the court held there was no voluntary abandonment. Commonwealth v. Jeffries, 454 Pa. 320, 311 A.2d 914 (Supreme Court of Pennsylvania, 1973).

Reasonable Expectation of Privacy

As we have seen in the discussion of the open fields doctrine, since the U.S. Supreme Court decision in Katz v. U. S., the courts increasingly have analyzed the legality of warrantless searches and seizures in terms of whether they are intrusions upon the defendant's reasonable expectation of privacy. This trend has extended also to cases involving vacated or discarded property. The Minnesota Supreme Court explained the new trend:

> In the law of property, the question * * * is whether the owner has voluntarily, intentionally, and unconditionally relinquished his interest in the property so that another, having acquired possession, may successfully assert his superior interest. In the law of search and seizure, however, the question is whether the defendant has, in discarding the property, relinquished his reasonable expectation of privacy so that its seizure and search is reasonable within the limits of the Fourth Amendment. In essence, what is abandoned is not necessarily the defendant's prop-

erty, but his reasonable expectation of privacy therein. City of St. Paul v. Vaughn, 306 Minn. 337, 346, 237 N.W.2d 365, 370–71 (Minnesota Supreme Court, 1975).

In a case involving supposedly vacated premises, law enforcement officers were investigating a possible arson in a building gutted by fire. The fire occurred on April 14, 1968, and the officers entered the building, made observations, and took photographs on April 24, 1968. Evidence showed that the house was boarded up on April 14. Thereafter the owner went to the house every day, and both she and the defendant kept some of their personal effects in the house. The defendant claimed that the observations and photographs of the officers were a product of an illegal search and seizure.

The court said:

> The uncontradicted evidence before the court was that the building was not abandoned. On April 24, 1968, it still contained personal effects and had been boarded up to keep the public out.
>
> The test to be used in determining whether a place is a constitutionally protected area within the meaning of the Fourth Amendment is * * * "whether the person has exhibited a reasonable expectation of privacy, and, if so, whether that expectation has been violated by unreasonable governmental intrusion." In the instant matter the owner of the dwelling house clearly demonstrated her expectation of privacy as to the interior of the house and its contents by boarding up the doorways, which were damaged by fire. That expectation was violated by the intrusion of the police on April 24, 1968. Swan v. Superior Court, County of Los Angeles, 8 Cal.App.3d 392, 396, 87 Cal.Rptr. 280, 282 (California Court of Appeal, 1970).

The question of the extent of a person's reasonable expectation of privacy in discarded *objects* has recently been the subject of differing opinions by the courts. The controversy has centered around the search and seizure of trash or garbage by law enforcement officers. In one of the leading cases in this area, law enforcement officers, acting without a warrant, found marijuana in a trash can in the open back yard area of defendant's residence. The court held that the marijuana in the trash can was not abandoned for the following reasons:

> As we have seen, the trash can was within a few feet of the back door of defendants' home and required trespass for its inspection. It was an adjunct to the domestic economy. * * * Placing the marijuana in the trash can, so situated and used, was not an abandonment unless as to persons authorized to remove the receptacle's contents, such as trashmen. * * * The marijuana itself was not visible without "rummaging" in the receptacle. So far as appears defendants alone resided at the house. In the light of the

> combined facts and circumstances it appears that defendants exhibited an expectation of privacy, and we believe that expectation was reasonable under the circumstances of the case. We can readily ascribe many reasons why residents would not want their castaway clothing, letters, medicine bottles or other telltale refuse and trash to be examined by neighbors or others, at least not until the trash has lost its identity and meaning by becoming part of a large conglomeration of trash elsewhere. Half truths leading to rumor and gossip may readily flow from an attempt to "read" the contents of another's trash. People v. Edwards, 71 Cal.2d 1096, 1104, 80 Cal.Rptr. 633, 638, 458 P.2d 713, 718 (Supreme Court of California, 1969).

Other courts have generally agreed with the holding in the *Edwards* case, and found a violation of the defendant's reasonable expectation of privacy where the trash can was located within the curtilage of defendant's house. Ball v. State, 57 Wis. 653, 205 N.W.2d 353 (Supreme Court of Wisconsin, 1973).

Where the trash can is placed adjacent to the street for collection, however, courts have differed greatly as to whether a person has a reasonable expectation of privacy in the trash. One court, relying on the *Edwards* case, has said that placement of trash on the sidewalk for collection is not necessarily an abandonment of it to the police or the general public. Among the court's reasons for not considering the contraband found in the barrels abandoned was that the contraband was concealed in paper sacks within the barrels and it was not visible without emptying or searching through the barrels. Also, the court said that many municipal ordinances prohibit unauthorized persons from tampering with trash containers, refuting the view that the contents of one's trash barrels become public property when placed on the sidewalk for collection. People v. Krivda, 5 Cal.3d 357, 96 Cal.Rptr. 62, 486 P.2d 1262 (Supreme Court of California, 1971).

Another court has taken the opposite view, and in a similar fact situation, held that the defendant abandoned the property. "The town ordinance simply cannot change the fact that he 'threw [these articles] away' and thus there 'can be nothing unlawful in the Government's appropriation of such abandoned property.' " U. S. v. Dzialak, 441 F.2d 212, 215 (2d Circuit Court of Appeals, 1971).

It is difficult to set forth any definite guidelines for the law enforcement officer with regard to the determination of when a person has a reasonable expectation of privacy in discarded or vacated property. Suffice it to say that before an officer conducts a warrantless search and seizure of such property, he should look for any indications that a person expects privacy in the property, and determine as best he can whether that expectation is reasonable. It is strongly recommended that officers get a search warrant before searching for and seizing objects in trash cans which are located within the curtilage of a house. The same advice applies to trash cans located outside the curtilage or which have been set out for collection, unless there is an emergency, or there are clear indications that the trash has been completely abandoned.

Abandoned Property—Summary

A law enforcement officer, without probable cause, warrant, or other legal justification may retrieve items of evidence which have been abandoned by their owners, without violating Fourth Amendment rights. Property has been abandoned when the owner has voluntarily relinquished all title, possession, or claim to it. Among the factors which the courts rely on in determining whether a given object has been abandoned by its owner are the following:

1. Place where property was left—As a general rule, if an object is voluntarily discarded inside the curtilage, it will not be considered abandoned; if discarded outside the curtilage, it will be considered abandoned. Objects left on premises, however, may be considered abandoned, if the premises themselves have been voluntarily vacated or abandoned.
2. Indications of intent to abandon—Indications of intent to abandon *premises* can be divided into positive acts and omissions. Positive indications of intent to abandon include removing personal belongings, paying final rent and other bills, turning in keys, quitting local employment, and taking leave of friends. Omissions indicating intent to abandon include failing to pay rent for a long time, long absence from premises, failure to communicate with anyone regarding premises, and failure to attend to or care for premises. Intent to abandon an *object* is indicated by leaving the object unattended for an unreasonable period of time, discarding the object out of consciousness of guilt or fear of apprehension, and allowing the object to be taken away in the ordinary course of events, without objection. Intentional concealment of an object is not considered an indication of intent to abandon. Intent to abandon *vehicles* is determined by the same considerations as those for premises and objects.
3. Lawfulness of police behavior—Objects discarded as a direct result of the unlawful presence or activity of a law enforcement officer will not be considered voluntarily abandoned.
4. Reasonable expectation of privacy in the property—Even though property has been vacated or thrown away, under

> certain circumstances, a person may reasonably retain an expectation of privacy with respect to the property. Such property is not considered abandoned and a search and seizure of it, without a warrant or probable cause, will be illegal.

Determining whether property is abandoned is similar to determining whether it is in the open fields, in that both require a consideration not only of a person's property rights, but also of his rights of privacy. Such determinations will always be difficult for the courts as well as for law enforcement officers. It is recommended that in the absence of an emergency, officers obtain a search warrant whenever possible.

PART THREE

ADMISSIONS AND CONFESSIONS, STOP AND FRISK, AND PRE-TRIAL IDENTIFICATION PROCEDURES

9

ADMISSIONS AND CONFESSIONS

Since the U.S. Supreme Court decision in the case of Miranda v. Arizona, 384 U.S. 436, 86 S.Ct. 1602, 16 L.Ed.2d 694, in June of 1966, the name *Miranda* has become very familiar to law enforcement personnel throughout the United States. The *Miranda* decision radically changed the course of law enforcement in the area of admissions, confessions, and interrogations, and in the process created a great deal of turmoil. The rash of lower court decisions interpreting various aspects of the *Miranda* decision indicates the degree of confusion and misunderstanding that followed in its wake.

Although many of the questions arising from the *Miranda* decision have now been resolved by the courts, there is still a great deal of misunderstanding concerning the practical applications of *Miranda*. This chapter will discuss the *Miranda* case, its background, its meaning, and its implications for law enforcement officers. A large number of court decisions will be cited, and it is strongly suggested that the law enforcement officer read the *Miranda* decision as well as several of the lower court decisions in order to fully appreciate the way in which the courts handle problems in this area of the law.

HISTORICAL BACKGROUND

Prior to 1964, the principal test for the admissibility of a defendant's admission or confession in court was its "voluntariness". That is, the confession had to have been given voluntarily and not as a result of threats, promises, force or any form of pressure, physical or psychological. Courts determined voluntariness by looking to the "totality of the circumstances" surrounding the confession in each case. Under this test, significant factors to be considered were actions of the interrogators (e. g. promises, threats, brutality), omissions of the interrogators (e. g. failure to bring before a magistrate, failure to warn of the right to remain silent), and inherent weaknesses of the accused himself (e. g. education, mental capacity). Payne v. Arkansas, 356 U.S. 560, 78 S.Ct. 844, 2 L.Ed.2d 975 (U.S. Supreme Court, 1958); Fikes v. Alabama, 352 U.S. 191, 77 S.Ct. 281, 1 L.Ed. 2d 246 (U.S. Supreme Court, 1957).

In June, 1964, a major change in the law took place. In the case of Escobedo v. Illinois, 378 U.S. 478, 84 S.Ct. 1758, 12 L.Ed.2d 977 (1964), the U.S. Supreme Court held that

> where * * * the investigation is no longer a general inquiry into an unsolved crime but has begun to focus on a particular suspect, the suspect has been taken into police custody, the police carry out a process of interrogations that lends itself to eliciting incriminating statements, the suspect has requested and been denied an opportunity to consult with his lawyer, and the police have not effectively warned him of his absolute constitutional right to remain silent, the accused has been denied "the Assistance of Counsel" in violation of the Sixth Amendment to the Constitution as "made obligatory upon the States by the Fourteenth Amendment," * * * and that no statement elicited by the police during the interrogation may be used against him at a criminal trial. 378 U.S. at 491, 84 S.Ct. at 1765, 12 L.Ed.2d at 986.

Escobedo was significant because it did not follow a "totality of the circumstances" approach. Instead, the Court took a circumstance it had previously regarded as one factor among many and made it the single determinative factor in all cases in which it occurs. The Court said:

> [W]hen the process shifts from investigatory to accusatory—when its focus is on the accused and its purpose is to elicit a confession * * * the accused must be permitted to consult with his lawyer. 378 U.S. at 492, 84 S.Ct. at 1766, 12 L.Ed.2d at 987.

This has come to be known as the *Escobedo* "focus of investigation" test.

Miranda v. Arizona decided two years later in June of 1966, again rejected the "totality of the circumstances" approach and extended the *Escobedo* decision. In short, the *Miranda* Court required that under certain specific conditions certain specified procedures must be followed, or any statements by a defendant will be inadmissible in court even if the statements were voluntary. Of course, if an admission or confession is involuntary for whatever reason, it will be inadmissible in court despite compliance with the *Miranda* requirements. Courts will carefully evaluate all the circumstances of an interrogation in determining voluntariness. Thus, even though *Miranda* requirements are met, a statement obtained through force, threat, promises, or any other form of coercion will be involuntary and therefore inadmissible.

Another indication of involuntariness is a delay between the arrest of a defendant and his appearance before the magistrate, during which time an admission or confession is obtained. People v. Carbonaro, 21 N.Y.2d 271, 287 N.Y.S. 385, 234 N.E.2d 433 (Court of Appeals of New York, 1967). If such an illegal detention is flagrant and purposely designed to elicit an admission or confession the statement will be inadmissible in court in some states. Williams v. State, 264 Ind. 664, 348 N.E.2d 623 (Indiana Supreme Court, 1976). Federal courts are governed by the cases of McNabb v. U. S., 318 U.S. 332, 63 S.Ct. 608, 87 L.Ed. 819 (U.S. Supreme Court, 1943), and Mallory v. U. S., 354 U.S. 449, 77 S.Ct. 1356, 1 L.Ed.2d 1479 (U.S. Supreme Court, 1957), which held that *any* admission or confession obtained during an unreasonable delay between arrest and appearance before a magistrate will be inadmissible in court.

Admissibility of admissions and confessions is therefore treated differently from admissibility of evidence seized as the result of a consent search. Evidence resulting from a consent search is admissible if the "totality of the circumstances" shows that the consent was voluntary. An admission or confession is admissible if (1) the "totality of the circumstances" shows that the statement was voluntary, *and* (2) the *Miranda* requirements have been complied with.

We turn now to a discussion of the requirements outlined in the *Miranda* decision.

MIRANDA—FACTS AND HOLDING

The Court's opinion in Miranda v. Arizona actually covers three other cases besides *Miranda,* all dealing with the admissibility of statements obtained from an individual who is subjected to custodial police interrogation. A brief description of the facts of each case is helpful in understanding the scope of the opinion.

In Miranda v. Arizona, the defendant was arrested at his home for rape and taken into custody at a police station where he was identified by the complaining witness. There he was interrogated and within two hours signed a written confession. At no time was he informed of his right to consult with an attorney, to have an attorney present during the interrogation, or of his right not to be compelled to incriminate himself. In Vignera v. New York, the defendant was picked up in connection with a robbery and taken to detective squad headquarters where he was interrogated and confessed. He was then locked up. He was questioned again about eight hours later and at that time gave a written statement. At no time was he informed of any of his rights. In Westover v. U. S., the defendant was arrested by municipal police as a robbery suspect. The F.B.I. conducted an interrogation that same afternoon in an interrogation room in the municipal police department. After two hours, the defendant signed two confessions. The Court noted that the F.B.I. interrogation was conducted following the interrogation by municipal police in the same police station—in the same compelling surroundings. In California v. Stewart, the defendant was arrested at his home where police found robbery proceeds. He was then taken to a police station and placed in a cell where over a period of five days he was interrogated nine times. The Court noted that the defendant was isolated with his interrogators at all times except when he was being confronted by an accusing witness.

The purpose of the above fact summaries is to indicate the type of situation to which the Court was addressing itself. In each case the defendant was questioned by police officers, detectives, or a prosecuting attorney in a room in which he was cut off from the outside world. In none of the cases was the defendant given a full and effective warning of his rights at the outset of the interrogation process. In all of the cases, the questioning elicited oral statements, and in three of them, signed statements resulted as well. These statements were admitted into evidence at trial. Thus, all the cases share the features of incommunicado interrogation of individuals in a police-dominated atmosphere, resulting in self-incriminating statements without full warnings of constitutional rights.

The *Miranda* Court, having reviewed the facts in each case, then discussed specific police interrogation techniques as prescribed in police manuals. In condemning these techniques, the Court said:

> It is obvious that such an interrogation environment is created for no purpose other than to subjugate the individual to the will of his examiner. This atmosphere carries its own badge of intimidation. To be sure, this is not physical intimidation, but it is equally destructive of human dignity. The current practice of incommunicado interrogation is at odds with one of our Nation's most cherished principles—that the individual may not be compelled to incriminate himself. Unless adequate protective devices are employed to dispel the compulsion inherent in custodial surroundings, no statement obtained from the defendant can truly be the product of his free choice. 384 U.S. at 457–58, 86 S.Ct. at 1619, 16 L.Ed.2d at 714.

The Court then went on to establish procedural safeguards to protect the individual's privilege against self-incrimination. These safeguards take the form of the *Miranda* warnings so familiar to all law enforcement personnel.

Briefly stated, whenever an individual is taken into custody or otherwise deprived of his freedom of action by police authorities in any significant way, he *must* be given the following warnings before any questioning takes place:

1. He must be informed clearly and unequivocally that he has the right to remain silent.
2. The warning of the right to remain silent must be accompanied by the explanation that anything said can and will be used against the individual in court.
3. The individual must be informed that he has the right to consult with a lawyer and to have the lawyer with him during interrogation.
4. He must be told that if he is indigent and cannot afford a lawyer, a lawyer will be appointed to represent him.

Opportunity to exercise these rights must be afforded the individual throughout the interrogation. After such warnings have been given, and such opportunity has been afforded him, the individual may knowingly and intelligently waive these rights and agree to answer questions or make a statement. But unless and until such warnings and waiver are demonstrated by the prosecution at trial, no evidence obtained as a result of interrogation can be used against him.

MIRANDA—ISSUES

The *Miranda* decision has raised many questions, but in general, the issues can be divided into two categories:

1. The first category is whether *Miranda* requirements apply to the particular case. Under this general heading the issues are whether the defendant was in custody, whether his statements were the result of interrogation, whether the interrogator was a law enforcement officer or agent, and whether the seriousness of the offense has any bearing.
2. The second category is whether *Miranda* requirements have been met in cases in which they apply. Under this general heading the issues are whether the warnings were adequate, whether rights were clearly waived, whether the suspect was competent to waive his rights, and whether more than one interrogation is allowed under *Miranda*.

In short, the major issues of *Miranda* can be said to center around the meaning of four words: "custody," "interrogation," "warning," and "waiver." The remainder of this chapter will be devoted to a discussion of these issues as well as some additional miscellaneous issues.

CUSTODY

Law enforcement officers often have difficulty determining when a person is in "custody" or is "deprived of his freedom of action in a significant way" so as to entitle him to the *Miranda* warnings. One of the reasons for this difficulty is that the meaning of the word custody depends upon a consideration of a variety of circumstances. A safe policy to follow is to give the warnings whenever there is any doubt whether or not they apply. However, there are several situations under which the warnings are clearly not required. The following discussion of particular facts and circumstances should help to clarify this issue for the law enforcement officer.

Focus of Investigation

The *Miranda* decision has been generally understood to have abandoned the "focus of investigation" test of the *Escobedo* case to determine when an interrogated suspect is entitled to warnings. Lowe v. U. S., 407 F.2d 1391, 1396 (9th Circuit Court of Appeals, 1969). The test now, under *Miranda,* is whether the individual being questioned is in custody or has been deprived of his freedom of action in any significant way. Therefore, it has generally been held that even though (1) an officer knows the suspect committed the crime, or (2) he intends to arrest the suspect at the end of the questioning, or (3) he would not allow the suspect to leave if he tried, *Miranda* warnings need not be given if the interview is not otherwise custodial. State v. Hall, 12 Ariz.App. 147, 468 P.2d 598 (Court of Appeals of Arizona, 1970); People v. Hazel, 252 Cal.App.2d 412, 60 Cal.Rptr. 437 (California Court of Appeal, 1967). Also, the U. S. Supreme Court has stated that, even though a suspect is clearly the focus of a criminal investigation, he need not be given *Miranda* warnings if he is not otherwise in custody or deprived of his freedom of action in any significant way. Beckwith v. U. S., 425 U.S. 341, 96 S.Ct. 1612, 48 L.Ed.2d 1 (1976).

Many courts have adopted an "objective" test of custody, i. e., whether under the circumstances of the case, a reasonable man would reasonably believe himself to be in custody or deprived of his freedom of action in any significant way. Under this "objective" test, a court will not accept a suspect's mere assertion that he considered himself in custody or deprived of his freedom of action, but will look at all the circumstances to determine the reasonableness of this belief. Freije v. U. S., 408 F.2d 100 (1st Circuit Court of Appeals, 1969).

The focus concept, however, may still have some vitality as one of the circumstances to be considered by the court in determining the custody issue. In a case in which three agents interviewed a suspect in his home, the court, discussing the custody issue, said that in the absence of actual arrest, something must be said or done by the authorities either in their manner or approach or in the tone or extent of their questioning, which indicates that they would not have heeded a request to depart or allowed the suspect to do so. The court went on to say:

> This is not to say that the amount of information possessed by the police and the consequent acuity of their "focus," is irrelevant. The more cause for believing the suspect committed the crime, the greater the tendency to bear down in interrogation and to create the kind of atmosphere of significant restraint that triggers Miranda * * *. U. S. v. Hall, 421 F.2d 540, 545 (2nd Circuit Court of Appeals, 1969).

Therefore, it would seem that an interview with a suspect could initially be non-custodial in all respects. However, as the questioning became more intense and pointed, a reasonable person might feel that he was no longer free to go about his affairs. A court might decide that, at this time, the person was significantly deprived of his freedom of action and thus entitled to *Miranda* warnings.

To summarize, in ascertaining whether *Miranda* warnings are required, the existence of "custody" or "deprivation of freedom of action in a significant way" is to be determined from a consideration of all the facts and circumstances, one of which may be the "focus" of the investigation on the suspect. We turn now to the various other facts and circumstances upon which a determination of custody may be based.

Place of Interrogation

Court decisions interpreting the *Miranda* requirements have indicated that the place of interrogation is a vital, though not conclusive, factor in determining custody. The following is a discussion of cases which have placed strong reliance on the place of interrogation in determining the question of custody.

Police Stations and Police Vehicles

In all four of the cases decided in the *Miranda* opinion (discussed earlier), the suspect was questioned in a police station after arrest. There would seem to be little question that custody exists in this type of situation. Other courts have held that even if the person is not arrested but is present at a police station for questioning at the command of the police, he is in custody for purposes of *Miranda.* U. S. v. Pierce, 397 F.2d 128 (4th Circuit Court of Appeals, 1968).

Nevertheless, there have been numerous cases in which the presence of a suspect at a police station was clearly non-custodial. Police station interrogation has been held non-custodial where the person questioned was present as a witness. Clark v. U. S., 400 F.2d 83 (9th Circuit Court of Appeals, 1968). Interrogation has also been held non-custodial where the person questioned came to the police station voluntarily, either on his own initiative or at police request.

In Oregon v. Mathiason, 429 U.S. 492, 97 S.Ct. 711, 50 L.Ed.2d 714 (1977), the U.S. Supreme Court dealt with the issue and held that a suspect is not necessarily in custody even though he is questioned in a police station. In that case the defendant, a parolee, was a suspect in a burglary. A state police officer asked him to come to the state police offices "to discuss something." When the defendant arrived, the officer took him into a closed office and told him that he was not under arrest. The officer then informed him that he was a suspect in the burglary and falsely stated that his fingerprints had been found at the scene. Within five minutes, the defendant confessed to the burglary. He left the office one half-hour later.

The Court held that the *Miranda* warnings were not required because the defendant was not in custody.

> In the present case, however, there is no indication that the questioning took place in a context where respondent's freedom to depart was restricted in any way. He came voluntarily to the police station, where he was immediately informed that he was not under arrest. At the close of a one half-hour interview respondent did in fact leave the police station without hindrance. It is clear from these facts that Mathiason was not in custody "or otherwise deprived of his freedom of action in any significant way."
>
> * * *
>
> Any interview of one suspected of a crime by a police officer will have coercive aspects to it, simply by virtue of the fact that the police officer is part of a law enforcement system which may ultimately cause the suspect to be charged with a crime. But police officers are not required to administer Miranda warnings to everyone whom they question. Nor is the requirement of warnings imposed simply because the questioning takes place in the station house, or because the questioned person is one whom the police suspect. Miranda warnings are required only where there has been such a restriction on a person's freedom as to render him "in custody." It was that sort of coercive environment to which Mir-

anda by its terms was made applicable, and to which it is limited. 429 U.S. at 495, 97 S.Ct. at 714, 50 L.Ed.2d at 719.

Cases dealing with the questioning of suspects in police vehicles have provided few guidelines for the law enforcement officer. The safest policy to follow in the police station or vehicle interrogation situation is to give the *Miranda* warnings, unless the individual is clearly there voluntarily.

Jails

The generally accepted rule is that if a suspect is incarcerated in a jail or prison, he is in custody for purposes of any interrogation. Thus, a person who was incarcerated in a penitentiary for one offense was held to be in custody for purposes of interrogation conducted by I.R.S. agents with respect to another offense. Mathis v. U. S., 391 U.S. 1, 88 S.Ct. 1503, 20 L.Ed.2d 381 (U.S. Supreme Court, 1968).

Homes

Ordinarily, interrogation in a suspect's home is non-custodial. The reasoning is that the person is in familiar surroundings and there is an absence of a "police-dominated atmosphere." However, this principle is not absolute. In the landmark case of Orozco v. Texas, 394 U.S. 324, 89 S.Ct. 1095, 22 L.Ed.2d 311 (U.S. Supreme Court, 1969), a suspect was questioned at 4:00 A.M. in his bedroom by four officers, one of whom later testified that the suspect was under arrest. The Court held that even though the questioning was brief and the suspect was in familiar surroundings, there was a custodial interrogation. The key factors in the decision were the time of the interrogation, the number of officers present, and the somewhat unclear evidence of formal arrest.

Usually cases of interrogation at homes involve less severe circumstances than those of the *Orozco* case. Courts generally hold that questioning a suspect in his own home without arrest is not custodial interrogation, as long as there has been no coercive conduct by law enforcement officers. U. S. v. Agy, 374 F.2d 94 (6th Circuit Court of Appeals, 1967).

Places of Business

Interrogation of a suspect at his place of business is usually held to be non-custodial. Like the home, the place of business represents a familiar surrounding. Archer v. U. S., 393 F.2d 124 (5th Circuit Court of Appeals, 1968).

Stores, Restaurants, and Other Public Places

Public places such as stores, restaurants, and bars are not always considered to be as familiar to a suspect as his home or office. Nevertheless, courts usually find that an interrogation conducted in such places is non-custodial. The reasons usually given are that the suspect is in a place of his own choosing and is not isolated from the outside world. Also there is generally an absence of a police-dominated atmosphere in public places. Lucas v. U. S., 408 F.2d 835 (9th Circuit Court of Appeals, 1969).

Hospitals

Questioning of a suspect confined in a hospital as a patient but not under arrest is not usually held to be a custodial interrogation. State v. Zucconi, 50 N.J. 361, 235 A.2d 193 (New Jersey Supreme Court, 1967). The reasons usually relied on are the lack of a compelling atmosphere, the routine nature of the questioning, and the lack of any deprivation of freedom. However, this is not a hard and fast rule, and factors such as intense and pointed questioning or a very sick or highly drugged suspect might cause a hospital interview to be held custodial in nature. State v. Ross, 183 Neb. 1, 157 N.W.2d 860 (Supreme Court of Nebraska, 1968).

Automobiles

Most instances in which a suspect is questioned in his automobile are usually dealt with as "on-the-scene" questioning or as a traffic stop. Both of these situations are discussed later in the chapter. Some cases emphasize that a suspect in his own car is in familiar surroundings. Under any of these rationales, the courts generally find a lack of custody.

Crime Scenes

The *Miranda* decision itself gives some guidance to the law enforcement officer regarding whether warnings are required when investigating the scene of a crime. The Court said that its decision was:

> not intended to hamper the traditional function of police officers in investigating crime. * * * General on-the-scene questioning as to facts surrounding a crime or other general questioning of citizens in the fact-finding process is not affected by our holding. It is an act of responsible citizenship for individuals to give whatever information they may have to aid in law enforcement. In such situations the compelling atmosphere inherent in the process of in-custody interrogation is not necessarily present. 384 U.S. at 477–78, 86 S.Ct. at 1629–30, 16 L.Ed.2d at 725–26.

In general, courts have held that the questioning of a suspect near the scene of a crime prior to arrest is not custodial interrogation. People v. Schwartz, 30 A.D.2d 385, 292 N.Y.S.2d 518 (Supreme Court of N.Y., Appellate Division, 1968). An example of crime scene questioning in a homicide situation is a case in which the defendant shot the victim in the defendant's home. The police arrived at the scene and asked what happened. The defendant replied that he shot the victim. The court held that the defendant was not in custody or deprived of his freedom in any significant way and that *Miranda* warnings were not required. "We do not interpret this important decision [*Miranda*] to exclude statements made at the scene of an investigation when nobody has been arrested, detained, or charged." State v. Oxentine, 270 N.C. 412, 415, 154 S.E.2d 529, 531 (Supreme Court of North Carolina, 1967). * * *

It is likely that a law enforcement officer would be allowed to briefly detain all potential witnesses at the scene of a crime for questioning and this questioning would not come within the scope of *Miranda*. An innocent citizen witness directed by an officer not to leave the scene of a crime is not likely to consider himself in custody or under arrest and it is unlikely that a court would so consider him. Arnold v. U. S., 382 F.2d 4 (9th Circuit Court of Appeals, 1967).

Brief Street Encounters

Another form of investigative questioning occurs when an officer makes inquiries of persons who are acting suspiciously. An example of this is a case in which a suspect was walking on a highway near a car known to be stolen and officers stopped him and asked him if the car was his. The suspect made incriminating statements in response. The court held that this situation did not require the giving of *Miranda* warnings, and the statements were admissible in court. State v. Whitney, 72 Wash.2d 122, 431 P.2d 711 (Supreme Court of Washington, 1967).

There are several reasons why courts do not require *Miranda* warnings before brief "on-the-scene" questioning during a street encounter. One basic reason is that law enforcement officers should be allowed to resolve suspicious situations by asking simple questions of a suspect, without having to explain all of his rights to him. Also, there is usually an absence of a compelling police-dominated atmosphere in a brief street encounter. The major reason, however, is that usually the questioning is merely investigative in nature. More will be said about *Miranda* warnings at brief investigative street encounters in Chapter 10.

It is important at this stage of the discussion to reiterate that the place where the interrogation occurs is only one factor to be considered in determining whether the person questioned is in custody for purposes of *Miranda.* Many of the cases cited above might have been decided differently if other surrounding facts and circumstances had been different. We turn now to a discussion of some of those other facts and circumstances.

Time of Interrogation

An interrogation carried out in a non-compelling setting during business hours is less likely to be considered custodial than one carried out during odd hours of the day. For example, the time of the interrogation was a significant factor in holding the interrogation at the suspect's home to be custodial in the *Orozco* case (see above under *Homes*). Had the questioning of the suspect taken place during business hours, the decision might have gone the other way. It is not unlikely that a reasonable man would consider his freedom significantly restrained when approached by police for questioning in the early hours of the morning.

Presence of Other Persons

The language of the *Miranda* decision expressly indicated a concern for the suspect who is "cut off from the outside world." 384 U. S. at 445, 86 S.Ct. at 1612, 16 L.Ed.2d at 707. Courts have taken this to mean that the presence of family, friends, or neutrals during the questioning of a suspect may cause it to be considered non-custodial. People v. Butterfield, 258 Cal.App.2d 586, 65 Cal.Rptr. 765 (California Court of Appeal, 1968). Correspondingly, the deliberate removal of a suspect from the presence of his family and friends is indicative of custody. Commonwealth v. Sites, 427 Pa. 486, 235 A.2d 387 (Pennsylvania Supreme Court, 1967). Some courts speak of a "balance of power" and find custody to exist in cases where the sheer number of police indicates a police-dominated atmosphere. State v. Ross, 183 Neb. 1, 157 N.W.2d 860 (Nebraska Supreme Court, 1968); Orozco v. Texas, 394 U.S. 324, 89 S.Ct. 1095, 22 L.Ed.2d 311 (U.S. Supreme Court, 1969).

Suspect Under Arrest or Restraint

If a suspect is told he is under arrest, then he is definitely in custody for *Miranda* purposes. Duckett v. State, 3 Md.App. 563, 240 A.2d 332 (Court of Special Appeals of Maryland, 1968). Of course, this also works the other way around, and the officer who tells a suspect that he is not under arrest and is free to leave at any time has fairly definitely established that the interview is non-custodial. U. S. v. Manglona, 414 F.2d 642 (9th Circuit Court of Appeals, 1969).

Short of actual arrest, the courts have generally recognized that the physical restraint of the suspect is a significant factor in determining questions of custody. In cases where physical restraint was present, courts have almost invariably found custody. State v. Saunders, 102 Ariz. 565, 435 P.2d 38 (Supreme Court of Arizona, 1967). By the same token, an absence of physical restraint has led several courts to conclude that the defendant was not under arrest or in custody. People v. Merchant, 260 Cal.App.2d 875, 67 Cal.Rptr. 459 (California Court of Appeal, 1968).

If an officer holds a gun on a suspect, he clearly creates a custodial situation. People v. Shivers, 21 N.Y. 118, 233 N.E.2d 836 (N. Y. Court of Appeals, 1967). However, if the suspect is himself armed, a court is unlikely to find that he was in custody. Yates v. U. S., 384 F.2d 586 (5th Circuit Court of Appeals, 1967). This is a potentially important situation because armed offenders often make damaging admissions while holding off the police.

The absence of other incidents of arrest such as frisk or search, fingerprinting, photographing, and other booking procedures tend to indicate a non-custodial interview. Hicks v. U. S., 382 F.2d 158 (District of Columbia Circuit Court of Appeals, 1967); U. S. v. Thomas, 396 F.2d 310 (2nd Circuit Court of Appeals, 1968). The use of these procedures may of course lead to the contrary conclusion. People v. Ellingsen, 258 Cal.App.2d 535, 65 Cal.Rptr. 744 (California Court of Appeal, 1968).

Duration and Nature of Questioning

The duration and nature of the interrogation is very significant in determining custody for purposes of *Miranda*. Most of the cases which allowed questioning without warnings at crime scenes and during brief street encounters relied on the fact that the questioning was of short duration and involved only a few general investigative questions. Such, brief, routine police inquiries generally indicate a non-custodial interview for the purpose of clarifying a suspicious situation.

An example of this type of situation is a case in which an officer stopped a car being driven by defendant in an unusual manner. A passenger in the car was injured and bleeding. The driver gave suspicious answers to the officer's questions. When the officer asked the passenger if he had been beaten and by whom, the passenger mumbled something and pointed at the driver. The officer then asked the driver if he had beaten the passenger and the driver said yes. The court held that the officer acted properly by asking routine questions to clarify the situation. The court found that *Miranda* warnings were unnecessary, pointing out that warnings hamper and perhaps demean routine police investigation, and make cooperative citizens nervous. Allen v. U. S., 390 F.2d 476 (District of Columbia Circuit Court of Appeals, 1968).

Interview Initiated by Suspect

If a suspect summons the police or initiates the interview, or both, a court is likely to hold that the interview was non-custodial. The element of compulsion is lacking and the statements are not entirely the product of police action.

An example of this situation is a case in which a defendant waved down a police car, voluntarily got into the car, and stated to the police that he had just shot a person attempting a robbery. The court held that police questioning of the defendant about the incident, in the police car, was not custodial and did not require *Miranda* warnings. People v. Lee, 33 A.D.2d 397, 308 N.Y.S.2d 412 (N. Y. Court of Appeals, 1970).

Statements to Undercover Agents or Informants

A suspect who does not know he is speaking to a law enforcement officer cannot be said to have a reasonable belief that he is in custody. Therefore, situations involving undercover agents or informants are clearly non-custodial in all respects. Hoffa v. U. S., 385 U.S. 293, 87 S.Ct. 408, 176 L.Ed.2d 374 (U. S. Supreme Court, 1966); People v. Ward, 266 Cal.App.2d 241, 72 Cal.Rptr. 46 (California Court of Appeal, 1968).

Traffic Stops

The questioning of a driver of a vehicle stopped for traffic violations or for general investigation is generally held by courts to be non-custodial. The reasons for this are that a traffic stop is very similar to an "on-the-scene" street encounter in that the questions are usually brief and general. Also, for most drivers, being stopped for a traffic violation is a fairly common occurrence, and it is not likely that a person would reasonably believe himself to be under arrest or in custody in such a situation. Lowe v. U. S., 407 F.2d 1391 (9th Circuit Court of Appeals, 1969).

Statements Arising Out of a Stop and Frisk

Although the issue is not settled, most courts seem to agree that a short period of on-the-scene questioning in connection with a stop and frisk does not require *Miranda* warnings.

The rationale behind this is that formal custody does not exist in stop and frisk. In addition, the *Miranda* opinion specifically refers to a deprivation of freedom of action in any *significant* way. A stop and frisk is a deprivation of freedom of action but in most cases is not a significant deprivation and thus *Miranda* should not be applicable. People v. Manis, 268 Cal.App.2d 653, 74 Cal.Rptr. 423 (California Court of Appeals, 1969). Again, a determination of whether there is custody or a significant deprivation of freedom of action depends on all the surrounding facts and circumstances, and no definite rule can be formulated in the stop and frisk situation. For a further discussion of *Miranda* in the stop and frisk situation, see Chapter 10.

Determination of Custody—Summary

As the foregoing discussion indicates, the determination of whether an interrogation is custodial for purposes of *Miranda* requires a consideration of many factors. No one can predict for sure how a court will react to a given set of facts and circumstances in deciding whether *Miranda* warnings are required. As was mentioned earlier, the safe procedure is to give the warnings whenever there is doubt as to whether they apply.

Miranda is designed to protect the individual and inform him of his rights, but it is not intended to hamper effective law enforcement. The cases discussed above clearly indicate that law enforcement officers may ask routine questions, investigate suspicious circumstances, enlist the aid of cooperative citizens, etc., without being required to give *Miranda* warnings in every instance. Making the proper decision in borderline cases will require a combination of knowledge, experience, and confidence.

INTERROGATION

Once it has been determined whether or not a suspect is in custody for *Miranda* purposes, the question arises whether or not he is being subjected to interrogation. Interrogation is the questioning of an individual suspected of a crime with the intent of eliciting incriminating statements from him. There are several situations, however, in which a person converses with or relates information to law enforcement officers, which are not considered to be "interrogation" for *Miranda* purposes and thus do not require the warnings.

Volunteered Statements

The most obvious of the situations in which *Miranda* warnings are not required is the volunteered statement—the statement which is made but *not* in response to questioning by a law enforcement officer. In the *Miranda* opinion, the Court stated that "[v]olunteered statements of any kind are not barred by the Fifth Amendment and their admissibility is not affected by our holding today." 384 U.S. at 478, 86 S.Ct. at 1630, 16 L.Ed.2d at 726.

Volunteered statements often occur when a person simply walks up to a police officer on the street or into a police station and makes damaging admissions. People v. Hines, 66 Cal.2d 348, 57 Cal.Rptr. 757, 425 P.2d 557 (California Supreme Court, 1967). Volunteered statements occur more frequently, however, when a person is in custody. And they may occur at any time while the person is in custody, whether before, during, or after interrogation. Dick v. U. S., 395 F. 2d 89 (9th Circuit Court of Appeals, 1968).

Volunteered statements may occur during interrogation when the suspect makes a damaging statement that does not respond to an officer's question. For example, an officer asked defendant where the key to his car was, so the car could be moved off the street and put in storage. Defendant replied that the car had been stolen. The court held that the statement that the car was stolen was not responsive to the inquiry about the key and was completely voluntary. Parson v. U. S., 387 F.2d 944 (10th Circuit Court of Appeals, 1968).

Furthermore, officers are not required to interrupt a volunteered statement in order to warn a suspect of his rights. The *Miranda* decision specifically states that "[t]here is no requirement that police stop a person who enters a police station and states that he wishes to confess to a crime, or a person who calls the police to offer a confession or any other statement he desires to make." 384 U.S. at 478, 86 S.Ct. at 1630, 16 L.Ed.2d at 726.

Clarifying Questions

Since most volunteered admissions are not very detailed, an officer may try to clarify exactly what is being said. Courts have held that a statement is volunteered even if some questions are asked by police. The questions, however, must not be designed to expand upon what the person originally intended to say, but must be merely to clear up or explain the person's statement. People v. Sunday, 275 Cal.App.2d 473, 79 Cal.Rptr. 752 (California Court of Appeal, 1969).

An example of this is a case in which a man walked into a police station and said "I done it; I done it; arrest me; arrest me." The officer asked him what he had done and the man said he killed his wife. Then the officer asked him how, and he replied, "With an axe, that's all I had." The court held that this type of clarifying questioning was permitted by *Miranda*. People v. Savage, 102 Ill.App.2d 477, 479, 242 N.E.2d 446, 447 (Illinois Court of Appeals, 1968).

Brief and Routine Questions

In the discussion of "custody" earlier, the fact that the questioning of a person was brief and routine was usually indicative of a lack of custody. Courts have also held that brief and routine questioning is not "interrogation" under *Miranda*, even if the suspect is in custody.

Routine questions asked during the booking of a suspect by the booking officer have usually been held not to be interrogative in nature. Toohey v. U. S., 404 F.2d 907 (9th Circuit Court of Appeals, 1968). However, this is not a hard and fast rule, and since the suspect is in a police station, probably involuntarily, it is safer to give the *Miranda* warnings in this situation.

Brief routine questions are asked by officers in a great variety of situations. Most courts have taken the view that *Miranda* warnings are only required when law enforcement officers demand answers in an authoritative manner from persons in custody. State v. Travis, 25 Or. 213, 441 P.2d 597 (Oregon Supreme Court, 1968). Therefore, the simple, everyday investigative question does not constitute interrogation. Usually, if an officer is not focusing on or trying to incriminate the person questioned, the courts will not require *Miranda* warnings.

Spontaneous or Emergency Questions

When questions are asked by law enforcement officers spontaneously, impulsively, or in response to emergency circumstances, they are usually held to be non-interrogative. An example of this is a case in which a jailer and a guard were called to a cell area where they found one prisoner near death from strangling. While tending to the injured prisoner, they asked the defendant, who was also a prisoner, about the incident and received incriminating replies. The court held that this questioning was not a deliberate effort to elicit damaging evidence but rather was spontaneous on-the-scene questioning by an astonished jailer. People v. Morse, 70 Cal.2d 711, 452 P.2d 607 (California Supreme Court, 1969).

Similarly, where the interest of the officer is his own self-protection, he may ask if the suspect is armed or where his weapon is. Ballew v. State, 246 Ark. 1191, 441 S.W.2d 453 (Arkansas Supreme Court, 1969).

Confrontation of Suspects With Evidence

In general, it is proper for a law enforcement officer to confront a suspect with the evidence against him or with the other facts of a case. Often, after such a confrontation, a suspect may confess to a crime or make damaging admissions. The question under *Miranda* is whether these statements made by the suspect are volunteered statements or the product of a form of "silent interrogation."

Courts have decided the issue both ways depending on the circumstances of individual cases. When there is no verbal interrogation and the suspect is merely confronted with evidence, an accomplice, scientific reports, etc., courts have held that damaging admissions made after the confrontation were not the products of interrogation. People v. Doss, 44 Ill.2d 541, 256 N.E.2d 753 (Illinois Supreme Court, 1970); State v. Burnett, Mo., 429 S.W.2d 239 (Missouri Supreme Court, 1968). When, however, along with a confrontation, there is subtle coercion or a deliberate effort on the part of police to break down defendant's refusal to talk, courts have expressed disapproval and have held resulting statements inadmissible in court. State v. LaFernier, 37 Wis.2d 365, 155 N.W.2d 93 (Wisconsin Supreme Court, 1967).

Statements Responding to Statements by Officers

An officer will often receive an incriminating reply to his mere comment or statement which is not a question. Since there is usually no intent to elicit incriminating information by officers in this situation, such statements by suspects are usually held not to be the product of interrogation. U. S. v. Pellegrini, 309 F.Supp. 250 (U. S. District Court, Southern District of N. Y., 1970). If, however, officers' statements are deliberately directed toward obtaining incriminating information, courts will consider the statements as tantamount to interrogation. Brewer v. Williams, 430 U.S. 387, 97 S.Ct. 1232, 51 L.Ed.2d 424 (U. S. Supreme Court, 1977).

Interrogation by Private Citizens

The warning requirements of *Miranda* apply only to custodial interrogations conducted by *law enforcement officers*. Therefore, damaging admissions made by a suspect in response to interrogation by private citizens will be admissible in court despite a lack of warnings. Yates v. U. S., 384 F.2d 586 (5th Circuit Court of Appeals, 1967). However, it is universally held that law enforcement officers are forbidden from using private citizens as their agents in order to escape the *Miranda* rule. Commonwealth v. Bordner, 432 Pa. 405, 247 A.2d 612 (Pennsylvania Supreme Court, 1968).

WARNING

The warnings which must be given whenever a person is in custody or is deprived of his freedom of action in a significant way for questioning have been stated earlier in this chapter, but will be stated again for emphasis.

1. He must be informed clearly and unequivocally that he has the right to remain silent.

2. The warning of the right to remain silent must be accompanied by the explanation that anything said can and will be used against the individual in court.

3. The individual must be informed that he has the right to consult with a lawyer and to have the lawyer with him during interrogation.

4. He must be told that if he is indigent and cannot afford a lawyer, a lawyer will be appointed to represent him.

Manner of Giving Warnings

Miranda warnings must be stated clearly and in an unhurried manner—so that the individual understands his rights and feels free to claim them without fear. The warnings should not be given in a careless, indifferent, and superficial manner.

When warnings are given to an illiterate or subnormal person, they must be given in language which he can comprehend and on which he can knowingly act. This may involve taking extra pains to explain and interpret the warnings. The crucial test is whether the words used by the officer, in view of the age, intelligence, and demeanor of the individual being interrogated, convey a clear understanding of all his rights. Anderson v. State, 6 Md.App. 688, 253 A. 2d 387 (Maryland Court of Special Appeals, 1969).

The warnings must be given before any questioning begins but they need not be repeated as the questioning focuses on different crimes or after a short break in the questioning. State v. Davidson, 252 Or. 617, 451 P.2d 481 (Supreme Court of Oregon, 1969).

Does the Suspect Require Warnings?

Suspect Knows His Rights

The *Miranda* opinion made it very clear that law enforcement officers are not to assume that any suspect knows his rights:

> The Fifth Amendment privilege is so fundamental to our system of constitutional rule and the expedient of giving an adequate

> warning as to the availability of the privilege so simple, we will not pause to inquire in individual cases whether the defendant was aware of his rights without a warning being given. Assessments of the knowledge the defendant possessed, based on information as to his age, education, intelligence, or prior contact with authorities, can never be more than speculation; a warning is a clearcut fact. More important, whatever the background of the person interrogated, a warning at the time of the interrogation is indispensable to overcome its pressures and to insure that the individual knows he is free to exercise the privilege at that point in time. 384 U.S. at 468–69, 86 S.Ct. at 1625, 16 L.Ed.2d at 720.

Suspect Is Not Indigent

If a suspect is known to be financially able to afford a lawyer, it is not necessary that he be given the warning that a lawyer will be appointed for him in case of indigency. He must, however, be given all the other warnings.

The law enforcement officer may not always be able to determine a person's financial status. But, as the *Miranda* Court stated, "the expedient of giving a warning is too simple and the rights involved too important to engage in *ex post facto* inquiries into financial ability when there is any doubt at all on that score." (emphasis supplied) 384 U.S. at 473, 86 S.Ct. at 1627, 16 L.Ed.2d at 723. Therefore, it is recommended that the complete set of warnings be given to every suspect requiring them.

Suspect Has an Attorney Present

The *Miranda* opinion seems to say that the warnings are not required to be given to a person who has an attorney present with him:

> The presence of counsel * * * would be the adequate protective device necessary to make the process of police interrogation conform to the dictates of the privilege. His presence would insure that statements made in the government-established atmosphere are not the product of compulsion. 384 U.S. at 466, 86 S.Ct. at 1623, 16 L.Ed.2d at 719.

Again, however, as a practical matter, it is a wiser and safer policy for the law enforcement officer to warn the suspect anyway. He may later claim that his lawyer was incompetent or that he had not actually been officially retained.

WAIVER

A waiver is a voluntary and intentional relinquishment of a known right. The determination of whether or not a suspect has fully and effectively waived his rights for purposes of *Miranda* presents many problems for the law enforcement officer. The only clear-cut rule is that a waiver cannot be inferred from silence. As stated by the Supreme Court in *Miranda*, "a valid waiver will not be presumed simply from the silence of the accused after warnings are given. * * *" 384 U.S. at 475, 86 S.Ct. at 1628, 16 L.Ed.2d at 724. This rule has been followed closely by the lower courts. Moore v. U. S., 401 F.2d 533 (9th Circuit Court of Appeals, 1968). Outside of this, however, there are few concrete guidelines for the law enforcement officer to help him determine whether or not he has obtained a valid waiver from a suspect and can begin questioning him.

The safest procedure for the law enforcement officer, after the *Miranda* warnings have been given, is to ask the suspect if he understands the rights that have been explained to him. Then the officer should ask the suspect if he wishes to talk without consulting a lawyer or having a lawyer present during questioning. If the officer receives an affirmative answer to both questions, he should carefully note the exact language in which the answer was given in order to preserve it for possible future use in court. He may then proceed with the interrogation of the suspect.

If possible, the officer should always try to obtain a written waiver of rights from the suspect before questioning. A written waiver is almost always held to be sufficient if the suspect is literate and there is no evidence of police overbearance. Menendez v. U. S., 393 F.2d 312 (5th Circuit Court of Appeals, 1968). The following form is suggested for this purpose:

Waiver of Rights

I have had my rights explained to me and I understand what my rights are.

I am willing to answer questions and make a statement.

I do not want a lawyer at this time.

I understand and know what I am doing.

No promises or threats have been made to me and no pressure or coercion of any kind has been used against me.

Signed

Time Date

Witness

Witness

[B9604]

If a written statement is obtained as a result of questioning, it should also be signed by the suspect and witnesses. The statement should indicate the place, date, and time the statement was commenced and the place, date, and time the statement was signed by the suspect.

As a further substantiation of the validity of the waiver, it is suggested the the law enforcement officer ask the suspect to sign the following form after a written statement is obtained:

Reaffirmation of Waiver

The entire statement I have just made and signed consisting of ______ pages was made by me after I carefully considered the rights I was giving up in making the statement.

At no time while I was making the statement did I decide to or indicate any desire to reclaim any of those rights.

Signed

Time Date

Witness

Witness

[B9600]

In practical application, it is not always possible for the law enforcement officer to obtain written waivers or clear-cut oral waivers. Suspects may express themselves through an infinite variety of words and actions, some of which may be held by a court to be a valid waiver of rights and some not. Often suspects will be indecisive and never quite get to the point of either claiming or waiving rights. This presents a difficult problem for the law enforcement officer. The following discussion will attempt to meet this problem and will consider various situations involving waivers that have arisen and how they have been treated by courts.

Words and Actions Indicating Waiver

When a defendant has been fully informed of his rights, any reasonable oral statement of understanding and willingness to speak is usually acceptable as a waiver of rights. Examples of valid waivers are cases in which, after warnings, a suspect said, I "might as well tell you about it.", U. S. v. Boykin, 398 F.2d 483, 484 (3rd Circuit Court of Appeals, 1968); "I'll tell you.", State v. Kremens, 52 N.J.

303, 307, 245 A.2d 313, 315 (New Jersey Supreme Court, 1968); or "I know all that.", State v. Brown, 250 La. 1125, 1140, 202 So.2d 274, 279 (Supreme Court of Louisiana, 1967). Courts have also approved non-verbal waivers such as nods and shrugs. Mullaney v. State, 5 Md.App. 248, 246 A.2d 291 (Maryland Court of Appeals, 1968). After receiving a waiver in any of these forms, the law enforcement officer may begin questioning the suspect.

Often a suspect will indicate that he understands his rights and then simply begin to make a statement without any other verbal or non-verbal indication of willingness to waive his rights and speak. Most courts have held that once the suspect has been informed of his rights and indicates that he understands those rights, his choosing to speak without a lawyer present is sufficient evidence that he knows his rights and chooses to waive them. People v. Johnson, 70 Cal.2d 541, 75 Cal.Rptr. 401, 450 P.2d 865 (California Supreme Court, 1969); U. S. v. Osterburg, 423 F.2d 704 (9th Circuit Court of Appeals, 1970). However, this rule is probably valid only if the statement of the suspect follows closely after he indicates his understanding of the warnings. Billings v. People, 171 Colo. 236, 466 P.2d 474 (Colorado Supreme Court, 1970).

A suspect who states that he will talk to a lawyer at some time in the future but agrees to answer questions without a lawyer has waived his right to counsel. Thompson v. State, Fla., 235 So.2d 354 (District Court of Appeal of Florida, 1970). Also, a request to see someone other than a lawyer is not considered to be an assertion of rights under *Miranda*, although a denial of such a request may have some bearing on the voluntariness of the statements. State v. Franklin, 103 R.I. 715, 241 A.2d 219 (Rhode Island Supreme Court, 1968). Similarly, a request for counsel made by a suspect to a friend or relative is not the same as a request to the police. Therefore, even if the police are aware of such a request, it does not operate as an exercise of *Miranda* rights. People v. Smith, 108 Ill.App.2d 172, 246 N.E.2d 689 (Appellate Court of Illinois, 1969).

The California Supreme Court held, however, that a minor's request to see his parents is equivalent to an adult's request to see an attorney under *Miranda*. People v. Burton, 6 Cal.3rd 375, 99 Cal. Rptr. 1, 491 P.2d 793 (1971). Officers should cease questioning a minor who has made such a request until his parents or an attorney is present. Otherwise, any statements taken may be held inadmissible.

Suspect Refuses to Sign Written Statements or Waivers

A suspect's refusal to sign either a written waiver or a written statement has generally been held not to affect the validity of the suspect's waiver with respect to the admissibility of oral statements he has made. Cummings v. U. S., 398 F.2d 377 (8th Circuit Court of Appeals, 1968); Pettyjohn v. U. S., 419 F.2d 651 (District of Columbia Circuit Court of Appeals, 1969). This assumes of course that a valid oral waiver has been obtained.

However, when a suspect indicates, after giving a valid written or oral waiver, that he does not want any notes taken, this may suggest that the suspect erroneously believes that his oral statements cannot be used against him in court. In this case, the law enforcement officer should tell him that oral statements can be used against him in court. Otherwise, a court might hold the waiver invalid. Frazier v. U. S., 419 F.2d 1161 (District of Columbia Circuit Court of Appeals, 1969).

Denial of Access to Retained Counsel

If officers fail to notify an attorney retained by a suspect before they interrogate the suspect, any admission or confession obtained may be inadmissible in court even though the suspect was given warnings and waived his right to counsel:

> Under these circumstances, the interrogation was made without an informed waiver of the defendant's right to the assistance of counsel and to remain silent. When counsel has been retained to represent a prisoner, the governmental authorities cannot deny the lawyer reasonable access to his client, nor may they ignore his request that he be allowed to confer with his client prior to, if not during, the interrogation. State v. Jackson, La., 303 So.2d 734, 737 (Louisiana Supreme Court, 1974).

OTHER MIRANDA ISSUES

Fourth Amendment Violations

Even though a law enforcement officer has satisfied all the *Miranda* requirements discussed in this chapter, a statement may still be inadmissible in court if it is taken in violation of a person's Fourth Amendment rights. The leading case on this subject is Katz v. U. S., 389 U.S. 347, 88 S.Ct. 507, 19 L.Ed.2d 576 (1968), a landmark decision of the U. S. Supreme Court. In that case, the defendant was eavesdropped on in a telephone booth by federal agents, who had attached an electronic listening and recording device to the outside of the booth. The Court held that despite the lack of an intrusion into a constitutionally protected area, the defendant's statements were inadmissible in court because they were taken in violation of his reasonable expectation of privacy. The Court said:

> [O]nce it is recognized that the Fourth Amendment protects people—and not simply "areas"—against unreasonable searches and seizures, it becomes clear that the reach of that Amendment cannot turn upon the presence or absence of a physical intrusion into any given enclosure. 389 U.S. at 353, 88 S.Ct. at 512, 19 L.Ed. 2d at 583.

The *Katz* "reasonable expectation of privacy" standard has been applied to a great variety of cases involving the Fourth Amendment, some of which are discussed elsewhere in this book. For purposes of this chapter, officers must not violate a person's reasonable expectation of privacy when obtaining statements from him. Otherwise the statements may be inadmissible in court, even though *Miranda* requirements have been fulfilled.

Examples of court applications of the "reasonable expectation of privacy" test will be presented to give officers a clearer idea of their rights and duties. In Halpin v. Superior Court, 6 Cal.3rd 885, 101 Cal.Rptr. 375, 495 P.2d 1295 (California Supreme Court, 1972), the incarcerated defendant's wife visited him at the jail during regular visiting hours. A detective allowed the defendant and his wife to use his office to converse, and the detective left the office. The conversation was secretly taped and was used in court against the defendant. The court ruled the tapes inadmissible, stating that law enforcement officers may not deliberately create an expectation of privacy so that the prisoner and his visitor will be "lulled" into believing their conversations will be confidential.

In U. S. v. Fisch, 474 F.2d 1071 (9th Circuit Court of Appeals, 1973), law enforcement officers were investigating a narcotics smuggling operation. The officers obtained a motel room adjacent to that of the suspects and, by listening at the door, the officers heard a discussion of criminal acts. They used no electronic devices and committed no trespass. The court ruled that the statements were admissible, holding that the defendants had no justifiable expectation of privacy in their conversations. The court emphasized that the individual's interest in privacy must be balanced against the public's interest in the investigation and prosecution of crime:

> Upon balance, appraising the public and private interests here involved, we are satisfied that the expectations of the defendants as to their privacy, even were such expectations to be considered reasonable despite their audible disclosures, must be subordinated to the public interest in law enforcement. In sum, there has been no justifiable reliance, the expectation of privacy not being "one that society is prepared to recognize as 'reasonable.'" 474 F.2d at 1078–79.

Multiple Interrogations

In the *Miranda* opinion, the Court said:

> Once warnings have been given, the subsequent procedure is clear. If the individual indicates in any manner, at any time prior to or during questioning, that he wishes to remain silent, the interrogation must cease. At this point he has shown that he intends to exercise his Fifth Amendment privilege; any statement taken after the person invokes his privilege cannot be other than the product of compulsion, subtle or otherwise. Without the right to cut off questioning, the setting of in-custody interrogation operates on the individual to overcome free choice in producing a statement after the privilege has been once invoked. If the individual states that he wants an attorney, the interrogation must cease until an attorney is present. At that time the individual must have an opportunity to confer with the attorney and to have him present during any subsequent questioning. If the individual cannot obtain an attorney and he indicates that he wants one before speaking to police, they must respect his decision to remain silent. 384 U.S. at 473–74, 86 S.Ct. at 1627–28, 16 L.Ed.2d at 723.

The quoted language states clearly that once a suspect indicates either his desire to remain silent or his desire for an attorney, all questions must stop, at least until the suspect confers with an attorney. Despite this seeming clarity, under certain circumstances, some courts have allowed second attempts to question after a suspect has claimed his rights. U. S. v. Brady, 421 F.2d 681 (2nd Circuit Court of Appeals, 1970). The rationales for these holdings have varied according to the circumstances of each case. Other courts have just as vehemently rejected this approach, adhering closely to the guidelines of *Miranda*. People v. Fioritti, 68 Cal.2d 714, 68 Cal.Rptr. 817, 441 P.2d 625 (Supreme Court of California, 1968).

The safest procedure for the law enforcement officer is to cease questioning entirely when the suspect either expresses a desire to remain silent or to have an attorney present after he is given warnings. However, if the suspect himself initiates a second conversation with police, courts have generally approved further interrogation. People v. Sunday, 275 Cal.App.2d 473, 79 Cal.Rptr. 752 (California Court of Appeal, 1969).

The U. S. Supreme Court has allowed, under limited conditions, a second interrogation of a suspect who has exercised his *Miranda* right of silence after being given warnings. In Michigan v. Mosley, 423 U.S. 96, 96 S.Ct. 321, 46 L.Ed.2d 313 (1975), the defendant was arrested early in the afternoon in connection with certain robberies and given the *Miranda* warnings by a police detective. After indicating that he understood the warnings, the defendant declined to discuss the robberies, and the detective ceased the interrogation. Shortly after 6:00 P.M. the same day, after giving the *Miranda* warnings, a different police detective questioned the defendant about a murder that was unrelated to the robberies. The defendant made an incriminating statement which was used against him at his trial. He was convicted of the murder.

The Court held that the admission into evidence of the defendant's statement did not violate *Miranda* principles. Even though the *Miranda* opinion states that the interrogation must cease when the person in custody indicates that he wishes to remain silent, the Court in the *Mosley* case held that "neither this passage nor any other passage in the *Miranda* opinion can sensibly be read to create a per se proscription of indefinite duration upon any further questioning by any police officer on any subject, once the person in custody has indicated a desire to remain silent." 423 U.S. at 102–03, 96 S.Ct. at 326, 46 L.Ed.2d at 320–21. The Court then gave several reasons why it allowed the second interrogation in the *Mosley* case. The defendant's right to cut off questioning had been "scrupulously honored" by the first detective. The detective ceased the interrogation when the defendant refused to answer and did not try to wear down his resistance by repeated efforts to make him change his mind. The second interrogation was directed toward a different crime with a different time and place of occurrence. Also the second interrogation began after a significant time lapse and after the defendant had been given a fresh set of warnings.

In U. S. v. Olof, 527 F.2d 752 (9th Circuit Court of Appeals, 1975), the court held that a second interrogation by federal agents, three hours after the defendant had refused to make a statement after being given the *Miranda* warnings, violated the defendant's rights. Although the agents gave the defendant fresh warnings, they pressured him to cooperate and they questioned him about the same crime as after the first warnings.

These cases suggest the following guidelines for custodial interrogation of a person who has exercised his *Miranda* right to remain silent:

1. The person's right to terminate questioning at the initial interrogation should be promptly honored;
2. A significant amount of time should separate the first and second interrogation attempts;
3. The person should be given complete *Miranda* warnings again; and
4. No pressure to cooperate or other illegal tactics should be employed.

Often, a suspect may waive his rights, submit to interrogation, and after an interval of time, police may wish to interrogate him again. The general rule is that warnings need not be repeated at the second interrogation. People v. Hill, 66 Cal.2d 536, 58 Cal.Rptr. 340, 426 P.2d 908 (California Supreme Court, 1967). However, a few courts have required a repetition of the warnings under certain circumstances, and since it is such a simple procedure, it is recommended that the law enforcement officer repeat the warnings before each questioning session just to be safe. The Supreme Court of Pennsylvania listed five significant factors in determining whether an accused must be reinformed of his constitutional rights:

> (1) the time lapse between the last *Miranda* warnings and the accused's statement; (2) interruptions in the continuity of the interrogation; (3) whether there was a change of location between the place where the last *Miranda* warnings were given and the place where the accused's statement was made; (4) whether the same officer who gave the warnings also conducted the interrogation resulting in the accused's statement; and (5) whether the statement elicited during complained of interrogation differed significantly from other statements which had been preceded by *Miranda* warnings. Commonwealth v. Wideman, 460 Pa. 699, 706–08, 334 A.2d 594, 598 (1975).

Competency of Suspect

A question that sometimes arises with respect to warning and waiver is whether or not the suspect is competent or capable of understanding his rights and of waiving them. Persons who might not be considered competent to waive their rights are those in pain of injury, those in shock, the insane or mentally defective, those under the influence of alcohol, drugs, or medicine, or the very young or old. Courts have usually looked at the totality of the circumstances in each case to determine whether a suspect was capable of understanding his rights and capable of voluntarily waiving them. Mossbrook v. U. S., 409 F.2d 503 (9th Circuit Court of Appeals, 1969). Therefore, no single factor would ordinarily be determinative of the issue.

Since no definite rules can be laid out to guide the law enforcement officer on this issue, he must proceed with caution. If a suspect is youthful or impaired in any of the ways mentioned above, the officer should take extra pains in explaining the meaning of the warnings to him. It is probably better to wait until a person under the influence of drugs or alcohol is back to normal before attempting to warn and question him. Officers should also delay the questioning of persons who are emotionally upset. In Sample v. Eyman, 469 F.2d 819, 821 (9th Circuit Court of Appeals, 1972), the court held that "once it has been determined that a person taken into custody is too upset to assert or waive his rights knowingly and intelligently under *Miranda*, all questioning should cease until such time as that person is clearly capable of so responding."

A juvenile is usually competent to waive his rights but it is advisable for the officer to try and obtain the waiver in the presence of and with the advice and consent of a parent or guardian. The Indiana Supreme Court held that a juvenile's waiver of his *Miranda* rights was invalid because he was not given an opportunity to have his parents or guardian present. The court said:

> We hold therefore that a juvenile's statement or confession cannot be used against him at a subsequent trial or hearing unless both he and his parents or guardian were informed of his rights to an attorney and to remain silent. Furthermore, the child must be given an opportunity to consult with his parents, guardian or an attorney representing the juvenile as to whether or not he wishes to waive those rights. After such consultation the child may waive his rights if he so chooses, provided, of course, that there are no elements of coercion, force, or inducement present. Lewis v. State, 259 Ind. 431, 439, 288 N.E.2d 138, 142 (1972).

Unless the officer is positive that the suspect is incapable of understanding and waiving his rights, he should not refrain from trying to obtain a lawful confession from him. It is the duty of the courts, not the law enforcement officer, to finally determine whether or not there was an intelligent and knowing waiver and a voluntary and trustworthy confession.

Misdemeanors and Other Proceedings

Miranda has been held to be inapplicable to misdemeanors involving only fines or small jail penalties. This includes most minor traffic offenses. State v. Zucconi, 93 N.J.Super. 380, 226 A.2d 16 (Superior Court of New Jersey, 1967); State v. Pyle, 19 Ohio St.2d 64, 249 N.E.2d 826 (Supreme Court of Ohio, 1969). The New Jersey Supreme Court stated the reasons why *Miranda* rules are inapplicable to motor vehicle violations:

1. The type of police questioning used in motor vehicle violations is not ordinarily the lengthy incommunicado interrogation at which *Miranda* was aimed. Usually the questions are simple, standard, and directed toward filling out routine police reports.
2. Usually traffic violations are not serious enough to warrant the time-consuming inconvenience to the administration of justice.
3. It would be impossible to provide sufficient numbers of lawyers for all the motor vehicle violators who would be likely to

> request legal advice. State v. Macuk, 57 N.J. 1, 268 A.2d 1 (Supreme Judicial Court of New Jersey, 1970).

However, where the suspect may be exposed to a substantial term of imprisonment for a misdemeanor, *Miranda* has been held to be applicable. Commonwealth v. Bonser, 215 Pa.Super. 452, 258 A.2d 675 (Superior Court of Pennsylvania, 1969).

Other proceedings to which *Miranda* has been held inapplicable are customs procedures, civil commitments, extradition proceedings, license revocation proceedings, and interviews between probation officer and probationer. It is fairly safe for the law enforcement officer to assume that, unless the suspect is subject to a possible substantial criminal penalty, *Miranda* warnings are not necessary.

Statements Obtained After Defendant Formally Charged

In Massiah v. U. S., 377 U.S. 201, 84 S.Ct. 1199, 12 L.Ed.2d 246 (U. S. Supreme Court, 1964), after the defendant was indicted, federal agents obtained incriminating statements from him in the absence of his counsel. While the defendant was free on bail, his co-defendant, in cooperation with the federal agents, engaged the defendant in conversation in the presence of a hidden radio transmitter. The Court held that the statements were inadmissible because the defendant was denied the basic protection of the right to assistance of counsel.

The *Massiah* decision has become less significant in recent years because the *Miranda* decision has resulted in courts shifting their emphasis from the Sixth Amendment to the Fifth Amendment. Nevertheless, as stated by the Fifth Circuit Court of Appeals:

> [I]t [*Massiah*] retains its vitality and stands as a supplement to *Miranda: Massiah* teaches that although the government may properly continue to gather evidence against a defendant after he has been indicted, it may not nullify the protection *Miranda* affords a defendant by using trickery to extract incriminating statements from him that otherwise could not be obtained without first giving the required warnings. Today *Massiah* simply means that after indictment and counsel has been retained the Fifth Amendment prevents law enforcement authorities from deliberately eliciting incriminating statements from a defendant by the surreptitious methods used in that case. U. S. v. Hayles, 471 F.2d 788, 791 (1973).

The U. S. Supreme Court recently affirmed the continuing validity of the *Massiah* case in Brewer v. Williams, 430 U.S. 387, 97 S.Ct. 1232, 51 L.Ed.2d 424 (1977). In that case, the defendant, who had been arrested, arraigned, and jailed in Davenport, Iowa for abducting a 10-year old girl in Des Moines, Iowa, was being transported by police to Des Moines to talk to his lawyer there. Both his Des Moines lawyer and the lawyer at his Davenport arraignment advised him not to make any statements until after consulting with his Des Moines lawyer. The police officers who were to accompany him on the trip agreed not to question him during the trip. Nevertheless, one of the police officers, who knew that the defendant was a former mental patient and was deeply religious, suggested that the defendant reveal the location of the girl's body because her parents were entitled to a Christian burial for the girl who was taken away from them on Christmas Eve. The defendant eventually made several incriminating statements during the trip and finally directed the police to the girl's body.

The U. S. Supreme Court, citing *Massiah*, held that a person against whom adversary proceedings have commenced has a right to legal representation when the government interrogates him. Since the officer's "Christian burial" speech was tantamount to interrogation and the defendant had been formally charged, the defendant was entitled to the assistance of counsel at the time he made the incriminating statements. The Court found that the defendant did not waive his right to counsel, and therefore held any evidence relating to or resulting from his statements inadmissible.

EFFECT OF MIRANDA IN COURT

As stated earlier, statements taken in violation of *Miranda* requirements will be inadmissible in court to prove the defendant's guilt of crime. In recent years, however, courts have allowed the use of statements taken in violation of *Miranda* for purposes other than the proof of the defendant's guilt. In Harris v. New York, 401 U.S. 222, 91 S.Ct. 643, 28 L.Ed.2d 1 (U. S. Supreme Court, 1971), and Oregon v. Hass, 420 U.S. 714, 95 S.Ct. 1215, 43 L.Ed.2d 570 (U. S. Supreme Court 1975), the Court admitted testimony of previous inconsistent statements taken from a defendant in violation of his *Miranda* rights solely for the purpose of impeaching the defendant's testimony at trial. Stressing that the trustworthiness of the defendant's earlier conflicting statements must satisfy legal standards, the Court in *Harris* said:

> The shield provided by *Miranda* cannot be perverted into a license to use perjury by way of a defense, free from the risk of confrontation with prior inconsistent utterances. We hold, therefore, that petitioner's credibility was appropriately impeached by use of his earlier conflicting statements. 401 U.S. at 226, 91 S.Ct. at 646, 28 L.Ed.2d at 5.

Officers should not interpret the *Harris* and *Hass* cases as providing an opportunity to get around the requirements of the *Miranda* case. An admission or confession obtained in compliance with *Miranda* is much more valuable to the prosecution than an illegally obtained statement to be used only for impeachment. Therefore, officers should carefully comply with the *Miranda* requirements in order to obtain convincing evidence of guilt in the form of an admissible confession. Also, it should be emphasized that *involuntary* statements obtained from a defendant cannot be used for any purpose in a criminal trial. The U. S. Supreme Court has stated that "*any* criminal trial use against a defendant of his *involuntary* statement is a denial of due process of law, 'even though there is ample evidence aside from the confession to support the conviction.'" Mincey v. Arizona, 437 U.S. 385, 398, 98 S.Ct. 2408, 2416, 57 L.Ed.2d 290, 303 (1978).

In U. S. v. Hale, 422 U.S. 171, 95 S.Ct. 2133, 45 L.Ed.2d 99 (1975), and Doyle v. Ohio, 426 U.S. 610, 96 S.Ct. 2240, 49 L.Ed.2d 91 (1976), the U. S. Supreme Court held that a defendant's silence after receiving the *Miranda* warnings could not be used against him at trial for the purpose of impeaching his trial testimony. The Court quoted the *Hale* case in the *Doyle* case as follows:

> "[W]hen a person under arrest is informed as *Miranda* requires, that he may remain silent, that anything he says may be used against him, and that he may have an attorney if he wishes, it seems to me that it does not comport with due process to permit the prosecution during the trial to call attention to his silence at the time of arrest and to insist that because he did not speak about the facts of the case at that time, as he was told he need not do, an unfavorable inference might be drawn as to the truth of his trial testimony * * *." 426 U.S. at 619, 96 S.Ct. at 2245, 49 L.Ed.2d at 98.

Another effect of a *Miranda* violation is that it may cause evidence seized in a subsequent search and seizure to be held inadmissible. In People v. Superior Court (Keithley), 13 Cal.3d 406, 118 Cal. Rptr. 617, 530 P.2d 585 (California Supreme Court, 1975), the court held that consent to search obtained after questioning conducted in violation of *Miranda* was the product of illegal conduct. The consent search was declared invalid. Officers, therefore, should strictly follow the *Miranda* requirements or risk the exclusion not only of statements obtained but also of evidence seized in a subsequent search. U. S. v. Cassell, 452 F.2d 533 (7th Circuit Court of Appeals, 1971).

SUMMARY

The problems created for the law enforcement officer by *Miranda* can be simplified if the officer knows what is required of him and approaches each situation systematically. The first question he should ask is whether the *Miranda* requirements are applicable to his particular case. To make this determination, the officer must ask whether the defendant is in custody, whether his statements are the product of interrogation, whether the person asking questions is a law enforcement officer, and whether the offense is serious enough to require *Miranda* warnings.

Once these questions have been answered in the affirmative, the officer must concentrate on satisfying the requirements of *Miranda*. He must make sure that adequate warnings are administered, and that a clear manifestation of waiver is obtained and recorded. Other issues of concern are whether the suspect is competent to waive his rights and whether multiple interrogations are consistent with *Miranda*. Also, even though the *Miranda* requirements are fully satisfied, a statement that is involuntary because of threat, force, coercion, or other reason, will be inadmissible in court.

A careful study of this chapter along with a selective reading of cited cases should prepare the officer for any *Miranda* problem that arises in the course of his duties.

*

10

STOP AND FRISK

In recent years, "stop and frisk" has become a major subject of comment and controversy in the field of law enforcement. This is not because it is a new procedure. In fact, it has been a long recognized procedure for law enforcement officers to stop suspicious persons for questioning and, occasionally, to search these persons for dangerous weapons. Nevertheless, it has taken the law and the courts a long time to respond to this practice and, as a result, "stop and frisk" has only recently been given judicial approval by the U. S. Supreme Court. This approval was given in 1968, in the case of Terry v. Ohio, 392 U.S. 1, 88 S.Ct. 1868, 20 L.Ed.2d 889 (1968), and its companion cases of Sibron v. New York and Peters v. New York, 392 U.S. 40, 88 S.Ct. 1889, 20 L.Ed.2d 917 (U. S. Supreme Court, 1968).

Before discussing these three cases, it is worthwhile to define "stop and frisk" and to distinguish it from an arrest. As we said in Chapter I, an arrest is "the apprehension or detention of the person of another in order that he may be forthcoming to answer for an alleged or supposed crime." State v. MacKenzie, 161 Me. 123, 137, 216 A.2d 24, 32 (Supreme Judicial Court of Maine, 1965). "Stop and frisk" also involves a detention or restraint of a person. It is, however, a much less severe and less extensive restraint than that of an arrest. Also, "stop and frisk" does not have as one of its purposes bringing a person forth to answer for a crime. As a preliminary definition, "stop and frisk" is a police practice involving the temporary detention, questioning, and limited search of a person suspected of criminal activity. It is initiated on something less than probable cause for the purposes of crime prevention and investigation and for the protection of the law enforcement officer carrying out the investigation.

This definition will be refined throughout the chapter through the discussion of the *Terry, Sibron,* and *Peters* cases and several others which have followed from 1968 to the present. An attempt will be made to set forth guidelines for the law enforcement officer to follow in his daily duties. However, officers should remember that this is a very sensitive and complex area of the law and many questions regarding stop and frisk still have not been answered. As a result, clearcut procedures for all situations are not available. These problem areas will have to be dealt with in the future as the courts resolve them on a case by case basis.

DISCUSSION OF THE TERRY, SIBRON, AND PETERS CASES

Terry v. Ohio

In the *Terry* case, a police detective with 39 years experience observed two men alternately pacing back and forth five or six times in front of a store window, each time peering into the store and returning to a corner to confer. The two men were joined briefly by a third man. When he walked away, the first two resumed their pacing, peering, and conferring. When the third man rejoined them again, the detective, suspecting that the men were "casing" the store for an armed robbery, approached them, identified himself, and asked their names. When the men "mumbled something," the detective grabbed Terry, spun him around in order to place him between the other two suspects and himself, and patted down the outside of his clothing. Feeling a pistol in Terry's coat pocket, the officer seized it and patted down the outer clothing of the other two men. One more weapon was found. Terry and the other man were arrested and convicted of carrying concealed weapons. They appealed, claiming that the weapons were obtained by means of an unreasonable search and should not have been admitted into evidence at their trial.

The U. S. Supreme Court affirmed the convictions. The Court said that even though "stop" and "frisk" represented a lesser restraint than a traditional "arrest" and "search", the procedure is still governed by the Fourth Amendment. However, stop and frisk is not subject to as stringent a limitation as a traditional full arrest and search. Rather than apply the "probable cause" standard to stop and frisk, the constitutional test that is applied is whether or not this type of search and seizure is an "unreasonable" one.

In discussing the reasonableness of the officer's actions in this case, the Court first mentioned the long tradition of armed violence of American criminals and the number of law enforcement officers killed or wounded in action. In light of this, the Court recognized the law enforcement officer's need to protect himself when suspicious circumstances indicate possible criminal activity by potentially dangerous persons, but when probable cause for an arrest is lacking. In these situations, the Court felt it would be unreasonable to deny an officer the authority to take necessary steps to determine whether a suspected person is armed and to neutralize the threat of harm. The Court concluded that

> where a police officer observes unusual conduct which leads him reasonably to conclude in light of his experience that criminal activity may be afoot and that the persons with whom he is dealing may be armed and presently dangerous, where in the course of investigating this behavior he identifies himself as a policeman and makes reasonable inquiries, and where nothing in the initial stages of the encounter serves to dispel his reasonable fear for his own or others' safety, he is entitled for the protection of himself and others in the area to conduct a carefully limited search of the outer clothing of such persons in an attempt to discover weapons which might be used to assault him. 392 U.S. at 30, 88 S.Ct. at 1884–85, 20 L.Ed.2d at 911.

Sibron v. New York

The *Sibron* case arose from another instance of police surveillance, in which a uniformed patrolman observed Sibron in the company of several known drug addicts during an eight hour period. The officer did not see anything pass between Sibron and the others, nor did he hear any of their conversation. Sibron later entered a restaurant where he spoke to three other known addicts but again nothing was observed to pass between them.

On the basis of these actions alone, the policeman accosted Sibron with the remark, "You know what I am after." Sibron mumbled a reply and began to reach into his pocket. The policeman intercepted his hand, reached into the same pocket, and discovered envelopes containing heroin. Sibron was convicted of unauthorized possession of narcotics and appealed on the basis that the seizure was made in violation of his Fourth Amendment rights.

The Supreme Court found that the policeman in the *Sibron* case did not have probable cause to make an arrest and therefore could not justify the search as incident to arrest. The officer knew nothing of the conversations between Sibron and the others, and saw nothing pass between them. All he had to go on was the fact that the others were addicts. This was not enough. "The inference that persons who talk to narcotics addicts are engaged in criminal traffic in narcotics is simply not the sort of reasonable inference required to support an intrusion by the police upon an individual's personal security." 392 U.S. at 62, 88 S.Ct. at 1902, 20 L.Ed.2d at 934. There was no basis to arrest until after the unlawful search.

Moreover, nothing on the record gave the slightest impression that the officer thought that Sibron might be armed. The officer could therefore not justify his actions on the grounds of self-protection. The *Terry* case certainly did not authorize a routine frisk of everyone seen on the street or encountered by an officer. The officer in *Sibron* was apparently after narcotics and nothing else. His search was therefore unreasonable under the standards announced in the *Terry* case.

Since there was neither probable cause to arrest nor sufficient justification to frisk, the heroin seized by the officer was not admissible in evidence and the conviction of Sibron was reversed.

Peters v. New York

In the *Peters* case, an off-duty patrolman heard a noise outside his apartment door. He saw two men tiptoeing furtively about the hallway, neither of whom he recognized although he had lived in the building for twelve years. After telephoning the police, he entered the hallway with his gun drawn, slamming the door behind him. The two suspects fled down the stairs and the patrolman gave chase. He caught up with the defendant, questioned him, and patted down his clothing. In the course of the frisk, the officer discovered a hard object which he believed could be a weapon. It turned out to be an envelope containing burglar's tools. Peters was convicted of possessing burglar's tools.

The Supreme Court affirmed the conviction of Peters. However, the decision was not based upon the officer's authority to "stop and frisk." Rather, the Court felt that the facts were strong enough to give the officer probable cause to *arrest* the defendant for attempted burglary, and for purposes of the Fourth Amendment, the search was properly incident to a lawful arrest. Emphasis was placed by the Court on the defendant's furtive action and his flight in establishing probable cause. The Court said in this respect:

> It is difficult to conceive of stronger grounds for an arrest, short of actual eyewitness observation of criminal activity. * * * [D]eliberately furtive actions and flight at the approach of strangers or law officers are strong indicia of *mens rea*, and when coupled with specific knowledge on the part of the officer relating the suspect to the evidence of crime, they are proper factors to be considered in the decision to make an arrest. * * * 392 U.S. at 66–67, 88 S.Ct. at 1904, 20 L.Ed.2d at 937.

Thus, in this case, questions of the reasonableness of the stop and the frisk did not come up because there was probable cause to arrest and the search was justified as incident to the arrest.

We turn now to a discussion of some general principles regarding "stop and frisk" which can be derived from the *Terry, Sibron* and *Peters* decisions. When possible, an effort will be made to set forth guidelines and suggestions to aid the law enforcement officer in determining what action to take, if any, in a "stop and frisk" situation. Direct quotations from the *Terry, Sibron* and *Peters* decisions will be used whenever appropriate, because it is important that law enforcement officers become familiar with the exact language of the Court in these important cases.

THE REASONABLENESS STANDARD

In order to fully understand the reasons for the restrictions placed on law enforcement officers in stop and frisk situations, it is vitally important for the law enforcement officer to realize that "stop and frisk" procedures are serious intrusions upon an individual's privacy and therefore are governed by the Fourth Amendment to the Constitution, prohibiting unreasonable searches and seizures. As the Supreme Court stated in the *Terry* case:

> It is quite plain that the Fourth Amendment governs "seizures" of the person which do not eventuate in a trip to the station house and prosecution for crime—"arrests" in traditional terminology. It must be recognized that whenever a police officer accosts an individual and restrains his freedom to walk away, he has "seized" that person. And it is nothing less than sheer torture of the English language to suggest that a careful exploration of the outer surfaces of a person's clothing all over his or her body in an attempt to find weapons is not a "search." Moreover, it is simply fantastic to urge that such a procedure performed in public by a policeman while the citizen stands helpless, perhaps facing a wall with his hands raised, is a "petty indignity." It is a serious intrusion upon the sanctity of the person, which may inflict great indignity and arouse strong resentment, and it is not to be undertaken lightly. 392 U.S. at 16–17, 88 S.Ct. at 1877, 20 L.Ed.2d at 903.

This passage serves to emphasize that the Fourth Amendment applies to "stop and frisk" procedures as it does to any other search and seizure. Despite the fact that a stop and frisk is a lesser form of intrusion or interference, it is still constitutionally protected. However, the Fourth Amendment does not apply to stop and frisk in the same way that it does in traditional search and seizure law. In a traditional search and seizure or arrest situation, a law enforcement officer would have to determine whether probable cause existed before he could justify a particular search, seizure, or arrest. This would be true whether a warrant was being sought or whether the situation fell within certain exceptions to the warrant requirement.

This is not the case, however, with stop and frisk. Here we deal with the many and varied situations in which a law enforcement officer must take swift action based on brief on-the-scene observations. This type of police conduct has not historically been subjected to the warrant procedure, nor could it be as a practical matter. The police conduct in a stop and frisk situation must therefore be tested, not by a probable cause standard, but under the Fourth Amendment's general prohibition against unreasonable searches and seizures.

The question for the law enforcement officer then becomes whether or not it is reasonable, in a particular set of circumstances, for him to seize a person and subject him to a limited search of his person when there is no probable cause to arrest.

Competing Interests

To help in answering this question of reasonableness, it is worthwhile to consider the competing interests involved in a stop and frisk situation. On one side there is the individual's privacy and his right to be free from unreasonable searches and seizures. In the words of the Supreme Court:

> Even a limited search of the outer clothing for weapons constitutes a severe, though brief, intrusion upon cherished personal security, and it must surely be an annoying, frightening, and perhaps humiliating experience. * * * 392 U.S. at 24–25, 88 S.Ct. at 1881–82, 20 L.Ed.2d at 908.

On the other side are the governmental interests involved. One of these is effective crime prevention and detection.

The other governmental interest, and the one with which the *Terry* Court was most concerned, is the interest of the police officer in taking steps to assure himself that the person with whom he is dealing is not armed with a weapon that could be used against him:

> Certainly it would be unreasonable to require that police officers take unnecessary risks in the performance of their duties. American criminals have a long tradition of armed violence, and every year in this country many law enforcement officers are killed in the line of duty, and thousands more are wounded. * * * 392 U.S. at 23, 88 S.Ct. at 1881, 20 L.Ed.2d at 907.

With these competing interests in mind, the law enforcement officer must evaluate each situation and determine for himself what action, if any, is justified by the circumstances. This determination can be broken down into two considerations:

1. Whether *any* police interference at all is justified by the circumstances; and
2. If so, *how extensive* an interference do those circumstances justify.

In setting out guidelines to help the law enforcement officer answer these questions, the "stop" aspect and the "frisk" aspect will be considered separately. The reason for this is that the "stop" and the "frisk" each have different purposes behind them, different sets of circumstances which will justify them, and different consequences for the individual who is subjected to the procedure.

DETERMINATION OF WHETHER TO STOP

The Supreme Court has recognized that stopping persons for the purpose of investigating possible criminal activity is necessary to the government's interest in effective crime prevention and detection:

> [I]t is this interest which underlies the recognition that a police officer may in appropriate circumstances and in an appropriate manner approach a person for purposes of investigating possibly criminal behavior even though there is no probable cause to make an arrest. * * * 392 U.S. at 22, 88 S.Ct. at 1880, 20 L.Ed.2d at 906–07.

Given this authority, the law enforcement officer must determine under what circumstances it is appropriate for him to stop a person for investigation. The officer may consider many factors. The following is a partial list of possible indications of criminal behavior which the officer should consider in deciding to make the initial stop:

1. The suspect is known to have a felony record.
2. The suspect fits a "wanted" notice.
3. The suspect makes furtive or evasive movements.
4. The suspect's actions are unusual for the time of day or night.
5. The suspect's clothing is peculiar or inappropriate, e. g., a coat on a hot day.
6. The suspect's vehicle is peculiar in some respect, e. g., clean license on a dirty car.
7. The suspect is in an unusual place or is acting strangely.

Any one of these things alone may not give the officer sufficient grounds to stop a person. However, a combination of these factors and/or others, evaluated in light of the officer's experience, may cause the officer to decide that an investigation is warranted.

The important thing for the officer to remember is that he must be able to justify any investigative stop by showing concrete facts and circumstances indicating possible criminal activity which caused him to decide to take action. As the Supreme Court said in *Terry*:

> [I]n justifying the particular intrusion the police officer must be able to point to specific and articulable facts which, taken together with rational inferences from those facts, reasonably warrant that intrusion. * * * 392 U.S. at 21, 88 S.Ct. at 1880, 20 L.Ed.2d at 906.

This means that a court will not accept a mere statement or conclusion by an officer that he was suspicious of criminal activity. The officer must be able to back up his conclusion by reciting the specific facts which led him to that conclusion. Furthermore, the officer's decision to initiate a stop will be judged against the following objective standard:

> [W]ould the facts available to the officer at the moment of the seizure or the search "warrant a man of reasonable caution in the belief" that the action taken was appropriate? * * * 392 U.S. 21–22, 88 S.Ct. at 1880, 20 L.Ed.2d at 906.

This objective standard is really very similar to the standard imposed upon law enforcement officers in traditional search and seizure or arrest situations. For example, assume that an officer is attempting to obtain a warrant for a person's arrest. Since probable cause is required to obtain that warrant, the officer will have to produce specific, reliable facts sufficient to support a reasonable belief *that a specific crime has been or is being committed.* In the stop and frisk situation, no crime has been committed—there is only a possibility that criminal activity is under way, perhaps only in the planning stage. However, the officer must still come up with concrete, reproducible facts indicating a *possibility of impending criminal activity* to justify his initial intrusion. The element common to the two situations is that the officer must be able to justify his action to a magistrate's or a judge's independent judgment, detached from the heat and excitement of the moment of the seizure or search. The only difference then is in the information that has to be given, and in the case of an investigative stop, the officer need only show facts indicating the possibility that criminal behavior is afoot.

Extent of Stop

Once an officer has determined that the circumstances justify his interfering with an individual to investigate possible criminal activity, the question arises to what extent do those circumstances allow him to interfere, In other words, how long may the person be detained and how much questioning may he be subjected to? This question can only be dealt with in general terms because the Supreme Court has not yet set forth any detailed guidelines.

An investigative stop can range from a friendly encounter with no imposed restraint or interference, to an angry confrontation resulting in the use of force or violence. Again the officer's actions must at all times be justified by the circumstances. He must be able to point to specific concrete facts and circumstances to indicate that the extent of his interference with an individual was reasonable.

For instance, an officer's initial questioning of a suspect may assure the officer that no further investigation is necessary. As an example, a law enforcement officer observed a young man carrying a flashlight and a small box walking on the sidewalk of a residential street at 2:40 A.M. The officer passed him in the patrol car and then stopped to ask him what he was doing. He replied that he was collecting night crawlers for fishing bait. The officer wished him luck and drove on.

On the other hand, the answers given by the stopped person may cause the officer to believe more strongly that something is amiss. In this situation he is permitted to investigate further or, if he has probable cause at the time, to arrest the person.

For example, an officer saw the defendant wearing one topcoat and carrying another. The defendant seemed to be attempting to hide something under the coat he carried. Considering this behavior suspicious, the officer stopped defendant and asked him what he had under his coat. Defendant replied that he had a tape recorder. When the officer asked him to identify himself he handed the officer a driver's license describing an older person of a different race. The officer then arrested the defendant.

The court held that the initial suspicious circumstances justified at least the mere questioning of the defendant by the officer. Then, when the officer checked the license, he had "probable cause not only to investigate further but to place the appellant under arrest with the very reasonable belief that the appellant's possession indicated, at the least, receiving stolen goods." Commonwealth v. Howell, 213 Pa.Super. 33, 41, 245 A.2d 680, 684 (Superior Court of Pennsylvania, 1968).

Other cases dealing with the extent of the stop will be discussed later in the chapter.

DETERMINATION OF WHETHER TO FRISK

The determination by a law enforcement officer of whether or not to "frisk" a suspect is a separate issue from the determination of whether or not to stop. There is a different governmental interest to be served and there is a different set of factors to be considered by the officer.

The governmental interest that is served by giving police the authority to frisk is that of protecting the officer and others from possible violence by persons being investigated for crime. As the Supreme Court said:

> [W]e cannot blind ourselves to the need for law enforcement officers to protect themselves and other prospective victims of violence in situations where they may lack probable cause for an arrest. * * * 392 U.S. at 24, 88 S.Ct. at 1881, 20 L.Ed.2d at 907–08.

Balanced against this interest is the invasion of privacy which would necessarily result from giving police the right to frisk suspects. The Supreme Court expressed its concern for this in the following language:

> We must still consider, however, the nature and quality of the intrusion on individual rights which must be accepted if police officers are to be conceded the right to search for weapons in situations where probable cause to arrest for crime is lacking. * * * 392 U.S. at 24, 88 S.Ct. at 1881, 20 L.Ed.2d at 908.

As we noted earlier, the Court considers the stop and frisk procedure to be a serious intrusion on a person's privacy, possibly inflicting great indignity and arousing strong resentment.

Taking both sides of the issue into consideration, the Court set out a limited authority for a protective frisk by law enforcement officers in the following terms:

> Our evaluation of the proper balance that has to be struck in this type of case leads us to conclude that there must be a narrowly drawn authority to permit a reasonable search for weapons for the protection of the police officer, where he has reason to believe that he is dealing with an armed and dangerous individual, regardless of whether he has probable cause to arrest the individual for a crime. * * * 392 U.S. at 27, 88 S.Ct. at 1883, 20 L.Ed.2d at 909.

Limited Authority

The most important thing for the law enforcement officer to remember is that his authority to frisk is a limited and narrowly drawn authority. The officer does *not* have the right to frisk everyone that he stops to investigate the possibility of criminal activity. Before he decides to conduct any frisk, the officer must have "reason to believe that he is dealing with an armed and dangerous individual." This does not mean that the officer must be absolutely certain that the individual is armed. Rather the issue is "whether a reasonably prudent man in the circumstances would be warranted in the belief that his safety or that of others was in danger. * * * " 392 U.S. at 27, 88 S.Ct. at 1883, 20 L.Ed.2d at 909.

Thus, the officer is governed by an objective standard as he is in determining whether to stop. He must be able to justify his search or frisk of the individual by pointing to specific facts and "specific reasonable inferences which he is entitled to draw from the facts in light of his experience." 392 U.S. at 27, 88 S.Ct. at 1883, 20 L.Ed.2d at 909.

There are many factors which an officer may take into consideration in deciding whether or not it is appropriate to frisk a person. Some things will carry more weight with one officer than another because of differences in experience and knowledge. The following is a partial list of things to be considered in deciding whether or not to frisk an individual.

1. The suspected crime involves the use of weapons.
2. The suspect is nervous or "rattled" over being stopped.
3. There is a bulge in the suspect's clothing.
4. The suspect's hand is concealed in his pocket.
5. The suspect does not present satisfactory identification or an adequate explanation for his whereabouts.
6. The area the officer is operating in is known to contain armed persons.

Any one of these things taken alone may not give sufficient grounds to frisk a suspect, but a combination of these elements or others, evaluated in light of the officer's knowledge and experience, might provide a justification to frisk. Specific cases dealing with situations in which a frisk was or was not authorized will be discussed in a later section of this chapter.

Scope of Search

A further limitation on a law enforcement officer's frisk authority relates to the scope or extent of the search allowed. The Supreme Court requires a frisk to be "a *reasonable* search for weapons for the protection of the police officer." (emphasis supplied) 392 U.S. at 27, 88 S.Ct. at 1883, 20 L.Ed.2d at 909. Since the *only* justifiable purpose of a frisk is the protection of the officer and others, the search must be limited to what is minimally necessary for his protection. Therefore, the frisk must initially be limited to a patdown of the *outer* clothing. There is no authority to reach inside clothing or into pockets in the *initial* stages of a frisk. During the patdown, if the officer detects an object which feels like it might be a weapon, he may then reach inside the clothing or pocket and seize it. If it turns out that it is not a weapon, but instead some other implement of crime (such as burglar's tools) that implement would be admissible in evidence for the crime to which it related (e. g. attempted burglary). However, if the officer does not feel an object which seems to be a weapon, but instead feels a package or bulge which he believes might be evidence of some other crime (such as possession of narcotics or lottery tickets), he may not seize the package or object. The search must end at this point. The reason for this is that the only authorized purpose for a frisk is the protection of the officer and others, *not* to obtain evidence for use at a subsequent trial. If the officer feels no weapon-like object during the course of his pat-down, he can no longer reasonably fear that the person is armed. Therefore, any further search without probable cause would exceed the purpose of the frisk, namely, the protection of the officer. Such a search would be unreasonable under the Fourth Amendment and any evidence obtained through it would be inadmissible.

SPECIFIC CIRCUMSTANCES IN STOP AND FRISK

Since the term "stop and frisk" covers an infinite variety of possible situations, a mere statement of general guidelines may not be sufficient to clearly indicate what behavior is or is not appropriate for a law enforcement officer in a given situation. Therefore, we will now consider specific fact situations involving "stop and frisk" and discuss the ways in which courts throughout the country have responded to these situations. We will cite actual court cases and go into the reasoning of why the court felt that the actions of the law enforcement officer in each case were either reasonable or unreasonable. In each situation, an attempt will be made to emphasize (1) the indications of possible criminal behavior which caused the officer to stop the suspect in the first place, and (2) the circumstances which caused the officer to reasonably believe that his safety or that of others was in danger, thus necessitating a frisk of the suspect.

The cases to be discussed will be grouped under various headings, each indicating the chief factor which caused a law enforcement officer to either stop or to frisk a suspect. In most cases, this will not be the only factor present in a case, but it is a convenient way of classifying the cases and should help to make the presentation more meaningful.

Bulge

In a District of Columbia case, two officers in plain clothes approached the entrance of a delicatessen to investigate a robbery of an earlier date. On their way into the store they passed by defendant who was standing outside. Inside the store, the officers overheard the store owner and some other people discussing the defendant and a companion, who was concealed behind a truck nearby. It was mentioned that they were acting in a suspicious manner. The owner went outside and told defendant that everyone was watching him and that he had better leave.

The officers then approached defendant, identified themselves, and asked for his identification. Defendant said, "Why? My name is Lee." When the officers again requested some identification, defendant reached back with his left hand into his left rear pocket to get his wallet. At this point a bulge was observed under the defendant's shirt, sticking in the waistband of his pants. The object was immediately seized and it turned out to be a loaded pistol.

The court found the "stop and frisk" in this instance to be a reasonable one. With respect to the "stop," the court said that the action of the officers here

> is the kind of momentary contact which is and must be recognized as necessary to a sound police-community relationship and its commensurate effective law enforcement. It cannot be said that the accused was so inconvenienced or restricted that the delicate balance between individual freedom and legitimate police activity has been unduly weighted against him. * * * U. S. v. Lee, D.C. App., 271 A.2d 566, 567–68 (District of Columbia Court of Appeals, 1970).

In approving the seizure of the gun, the court stated that the officer

> had no other choice. He was justifiably concerned for his own safety when the accused revealed that he had something concealed under his waistband. * * * Surely then, under the considerations discussed in Terry v. Ohio, supra, the in-depth search for and seizure of the gun was reasonable—clearly as reasonable as the in-depth search for and seizure of Terry's gun when its presence was discovered by Officer McFadden's sense of touch during the so-called "frisk." * * * 271 A.2d at 568.

Hand Concealed in Pocket

During a routine investigation for a traffic violation, an officer was informed from police headquarters via radio that the car and driver he was investigating were carrying forged prescriptions for narcotic drugs. Defendant, a passenger in the car, while talking with the officer, voluntarily got out of the car with his right hand concealed in his coat pocket. The officer requested defendant to remove his hand from his pocket. Upon his refusal, the officer removed the hand and frisked defendant. At no time did the officer go into any hidden places upon defendant's person. However, clutched in the removed hand was a small yellow envelope which the officer seized. Upon observing its contents, the officer arrested defendant for the possession of heroin.

This case presents no problems as far as the initial stop is concerned. The facts indicate that it was a routine traffic investigation. The information received over the police radio certainly gave the officer good reason to at least investigate the situation further.

The real question in this case is whether the frisk was reasonable. On this issue the court said:

> A person does not ordinarily alight from an automobile with a hand inserted in a pocket. When the hands are free such person has better maneuverability to accomplish this task. Thus when the hand didn't come out after one or more routine questions by the officer, he certainly by this time had probable cause to initiate reasonable precaution for his own safety. Under such facts and circumstances the frisk for weapons was not unreasonable. State v. Henry, 23 Ohio Misc. 367, 368, 256 N.E.2d 269, 270 (Court of Common Pleas of Ohio, 1969).

Thus, the court felt in this case that based upon all of the facts and circumstances presented, the officer had reasonable grounds to believe that defendant was armed and dangerous. Furthermore, the court held that the heroin taken from defendant was admissible in evidence against him because as a result of a reasonable frisk, defendant *himself* brought the envelope containing the heroin from his pocket, after which it was then in plain view.

Admission by Defendant

While driving an automobile, the defendant was stopped by a police officer for speeding. After stopping the vehicle, the officer walked up to it. The defendant got out holding his right hand in the pocket of his knee-length coat. The pocket was baggy and sagged. The officer grabbed the defendant's arm and asked him if he had a gun. The defendant answered "yes." The officer then removed the gun and arrested the defendant.

Here, again, the court assumed, without discussion, that the stop was reasonable because it was a routine traffic stop. In dealing with the frisk, the court cited Terry v. Ohio:

> Terry v. Ohio * * * tells us that when a police officer has reason to believe that he is dealing with an armed individual he has a right to search for weapons regardless of whether he has probable cause to arrest that individual for a crime. Here the

> officer did not merely think he was dealing with an armed person—he knew he was. State v. Hall, 4 Or.App. 30, 31, 476 P.2d 930, 931 (Court of Appeals of Oregon, 1970).

The gun was held to be admissible in evidence and the defendant's concealed firearm conviction was upheld.

Information from Informants

Two officers were cruising in a patrol car at about 9:00 at night. As they proceeded along a street, a taxicab driver coming from the opposite direction hailed them and said, "I just saw a guy up the street tuck a gun inside his belt." The cabdriver pointed to three men down a street which was otherwise empty. He did not say which of the men he had seen with the gun.

The officers drove up to the three men, stopped them, searched the defendant, and found a gun in his left coat pocket. The other two men were also searched and the officers seized a knife from one and narcotics paraphernalia from the other. All three were arrested.

The "stop and frisk" was found to be reasonable. The court found that there were but two courses open to the officers: (1) to let the three men pass in the night because the officers were not told which of the three had the gun and therefore they may have lacked the legal authority to search any of them, or (2) to stop the three and determine which, if any, was carrying a weapon. The officers were justified in taking the latter action.

The court said:

> In stopping the three the police were not required to confine their efforts to interrogation to the crucial question. Based on the information they had, there was only one realistic way to proceed and that was the usual method of "frisking" or, if a bulge were noticed, of seizing the gun. * * *
>
> A forcible stop of the three was warranted and the necessity to frisk appellant (and the other two) for a weapon was immediate if the stop was to have meaning. Questions leading toward a frisk might have brought a shooting. Gaskins v. U. S., D.C.App., 262 A.2d 810, 811–12 (District of Columbia Court of Appeals, 1970).

In Adams v. Williams, 407 U.S. 143, 92 S.Ct. 1921, 32 L.Ed.2d 612 (U. S. Supreme Court, 1972), a law enforcement officer on patrol in his cruiser was approached by a person known to him. He was told that an individual seated in a nearby vehicle had a gun at his waist and was carrying narcotics. The officer approached the vehicle, tapped on the window, and asked the occupant (the defendant) to open the door. When the defendant rolled down the window instead, the officer reached in and removed a pistol from the defendant's waistband and then arrested him.

The Court held that the officer acted justifiably in responding to the informant's tip:

> The informant was known to him personally and had provided him with information in the past. This is a stronger case than obtains in the case of an anonymous telephone tip. The informant here came forward personally to give information that was immediately verifiable at the scene. Indeed, under Connecticut law, the informant herself might have been subject to immediate arrest for making a false complaint had Sgt. Connolly's investigation proven the tip incorrect. Thus, while the Court's decisions indicate that this informant's unverified tip may have been insufficient for a narcotics arrest or search warrant, the information carried enough indicia of reliability to justify the officer's forcible stop of Williams.
>
> In reaching this conclusion, we reject respondent's argument that reasonable cause for a stop and frisk can only be based on the officer's personal observation, rather than on information supplied by another person. Informants' tips, like all other clues and evidence coming to a policeman on the scene, may vary greatly in their value and reliability. One simple rule will not cover every situation. Some tips, completely lacking in indicia of reliability, would either warrant no police response or require further investigation before a forcible stop of a suspect would be authorized. But in some situations—for example, when the victim of a street crime seeks immediate police aid and gives a description of his assailant, or when a credible informant warns of a specific impending crime—the subtleties of the hearsay rule should not thwart an appropriate police response. 407 U.S. at 146–47, 92 S.Ct. at 1923–24, 32 L.Ed.2d at 617–18.

Under the Adams v. Williams case, an officer may stop a person suspected of possible criminal activity based on an informant's tip if the tip carries "enough indicia of reliability." This standard is less than the two-pronged *Aguilar* standard discussed in Chapter 3. Nevertheless, the officer must be able to give specific reasons why he believed that the tip was reliable. As the Adams v. Williams case indicated, an anonymous telephone tip would probably not be sufficiently reliable.

Officers may rely upon a police radio dispatch to obtain facts to justify the stop of a person or vehicle. If, however, it is later stermied that the person relaying the information over the radio had no factual foundation for the message, the stop will be ruled illegal. In

U. S. v. Robinson, 536 F.2d 1298 (9th Circuit Court of Appeals, 1976), the court said:

> We recognize that effective law enforcement cannot be conducted unless police officers can act on directions and information transmitted by one officer to another and that officers, who must often act swiftly, cannot be expected to cross-examine their fellow officers about the foundation for the transmitted information. The fact that an officer does not have to have personal knowledge of the evidence supplying good cause for a stop before he can obey a direction to detain a person or a vehicle does not mean that the Government need not produce evidence at trial showing good cause to legitimate the detention when the legality of the stop is challenged. If the dispatcher himself had had founded suspicion, or if he had relied on information from a reliable informant who supplied him with adequate facts to establish founded suspicion, the dispatcher could properly have delegated the stopping function to Officer Holland. But if the dispatcher did not have such cause, he could not create justification simply by relaying a direction to a fellow officer to make the stop. 536 F.2d at 1299–1300.

Frisk of Traffic Offender's Passengers

When an officer makes a stop for a traffic offense and has sufficient specific facts to support his belief that he is confronted with a dangerous situation, he may frisk the traffic offender's passengers for weapons. The court in U. S. v. Tharpe, 536 F.2d 1098 (5th Circuit Court of Appeals, 1976), found sufficient facts to justify such a frisk under the following circumstances: (1) The driver showed the officer a false license; (2) The driver admitted being the "bad check" suspect of whom the officer had just been informed by radio; (3) The officer recognized the two passengers as burglary suspects; (4) The officer was alone; and (5) The arrest and frisk occurred late at night.

Routine Vehicle Checks

A law enforcement officer may stop a single motor vehicle traveling on a public highway for a routine traffic check to determine compliance with vehicle or traffic laws when he reasonably suspects a violation of those laws. If he does not reasonably suspect a violation, an officer may not stop a motor vehicle to determine compliance with vehicle or traffic laws, unless the stop is conducted according to nonarbitrary, nondiscriminatory, uniform, and systematic procedures for detecting violations. The stopping and uniform inspection of *all* vehicles at a roadblock, weighing station, or other checkpoint, for example, would ordinarily be a satisfactory means of inspecting vehicles when there is no suspicion that a particular vehicle is in violation.

In People v. Ingle, 36 N.Y.2d 413, 369 N.Y.S.2d 67, 330 N.E.2d 39 (Court of Appeals of New York, 1975), the defendant was lawfully operating his 23-year-old automobile, which was in apparently excellent condition and showed no external signs of defective equipment. A state trooper stopped the defendant in order to make a routine traffic check, although he had no information about the defendant or his vehicle. As he was inspecting the car, the trooper detected the smell of marijuana and found marijuana in a pouch on the front seat of the car.

The court, citing Terry v. Ohio, found that the stop for a routine traffic check was a limited seizure and thus was subject to constitutional requirements. In determining the constitutionality of the seizure, the court balanced the interest of the state in highway safety against the right of the citizen to be free from arbitrary state intrusion on his freedom of movement. Since the trooper did not reasonably suspect a violation, nor did he conduct the stop according to a uniform, systematic, nondiscriminatory procedure, the stop was arbitrary. As such, the stop was an unreasonable seizure under the constitution and the evidence derived from it was held inadmissible.

Ordering Driver Out of Vehicle

Once an officer has lawfully stopped a motor vehicle for a traffic violation, the officer may, for his own personal safety, order the driver out of the vehicle. The officer may do so even though he has no reason to suspect foul play from the particular driver at the time of the stop. The U. S. Supreme Court said:

> We think this additional intrusion can only be described as de minimis. The driver is being asked to expose to view very little more of his person than is already exposed. The police have already lawfully decided that the driver shall be briefly detained; the only question is whether he shall spend that period sitting in the driver's seat of his car or standing alongside it. Not only is the insistence of the police on the latter choice not a "serious intrusion upon the sanctity of the person," but it hardly rises to the level of a " 'petty indignity.' " * * * What is at most a mere inconvenience cannot prevail when balanced against legitimate concerns for the officer's safety. Pennsylvania v. Mimms, 434 U.S. 106, 111, 98 S.Ct. 330, 333, 54 L.Ed.2d 331, 337 (1977).

Once the driver is out of the car, the officer may, of course, frisk him if the officer has reason to believe that he is dealing with an armed and dangerous individual.

Violent Crime

Police received a report of an armed robbery minutes after it happened. It was about 3:30 A.M. and the officers on patrol in the area of the robbery had seen only one moving car in the vicinity. Police approached the car and noticed that one of the passengers fit the description of the robber given to them over the radio. The car was stopped and the two occupants were instructed to get out. No questions were asked at this moment, but one of the officers immediately began a pat-down search of the defendant for weapons. Bullets were found and the defendant was arrested.

The court found that the stop was justified by the information that the police had received over the radio:

> It is well established that circumstances short of probable cause to make an arrest may justify an officer's stopping motorists for questioning, and, if the circumstances warrant it, the officer may in self-protection request a suspect to alight from an automobile and to submit to a superficial search for concealed weapons. * * * People v. Anthony, 7 Cal.App.3d 751, 760, 86 Cal.Rptr. 767, 773 (California Court of Appeal, 1970).

The important point in this case, however, is that the court authorized an immediate frisk for weapons without any questions being asked:

> If the reason for the stop is an articulate suspicion of a crime of violence, and the officer has reason to fear for his personal safety, he may immediately proceed to make a pat-down search for weapons without asking any prior questions * * * " 'There is no reason why an officer, rightfully but forcibly confronting a person suspected of a serious crime, *should have to ask one question and take the risk that the answer might be a bullet.*' " * * * 7 Cal.App.3d at 760, 86 Cal.Rptr. at 773.

This case, therefore, stands for the principle that an officer need not ask questions before frisking a suspect if the nature of the crime being investigated is violent and the officer has a reasonable fear for his own safety.

Questionable Objects Felt in Frisk

Police had a certain residence under surveillance as a receiving point for marijuana shipments. They also had probable cause to arrest its occupant, although he was absent at the time.

Defendants entered the driveway of the residence in a car, proceeded up the driveway, and were attempting to back out when the police stopped them. The officers knew that the defendants were not occupants of the residence nor were they subjects of the investigation. Nevertheless, they caused defendants to be spread-eagled against the car and searched. One of the officers patted down the defendants' outer clothing and frisked the defendants' inner clothing. During the patdown and frisk of one defendant, the officer felt a lump in his shirt pocket. A further search disclosed that the lump was a plastic baggie containing marijuana seeds and a package of roll-your-own cigarette papers. Defendants were arrested and convicted of possession of marijuana.

The court approved the stop in this case, stating:

> Admittedly the police officers would have been derelict in their duty had they not stopped the defendants' vehicle to determine whether the occupant of the residence, or any other known subject of the investigation, was in the car. Likewise, the officers could have detained the defendants long enough to ascertain why they were on the premises. * * * People v. Navran, 174 Colo. 222, 226, 483 P.2d 228, 230 (Supreme Court of Colorado, 1971).

However, the court found the frisk in this case to be unreasonable:

> It is apparent that the search conducted herein was not the "reasonable search for weapons" contemplated by the *Terry* case. * * * The right to "stop and frisk" is not an open invitation to conduct an unlimited search incident to arrest or a means to effect a search to provide grounds for an arrest. Rather, it is a right to conduct a limited search for weapons. * * * The seeds and cigarette papers seized were not shown by any evidence produced at the hearing to have been taken from the defendants under circumstances which would permit a search for weapons. 174 Colo. at 229, 483 P.2d at 232.

In another case involving objects felt in a frisk, an officer received a broadcast that a murder had just been committed at a certain intersection. The officer proceeded to the scene of the crime and spotted defendant, who fit the description that the officer had received on his radio.

The officer stopped defendant and conducted a frisk for offensive weapons. Just after he started the search around defendant's waistband, defendant abruptly grabbed his outside upper jacket pocket. The officer moved defendant's hand away from the pocket and from the outside felt a round cylindrical object which he thought was a 12 gauge shotgun shell. He reached into the pocket to remove it and at the same time pulled out a marijuana cigarette. The cylindrical object turned out to be a lipstick container. Defendant was convicted of unauthorized possession of marijuana.

The reasonableness of the stop was not in question here. Certainly, the officer had a duty to investigate defendant on the basis of the description given over his police radio. The court addressed itself therefore to the reasonableness of the frisk. Without deciding if a shotgun shell alone could be used as a weapon, the court found that the officer could have reasonably believed that his safety was in danger and that the frisk was justified:

> Though there is some confusion in the record, it is susceptible of the inference that at the moment the officer had not yet eliminated the possibility that defendant was hiding a relatively short shotgun under his jacket. In any event a shotgun was not necessarily the only object which, in combination with a shell, could be used as a weapon. The officer could reasonably believe that any sharp object could be used as a detonator. * * * People v. Atmore, 13 Cal.App.3d 244, 247, 91 Cal.Rptr. 311, 313–14 (Court of Appeal of California, 1971).

The court further stated:

> Hindsight may suggest that, in order to combine maximum personal safety for the officer with a minimum invasion of defendant's privacy, the officer should first have ascertained what else defendant was carrying. We do not believe, however, that under the circumstances the officer was required to proceed in the coldly logical sequence which may suggest itself after the event. It appears from the record that his reaching into the pocket was almost a reflexive motion, provoked by defendant's sudden gesture toward the pocket and his own feeling of the contents. We cannot say that under all of the circumstances defendant's constitutional rights were violated. 13 Cal.App.3d at 247–48, 91 Cal.Rptr. at 314.

Other Unusual Circumstances

After a high speed chase, an officer stopped defendant's vehicle for speeding. The officer came up to the passenger side of the vehicle and asked defendant to get out of the vehicle. While the officer was at the car, he could smell alcohol. Defendant started to unbutton his coat. He turned towards the police officer and proceeded to take off his coat while he was still seated in the car. As he got out of the car he dropped the coat on the passenger seat where he had been sitting.

Since it was a cold November night, the officer thought it was peculiar for the defendant to remove his coat and the officer grabbed the coat as the defendant was getting out. As the officer started to follow defendant, he noticed a pistol on the passenger seat which had been covered by the overcoat. The pistol was introduced as evidence at defendant's trial and defendant was convicted of carrying a concealed deadly weapon.

On appeal, the court analyzed the reasonableness of both the stop and the frisk:

> The question then becomes whether or not the policeman acted legally when he reached into the car and picked up the defendant's coat. It should be noted that this case involves an incident where the police had a duty to act in stopping the vehicle. It is not a case of general exploratory investigation. Since the police had a duty to act, they also had a right to take reasonable measures to see that their safety was not endangered. * * * In view of the lateness of the hour, the high speed chase, the number of men in the car [3], the fact that the men had been drinking, the police acted reasonably in self protection in asking the gentlemen to get out of the car. Moreover, under these facts, it was reasonable for the police to conduct a limited pat-down search for weapons. A person cannot avoid such a search of his clothing by removing his clothing when it necessarily remains in the general vicinity where he is to remain. The police do not have to risk watching three men to make sure that they did not at any time go back to the clothing left in the car. And the mere fact that the coat was removed is another circumstance justifying a self protection frisk search. Modesti v. State, Del.Super., 258 A.2d 287, 288 (Superior Court of Delaware, 1969).

In another case, two police officers had received information over the police radio that a shooting had occurred. The suspects were described as two negroes in dark clothing and one Puerto Rican in light clothing. The officers proceeded to the area of the shooting and spotted a negro in dark clothing and a Puerto Rican in light clothing, walking together near the scene, acting normally. The only reason the police had to connect them with the reported shooting was that they were walking in the general area and they fit the limited description police had been given. The police had no information of the physical makeup or characteristics of the men they were seeking.

The officers stopped the two men and frisked them on the spot. A gun was found in defendant's belt and defendant was convicted of carrying a concealed deadly weapon.

The court discussed the "stop and frisk" aspects of the case together:

> A policeman may legally stop a person and question him. But he may not without a warrant restrain that person from walking away and "search" his clothing, unless he has "probable cause" to arrest that person or he observes such unusual and suspicious conduct on the part of the person who is stopped and searched that the policeman may reasonably conclude that criminal activity may be afoot, and that the person with whom he is dealing may be armed and dangerous. * * * Commonwealth v. Berrios, 437 Pa. 338, 340, 263 A.2d 342, 343 (Supreme Court of Pennsylvania, 1970).

The court felt that the circumstances disclosed in this case would *not* warrant a reasonably prudent man in the belief that his safety or that of others was in danger:

> If the policemen were constitutionally justified in searching Berrios under these circumstances, then every Puerto Rican wearing light clothing and walking with a negro in this area could likewise be validly searched. This, we cannot accept. 437 Pa. at 342, 263 A.2d at 344.

MISCELLANEOUS ISSUES IN STOP AND FRISK

Stop and Frisk and Miranda

As discussed in Chapter 9, the *Miranda* warnings must be given before any questioning of a person in custody or otherwise deprived of his freedom of action in any *significant* way. The question arises whether the warnings are required to be given before questioning in connection with a "stop and frisk."

Most courts seem to agree that a short period of on-the-scene questioning pursuant to a "stop and frisk" does not require the *Miranda* warnings. The reasoning behind this is that the *Miranda* decision was designed to protect against the dangers of compulsion which exist when a suspect is swept from familiar surroundings and questioned in a coercive, police-dominated atmosphere. This compelling atmosphere is usually not present in a stop and frisk situation. First of all, the questions in a stop and frisk situation are not considered to be interrogative but rather are usually neutral and brief in scope. Secondly, an ordinary stop and frisk situation does not involve taking a person into custody, nor does it involve a significant deprivation of his freedom of action. The key word here is *significant.* Although there is definitely a deprivation of a person's freedom of action, because the detention and questioning is brief, casual, and limited in scope, courts have usually not considered it significant enough to require the *Miranda* warnings.

This is not to say that questioning in connection with a stop and frisk could never require the warnings. Circumstances might develop which would create a coercive and compelling atmosphere resulting in a significant deprivation of a person's freedom of action. For example, if the police outnumber the suspects, questioning is sustained and accusatory, force is used, or other similar factors are present, alone or in combination, then very likely the warnings would be required.

It is difficult to formulate any definite rules for determining when questioning in connection with a stop and frisk will require the

Miranda warnings. Hopefully, the following cases will give some guidance.

Police officers had been alerted via radio to be on the lookout for a white Mustang with California license plates believed to be driven by a person involved in a robbery in a nearby town. When the officers spotted a car fitting that description, they stopped defendant, asked him for identification and asked if he had been in the town where the robbery occurred. Defendant replied that he had. No *Miranda* warnings had been given prior to the questions. Defendant was convicted of robbery and appealed.

The court felt there was nothing in the questioning which amounted to an in-custody interrogation calling for *Miranda* warnings:

> Miranda does not bar all inquiry by authorities without previous warnings * * * In our opinion Miranda was not intended to prohibit police officers from asking suspicious persons such things as their names and recent whereabouts without fully informing them of their constitutional rights. * * * Utsler v. State, 84 S.D. 360, 368, 171 N.W.2d 739, 743 (Supreme Court of South Dakota, 1969).

Another case illustrates that law enforcement officers do not have to give the *Miranda* warnings before asking questions related to their immediate physical protection. The police in this case had evidence that defendant had robbed a store at gunpoint and they were looking for him. By luck, several days after the robbery, one of the eye-witnesses recognized defendant in public and informed police of his whereabouts. Police then broke into defendant's apartment and placed him under arrest. One officer handcuffed defendant while the other proceeded to give him *Miranda* warnings. A third officer interrupted asking "Do you have the gun?" Defendant replied "I don't have the gun. I wouldn't be dumb enough to have it here." A jury subsequently found defendant guilty of armed robbery.

Defendant claimed on appeal that this potentially incriminating statement should not have been admitted in court because he had not been given the *Miranda* warnings. The court felt, however, that the questions were not designed to elicit incriminating information but were apparently for one reason only—the physical protection of the police. The police had good reason to believe defendant was armed and dangerous because he had an extensive past history of robbery and burglary.

The court cited the following passage from Terry v. Ohio:

> "[I]t would appear to be clearly unreasonable to deny the officer the power to take necessary measures to determine whether the person is in fact carrying a weapon and to neutralize the threat of

> physical harm." State v. Lane, 77 Wash.2d 860, 863, 467 P.2d 304, 306 (Supreme Court of Washington, 1970).

The court went on to say:

> Although Terry v. Ohio involved a "stop and frisk" situation which was tested by the reasonableness standard of the Fourth Amendment, we believe the concern there expressed is equally applicable when the Fifth Amendment is involved. Accordingly, we hold that it is not a violation of either the letter or spirit of *Miranda* for police to ask questions which are strictly limited to protecting the immediate physical safety of the police themselves and which could not reasonably be delayed until after warnings are given. * * * 77 Wash.2d at 863, 467 P.2d at 306.

Frisking of Persons of the Opposite Sex

The frisking of a person of the opposite sex presents a very delicate situation. On the one hand, there are certainly situations in which a law enforcement officer could reasonably fear that a person of the opposite sex presents a danger to the officer or to other persons. On the other hand, if routine frisk procedures are used on a person of the opposite sex, the officer may be subjected to a claim of indecent handling or the embarrassment of a law suit. Therefore, an examination of the outer clothing of a person of the opposite sex should not be undertaken without some degree of certainty that the person is armed. The officer may ask a person to remove an overcoat or other covering, and the officer may squeeze handbags or shoulder bags. Such bags may not be opened unless a weapon-like object is felt. Of course, if the person is subsequently arrested, the search and seizure of clothing, pockets, bags, and bundles is governed by the law of search incident to arrest. (See Chapter 4.)

It is difficult to give any specific guidelines on the frisking of persons of the opposite sex. Suffice it to say that the officer should use his or her common sense and discretion.

Packages

The variety of situations which are covered under the general category of stop and frisk is illustrated by a rather unusual U. S. Supreme Court case involving packages. A postal clerk advised a policeman that he was suspicious of two packages of coins which had just been mailed. The policeman immediately noted that the return address was fictitious and that the individual who mailed the packages had Canadian license plates. Later investigation disclosed that the addresses (one in California, the other in Tennessee) were under investigation for trafficking in illegal coins. Upon this basis, a search warrant for both packages was obtained, but not until the packages had been detained for slightly more than a day. Defendants were convicted of trafficking in illegal coins.

The Court upheld the warrantless detention of the packages while the investigation was made, recognizing nevertheless that a detention of mail could at some point become an unreasonable seizure of "papers" or "effects" within the meaning of the Fourth Amendment. The Court emphasized, however, that in this case the investigation was conducted promptly and that most of the delay was attributable to the fact that the Tennessee authorities could not be reached until the following day because of the time differential. U. S. v. Van Leeuwen, 397 U.S. 249, 90 S.Ct. 1029, 25 L.Ed.2d 282 (U. S. Supreme Court, 1970). The authority to detain for investigation, therefore, is not confined to persons but applies also to things.

SUMMARY

The law of "stop and frisk" as it applies to the law enforcement officer may be summarized as follows:

A law enforcement officer may intrude upon a person's freedom of action and "stop" him for purposes of investigating possible criminal behavior even though the officer does not have probable cause to arrest the person. The officer must, however, be able to point to specific circumstances which show that the investigation was appropriate. He may use his experience and training to explain why the circumstances indicated to him that possible criminal activity was afoot in a given situation.

The extent of the "stop" as to length of time, duration of questioning, and use of force, must also be reasonable under the circumstances.

A law enforcement officer may, upon less than probable cause, intrude upon a person's privacy for purposes of conducting a protective search for weapons or frisk. A frisk is not automatically authorized whenever there is a stop. The officer must be able to demonstrate that the circumstances reasonably indicated that the person might be armed. Also, the frisk must be very strictly limited to a protective purpose, although evidence of a crime obtained from a properly conducted frisk will be admissible in court.

The standard to be applied for both the stop and the frisk is whether the action taken by the officer was reasonable at its inception and limited in scope to the accomplishment of the lawful purpose.

The guidelines that the Supreme Court has set out in the area of "stop and frisk" have arisen from a careful balancing of the needs of the police in performing their function of protecting society and the needs of the individual in maintaining his constitutional liberties undiminished. There are still, however, many aspects of stop and frisk which need further clarification such as the appropriateness of the use of force, the significance of a refusal to answer questions, and the searching of automobiles. These issues, and others, will have to be resolved by the courts on a case by case basis.

*

11

PRE-TRIAL IDENTIFICATION PROCEDURES

Pre-trial criminal identification procedures, and in particular the lineup, have long been accepted law enforcement techniques. These procedures are necessary to help identify persons implicated in crimes and also to clear from suspicion those who are innocent. In 1967, the Supreme Court of the United States handed down three major decisions governing this area of the law. The three decisions were U. S. v. Wade, 388 U.S. 218, 87 S.Ct. 1926, 18 L.Ed.2d 1149 (1967), Gilbert v. California, 388 U.S. 263, 87 S.Ct. 1951, 18 L.Ed.2d 1178 (1967), and Stovall v. Denno, 388 U.S. 293, 87 S.Ct. 1967, 18 L. Ed.2d 1199 (1967). It would be worthwhile for the law enforcement officer to commit the names *Wade, Gilbert,* and *Stovall* to memory, because any discussion of the law in this area is sure to center around one or more of these cases. This chapter will attempt to set out guidelines for the law enforcement officer in light of these cases and others interpreting them.

Before beginning the discussion of the *Wade, Gilbert,* and *Stovall* cases, it will be helpful to define the terms *showup, lineup,* and *confrontation,* which will be used throughout the rest of this chapter. A *showup* is the presentation of a single suspect to a victim or witness of a crime for the purpose of identifying the perpetrator of the crime. A *lineup* is the presentation at one time of several persons including a suspect to a victim or witness of a crime for the purpose of identifying the perpetrator of the crime. A lineup gives the victim or witness several alternate choices. A *confrontation* includes both showups and lineups and is any presentation of a suspect to a victim or witness of a crime for the purpose of identifying the perpetrator of the crime. These terms are also sometimes used in connection with photographic or voice identifications. Thus, for example, a photographic showup would be a presentation of a single photograph of a suspect to a victim or witness of a crime.

REQUIREMENT OF COUNSEL—THE WADE–GILBERT RULE

In the *Wade* and *Gilbert* decisions, the Supreme Court decided that a pre-trial confrontation of a suspect of a crime with witnesses or victims of the crime was a critical stage in the legal proceedings against the suspect. As such, the Court ruled that a suspect has a right to the presence of a lawyer at the confrontation if he so desires. Furthermore, if the suspect is unable to afford his own lawyer, he is entitled to have one appointed for him by the court. This ruling is an extension of the right of every accused person to have the assistance of counsel for his defense at all critical stages of his criminal prosecution, a right guaranteed by the Sixth Amendment to the Constitution.

Basis of Court's Decision

The Supreme Court's reasoning in these cases was based (1) on the inherent unreliability of eyewitness identifications and (2) on the possibility of detrimental suggestions made to witnesses either by police officers themselves or through unfair procedures at the confrontation. It was felt that having a suspect's counsel present at the confrontation with witnesses would prevent possible misconduct on the part of the police or others. Also, the attorney would have first-hand knowledge of what took place at the identification proceedings and could thereby conduct an intelligent cross-examination of witnesses at the trial and bring out any improprieties which might have occurred at the confrontation.

Waiver of Right to Counsel

A suspect may waive his right to the presence of counsel at a pre-trial confrontation. Before the suspect can intelligently and understandingly waive his right to presence of counsel, he should be clearly advised of his rights. The following suggested Warning and

Waiver form should effectively satisfy the standards of the United States Supreme Court:

Name	Address
Age	Place
Date	Time

WARNING

Before appearing at any confrontation with any witnesses being conducted by (Name of Police Department) in relation to (Description of Offense), you must understand your legal rights.

The results of the confrontation can and will be used against you in court.

You have the right to the presence and advice of an attorney of your choice at any such confrontation.

If you cannot afford an attorney and you want one, an attorney will be appointed for you at no expense, before any confrontation is held.

WAIVER

I have been advised of my right to the advice of an attorney and to have an attorney present at any confrontation with witnesses, and that if I cannot afford a lawyer, one will be appointed for me before any such confrontation occurs. I understand these rights.

I do not want a lawyer and I understand and know what I am doing.

No promises have been made to me and no pressures of any kind have been used against me.

Signature of Suspect

CERTIFICATION

I, (Name of Officer), hereby certify that I read the above warning to (Name of Suspect) on (Date), that he indicated that he understood his rights, and signed the WAIVER form in my presence.

Signature of Officer

Witness

[B9601]

Substitute Counsel

If a suspect requests the advice and presence of his own lawyer and his lawyer is not immediately available, a substitute lawyer may sometimes be called for the purpose of the confrontation. Zamora v. Guam, 394 F.2d 815 (9th Circuit Court of Appeals, 1968). As stated in U. S. v. Wade:

> Although the right to counsel usually means a right to the suspect's own counsel, provision for substitute counsel may be justified on the ground that the substitute counsel's presence may eliminate the hazards which render the lineup a critical stage for the presence of the suspect's own counsel. 388 U.S. at 237 n. 9, 87 S.Ct. at 1938 n. 9, 18 L.Ed.2d at 1163–64 n. 27.

CHECK LIST FOR LINEUP IDENTIFICATIONS

The following guidelines may be helpful in conducting a lineup identification after the suspect has been advised of his right to counsel and counsel has been retained or waived.

1. No lineup identification should be conducted without discussing the legal advisability of it with the prosecuting attorney.

2. A person in custody may be compelled to participate in a lineup without violating his Fourth or Fifth Amendment rights. Most courts have reasoned that once a person is in custody, his liberty is not further infringed by presenting him for witnesses to view. People v. Hodge, 186 Colo. 189, 526 P.2d 309 (Supreme Court of Colorado, 1974). Also, his right against compulsory self-incrimination is not violated by a lineup, because he is not compelled to utter any words of a testimonial or communicative nature.

Compelling a person who is not in custody to appear in a lineup involves a much greater intrusion on his liberty, and is usually only done by order of the court or the grand jury or by authority of statute in some states. Some courts have upheld the ordering of a person or persons not in custody to appear in a lineup in serious cases in which the public interest in law enforcement outweighed the privacy interests of the person. Wise v. Murphy, D.C.App., 275 A.2d 205 (District of Columbia Court of Appeals, 1971). Other courts have held that a person not in custody cannot be ordered to participate in a lineup without probable cause to arrest. Alphonso C. v. Morgenthau, 50 A.D.2d 97, 376 N.Y.S.2d 126 (Supreme Court of New York, Appellate Division, 1975).

3. Insofar as possible, all persons in the lineup should be of the same general weight, height, age, and race, and have the same general physical characteristics. Also, they should be dressed similarly. A

defendant may be required to wear distinctive clothing at the lineup. U. S. v. King, 433 F.2d 937 (9th Circuit Court of Appeals, 1970). Also a defendant may be required to shave, trim his hair, or even grow a beard before participating in a lineup. U. S. v. O'Neal, 349 F. Supp. 572 (U. S. District Court, Northern District of Ohio, 1972). If a suspect fails to cooperate with identification procedures or attempts to change his appearance, the officer conducting the lineup should keep a careful record of these acts.

4. Should any body movement, gesture, or verbal statement be necessary, this should also be done uniformly. Any movement, gesture, or statement should be made one time only by each person in the lineup, and repeated only at the express request of the observing witness or victim. Again, the officer conducting the lineup should keep a careful record of a suspect's failure to cooperate.

5. A color photograph of the lineup should be taken and developed as soon as possible. A copy of such photograph should be made available immediately to the suspect's counsel.

6. The names of all persons participating in the lineup should be recorded and preserved together with the names of the officers conducting the lineup.

7. A record should be made of the suspect's waiver of his right to counsel and voluntary participation in the lineup. If counsel is present, his name should be recorded.

8. If the suspect has chosen to have an attorney present at the lineup proceedings, the attorney should be given every opportunity to observe all the proceedings, to take notes, and to tape record the identification process in whole or part. If the attorney has any suggestions which might improve the fairness of the proceedings, the officer in charge may follow them if they are reasonable and practicable. However, the attorney should not control the proceedings in any way.

The suspect's counsel must be made aware that an identification is taking place. His mere presence will not satisfy the *Wade-Gilbert* rule. In a case in which the suspect and his attorney were unaware that witnesses had identified the suspect during his arraignment, the suspect's right to counsel was held to be violated. Mason v. U. S., 414 F.2d 1176 (District of Columbia Circuit Court of Appeals, 1969). Counsel's purpose is to ensure that the identification is conducted fairly and to reconstruct the procedures at trial. He can do neither if he is unaware that an identification is taking place.

9. The witness or victim attending the lineup should be advised of the purpose for which it is being conducted, but the officer should not suggest that the suspect is one of those in the lineup or even that the suspect is in police custody.

10. All witnesses who are to view the lineup should be prevented from seeing the suspect in custody, particularly in handcuffs, or in any other circumstances that would indicate to the witness the identity of the suspect in question.

11. All efforts should be made to prevent a witness from viewing any photographs of the suspect prior to the lineup. If a witness has viewed photographs prior to a lineup, the officer conducting the lineup should inform the suspect's counsel and the court of any identification of suspect's photograph, any failure to identify the suspect's photograph, and any identification of the wrong photograph.

12. Before viewing the lineup, each witness should be required to give a description of the perpetrator of the crime in writing to the officer in charge of the lineup. A copy should be made available to defense counsel.

13. If more than one person is called to view a lineup, the persons having already viewed it should not be allowed to converse with other witnesses or victims prior to their viewing the lineup. It is good practice to keep witnesses who have viewed the lineup in a room separate from witnesses who have not yet viewed the lineup.

14. Should there be more than one witness, only one witness at a time should be present in the room where the lineup is being conducted.

15. The officer in charge of the lineup should not engage in unnecessary conversation with witnesses nor permit un-needed persons in the lineup room. A suggested group of people would be the witness, the officer conducting the lineup, the prosecuting attorney, the suspect's attorney, and possibly an investigator.

16. Use of a one-way mirror in a lineup, so that the suspect is unable to know what occurs on the other side of the mirror, has been held to be a prima facie violation of constitutional due process. This simply means that a lineup identification in which a one-way mirror is so used will be illegal, unless the officer in charge of the lineup can show that particularly compelling or exigent circumstances made the practice necessary. State v. Northup, Me., 303 A.2d 1, 5 (Supreme Judicial Court of Maine, 1973). When the suspect's counsel is present, one-way mirrors may be permitted because counsel can observe the conduct of the lineup and preserve the suspect's rights. A one-way mirror may also be used to protect witnesses who fear retaliation. Commonwealth v. Lopes, 362 Mass. 448, 287 N.E.2d 118 (Massachusetts Supreme Court, 1972).

17. The officer in charge should make complete notes of everything which takes place at the lineup and then make an official report of all the proceedings to be filed in his department's permanent records. A copy should be made available to the suspect's attorney.

18. Each witness, as he appears in the room where the lineup is being conducted, should be handed a form for use in the identification. The form should be signed by the witness, the defense counsel and the law enforcement officer conducting the lineup. A suggested identification form follows:

WITNESS LINEUP IDENTIFICATION FORM

The positions of the persons in the lineup will be numbered left to right, beginning with 1 on your left.

A. If you have previously seen one or more of the persons in the lineup, place an X in the appropriate square (or squares) corresponding to the number of the person in the lineup.

B. Then sign your name and fill in the date.

C. When completed, hand this sheet to the officer.

1	2	3	4	5	6	7
( )	( )	( )	( )	( )	( )	( )

____
Signature of Witness

____
Date and Time

____
Signature of Law Enforcement Officer

____
Signature of Attorney for Suspect

[B9602]

19. A copy of this identification form should be given to the suspect's attorney at the completion of the viewing of the lineup by each individual witness.

20. Law enforcement officers must disclose to the court any evidence which might affect the accuracy of the identification. Failure to do so may be a violation of the suspect's due process rights.

21. Even when the suspect's counsel is not required at a lineup (See the next section on EXCEPTIONS TO THE WADE-GILBERT RULE), officers should allow counsel to be present in order to minimize subsequent challenges to the fairness of the lineup. State v. Taylor, 60 Wis.2d 506, 210 N.W.2d 873 (Wisconsin Supreme Court, 1973).

EXCEPTIONS TO THE WADE–GILBERT RULE

The *Wade* and *Gilbert* decisions have caused much controversy and have generated many conflicting opinions in subsequent court decisions. Some lower courts have limited *Wade* and *Gilbert* to their particular facts. Others have created exceptions to the broad holdings implicit in the decisions. An attempt to indicate some of these exceptions follows.

Identifications Conducted Before the Initiation of Adversary Judicial Proceedings

Kirby v. Illinois

The *Wade* and *Gilbert* decisions have generated various interpretations among lower courts with respect to the question—at what stage of a criminal proceeding does a suspect have a right to counsel at an identification procedure. Both the *Wade* and *Gilbert* decisions dealt with identification procedures which took place after the suspect had already been indicted. Some lower courts, interpreting these decisions literally, restricted the right of presence of counsel only to lineups and showups occurring after the formal filing of charges. People v. Palmer, 41 Ill.2d 571, 244 N.E.2d 173 (Supreme Court of Illinois, 1969). Other courts, however, reasoned that since the purpose of counsel's presence is to avert prejudice to the suspect and assure meaningful cross-examination of witnesses at trial on the issue of identification, counsel should be required whether the lineup or showup occurs before or after the formal filing of criminal charges. People v. Fowler, 1 Cal.3d 335, 82 Cal.Rptr. 363, 461 P.2d 643 (Supreme Court of California, 1969).

The U. S. Supreme Court cleared up the controversy in its decision in the case of Kirby v. Illinois, 406 U.S. 682, 92 S.Ct. 1877, 32 L.Ed.2d 411 (1972). In the *Kirby* case, the Court stated that the right to counsel attaches to lineups and showups held "at or after the initiation of adversary judicial criminal proceedings—whether by way of formal charge, preliminary hearing, indictment, information or arraignment." 406 U.S. at 689, 92 S.Ct. at 1882, 32 L.Ed.2d at 417. It is clear then that a law enforcement officer is not required to warn a suspect of his right to counsel at a confrontation with witnesses or to provide him with counsel at such confrontation, if the suspect has not been formally charged with a crime.

Courts differ, however, in their interpretations of when a suspect has been formally charged with a crime. The Supreme Court of Pennsylvania, for example, affords an accused a right to counsel at all lineups held after arrest. Commonwealth v. Richman, 458 Pa. 167, 320 A.2d 351 (1974). In People v. Blake, 35 N.Y.2d 331, 361

N.Y.S.2d 881, 320 N.E.2d 625 (Court of Appeals of New York, 1974), the court concluded that a complaint for an arrest warrant triggers the right to counsel since it is an "accusatory instrument." Other courts have held that the issuance of an arrest warrant triggers the right to counsel. U. S. ex rel. Robinson v. Zelker, 468 F.2d 159 (2d Circuit Court of Appeals, 1972). Each officer must determine at what point in the criminal justice process the right to counsel at pre-trial identification procedures attaches in his jurisdiction.

It should be noted, however, that just because a suspect does not have a right to counsel at a confrontation with witnesses, he does not lose his right to have the identification procedure conducted in a fair and impartial manner. The Court in the *Kirby* case said:

> What has been said is not to suggest that there may not be occasions during the course of a criminal investigation when the police do abuse identification procedures. Such abuses are not beyond the reach of the Constitution. As the Court pointed out in *Wade* itself, it is always necessary to "scrutinize *any* pretrial confrontation * * *" 388 U.S. at 227, 87 S.Ct. at 1932. The Due Process Clause of the Fifth and Fourteenth Amendments forbids a lineup that is unnecessarily suggestive and conducive to irreparable mistaken identification. Stovall v. Denno, 388 U.S. 293, 87 S.Ct. 1967, 18 L.Ed.2d 1199; Foster v. California, 394 U.S. 440, 89 S.Ct. 1127, 22 L.Ed.2d 402. When a person has not been formally charged with a criminal offense, *Stovall* strikes the appropriate constitutional balance between the right of a suspect to be protected from prejudicial procedures and the interest of society in the prompt and purposeful investigation of an unsolved crime. 406 U.S. at 690–91, 92 S.Ct. at 1883, 32 L.Ed.2d at 418–19.

Stovall v. Denno

The case of Stovall v. Denno, 388 U.S. 293, 87 S.Ct. 1967, 18 L. Ed.2d 1199 (U. S. Supreme Court, 1967) mentioned in the above quote from the *Kirby* case, is of vital importance to law enforcement officers and deserves further discussion here. The basic holding of the case is that the Due Process Clause of the Fifth and Fourteenth Amendments to the Constitution forbids any pre-trial identification procedure that is unnecessarily suggestive and conducive to irreparable mistaken identification. For the law enforcement officer, this simply means that *all* lineups and showups must be conducted in a fair and impartial manner. The word *all* is emphasized because the *Stovall* test applies whether or not a suspect is represented by an attorney at the identification procedure.

The *Stovall* case is particularly important to law enforcement officers with respect to lineups or confrontations occurring *before* the initiation of adversary judicial criminal proceedings against a suspect. Courts will carefully scrutinize identification procedures for fairness and impartiality in these instances, because the suspect is without the benefit of an attorney to protect his rights. Therefore, when a law enforcement officer conducts a *lineup* to identify a suspect, before the suspect has been formally charged, the officer should follow carefully the recommended procedures in the Check List for Lineup Identifications. When a *showup* rather than a lineup is used the officer must be extra careful to ensure that identification procedures are fair and impartial. A common type of showup is the on-the-scene showup in which the suspect is arrested or apprehended at or near the scene of the crime and is immediately brought before victims or witnesses by a law enforcement officer for identification purposes. It is clear that as long as adversary judicial criminal proceedings have not been initiated, the suspect has no right to counsel at this type of confrontation. The question arises, however, whether an on-the-scene showup satisfies the *Stovall* requirements of fairness and impartiality.

Although courts differ on this question, the prevailing view seems to be that practical considerations may justify a prompt on-the-scene showup under the *Stovall* test. In the case of Russell v. U. S., 408 F.2d 1280 (District of Columbia Circuit Court of Appeals, 1969), the court said that the delay required to assemble a lineup "may not only cause the detention of an innocent suspect; it may also diminish the reliability of any identification obtained." 480 F.2d at 1284. Immediate identifications are desirable because memories are fresh and the suspect has no opportunity to change his clothes or appearance. Furthermore, if a suspect is innocent, a prompt on-the-scene showup enables the police to continue their search for the real offender unhampered by delay. The court in the *Russell* case suggested that only "fresh" on-the-scene identifications which occur within minutes of the witnessed crime would satisfy the *Stovall* standard. The District of Columbia Circuit Court of Appeals discussed "on-the-scene" showups in the case of Bates v. U. S., 405 F.2d 1104 (1968):

> There is no prohibition against a viewing of a suspect alone in what is called a one-man showup" when this occurs near the time of the alleged criminal act; such a course does not tend to bring about misidentification but rather in some circumstances to insure accuracy. The rationale underlying this is in some respects not unlike that which the law relies on to make an exception to the hearsay rule, allowing spontaneous utterances a standing which they would not be given if uttered at a later point in time. An early identification is not error. Of course, proof of infirmities and subjective factors, such as hysteria of a witness, can be explored on cross-examination and in argument. Prudent police work would confine these on-the-spot identifications to situations in

> which possible doubts as to identification needed to be resolved promptly; absent such need the conventional lineup viewing is the appropriate procedure. 405 F.2d at 1106.

It is therefore suggested that law enforcement officers only use on-the-scene showups when the suspect can be shown to the witness minutes after the crime has occurred. Also, the officer should be careful not to coach the witness or add in any way to the already inherent suggestiveness of the on-the-scene identification. If there is a significant delay between the commission of the crime and the confrontation, the officer should take the suspect to the station and conduct a lineup in accordance with suggested procedures in the Check List for Lineup Identifications.

Neil v. Biggers

Despite the advice in the previous paragraph, law enforcement officers have often conducted showups several days, weeks, or even months after a crime has occurred. Before 1972, most courts, applying the standards of Stovall v. Denno, held that such delayed one-on-one confrontations were impermissably suggestive and violative of due process. Evidence of identifications made under these circumstances was held inadmissible in court.

In 1972, however, the U. S. Supreme Court decided the case of Neil v. Biggers, 409 U.S. 188, 93 S.Ct. 375, 34 L.Ed.2d 401, in which the Court concentrated on whether the identification was accurate or reliable despite the suggestiveness of the identification procedure. Neil v. Biggers involved a defendant who had been convicted of rape on evidence consisting in part of the victim's visual and voice identification of him at a station-house showup seven months after the crime. At the time of the crime, the victim was in her assailant's presence for nearly one-half hour and directly observed him indoors and under a full moon outdoors. She testified at trial that she had no doubt that the defendant was her assailant. She gave the police a thorough description of the assailant immediately after the crime which matched the description of the defendant. And she had made no identification of others presented at previous showups or lineups, or through photographs.

The Court, despite its concern about the seven-month delay between the crime and the confrontation, held that the central question was "whether under the 'totality of the circumstances' the identification was reliable even though the confrontation procedure was suggestive." 409 U.S. at 199, 93 S.Ct. at 382, 34 L.Ed.2d at 411. The Court listed the following five factors to be considered in evaluating the likelihood of misidentification:

1. The opportunity of the witness to view the criminal at the time of the crime;
2. The witness's degree of attention;
3. The accuracy of the witness's prior description of the criminal;
4. The level of certainty demonstrated by the witness at the confrontation; and
5. The length of time between the crime and the confrontation.

Applying these facts to the facts of the case, the Court found no substantial likelihood of misidentification and held the evidence of the identification admissible in court.

Manson v. Brathwaite

In the case of Manson v. Brathwaite, 432 U.S. 98, 97 S.Ct. 2243, 53 L.Ed.2d 140 (U. S. Supreme Court, 1977), the Court added an additional factor to be considered by courts in determining the admissibility of identification evidence—the corrupting effect of the suggestive identification itself. The *Brathwaite* case involved an undercover drug officer's viewing of a single photograph of a drug crime suspect which had been left in his office by a fellow officer. Two days had elapsed between the crime and the viewing of the photograph. After finding that the single photographic display was unnecessarily suggestive the Court considered the five factors affecting the reliability of an identification set out in Neil v. Biggers. The Court found that the undercover officer was no casual observer, but a trained police officer; that he had sufficient opportunity to view the suspect for two or three minutes in natural light; that he accurately described the suspect in detail within minutes of the crime; that he positively identified the photograph in court as that of the drug seller; and that he made the photographic identification only two days after the crime.

The Court's analysis of the five factors indicated that the undercover drug officer was able to make an accurate identification of the defendant. The Court did not end its discussion at this stage as it did in the *Biggers* case, however. Instead, the Court took the additional step of analyzing the corrupting effect of the suggestive identification and then weighing that against the factors indicating reliability. The Court said:

> Although identifications arising from single-photograph displays may be viewed in general with suspicion, * * * we find in the instant case little pressure on the witness to acquiesce in the sug-

gestion that such a display entails. D'Onofrio had left the photograph at Glover's office and was not present when Glover first viewed it two days after the event. There thus was little urgency and Glover could view the photograph at his leisure. And since Glover examined the photograph alone, there was no coercive pressure to make an identification arising from the presence of another. The identification was made in circumstances allowing care and reflection. 432 U.S. at 116, 97 S.Ct. at 2254, 53 L.Ed.2d at 155.

Under the totality of the circumstances, the Court held that the identification was reliable and that evidence of the identification was admissible in court.

It is worthwhile at this point to quote from the *Brathwaite* case because that case sets out the basic test for determining the admissibility of evidence of identifications which take place before the initiation of adversary criminal proceedings:

> We therefore conclude that reliability is the linchpin in determining the admissibility of identification testimony for both pre- and post-*Stovall* confrontations. The factors to be considered are set out in *Biggers*. 409 U.S. at 199–200, 93 S.Ct. at 382. These include the opportunity of the witness to view the criminal at the time of the crime, the witness' degree of attention, the accuracy of his prior description of the criminal, the level of certainty demonstrated at the confrontation, and the time between the crime and the confrontation. Against these factors is to be weighed the corrupting effect of the suggestive identification itself. 432 U.S. at 114, 97 S.Ct. at 2253, 53 L.Ed.2d at 154.

The lesson of the *Biggers* and *Brathwaite* cases for law enforcement officers would appear to be that even though an officer conducts an unnecessarily suggestive identification procedure, all is not lost, because evidence of the identification may still be admitted in court if the identification is otherwise reliable. This will indeed be the result in many cases. Officers, however, should not read the *Biggers* and *Brathwaite* cases to mean that they need no longer be concerned about conducting fair and impartial identification procedures. As the Court stated in the *Brathwaite* case:

> [I]t would have been better had D'Onofrio presented Glover with a photographic array including "so far as practicable * * * a reasonable number of persons similar to any person then suspected whose likeness is included in the array." * * * The use of that procedure would have enhanced the force of the identification at trial and would have avoided the risk that the evidence would be excluded as unreliable. 432 U.S. at 117, 97 S.Ct. at 2254, 53 L.Ed. 2d at 155.

Since the officer has control over the conduct of the identification procedure, but has little or no control over the five factors determining the reliability of the identification he should conduct all identification procedures fairly and impartially. Therefore, in order to avoid the risk that identification evidence will be excluded as unreliable, officers should follow as closely as possible the check list for lineup identifications set out earlier in this chapter or, when photographs are used, the guidelines on photographic identifications appearing later in this chapter.

Emergency Identifications

It is fairly well settled law that when there are emergency circumstances (e. g., a witness believed to be dying), a relaxation of the right to counsel rule and the *Stovall* "fairness" rule may be allowed when necessary to prevent the loss of vital evidence. In an illustrative case, a defendant who was being held in jail on a charge of robbing a store, was presented to a hospitalized victim of a separate assault and robbery offense which was under investigation. There was some question whether the defendant had retained a lawyer on the store robbery charge. In any event, no lawyer was contacted for the identification proceeding in the separate assault and robbery crime. The defendant was transported to the hospital by a deputy sheriff. The victim spontaneously and positively identified the defendant as his assailant. The defendant claimed that he should have been represented by a lawyer at this pretrial confrontation with the victim.

The court applied the *Stovall* test and decided that a claimed violation of constitutional rights in the conduct of a confrontation with a witness depends on the totality of the circumstances surrounding it. In this case, the circumstances surrounding the identification were not unnecessarily suggestive and conducive to irreparable mistaken identification: (1) No preliminary statements were made to the victim; (2) The victim's words of identification were spontaneous and positive; (3) The defendant said nothing in the presence of the victim; (4) The case was merely in the investigatory stage; (5) The critically injured victim (thought to be dying) was about to be moved to a distant hospital. Under these emergency conditions, the fact that a lawyer was not present did not void the identification. Trask v. Robbins, 421 F.2d 773 (1st Circuit Court of Appeals, 1970).

It should be noted that the *Trask* case was decided before the 1972 U. S. Supreme Court decision in Kirby v. Illinois. Under the rule of the *Kirby* case, the defendant in the *Trask* case would not have been entitled to a lawyer at the showup even if there was no emergency, because the showup was conducted before formal charges were brought against the defendant. Nevertheless, the showup would still have had to satisfy the *Stovall* fairness test. Furthermore, even if formal charges had been brought against the defendant, it is very likely that, in the genuine emergency that existed, the court still would have allowed an exception to the rule requiring presence of counsel at confrontations. Therefore, when there is a genuine emergency, accompanied by a strong risk that identification evidence will be lost forever if a showup is not conducted immediately, the law enforcement officer should conduct the showup immediately and take careful notes of all the surrounding circumstances.

PHOTOGRAPHIC IDENTIFICATIONS

An often used and accepted method of police investigation is the showing of mug shots or photographs to witnesses to aid in identifying or eliminating suspects. The U. S. Supreme Court in the case of Simmons v. U. S., 390 U.S. 377, 88 S.Ct. 967, 19 L.Ed.2d 1247 (1968), has approved this procedure, subject to the same standards of fairness set out in Stovall v. Denno. Furthermore, the U. S. Supreme Court has held that there is no right to counsel at any photographic identification procedure, whether it is held before or after the initiation of adversary judicial criminal proceedings. U. S. v. Ash, 413 U.S. 300, 93 S.Ct. 2586, 37 L.Ed.2d 619 (1973).

Each case, therefore, must be decided on the total circumstances surrounding it and the identification evidence will be excluded in court "only if the photographic identification procedure was so impremissibly suggestive as to give rise to a very substantial likelihood of irreparable misidentification." 390 U.S. at 384, 88 S.Ct. at 971, 19 L.Ed.2d at 1253. The following guidelines, based on the *Simmons* case, are suggested for photographic identifications.

1. More than one photograph should be shown to a witness. In the *Simmons* case, six photographs were shown to several witnesses, and the Supreme Court suggested that even more than six would be preferable.

2. The people appearing in the photographs should be of the same general age, height, weight, and color of hair and skin.

3. No group of photographs should be arranged in such a way that the photograph of a single person reoccurs or is in any way emphasized.

4. If there are two or more suspects, no two should appear together in a group photo.

5. Witnesses should be handled in a manner similar to that suggested in the Check List for Lineup Identifications (above).

6. If there are several witnesses, the Supreme Court suggests that only some of them be shown the photographs, in order to obtain an initial identification. Then the suspect could later be displayed to the remaining witnesses in a more reliable lineup at which counsel for the suspect is present.

7. The officer in charge should keep careful notes of all remarks of witnesses while viewing photos, and of all identifications and mistakes in identification.

8. After the photographs have been shown to the witnesses, they should be numbered and preserved as evidence.

9. After a witness selects a photograph from a photographic display, that witness should not be shown the same photograph in later photographic displays. Such a procedure would tend to fix the image of the photograph in the witness's mind and blur the image actually perceived at the crime. U. S. v. Eatherton, 519 F.2d 603 (1st Circuit Court of Appeals, 1975).

10. Photographs of suspects in the act of committing the crime (such as bank robbery surveillance photographs) do not present any problems of suggestiveness and mistaken identification. Courts have held that presenting such photographs to witnesses shows the actual perpetrator of the crime in the act rather than suggesting a number of possible perpetrators. The photographs refresh the witness's memory of the actual crime and thereby strengthen the reliabiltiy of his in-court identification. U. S. v. Evans, 484 F.2d 1178 (2nd Circuit Court of Appeals, 1973).

11. Mug shots should not be used together with other photographs for identification purposes. Mug shots may prejudice a suspect by implying that he has criminal record.

12. Photographic identification should not be used once a suspect's identity is known and he is in police custody. A lineup should be used in these circumstances because lineups are more accurate than photographic identifications. State v. Wallace, La., 285 So.2d 796 (Louisiana Supreme Court, 1973).

It must be remembered that these guidelines are only suggested and that different circumstances may require different identification procedures. The key factor to keep in mind is that the totality of the circumstances surrounding the identification must not be so overly suggestive as to cause a substantial likelihood of irreparable misidentification. Of course, as indicated in the case of Manson v. Brathwaite, discussed earlier in this chapter, courts will look beyond the mere fact of a suggestive photographic identification procedure in determining whether there was a substantial likelihood of irreparable misidentification. Courts will analyze each case with respect to the five factors determining the reliabilty of the identification as set out in Neil v. Biggers. Courts will then weigh those factors against the corrupting effect of the suggestive identification as was done in Manson v. Brathwaite. Law enforcement officers should follow the guidelines for photographic identifications set out in this section to minimize the suggestiveness of identification procedures and to ensure that identification evidence will not be excluded as unreliable.

EFFECT OF IMPROPER IDENTIFICATION PROCEDURE

In order to enforce the standards set out by the U. S. Supreme Court with respect to pre-trial identifications, certain rules have been established for the admission of identification evidence in court. If a pre-trial identification is made in violation of a defendant's right to counsel or if the identification is unreliable and thereby violates a defendant's due process rights, the court must exclude at trial:

1. Any evidence of the pre-trial identification presented as a part of the prosecution's direct case; and
2. Any identification of the perpetrator of the crime made by a witness in court.

If, however, the prosecution can establish by clear and convincing evidence that a witness had a source independent from the illegal confrontation for identifying the perpetrator of the crime, the court may allow in-court identification testimony. A judge will find that an in-court identification has an independent source when he is convinced that the identifying witness, by drawing on his memory of the crime and his observations of the defendant during the crime, has such a clear and definite image of the defendant that he is able to make an identification without being affected by the illegal confrontation. Some of the factors considered by judges in determining independent source are:

1. Opportunity for observation during the crime;
2. Prior knowledge of the identity of the perpetrator of the crime;
3. Accuracy of the witness's description of the perpetrator given to the police;
4. Failure of the witness to identify the defendant at prior confrontations;
5. Identification of a person other than the defendant prior to the confrontation;
6. Lapse of time between the crime and the confrontation; and
7. Differences of opinion among witnesses.

Law enforcement officers should obtain information on these factors from witnesses and record the information in their reports. Officers should obtain as much detail as possible, because strong evidence of an independent source for identification of a criminal can salvage an improperly conducted identification procedure. Such evidence can often mean the difference between winning and losing a case.

SUMMARY

A criminal suspect has a right to counsel at all lineups and showups *after* the initiation of adversary judicial proceedings against him. The emergency showup is the only possible exception to this rule. In every other case, the suspect should be warned of his right to counsel in accordance with the form provided. All formal confrontations should be conducted in accordance with the guidelines in the Check List for Lineup Identifications.

If a lineup or showup is conducted *before* adversary judicial proceedings are initiated against a suspect, the suspect is *not* entitled to the presence or advice of counsel. Nevertheless, *all* pre-trial identification procedures, whether lineups or showups, must be conducted in accordance with due process, which forbids any pre-trial identification procedure that is unnecessarily suggestive and conducive to irreparable mistaken identification. As further interpreted by the U. S. Supreme Court, the due process test can be simply state as requiring that all pre-trial identifications be reliable in the totality of the circumstances or evidence of the identification will be inadmissible in court. Factors to be considered in determining reliability are the opportunity of the witness to view the criminal at the time of the crime, the witness's degree of attention, the accuracy of his prior description of the criminal, the level of certainty demonstrated at the confrontation, and the time between the crime and the confrontation. These factors are to be weighed against the corrupting effect of any suggestive identification.

To help insure reliable identifications, law enforcement officers must conduct all confrontations as fairly and impartially as possible. Officers are again advised to follow the guidelines in the Check List for Lineup Identifications.

A criminal suspect is *not* entitled to the presence or advice of counsel at *photographic* identification procedures no matter when they are held. Nevertheless, such procedures must also be conducted as fairly and impartially as possible. Officers are advised to follow the guidelines for photographic identifications provided in this chapter.

PART FOUR

PREPARATION OF A CASE FOR COURT

12

INVESTIGATION OF CRIME

One of the most important duties of the law enforcement officer is the investigation of crime. An investigation that is conducted in a careful, systematic, and professional manner contributes to the orderly, efficient, and just operation of the criminal justice system. A sloppy, unorganized investigation will almost certainly result in an inadequate presentation of the prosecution's case, and may thereby impair the just outcome of the trial.

The body of knowledge of criminal investigation techniques has been growing continuously over the years. Today nearly every crime requires different techniques to solve it. And there has been an increasing use of scientific devices such as the polygraph and the voice analysis machine. Large law enforcement agencies have even assigned certain officers to specialized duty as investigators. Some of these investigators have become further specialized in specific areas or techniques of criminal investigation.

It would be impossible, in a book on criminal procedure, to cover in detail any of the specialized aspects of criminal investigation. The purpose of this chapter, then, will be to discuss the basic techniques of criminal investigation which apply to most crimes and which every law enforcement officers needs to know. Throughout the chapter, these basic techniques will be related to the ultimate purpose of every investigation of crime—the presentation of evidence at trial.

INVESTIGATION IN GENERAL

At the first report of a crime the investigating officer has no clear idea of what happened, how, why, when, or where it happened, or who did it, The purpose of the investigation is to answer these questions, and to obtain proof of the answers in the form of evidence that is admissible in court. Obtaining this proof is similar to fitting together the pieces of a puzzle. The items will not be obtained by the investigating officer in any particular order, and therefore the officer's method must insure that he collects all the available "pieces" of the case. An orderly procedure is absolutely required and this chapter will attempt to set out a step by step approach to criminal investigation.

Before these detailed guidelines are set forth, however, a few preliminary considerations should be mentioned. First and foremost, the investigating officer must keep in mind at all times that the ultimate result of his investigation may be the determination of someone's guilt or innocence in court. Therefore, from the first report of a possible criminal offense, the investigating officer's thoughts and actions should be directed toward developing a case for possible trial. This attitude will not only encourage meticulous car in the acquisition of evidence but also will save the officer time and effort which might otherwise be wasted on irrelevancies.

Notebook

Note-taking is an essential part of the investigation and preparation of a case for prosecution. Every officer should have a loose-leaf notebook with him at all times to record his activities. Accurate and complete notes aid in the preservation and identification of physical evidence, the preparation of departmental reports, and may even be used to refresh the memory of the investigating officer on the witness stand at a subsequent trial. For these reasons, all facts connected with an investigation should be accurately recorded—conversations with witnesses or suspects, personal observations, descriptions of real evidence recovered, names of people and places, and times and dates of all actions taken by the officer.

There are a few basic note-taking techniques which will aid the investigating officer in keeping these records.

1. Notes must be legible, brief, complete, and accurate.

2. Notes should be made as soon as possible, i. e. while conducting the investigation and while the information is fresh in the investigating officer's mind.

3. Notes must be complete enough to answer the basic questions about a possible crime (who, what, when, where, why, how) and also to record the officer's actions, sense perceptions, and thoughts.

4. At a crime scene, all descriptive information should be recorded. This would include descriptions, locations, and positions of objects, and all relevant dimensions, distances, and measurements.

5. Enough notes should be made to fix the details of a crime permanently in the officer's memory. It is easier to discard unneeded notes than to try to recall something which was not written down at all through neglect or laziness.

6. Statements of all witnesses, victims, subjects, and suspects should be recorded fully along with their names and physical descriptions.

7. Any thing or person that is missing or unaccounted for should be carefully described.

8. Notes should be identified by the name of the officer, case number or file number, or some other effective means.

Camera

Besides a carefully kept notebook, another very useful tool is the camera. A series of photographs can convey aspects of a crime scene which cannot be adequately described in words. Careful photographs, taken from all angles in order to give a fair and complete representation of a scene, may be an invaluable aid afterwards in determining the guilt or innocence of an accused. It should be emphasized that the notebook and camera should be used together in order to be effective. More will be said about the uses of these investigative tools later in this chapter.

CRIME SCENE SEARCH

One of the most critical phases of criminal investigation is the preliminary investigation at the scene of the crime. It is at this stage that a case may be made or lost, depending upon the efficiency of the officers who conduct the investigation. Generally, preliminary investigation of a crime scene involves four major types of activities.

1. Protection of the scene of the crime.
2. Recognition of the evidence.
3. Collection and preservation of the evidence.
4. Expert examination and evaluation of the evidence.

Protection of the Scene of the Crime

A crime scene may be defined as the place where a particular crime took place. It might be a room where a homicide occurred, a house in which a burglary was committed, or a building or portion thereof which has been bombed. The reason for protecting a crime scene is to preserve evidence in its original condition and location.

The following procedures are suggested for protecting the scene of a crime:

1. Proceed to the scene of the crime as soon as possible after being notified of its commission. Promptness in responding may prevent possible disturbance or destruction of evidence by witnesses or curious bystanders.
2. Immediately upon arrival at the scene, the officer or officers responsible for the investigation should exclude all unauthorized or unnecessary personnel from the crime scene, being careful at the same time to identify and segregate possible witnesses and suspects. No one other than officers or officials with responsibilities relating to the investigation of the crime should be allowed upon the scene. This applies even to law enforcement officers of the investigating officer's own department who have no connection with the investigation.
3. The area and boundaries of the scene of the crime should be determined and blocked off accordingly. This may include an entire house and yard or, on occasion, might even include a whole city block. If so, the area should be roped off or barricaded and, if necessary, other officers should be employed to secure it. If the entire scene is inside a house, or a single room therein, doors and windows may be secured and an officer stationed at the door designated for entrance and exit.

Recognition of Evidence

The term "evidence" can be defined as something which tends to prove or disprove the matter in question, or to influence the belief respecting the matter. Evidence involves all the means by which any alleged fact may be established or disproved when submitted to investigation. "Real" or "physical" evidence is that furnished by *things*—physical objects which can be viewed or inspected. "Testimonial" evidence is oral or verbal evidence given by witnesses. A more detailed discussion of evidence appears in Chapter 14.

After the scene of a crime has been secured, investigation should start immediately. The investigating officer must concern himself first with finding out what happened, which usually means interviewing witnesses and possibly other officers who may have arrived at the scene before him. The techniques of effective interviewing will be covered later in this chapter.

From the information obtained in interviews, the investigating officer should be able to determine what type of real evidence is pertinent. He can then make a preliminary inventory of all objects found at the crime scene. He should remember that there is almost always evidence to be found at the scene of a crime and that his task is to recognize, collect, and preserve it.

The investigating officer must constantly remind himself that the evidence he gathers at the crime scene may be used later at a criminal trial. Therefore, as an aid to recognizing evidence, he should evaluate the preliminary information he has received from witnesses as well as his own personal observations, and attempt to determine what criminal charge or charges will probably be brought against the offender. He then should list the elements of each offense to be charged and compare his available evidence with the elements to be proved. Thus, he can determine what strengths and weaknesses there are in the evidence available at the moment and he can determine what directions to take in his subsequent investigation.

The investigating officer must use caution not to overlook any relevant piece of evidence. Even though he may think that some object which he uncovers is a minor article with no apparent bearing on the case, it later may prove to be an important piece of evidence. Therefore, even the most insignificant objects should be gathered, identified, and recorded. The following are some of the more common types of real evidence which may be found at the scene of a crime:

1. Blood or semen stains.
2. Fingerprints or footprint impressions.
3. Weapons or tools.
4. Shell casings.
5. Glass or wood fragments.
6. Hairs or fibers.
7. Debris, such as dirt and sand.
8. Clothing or pieces thereof.
9. Cigarette butts or packages, and matchbook covers.
10. Documents, such as suicide notes, checks, threatening letters, etc.

Collection and Preservation of Real Evidence

The actual picking up and carrying away of real evidence at a crime scene is an involved process. Before anything else, the investigating officer should be aware that there may be Fourth Amendment search and seizure requirements to be met before the scene may be searched. Discussion of these requirements may be found in Chapters 2 through 8. Once these requirements have been satisfied, the investigating officer may find the following guidelines helpful in collecting the evidence:

1. Plan and Organize the Investigation

An investigating officer should make a preliminary survey of the scene, determine what work must be done, and in what order. He should check his equipment and make sure it is sufficient to do the job. Then he should conduct a detailed examination of the scene, using care not to disturb or obliterate any evidence, and taking the time necessary to be thorough.

2. Photograph the Scene

Before any objects are moved or examined, the entire scene should be recorded on film. It is a good rule to take more photographs than seem necessary rather than too few. Too often, lack of enough photographs has hindered a court in determining the truth of a matter. A thorough photographic coverage of a scene often will call attention to matters that were missed in visual observation. Comprehensive photographs can also be of assistance in later study and reconstruction of the scene. At the very least, the following types of photographs should be taken at the crime scene:

(a) Photo of entry and exit.

(b) Photo of point of attack (body, safe, cash drawer, etc.)

(c) Overall photos of entire crime scene.

(d) Close-up photos of all evidentiary items.

(e) Overall views of the outside, showing entry and escape routes and general neighborhood surroundings. This would include a photo of the people standing around watching. They are potential witnesses or suspects.

(f) Color photos of human bodies, if any, blood stains, and any other evidentiary items which show color.

Investigating officers should be aware that in order to have a photograph admitted in evidence at a trial, the photograph must be identified by a witness and be verified by him on personal knowledge that it is a true and accurate portrayal of its subject matter. While it is not necessary that this witness be the photographer, the witness must have personal knowledge of the scene or object in question and be able to testify that it is correctly portrayed by the photograph. For this reason, chalk marks, arrows, and other types of identifying markers should not be included in the original photographs of the scene of a crime. If it is necessary to accent certain places, areas, or things in a photograph, such as skidmarks or the place where a dead body was found, this can be done after all the necessary preliminary photographs of the scene have been taken. A second set of pictures then can be taken of the scene with the accent markers properly placed.

Identifying records should be made of each photograph taken, indicating the object photographed, date and time, direction in which the camera was pointed, distance, and lens settings. Each photograph taken should have a number and this number should be placed on the back of the print along with the case number.

3. Sketch the Scene and Make Measurements

A sketch of the scene of the crime should be made, showing in accurate perspective all items of evidence, furniture, doors, and windows. A large sheet of paper should be used if a large area is involved. Usually an officer's notebook is not large enough for all necessary details.

Each item in the sketch should be identified, the direction north shown, and the date, time, and case number noted. A field sketch need not be a work of art but should be sufficiently accurate and detailed so that a scale diagram can be prepared from it if necessary for subsequent trial. The name and signature of the officer preparing the sketch should appear at the bottom of the sketch.

Accurate measurements should be made of all pertinent items, such as the size of a room, the length of skidmarks, the size of entry to a house or room, and distances between objects. Every item also should be properly located by accurate measurements. Measurements for locating items may be made by triangulation, that is, by measuring to an object from two different fixed points. It is important that all measuring instruments be checked over for accuracy.

4. Collect All Real Evidence

After records of the entire scene of the crime have been made by photographs, sketches, and notes, the collection of all items of real evidence should be accomplished. Different types of real evidence will require different procedures and different containers for collecting them. It is beyond the scope of this chapter to go into detail as to the precise procedures for collecting each type of real evidence. Therefore, the following brief guidelines will have to suffice.

(a) Where fingerprint evidence may exist, collecting it should be done before collection of other items of evidence. Latent fingerprint impressions should be dusted, photographed, and then lifted.

(b) Real evidence like footprints, tire tracks, and tool marks, which cannot be placed in containers and carried away, should be photographed, and then casted or molded.

(c) Other evidentiary items should be picked up and placed in suitable containers. Extreme care must be taken that the container selected will adequately protect the evidence. As each item is picked up, it should be carefully examined, and detailed notes should be made as to such things as size, color, shape, and location. Each item of evidence should be kept in a separate container to avoid confusion, intermingling, or possible contamination.

The officer who picks up any evidentiary item in this process should be responsible for its identification and submission for analysis or evaluation, in order to keep proof of the chain of possession to a minimum. The fewer the number of persons who have handled a piece of real evidence, the fewer the witnesses who will have to take the stand to establish its identity. A good practice is to have one officer assigned the responsibility for picking up evidentiary items.

5. Identify and Preserve All Items of Real Evidence

Each evidentiary item should be marked with the case number, time, date, and the officer's initials, if space permits. On extremely small items, the official's initials will suffice. It should be kept in mind that each item may have to be identified later in court.

Items which cannot be marked, such as liquids, new clothing, and valuable jewelry or antiques, can either have identification tags attached, or have the essential information contained on appropriate labels attached to their containers. Perishable items should be placed under refrigeration immediately. All liquids should be placed in sealed containers to avoid contamination and possible evaporation. All clothing and similar material which is damp from blood or other liquid stains should be air dried before packaging.

Extreme caution should be exercised in placing initials or other identifying marks on items which are to be sent to a laboratory for processing. They should not be placed where they will adversely affect proper analysis or examination. For example, a bullet to be sent into the laboratory for ballistic tests should not be marked anywhere but upon its base or nose, where comparison of land and groove markings will not be affected.

Real evidence should be stored in a place which is protected and to which there is only controlled access. The whereabouts of evidentiary items, and the conditions of the items from time of discovery until their presentation in court must usually be accounted for on the witness stand. If and when an item is removed by anyone from its designated storage place, he should be required to give a signed receipt showing the time, date, and reason for removal.

Expert Examination and Evaluation of the Evidence

Expert examination, analysis, and evaluation can be performed on most types of real evidence found at the scene of a crime. However, all the preliminary steps of collection, identification, preservation, and packaging should be performed before an item of evidence is sent to the laboratory. Then, extreme care should be exercised in sending the evidence along.

Every package of evidence sent to the laboratory should be accompanied by a letter, a copy of which should be placed in the case file. The letter should contain the following information:

1. Type of crime and names of victims and suspects.
2. Description in detail of each piece of evidence sent, along with all pertinent facts which may be helpful in making an examination, analysis, and evaluation.
3. Type of service desired.

Every state, and some large cities, have either a central crime laboratory or other laboratories which will analyze and evaluate criminal evidence for law enforcement agencies. It is up to each law enforcement officer to know which laboratories provide which services in his state. Also the Federal Bureau of Investigation has a large crime laboratory which provides its services free of charge to any law enforcement agency in the country. And it will furnish technicians to testify in local courts concerning their findings. The FBI Lab will process any kind of evidence, but will not handle anything that has been processed by any other lab. The address is: Federal Bureau of Investigation Laboratory, U. S. Department of Justice, Washington, D. C. 20535.

INTERVIEWING

As mentioned above, the interview with witnesses is often the way an investigating officer obtains preliminary information about what happened at a crime scene and gets an idea of what to look for in the way of real evidence. Interviews, however, are also an important source of information in themselves. In fact, testimonial evidence of witnesses in court is often more effective than physical evidence in proving a case. Therefore, it is essential that the investigating officer obtain as much information as possible from interviews.

Interviews should be conducted as soon as possible after the event in question, while facts and images are still fresh in the mind of witnesses. A witness's memory can be unduly influenced by the passage of time and discussions with other persons.

The basic goal of an interview is to get the person being interviewed to talk. The officer obtains no information when he himself is talking. Strokes of brilliance and clever questions which "pay off" are rare. What is needed is a good basic technique combined with persistence.

General Approach or Attitude

In order to make a good initial impression on the person interviewed, the investigating officer's appearance should be clean and neat, and he should attempt to avoid anything that would be offensive or distasteful to the interviewee (chewing gum, smoking a cigar, loudness, etc.). The officer's initial approach should be courteous and cordial in order to create a relaxed atmosphere. He should also convey an air of frankness and openness so the interviewee will not become unduly wary of trick questions or clever techniques on the officer's part. The officer must be patient and show an interest in both the person interviewed and the information given. He must also control his own emotions and not indicate his personal feelings and attitudes in such a way as to pass judgment on or intimidate a witness.

Preparation for Interview

Every interview requires some preparation. The amount of preparation in each case will depend upon the time available, the information at hand, and various other factors. In any case, the investigating officer should have in mind what information he wants to obtain from a particular interview. In a complex case, it may be desirable to make a list of the information to be sought. Time permitting, the officer may even want to find out general information about the interviewee from relatives and friends before contacting him.

Physical Aspects of Interview

An attempt should be made to schedule an interview for a time when the person to be interviewed is not busy and when he is free to devote full attention to the interview. Whenever possible, it is best to interview a witness in private, preferably in some neutral setting such as his home or office, where he is more likely to be relaxed and to feel comfortable. A police station usually is the least desirable place to conduct an interview. Also, it is generally best not to have relatives, friends, or telephones around, so that the witness can talk freely without being interrupted or overheard.

Investigating officers should realize that all interviews are time consuming and they should not be impatient. A witness should be given plenty of time when being interviewed so that he can give his whole story in as much detail as possible. The best procedure is to let the witness tell the story in his own words and later to narrow the questioning down to specifics, if necessary.

Notes should be taken during an interview unless it distracts the witness or appears to have an adverse effect on his willingness to talk. When notes are not taken initially, the interviewing officer should have the witness tell his whole story without interruption. Then the officer should go back over the main points and at this time take down notes. A statement may then be prepared to be signed by the witness using the notes as a basis. It may be better to use a tape recorder in some situations.

While the officer is interviewing the witness, he should be carefully observing and evaluating him in order to properly weigh his statement and to assess his future value as a witness in court. Some of the things to look for during the interview are the physical and emotional condition of the witness, his mental ability and education, his experience, and his apparent prejudices and biases.

Interrogation

Some of the suggestions concerning interviews are applicable also to interrogation of persons suspected or accused of having committed a particular crime. However, when a suspect or accused is in custody or deprived by officers of his freedom of action in any significant way, the rules set forth in the U. S. Supreme Court's *Miranda* decision govern the situation. A detailed discussion of the *Miranda* decision appears in Chapter 10.

Subsequent Investigation

After physical evidence has been gathered at the scene and available witnesses have been interviewed, further investigation may be necessary to piece together loose ends and clear up cloudy information. This may involve finding further witnesses, sifting and evaluating clues, and running down leads. Each crime presents its own problems of investigation, but the following general suggestions may be helpful:

1. Screen the neighborhood of the crime scene for additional witnesses and evidence.
2. Interview neighbors, relatives, and friends of victims and suspects in order to collect background information.

3. Circulate pertinent information to other law enforcement agencies, news media, and other possible victims, requesting their assistance.
4. Be on the alert for the commission of similar crimes, stolen vehicles, pawned articles, loose conversation, etc., which might lead to the identification of the guilty party.
5. Compare statements of witnesses and interview them again if necessary.
6. Maintain constant liaison with the prosecuting attorney for his assistance and counsel, particularly in matters pertaining to warrants, arrests, lineups, interrogation of suspects, and the filing of proper charges.

This last suggestion may be the most important of those listed and deserves further comment. It ties in closely with the previous advice of always keeping case preparation in mind while investigating a crime. Besides investigating the case carefully and thoroughly, and keeping in close communication with the prosecuting attorney, the investigating officer can greatly aid the prosecutor by efficiently organizing cases for court preparation. This includes all the suggestions discussed above such as note taking, photographing the scene, proper labeling and filing.

Case Summary Sheet

One further step that will bring all the information together is the preparation of a case summary sheet for the use of the prosecuting attorney. On this sheet would be a listing of all witnesses with a brief statement of their expected testimony. Also a concise summary of the facts of the case along with any diagrams and brief descriptions of physical evidence should be included.

The case summary sheet should be forwarded to the prosecuting attorney prior to trial so that he may have ample time to study it and arrange for a pre-trial conference with the investigating officer and witnesses. The purposes of such a conference usually are to:

1. Clear up uncertain or involved points.
2. Anticipate possible defenses.
3. Determine the possible need for additional evidence.
4. Determine the possible desirability of changing the charge or filing an additional charge.
5. Plan trial strategy.

After the pre-trial conference, the investigating officer's final contact with a case will be his testimony in court, if he is called to testify. Suggestions and guidelines to assist law enforcement officers in testifying in court appear in Chapter 15.

SUMMARY

The investigation of criminal cases is an essential step in the process of apprehending an offender and determining his guilt or innocence. An organized, well-documented approach is the only way to insure that every clue is uncovered and every important piece of information is brought to light at a subsequent trial. Such an approach, together with close cooperation between law enforcement officers, prosecuting attorneys, and community resources is essential to the effective presentation of cases in court and contributes to the just and efficient operation of the criminal justice system.

*

13

CRIMINAL COURT PROCEDURE

The topics that have been covered thus far, namely Arrest, Search and Seizure, Confessions, Pre-Trial Identifications, and Criminal Investigation, are part of the law enforcement officer's daily duties, and are therefore somewhat familiar to him. The officer, however, may not be as familiar with the law of criminal procedure that governs a case after it reaches the prosecuting attorney. As a case moves through pleadings, motions, jury selection, trial and appeal, the law enforcement officer may be ignored or be treated as just another witness in the proceedings. To him the entire process may look like a complex legal jumble involving the prosecuting attorney, the defense attorney, and the judge or magistrate. Since the law enforcement officer is an integral part of the criminal justice system and often testifies in court as a witness, it is worthwhile for him to understand what is going on and to know the meaning of the various words and phrases that are used by the judges and the attorneys.

Criminal court procedure in most states is governed by court rules and statutes. These rules and statutes are designed for use by judges and attorneys to ensure the just and efficient processing of criminal offenders. Many of the rules are quite involved and do not directly concern the law enforcement officer. Therefore, an effort will be made in this chapter to highlight pertinent court procedures and legal terms that will provide a comprehensive view of how the system works, without dwelling too heavily on details which are of little direct concern to the law enforcement officer.

To the extent possible, this chapter will present the different stages of criminal court procedure in chronological order, following a criminal case from beginning to end. The discussion will be limited to court procedures for serious offenses and will not discuss procedures for traffic offenses and other petty misdemeanors. Wherever certain aspects of criminal court procedure might be covered in another chapter, reference will be made to that chapter. Because the information in this chapter is general, and because criminal court procedure differs by state, officers should not take the information presented here as the authority for their state, but should consult their state's pertinent statutes or rules.

STRUCTURE OF THE COURT SYSTEM

Before discussing the preliminary proceedings in a criminal case, it will be helpful to first briefly outline the basic structure of the federal court system and of a typical state court system, and to briefly describe the criminal trial jurisdiction of the different courts. "Jurisdiction," as used here, simply means the authority of a court to deal with a particular case.

The federal court system is larger and more complex than any state court system, but the basic structures of the two court systems are similar. Both the federal system and the state systems consist of courts which have original jurisdiction over criminal matters and courts which have appellate jurisdiction. "Original jurisdiction" means the authority to deal with a case from the beginning, to try it, and to pass judgment upon the facts and the law. "Appellate jurisdiction" means the authority to deal with a case, not in its initial stages, but only after it has been finally decided by an inferior court, and then only to revise or correct the proceedings in the inferior court.

The federal court system is divided into 88 judicial districts, each served by a United States District Court. Each state has at least one district within it. The District Courts have original jurisdiction over criminal cases, and the great majority of federal criminal cases begin in the District Courts.

The U. S. Court of Appeals and the U. S. Supreme Court both have appellate jurisdiction in criminal matters. The Court of Appeals is an intermediate appellate court because its decision can be further appealed to the U. S. Supreme Court. There are eleven divisions or Circuits of the U. S. Court of Appeals throughout the country. The U. S. Supreme Court is the appellate court of last resort, meaning that it is a court from which there is no appeal.

The U. S. Supreme Court has original jurisdiction in certain limited areas, but its greatest workload is to review the decisions of the lower federal courts and the highest state courts. The most common way in which the Supreme Court exercises its appellate jurisdiction is through the granting of a "writ of certiorari." The granting of a writ of certiorari means that the Supreme Court, upon petition of a party, agrees to review a case decided by one of the Circuit Court of Appeals or by the highest court of a state. Certiorari is granted at the Court's discretion when a case presents questions whose resolution will have an immediate impact and import beyond the particular facts of the case. Some cases may also reach the U. S. Supreme Court by direct appeal, e. g., when a state court declares a statute unconstitutional or a federal court finds that the provisions of a state statute are contrary to the treaties, laws, or Constitution of the United States. Also, a few cases may reach the U. S. Supreme Court upon a certification from a United States Court of Appeals requesting instructions on procedure with respect to a particular point of law.

Besides the courts mentioned, the federal court system also includes a number of specialized courts which have been established to hear particular classes of cases. Examples are the U. S. Court of Claims, the U. S. Court of Customs and Patent Appeals, the U. S. Customs Court, and the U. S. Tax Court. In addition, there are quasi-judicial boards or commissions, which have special and limited jurisdiction under specific federal statutes.

A typical state court system has the same basic structure as the federal system. Courts of original jurisdiction are usually divided into (1) courts that try only misdemeanor cases and (2) higher courts that try both misdemeanors and felonies. The courts that try only misdemeanor cases are usually established on a local level and may be called municipal courts, traffic courts, minor criminal courts, district courts, or something similar. For purposes of this chapter, these courts will be called local courts. The courts with original jurisdiction over both misdemeanors and felonies are usually established on a county or regional level and may be called county courts, district courts, superior courts, or something similar. Generally the more serious criminal cases will be instituted in these courts. In some states these courts may also exercise a limited appellate jurisdiction over certain cases appealed from the local courts. For purposes of this chapter these county, regional, or district courts will be called county courts.

From the county court level, a case may proceed through one or more intermediate appellate courts until it reaches the highest court (or the court of last resort) of the state, usually called the state supreme court. If a case involves important constitutional issues, it may finally reach the U. S. Supreme Court for review. Generally the state supreme court also has the power to prescribe rules of pleading, practice, and procedure before itself and the other lower courts of the state.

PRELIMINARY PROCEEDINGS

The Complaint

Criminal process against a defendant formally begins with the complaint. The reason the word "formally" is used here is that persons can be arrested for an offense before a complaint is filed or a warrant is issued. Such an arrest would be considered the beginning of the criminal process. However, since the arrest without a warrant is considered an exception to the basic warrant requirement, the complaint is still considered the formal beginning of proceedings.

The complaint can serve a dual purpose in a criminal proceeding. If the defendant has been arrested without a warrant, the complaint is prepared, signed, and filed at the defendant's initial appearance before the magistrate. The complaint serves as the charging document upon which the preliminary examination will be held. If the defendant has not been arrested, and is not before the court, the complaint serves as the basis for determining whether there is probable cause to justify the issuance of a warrant for his arrest.

The complaint must be made on oath or affirmation, must state the essential facts of the offense being charged, must be in writing, and must be made before a judicial officer authorized to issue process in criminal cases. This officer is usually called a magistrate. The information in the complaint does not have to be derived from personal observation or experience, but may be based upon information from others or upon circumstantial evidence. Nevertheless the evidence put forth in the complaint must be strong enough to convince the magistrate that there is probable cause to believe that an offense has been committed and that the defendant committed it. A complete discussion of probable cause appears in Chapter 3.

Affidavits

Information which is not contained in the complaint or which comes from witnesses other than the complainant may be brought to the court's attention in the form of an affidavit. An *affidavit* is a sworn statement of the facts relied upon in seeking the issuance of a warrant. It need not be prepared with any particular formality. It is filed with the complaint and together they can provide a sufficient written record for a reviewing court to examine in determining whether probable cause existed for the issuance of a warrant.

Warrant or Summons Issued on the Complaint

Once the magistrate has determined from the complaint and accompanying affidavits that there is probable cause to believe that an offense has been committed and that the defendant committed it, he then will issue either a summons or a warrant for the defendant's arrest. Of course, if the defendant is already before the court, no summons or warrant is necessary.

Once the warrant is issued, the law enforcement officer must execute the warrant by arresting the defendant and bringing him before a magistrate as commanded in the warrant. A detailed discussion of arrest warrant procedure appears in Chapter 1.

Proceedings Before the Magistrate

Once a person has been arrested either with or without a warrant, he is required by statute to be brought before a magistrate "without unnecessary delay," or "forthwith," depending upon statutory language. The details of this procedure are also discussed in Chapter 1.

The purpose of bringing an arrested person before a magistrate without unnecessary delay is to inform him of the following things:

1. the charge against him;
2. his right to retain counsel; and
3. his right to have a preliminary examination.

Under some statutes, the defendant must be informed that he is not required to make a statement, and that any statement made by him may be used against him. Also, a few statutes require that the defendant be informed of his right to request the assistance of free counsel in case of indigency. He is then given reasonable time and opportunity to consult an attorney and is admitted to bail where appropriate.

Preliminary Examination

At the preliminary examination (also called the preliminary hearing), the magistrate must determine whether there is probable cause to believe that an offense was committed and that the defendant committed it. The purpose of the preliminary examination is to provide another judicial determination of the existence of probable cause and to protect the defendant from a totally baseless prosecution. Nevertheless, many defendants waive the preliminary examination, allowing their cases to go directly to the grand jury.

The preliminary examination consists mainly of the presentation of evidence against the defendant by the prosecuting attorney. The defense attorney may cross-examine witnesses against the defendant as well as introduce evidence in the defendant's behalf. If probable cause to believe that the defendant committed the offense is found,

STATE OF MAINE

Superior Court
Knox, ss

SUPERIOR COURT
CR- 120-79

STATE OF MAINE

Vs.

Moe Torboat, Jr.

INDICTMENT FOR VIOLATION
17-A OF M.R.S.A. SECTION 353

(THEFT Class B)

THE GRAND JURY CHARGES:

that Moe Torboat, Jr. of Camden, in the County of Knox and State of Maine, on the second day of February, 1978, in the Town of Warren, County of Knox and State of Maine, did commit theft by obtaining or exercising control over the property of Otto Mabeel, to wit, one Realistic stereo receiver of the value of fifty dollars; one Winchester single shot, .22 rifle of the value of fifty dollars; one Zenith 19-inch color TV of the value of three hundred dollars; one table lamp of the value of fifteen dollars; one CB radio converter of the value of thirty dollars; and one buzzay of the value of five dollars, all of the aggregate value of four hundred and fifty dollars, with intent to deprive said Otto Mabeel thereof.

A True Bill.

Date: July 5, 1979

Clay Potts
Foreman

CR-18

[B9585]

the defendant will be held to answer to the grand jury in the county where the trial is to be held. This is often called binding the defendant over to the grand jury. The magistrate may admit the defendant to bail at the preliminary examination or may continue, increase, or decrease his original bail. If no probable cause is found, the magistrate will dismiss the complaint and discharge the defendant.

The U. S. Supreme Court, in Gerstein v. Pugh, 420 U.S. 103, 95 S.Ct. 854, 43 L.Ed.2d 54 (1975), held that the Fourth Amendment requires a judicial determination of probable cause as a prerequisite to extended detention following arrest. Under this decision, an arrested person may not be held in custody for a substantial period of time on the decision of a prosecuting attorney or other non-judicial officer. The arrested person must be promptly afforded a probable cause determination at a preliminary examination presided over by a judicial officer. The preliminary examination need not be an adversary proceeding, however, and the arrested person need not be afforded a right to counsel, confrontation, cross-examination, or compulsory process for witnesses.

INDICTMENT AND INFORMATION

The indictment and the information are the documents that charge the defendant with an offense and upon which the defendant is brought to trial. The indictment and the information are very similar in nature and content. Each is a concise and definite written statement of the essential facts constituting the offense charged. The main difference between the indictment and the information is that the indictment is issued by a grand jury and signed by the foreman of the grand jury. The information is signed and sworn to by the prosecuting attorney without the approval or intervention of the grand jury. The laws governing when the indictment or the information is used differ from state to state.

There are a number of somewhat technical provisions in state statutes and rules that deal with drafting, amending, and joining indictments or informations and with joining offenses or defendants for trial together. These provisions are of direct concern only to judges and attorneys and will not be discussed here.

An example of a typical indictment appears on page 342.

Grand Jury

The grand jury usually consists of from 12 to 23 jurors, selected from their communities according to law to serve during the criminal term of the appropriate court. The duty of the grand jury is to receive complaints in criminal cases, hear the evidence put forth by the state, and find an indictment when they are satisfied that there is probable cause that the defendant has committed an offense. The concurrence of a specified number of grand jurors is required in order to find an indictment.

Grand jury proceedings are traditionally kept secret. During deliberations or voting, no persons other than the jurors are allowed to be present. When the grand jury is taking evidence, however, the attorneys for the state, the witnesses under examination, and an official court reporter may be present. Matters occurring before the grand jury, other than the deliberations or the votes of any juror, may be disclosed to the prosecuting attorney for use in performing his duties. Otherwise, these matters are to be kept secret, unless the court orders that they be disclosed.

The reasons for keeping grand jury proceedings secret can be summarized as follows:

1. To prevent the escape from the jurisdiction of someone who is not yet in custody but whose indictment may be contemplated;
2. To provide the utmost freedom for the grand jury in its deliberations and to protect them from outside influences;
3. To prevent tampering with witnesses who may testify before the grand jury and later appear at the trial of those indicted;
4. To encourage the free and unrestrained disclosure of information by persons who have information on the commission of crimes; and
5. To protect innocent persons who are exonerated of charges from disclosure of the fact that they were under grand jury investigation.

Waiver of Indictment

In some states a defendant who does not wish to be prosecuted by indictment may waive the indictment and be prosecuted by information. The waiver of an indictment procedure is of great advantage to a defendant who desires to plead guilty or *nolo contendere.* (These pleas will be discussed in further detail in this chapter.) In effect, the waiver of indictment procedure enables a defendant to begin serving a sentence immediately instead of having to wait for a grand jury, which sits only during the criminal term of court. The defendant can thereby secure his release from custody at an earlier date than he would if he had gone through the indictment procedure.

Warrant or Summons Issued on the Indictment

An indictment may sometimes be found against a defendant before he has been taken into custody and brought before the court. In these cases, upon the request of the attorney for the state, or by direction of the court, the clerk shall issue a summons or a warrant for the arrest of each defendant named in the indictment. This indicates no change of procedure for the law enforcement officer. He is required to execute the warrant or serve the summons in the same way as he would any other warrant or summons. Procedures for executing an arrest warrant or serving a summons appear in Chapter 1.

ARRAIGNMENT AND PREPARATION FOR TRIAL

The next step in the criminal proceeding, after an indictment or information is found, is the arraignment. The term "arraignment" is often confused with the initial appearance before a magistrate by a defendant who has been arrested. Part of the reason for the confusion is that in misdemeanor proceedings in many local courts, the two procedures are combined. The essence of the arraignment is that the defendant is *called upon to plead* to the charge against him after the substance of the charge is read to him. In local court misdemeanor proceedings, if there is no requirement of prosecution by indictment or information, the *complaint* is read to defendant and he pleads to the complaint. However, in courts where prosecution must be by indictment or information, the *indictment* or *information* is read to the defendant and he pleads to that. Therefore, in courts which require prosecution by indictment or information, the arraignment proceeding must be separate from the initial appearance before the magistrate.

Pleas

As mentioned above, the distinctive feature of arraignment is that the defendant is called upon to plead to the charge against him. Although the pleas available to the defendant differ from state to state, three of the most common pleas are:

1. Not guilty;
2. Guilty; and
3. *Nolo contendere* (no contest).

Each of these merits some explanation.

A plea of not guilty puts in issue all the material facts alleged in the indictment, information, or complaint. A defendant has a right to refuse to plead at all in which case the court must enter a plea of not guilty.

In order to plead guilty or *nolo contendere,* the defendant must obtain the consent of the court. Both of these pleas have the same effect on the defendant with one exception. They simply mean that the defendant does not wish to contest the charge but will submit to the judgment of the court. The exception is that a guilty plea may constitute an admission of guilt by the defendant and may be used against him in a *civil* action based on the same facts. A plea of *nolo contendere* is not an admission and cannot be used against the defendant in a civil action.

The court may not accept a plea of guilty or *nolo contendere* in a felony proceeding unless the court is satisfied, after inquiry, that the defendant committed the crime charged, and that the plea is made voluntarily with an understanding of the nature of the charge.

In some states, a plea of not guilty by reason of insanity may be entered. This plea is required if the defendant intends to raise the defense of insanity. A defendant may plead not guilty and not guilty by reason of insanity to the same charge. When a plea of not guilty by reason of insanity is entered, the court may, on petition, order the defendant committed to an appropriate institution for the mentally ill for examination. The insanity plea is rarely raised in a misdemeanor proceeding.

Motions

Before trial, there are many contentions and requests which the defendant may put forth by way of motions. These motions are heard by the court and may result in various forms of relief ranging from amending or curing a defect in the complaint, indictment, or information to discharging the defendant. Because most motions are primarily of concern to judges and attorneys, they will not be discussed in detail here. There are two pretrial motions, however, which are of direct concern to the law enforcement officer (1) the motion to suppress evidence, and (2) the motion to suppress a confession. These motions are made by a defendant who believes he is aggrieved by either an unlawful search and seizure, or an unlawfully obtained admission or confession. Some states do not allow one or both of these motions to be made before trial.

The purpose of a motion to suppress is twofold:

1. To enable the defendant to invoke the exclusionary rule and prevent the use of illegally obtained evidence at his trial; and
2. To enable the court to resolve the issue of the legality of a search and seizure or confession without interrupting the trial.

The motion to suppress is important to the law enforcement officer because the hearing on the motion is often the point in the proceedings at which an officer's performance in a case is carefully scrutinized by the court. If the defendant is able to prove that evidence was illegally obtained by an officer and if the evidence is essential to the prosecution's case, suppression of the evidence is likely to result in a dismissal of charges or the granting of a motion for judgment of acquittal. It is important, therefore, for the law enforcement officer to know the law not only at the time he conducts a search and seizure or obtains a confession, but also later when he may be called upon to justify his actions at a hearing on a motion to suppress.

Depositions

When a witness is unable to attend a criminal trial, and it is shown that his testimony is material to a just determination of the case, the court may order that a deposition of the witness be taken at any time after the filing of an indictment or information. A deposition involves taking the testimony of a witness out of court and preserving that testimony in writing for later use in court. It is used only in exceptional circumstances and not for the mere convenience of a witness or party. It may be requested by either the state or the defendant, and the opposing party is given the opportunity to attend the taking of the deposition.

A deposition, or a part thereof, may be used at a trial or hearing if it appears that any of the following circumstances exist:

1. The witness who gave the deposition is dead;
2. The witness is out of the state (unless, of course, the party offering the deposition caused the witness's absence);
3. The witness is unable to attend or testify because of sickness or infirmity; or
4. The party offering the deposition is unable to procure the attendance of the witnesses by subpoena.

Furthermore, depositions may be used even if the witness does testify at the trial, but only for the purposes of contradicting or impeaching his testimony.

Discovery

Discovery is the procedure by which a defendant in a criminal case petitions the court to allow him to inspect, copy, or photograph certain items which are in the possession of the prosecution. In order to obtain this right, the defendant must make a motion before the court and show that the items he seeks may be material to the preparation of his defense, and that his request is reasonable. The items sought may be books, papers, documents, or tangible objects, and may include written or recorded statements or confessions made by the defendant or a co-defendant, written or recorded statements of witnesses, and the results or reports of physical examinations and scientific tests, experiments, and comparisons.

There are considerable differences among states with respect to the conditions under which discovery is allowed and the items which are subject to discovery. Some states do not allow discovery at all. Other states allow discovery as a matter of right for certain items and even allow discovery by the prosecution in certain instances. The state of the law of discovery is constantly changing, but the trend appears to be in favor of broadening the right of discovery for both the defense and the prosecution.

It is worthwhile to mention the rationale behind the discovery procedure. Allowing the defendant access to information prior to trial can help to eliminate the concealment of evidence by the prosecution that could later result in the surprising of an unprepared defendant at trial. Discovery can assist in the fair and expeditious disposition of certain cases before trial. It can also assure a fuller presentation of evidence at trial.

The discovery procedure recognizes that there is a basic imbalance between the investigative resources of the defense and the prosecution. The state has at its disposal an investigative staff to assist in obtaining evidence. The state can also obtain the services of scientists and technicians to conduct tests and experiments. Furthermore, the state can conduct interrogations to obtain evidence, even though this method of investigation has been severely limited in recent years by court decisions. The defendant on the other hand goes to trial with very little evidence and must rely heavily on challenging and discrediting the prosecution's case. The right of discovery is designed to correct this imbalance and enable the defendant to more adequately prepare his defense.

Subpoena

The term "subpoena" is used to describe the process used to secure the attendance of witnesses or the production of books, papers, documents, or other objects at a criminal proceeding. The subpoena is issued by a judicial officer and it commands the person to whom it is directed to attend a trial, hearing, or deposition for the purpose of testifying at the proceeding or bringing with him a named document or object. A subpoena can be served by a law enforcement officer or any other adult person who is not a party to the proceedings.

VENUE

One final pretrial matter to be dealt with is the definition of the term "venue." Venue is often confused with jurisdiction. Jurisdiction refers to the authority of the court to deal with a particular case. For instance, a municipal court may have *jurisdiction* over misdemeanor offenses. Venue, on the other hand, merely refers to the *place* at which the authority of the court should be exercised. For example, some statutes require that the trial of certain types of cases be held in the geographic division of the court in which the offense was committed.

Most states have special rules relating to the proper venue for offenses that are committed on a boundary of two counties or offenses part of which is committed in one county and another part in another county. These technicalities will not be discussed here.

Change of Venue

Sometimes, because of heavy publicity or intense community feeling, a defendant may wish to have his case tried in a different place than the one authorized by statute. To enable him to do so, a procedure is provided for a defendant to make a motion for a change of venue. The motion usually must be made before the jury is impaneled or, in cases where there is no jury, before any evidence is received. Defendant must, of course, give adequate reasons in support of the motion. Typical grounds for granting a motion for change of venue are:

1. There is such prejudice in the county where the case is to be tried that defendant cannot obtain a fair and impartial trial there; or
2. Another location is much more convenient for the parties and witnesses than the intended place of trial, and the interests of justice require a transfer of location.

THE TRIAL

The United States Constitution and most state constitutions guarantee a defendant in a criminal prosecution a speedy, public, and impartial trial by jury. This guarantee means that a defendant must be provided a jury trial in all criminal prosecutions except those for petty offenses. If, however, a defendant does not wish to be tried by a jury, he may, with the approval of the court, waive in writing his right to a jury trial.

Trial Without a Jury

When a case is tried without a jury, the judge must perform the jury's function of weighing the evidence, determining the credibility of witnesses, and finding the facts, in addition to his regular duties as judge. He must also make a finding as to the guilt or innocence of the defendant based upon his view of the evidence. Outside of his performance of these jury functions in a non-jury trial, the judge's other regular duties are essentially the same in either a jury or a non-jury trial. Therefore, the remainder of this chapter will be concerned primarily with jury trials.

Selection of Jurors

Once it has been determined that the trial will be by jury, the next step in the criminal proceeding is the selection of the jurors. This step is very important because the jurors will be performing the crucial tasks of finding the facts, determining the credibility of witnesses, weighing the evidence, and ultimately issuing a verdict of guilty or not guilty. Because of the importance of the jury's function, there are detailed rules governing the selection of jurors. These rules are designed to protect the state or the defendant from a person who is prejudiced against its cause sitting as a member of the jury during the trial of the case.

The selection of the jury is accomplished by the court through an examination of prospective jurors on the jury panel or venire. The *jury panel* is a list of members of the community considered fit for jury service. The list is compiled by local officials, often according to statute. It must be indiscriminately drawn and must not *systematically* exclude any class of persons.

The examination of prospective jurors on the panel is commonly referred to as *voir dire*. The usual method of examination is to question the prospective jurors with regard to their feelings and views on various matters. The parties or their attorneys may conduct the examination unless the court elects to conduct the initial examination itself. If the court conducts the initial examination, the court must allow the parties or their attorneys to address additional questions to the prospective jurors on any subject which has not been fully covered and which is relevant to the juror's qualifications.

The purpose of the examination or *voir dire* is to determine whether any prospective juror is prejudiced about the case in any way. Typical questions asked relate to whether the prospective juror knows the defendant, the attorneys, or any of the witnesses; whether he has read about the case in the newspapers; and whether he has formed any opinions on the case.

If either attorney wishes to have a prospective juror dismissed on the basis of these questions or for any other reason, he may issue a challenge to that juror. There are two types of challenges available. One is a *challenge for cause* and it is directed toward the qualifications of a juror. Most states have statutes setting out the permissible grounds for a challenge for cause. Typical grounds are:

1. The juror is related to one of the parties;
2. The juror has given or formed an opinion in the case; or
3. The juror has a bias, prejudice, or particular interest in the cause.

Each party has an unlimited number of challenges for cause available to him assuming that he can establish the grounds for such a challenge to the satisfaction of the judge.

The other form of challenge is known as the *peremptory challenge*. Peremptory challenges are available to each party as a means for dismissing prospective jurors who may be qualified, but who for some other reason are felt to be undesirable by one party's attorney. No reason need be given for a peremptory challenge. Peremptory challenges have to be exercised with great care. It is often difficult to determine from a few questions whether a prospective juror will be receptive or antagonistic to a party's position. Furthermore, the number of peremptory challenges available to each side is limited in number.

Once all the challenges available to both the prosecution and defense are exercised, a jury of 12 remains and is sworn in by the judge to try the case. In some cases, additional jurors are selected as alternates, who sit in on the case but who do not enter deliberations unless one of the regular 12 jurors becomes ill or dies, or is unable to serve for some other reason. It should be noted that the parties may agree, with the approval of the court, to a jury of less than 12. This is rarely done, however, except in cases in which a juror dies during trial and there is no alternate to take his place. After administering an oath to the jurors, the judge admonishes the jurors to discuss the case with no one until the jury goes into deliberations to decide the case after hearing all the evidence.

Presentation of Evidence

Once the jury has been impaneled, the presentation of evidence begins with the opening statement of the prosecuting attorney. The prosecuting attorney gives an outline of what he intends to prove by the evidence he will present. Following this, the defense counsel makes an opening statement to the jury outlining what he intends to prove. Sometimes, however, the defense counsel will wait until the prosecutor has presented the state's evidence before giving his opening statement, thereby concealing the course of his defense until the government has disclosed its proof.

In either case, after the opening statement or statements are given, the prosecutor begins the introduction of the state's proof. The state is entitled to present its evidence first in a criminal case because it is the plaintiff and therefore has the burden of proof. The burden of proof means the duty to establish the truth of facts alleged in support of every element of the offense charged against the defendant. The burden of proof is upon the prosecution from the beginning to the end of the trial because of the presumption that the accused is innocent. Furthermore, the prosecution is required to prove the defendant's guilt *beyond a reasonable doubt.* Reasonable doubt is a term requiring little interpretation although various courts have attempted to formulate somewhat involved definitions which add little beyond its plain meaning. Suffice it to say that proof beyond a reasonable doubt requires that the guilt of the defendant be established to a reasonable, but not absolute or mathematical certainty. Probability of guilt is not sufficient.

Rules of Evidence

The rules of evidence govern which evidence will be admissible in court and which will be excluded. These rules are designed to ensure that only trustworthy, competent, and credible information is presented to the jury. The rules of evidence are discussed in Chapter 14.

Order of Presentation of Evidence

The order of presentation of evidence begins with the *direct examination* or *examination in chief* of the prosecution's first witness. This witness will be someone whom the prosecution has called. He will be expected to give evidence favorable to the state's position. The examination of the witness is designed to produce evidence that will prove the state's case against the defendant. A law enforcement officer is usually involved as a witness for the prosecution, sometimes as its only witness. For a discussion of the importance of the officer as a witness and various techniques and suggestions for testifying in court, see Chapter 15.

When the prosecutor is through questioning his witness, the defense counsel then has a right to question the same witness. This is known as *cross-examination.* Its purpose is either to discredit information given by the witness or to impeach his credibility as a witness. In some states, the defense attorney on cross-examination is limited to questioning the witness on matters raised by the prosecutor during direct examination. In other states, the defense attorney is not so limited, and he may cross-examine the witness concerning any matter which is relevant and material to an issue in question. The judge determines what is relevant and material.

After cross-examination, the prosecutor may wish to re-examine his witness in order to rehabilitate him in the eyes of the jury. This is called *redirect* examination. Unlike cross-examination, the scope of redirect examination is limited to those matters brought out in the previous examination by the adverse party. This same rule applies if the defense counsel wishes to conduct a recross-examination. This order of presenting evidence by direct examination, cross-examination, redirect, and recross is followed for all of the prosecutor's witnesses until all of the state's evidence has been presented.

Motion for Acquittal

After the prosecutor has presented the state's evidence, the defense counsel may move for a judgment of acquittal. A judgment of acquittal will be granted in cases in which the evidence is insufficient to sustain a conviction on the offense or offenses charged. This will usually mean that the judge has decided that reasonable men could not conclude that guilt has been proven beyond a reasonable doubt. If the motion is not granted at the close of the state's evidence, the defense may then offer its evidence. The motion for acquittal may be renewed at the close of all the evidence or, at the judge's discretion, it may be renewed after the jury returns a verdict or is discharged without having returned a verdict.

The Defendant's Evidence

Assuming that the court does not grant a motion for judgment of acquittal at the close of the prosecution's evidence, the defense counsel then has an opportunity to present his evidence. The defense may put forth one or more of several possible defenses to refute the proof offered by the state. Among the defenses available to the defendant are alibi, insanity, self-defense, and entrapment. In presenting any of these defenses, the defense counsel may call witnesses on direct examination. The prosecutor has a right to cross-examine each of the defense witnesses, just as the defense counsel had a right to cross-examine the state's witnesses.

The defendant may or may not choose to testify in his own behalf. He has an absolute constitutional right *not* to testify. If he does testify, he is treated much like any other witness. If he does not choose to testify, the prosecuting attorney is not permitted to comment upon his failure to testify to the jury. The basis for this principle is the constitutional privilege which protects a person from self-incrimination.

Rebuttal by the Prosecution

Assuming that a motion for judgment of acquittal is not granted at the close of defendant's evidence, the prosecution is entitled to present rebuttal proof at this time. Rebuttal proof is designed to controvert evidence presented by the defense and to rebut any special defenses raised. Rebuttal proof is limited to new matter brought out in the defendant's presentation of evidence. Law enforcement officers may be called as witnesses again at this stage of the prosecution to correct any errors or misleading impressions that might be left after the defendant's presentation of evidence.

Closing Arguments

After all the evidence has been presented, both the prosecutor and the defense attorney are allotted certain amounts of time, usually specified by statute or rule, for final argument. In the final argument, the attorney for each side attempts to convince the jury (in non-jury cases, the judge) of the correctness of his position. The attorney for the state presents his argument first and is followed by the attorney for the defense. The attorney for the state is then allowed to present a short rebuttal. Much leeway is given for the attorneys for both sides to use their wit and imagination to win the jury over to their respective positions. However, they are required to confine themselves to a discussion of the evidence presented and reasonable inferences to be derived from that evidence.

Instructions to the Jury

After the final arguments and before the jury retires for deliberations, the judge must give instructions to the jury regarding the law of the case. The attorney for each side is given an opportunity to submit written requests to the judge for particular instructions that he wishes to be given. In a typical case, the instructions will cover such matters as the respective responsibilities of the court and the jury, the presumption of innocence and the burden of proof, various evidentiary problems, a definition of the offense or offenses charged, additional clarification of the critical elements of these offenses, any defenses which are properly in the case, and the procedures to be followed in the jury room. The exact content of the instructions is a matter for the judge's discretion but the attorneys are given an opportunity to object to any portion of the charge or any omission therefrom.

The judge may summarize the evidence for the jury, help them recall details, and attempt to resolve the complicated evidence into its simplest elements. However, the judge may not express any opinion on any issue of fact in the case nor may he favor either side in summarizing the evidence.

Verdict

After receiving instructions, the jury retires to the jury room to begin deliberations on a verdict. The *verdict* is the decision of the jury as to the defendant's guilt or innocence and it must be unanimous. If the jurors are unable to agree on a verdict, a hung jury results. The jurors are then dismissed and the case must be either retried or dropped. If however, an agreement is reached, the jurors return to the courtroom and the verdict is read in open court by the jury foreman. Any party, or the court itself, may then request a *poll* of the jury. This simply involves asking each individual juror if he concurs in the verdict. The purpose of polling the jury is to make sure that the verdict was not reached as a result of the coercion or domination of one juror by some of his fellows or as a result of sheer mental or physical exhaustion of a juror. If, during the poll, it is found any juror did not concur in the verdict, the whole jury may be directed to retire for further deliberations or they may be discharged by the judge.

SENTENCE AND JUDGMENT

After the defendant's guilt or innocence has been determined, either by verdict of the jury or by a judge without a jury, the judge must enter a judgment in the case. The judgment is merely the written evidence of the final disposition of the case by the court. If the defendant is found not guilty or for some other reason is entitled to be discharged, the judgment is entered accordingly, and the defendant is free forever from any further prosecution for the crime for which he was tried. However, if the defendant is found guilty, the judge must pass sentence on the defendant before entering judgment.

The determination of the sentence is perhaps the most sensitive and difficult decision the judge has to make because of the effect it will have on the defendant's life. For this reason, most states have laws directing and guiding the judge in his determination. A typical provision requires the judge to impose sentence without unreasonable delay. This protects the defendant from a prolonged period of uncertainty as to his future. Also, before imposing sentence, the judge is usually required to address the defendant personally and ask him if he desires to be heard prior to the imposition of sentence. The defendant may be heard personally or by counsel or both. The purpose of this provision is to enable the defendant to present any information which may be of assistance to the court in determining his punishment.

Another typical statutory provision that is designed to assist the court in fixing sentence allows the court, in its discretion, to direct the state probation and parole board to make a pre-sentence investigation and report to the court before the imposition of sentence. This report will contain any prior criminal record of defendant and such other information on his personal characteristics, his financial condition, and the circumstances affecting his behavior as may be helpful to the court in reaching its decision.

The court has a number of alternatives open to it with respect to sentencing, depending largely on individual state criminal statutes. Some criminal statutes have mandatory sentences, some have fixed maximum and/or minimum sentences, and others leave the matter of sentencing to the judge. Therefore, depending upon the offense for which the defendant has been convicted, the court may have very broad discretion in fixing sentence, or no discretion whatsoever. It should be noted that, in a few states, the jury has power to fix the sentence as well as to determine guilt or innocence.

Probation

The court also has the power to place a defendant on probation provided he has been convicted of an offense not punishable by life imprisonment. Probation is usually controlled by statute. It is a procedure by which a person found guilty of an offense is released by the court, subject to conditions imposed by the court, without being committed to a state penal or correctional institution. Probation of a defendant is usually effected in one of two ways. The court may sentence the defendant, suspend the execution of the sentence, and place the defendant on probation; or the court may continue the matter for sentencing for a period of not more than two years and during that period place the defendant on probation. Once a defendant is placed on probation, he is under the control and supervision of the state probation and parole board, although still under the jurisdiction of the court.

In some states, a different type of probation may be imposed by the court for those caess that involve the violation of any statutes concerning controlled or illegal drugs or narcotics. In such cases, the court may impose sentence, place the defendant on probation, and require as a condition of probation that the defendant participate in programs at an approved drug treatment facility.

POST-TRIAL MOTIONS

After judgment has been entered, there are still several motions available to the defendant to challenge the decision of the court. One of these is the motion for judgment of acquittal, sometimes called a motion for "judgment notwithstanding the verdict." The statutes or rules in some states provide that this motion can be made after the jury has been discharged as long as it is made within a specified time after the discharge. Courts will usually not grant such a motion unless

1. the state's evidence was insufficient or nonexistent on a vital element of the offense charged; or
2. the indictment or information did not state a criminal offense under state law.

Another motion open to the defendant is the motion for a new trial. This motion may be made in addition to a motion for acquittal. When it is made alone, it is sometimes deemed to include a motion for judgment of acquittal. In the latter case, if the defendant moves for a new trial, the court in granting it may either enter a final judgment of acquittal or grant a new trial. A new trial may be granted by the court if it is required in the interest of justice. The usual ground for granting a new trial is the insufficiency of the evidence to support the verdict. Some courts have also considered errors of law and improper conduct of trial participants during the trial under the motion.

Another ground for granting a motion for a new trial, which carries with it a difference in procedure, is the discovery of new evidence. The procedural difference is an extended time period during which a motion for a new trial based on the ground of newly discovered evidence may be made. The time period varies from state to state but is usually longer than the period for a motion based on any other ground. The reason for this is to allow a reasonable amount of time for the discovery of new evidence. In order to justify the granting of a motion for a new trial on the ground of newly discovered evidence, it must be shown that the new evidence will probably change the result of the trial, that it could not have been discovered before the trial by the exercise of due diligence, that it is material to the issue, and that it is not merely cumulative or impeaching.

Either by motion of the defendant or by motion of the court, the defendant may obtain a revision or correction of his sentence. The power to revise a sentence is granted to enable the trial court to change a sentence which is inappropriate in a particular case, even though the sentence may be legal and was imposed in a legal manner. This power to revise a sentence includes the power to increase as well as to reduce the sentence.

In contrast with the power to revise, the power to correct a sentence is granted to enable the court to change a sentence because the sentence was either illegal or it was imposed in an illegal manner. An illegal sentence might be one which was in excess of the statutory maximum. An illegally *imposed* sentence might be one in which the defendant was not personally addressed by the judge and given an opportunity to be heard before sentencing, where such a procedure is required by statute. In any case, the court must exercise both its power to revise and its power to correct a sentence within specific time periods or the powers are lost.

REMEDIES AFTER CONVICTION

There are two major forms of relief for a defendant, after he has been convicted of a crime—*appeal* and *habeas corpus*. Each will be discussed separately here.

Appeal

A defendant has a right to appeal when he has been convicted of a crime and all of his post-trial motions have been denied by the trial judge. The procedure for a defendant to appeal his conviction varies from state to state, and will not be detailed here. It involves among other things, the filing of a notice of appeal, the designation of the parts of the trial record to be considered on appeal, the filing of a statement of points on appeal, the filing of briefs, and the arguing of the briefs before the appellate court. If a defendant is unable to afford a lawyer to handle his appeal, provision is made in state statutes or rules for a lawyer to be appointed by the court free of charge.

In some states, by statute, the prosecution is also given a right to appeal adverse decisions of the trial court. The prosecution's right to appeal, however, is usually much more limited than the defendant's right. Typical state statutes allow appeal by the prosecution of adverse rulings made *before* the jury hears the case or in cases in which the defendant has himself appealed. The procedure for appeal by the prosecution is essentially the same as it is for the defendant.

The important thing to remember about the appeal procedure is that it is *not* a retrial of the case, nor is it ordinarily a reexamination of factual issues. The determination of factual issues is the function of the jury or, in a non-jury case, of the lower court judge. The function of the appellate court in an appeal is primarily to review the *legal* issues involved in the case. A simple example will illustrate this point.

Suppose a law enforcement officer has obtained a confession from a defendant but has forgotten to give him his *Miranda* warnings prior to a custodial interrogation. During the trial of the case, the trial judge erroneously permitted the officer who obtained the confession to read it to the jury over the objection of the defense. The jury convicted the defendant. On appeal, the defendant argues that the trial judge committed an error of law in allowing the jury to hear the confession.

The appellate court would very likely reverse the conviction on the basis of the error of law made by the trial judge. Along with reversal, the usual procedure is to remand or send the case to the trial court for a new trial with instructions to exclude the confession from the jury in the new trial. A different jury would then hear the evidence in the case, without the tainted confession, and render another verdict.

Therefore, even though a conviction is reversed on appeal, it does not necessarily mean that the defendant is acquitted and can go free. It usually means simply that the defendant has won the right to be tried again.

If the appellate court finds that the trial court committed no errors of law, it will affirm the defendant's conviction. The defendant, however, may still have a chance for further appeal. If his appeal was heard in an intermediate appellate court, he has the possibility of an additional appeal to the highest appellate court in the state. If the defendant's appeal was heard in the highest appellate court in the state, he may still appeal to the U. S. Supreme Court. It should be noted that the U. S. Supreme Court and the highest appellate courts of some states have discretionary jurisdiction and may select the cases which they will hear. A defendant has no right to insist upon having his appeal heard by such a court.

Appeals may only be taken from cases which have come to a final judgment. This means that an appellate court will not decide any legal issues nor will it review the denial of any motions until the case has been finally disposed of by the trial court. The reason for this rule is to prevent unnecessary delays in the conduct of trials which would result if the parties could appeal issues during the course of a trial. There are some minor exceptions to the final judgment rule, but they will not be discussed here.

When an appellate court decides a case, it delivers a written opinion to explain and justify its decision. In this way the higher court explains the trial judge's errors and also informs the party losing the appeal that he has lost and why he has lost. The decisions of the appellate courts are compiled and published in books of reported court decisions, which can be found in law libraries. These reported decisions are used by attorneys and judges as authorities for arguing and deciding future cases which raise issues similar to those already decided.

Habeas Corpus

Federal Habeas Corpus for State Prisoners

A state prisoner may challenge his state conviction on constitutional grounds by means of a petition for a writ of habeas corpus in federal court. The federal statute governing the remedy is 28 U.S.C. 2254. Initially, the constitutional grounds for which habeas corpus relief could be granted were limited to those relating to the jurisdiction of the state court, but the United States Supreme Court extended the scope of the writ to all constitutional challenges by its decision in Fay v. Noia, 372 U.S. 391, 83 S.Ct. 822, 9 L.Ed.2d 837 (1963).

Recently, the United States Supreme Court again limited federal habeas corpus review of state prisoners' claims of violations of federal constitutional rights, holding that "where the State has provided an opportunity for full and fair litigation of a Fourth Amendment claim, a state prisoner may not be granted federal habeas corpus relief on the ground that evidence obtained in an unconstitutional search or seizure was introduced at his trial." Stone v. Powell, 428 U.S. 465, 494, 96 S.Ct. 3037, 3052, 49 L.Ed.2d 1067, 1088 (1976). With that limitation, however, other constitutional claims of state prisoners may be heard in a federal habeas corpus proceeding even though the claims have been fully adjudicated by a state court. Townsend v. Sain, 372 U.S. 293, 83 S.Ct. 745, 9 L.Ed.2d 770 (U. S. Supreme Court, 1963). Also, constitutional claims that were not adjudicated in a state court because the prisoner forfeited his remedy by failing to observe state procedural rules may nevertheless still be considered on habeas corpus by a federal court.

A defendant may forfeit his right to federal habeas corpus review of a constitutional claim if he *deliberately* fails to comply with valid state procedural requirements for enforcing that claim. Fay v. Noia, supra. Federal habeas corpus review may likewise be barred if he is unable to show cause for noncompliance with a state procedural rule and show some actual prejudice resulting from the alleged constitutional violation. Wainwright v. Sykes, 433 U.S. 72, 97 S.Ct. 2497, 53 L.Ed.2d 594 (U. S. Supreme Court, 1977).

A prisoner must exhaust available state remedies before a federal court will consider his claim on habeas corpus. This means that, if an appeal or other procedure to hear his claim is still available by right in the state court system, the prisoner must pursue that procedure before a federal habeas corpus application will be considered.

Post-Conviction Relief for Federal Prisoners

In 1948, Congress enacted a statute (28 U.S.C. § 2255) that was designed to serve as a substitute for habeas corpus for federal prisoners. The primary purpose of the statute was to shift the jurisdictions of the courts hearing habeas corpus applications. The basic scope of the remedy that had been available to federal prisoners by habeas corpus was not changed by the statute.

Section 2255 provides in part:

> A prisoner in custody under sentence of a court established by Act of Congress claiming the right to be released upon the ground that the sentence was imposed in violation of the Constitution or laws of the United States, or that the court was without jurisdiction to impose such sentence, or that the sentence was in excess of the maximum authorized by law, or is otherwise subject to collateral attack, may move the court which imposed the sentence to vacate, set aside or correct the sentence.
>
> * * *
>
> An application for a writ of habeas corpus in behalf of a prisoner who is authorized to apply for relief by motion pursuant to this section, shall not be entertained if it appears that the applicant has failed to apply for relief, by motion, to the court which sentenced him, or that such court has denied him relief, unless it also appears that the remedy by motion is inadequate or ineffective to test the legality of his detention.

The section 2255 remedy is similar to the habeas corpus remedy for state prisoners, discussed earlier. Although there are some significant distinctions between the two remedies, they are beyond the scope of this book and will not be discussed here.

State Post-Conviction Relief

Almost all states have post-conviction procedures permitting prisoners to challenge constitutional violations. These procedures may derive from statutes, court rules, or the common law. Many of these state remedies are as extensive in scope as federal habeas corpus for state prisoners. Other states provide much narrower remedies. The differences in post-conviction remedies among the states is also beyond the scope of this book and will not be discussed further here.

* * *

This concludes our discussion of criminal court procedure. The purpose of this chapter has been to provide law enforcement officers with a better understanding of some of the legal terms and procedures involved in a criminal case from the initial report of a crime through an appeal to the U. S. Supreme Court. Although much of the information does not bear directly on an officer's daily duties, the chapter will have served is purpose if it has helped him to better perceive his role in the entire criminal justice system and the importance of the proper performance of that role to the effective and just operation of the system.

*

14

EVIDENCE

A law enforcement officer should have basic knowledge of the rules of evidence. Although he does not need as complete a grasp of these rules as an attorney or a judge, he does need a working knowledge of the rules for the proper investigation and preparation of cases and for the proper presentation of testimony in court. If the officer knows what evidence will and will not be admissible in court, he can concentrate his time and efforts accordingly and not waste time gathering useless information. Likewise, if the officer presents the results of his investigation in court in a manner acceptable under the law, he will be a more effective witness.

At first the rules of evidence may seem to frustrate the purposes of the prosecutor or the law enforcement officer. Facts essential to the conviction of an offender may not be established simply because the evidence by which the prosecution proposed to prove them did not meet required standards. An analysis of the rules, however, shows that they are essential to ensure the just and efficient operation of the criminal justice. They guarantee that judgments which involve the life and liberty of the individual on the one hand, and the peace and security of the state, on the other will be based only upon evidence worthy of being believed and acted upon in such important matters. Looking at the rules in this light, one will observe that there are usually good, logical reasons for the admissibility or non-admissibility of evidence under the various circumstances covered by the rules.

DEFINITION AND CLASSIFICATION OF EVIDENCE

The term "evidence" can be defined as anything which tends to prove or disprove a matter in question, or to influence the belief respecting it. Evidence involves all the means by which the truth of an alleged fact is established or disproved to the finder of fact (judge or jury).

The words "testimony" and "proof" are often confused with the word evidence. *Testimony* is one type of evidence—the oral statements of witnesses. Evidence is a much broader term including writings, objects, photographs, demonstrations, and the like. The term *proof* is sometimes used interchangeably with the term evidence. The difference between the two is that proof is the effect or the result of evidence, and evidence is the means of offering proof.

The three major categories of evidence are (1) direct evidence, (2) circumstantial evidence, and (3) real evidence. Direct evidence refers to matters introduced in court through the oral statements of witnesses on the stand testifying to their own personal knowledge of the facts in issue. Their knowledge will have been acquired through their own senses of sight, hearing, smell, touch, or taste. A simple example will illustrate. Assume that a witness on the stand in a homicide trial says, "I saw the defendant point a pistol at the deceased. I saw him pull the trigger. The gun went off with a loud crack and the deceased fell to the floor." All the facts to which the witness testified were within his immediate experience. His testimony was direct evidence of how the deceased died and who killed him.

Circumstantial evidence (sometimes called indirect evidence) refers to evidence which does not *directly* prove a fact in issue, but raises a strong inference or suggestion as to the truth of that fact. When a crime is committed in secret, usually the only way it can be proved against the defendant is by circumstantial evidence. For example, if a man breaks into a house, ordinarily no one sees him and therefore there will be no direct evidence that he committed the act. However, if he is caught with the stolen goods after having been seen in the neighborhood, and he has bits of glass from a broken window on his clothing, these circumstances raise a strong inference that he committed the act in question. Circumstantial evidence generally must be added to other evidence in order to prove the fact in issue, but many pieces of circumstantial evidence can convict a defendant of the crime with which he is charged even if no one actually saw him commit the offense.

Real evidence (sometimes called physical evidence) is made up of things—objects of one kind or another that are associated with the offense. When items have been identified and then associated with an offense, they themselves constitute proof of facts which bear upon the matters in issue. For example, a shoe identified as belonging to the defendant is shown to match a footprint found at the scene of the offense. The shoe is introduced into evidence. It is real evidence tending to show that the defendant was at the place where the crime was committed. It should be noted that the shoe would also be circumstantial evidence that the defendant committed the offense. Other examples of real evidence would be a knife, a gun, a key, human hairs, fingerprints, photographs, documents, soil, paint chips, etc.

All of the above types of evidence are useful and admissible in the presentation of a case in court. Direct evidence from mature, careful witnesses is highly desirable, but crimes are often committed in secret, out of the sight and hearing of others. Hence, real and circumstantial evidence may be the only forms of proof available to the prosecutor. This should not discourage the prosecution. Real and circumstantial evidence may be more accurate and compelling than the direct testimony of a witness whose power of observation may be diminished and rendered inaccurate in the shock and excitement of seeing a crime committed before him.

RULES OF EVIDENCE

Evidence which can properly be admitted in court to prove a fact in issue is said to be admissible evidence. The introduction and admissibility of evidence in court is governed by various tests called the rules of evidence. These rules have been developed over the years by courts and legislative bodies. Under the rules, evidence is considered inadmissible if it does not have sufficient value to prove a fact in issue. It may lack this value because it is incompetent or unreliable (such as hearsay evidence and opinions of non-experts) or because it is not relevant or material to the proof of the fact in issue.

It is worthwhile to mention here that under the so-called "exclusionary rule," evidence may be excluded for reasons having nothing to do with the tendency of the evidence to prove facts in issue, but involving instead the manner in which the evidence was obtained. For example, if a murder weapon was found and seized in the defendant's room during the course of an illegal search, it will be excluded from evidence not because its admission into evidence would not tend to prove defendant's guilt but because it was illegally seized.

The difference between "admissibility" and "weight" of the evidence should be explained. *Admissibility* of evidence means the tendency of the evidence to prove a fact in issue under the various tests called the rules of evidence. *Weight* of the evidence means the tendency of the evidence to convince and persuade. For example, assume that defendant is accused of murder. His mother testifies that he was home reading on the night of the murder. The family doctor testifies that defendant was undergoing tests in his office on the night of the murder. The testimony of both the mother and the doctor would be *admissible* evidence. The testimony of the doctor, however, would be entitled to more *weight,* because he is a disinterested party, whereas the mother would be more likely to lie to protect her son. Admissibility of evidence is determined by the judge; weight of the evidence is for the jury to decide.

Following is a brief discussion of the workings of these rules of evidence.

Competency, Relevancy, and Materiality

Competent evidence is evidence which is reliable and adequate to prove a fact in issue. Testimony of a witness about an event which he observed is competent evidence. His presence at the event is sufficient to establish the reliability of his testimony. The testimony of a carpenter that a person died of a heart attack would not be competent evidence, however. Only a person with medical training and experience could give a reliable and adequate opinion on such a matter. Hearsay evidence is incompetent evidence unless it falls within one of the exceptions to the hearsay rule. The reasons why hearsay evidence is incompetent will be discussed later in the chapter.

A party proposing evidence often has to lay a *foundation* to establish the competency of certain types of evidence. For example, the party introducing a photograph of a crime scene must first show that the photograph is an accurate reproduction of the place depicted in the photograph. Otherwise the photograph would be unreliable because of the possibility of trick photography.

Relevant evidence is evidence which tends to shed light on the truth of a fact in issue. For example, in a murder trial, testimony that the defendant had a motive for killing the victim would be relevant evidence to prove that defendant did kill the victim. Also, evidence that the defendant owned the weapon with which the murder was accomplished would be relevant evidence that the defendant was the killer.

Material evidence is evidence of substantial importance in proving the truth of a fact in issue. If an item of evidence is relevant to an issue, but is so remotely connected to it as to be of little or no value, it is immaterial. For example, evidence that two years previous, the defendant's brother had committed a crime similar to the crime for which the defendant is being tried would be immaterial evidence. Evidence of the brother's crime, although arguably relevant, would be too unimportant and too remote to have any value in proving that the defendant committed a similar crime.

Relevancy and materiality are closely interconnected and are easily confused. Some courts treat the two as substantially the same in meaning and effect, and use them interchangeably.

Evidence must satisfy all three tests of competency, relevancy, and materiality in order to be admissible in court. The remainder of this chapter will discuss various facets of the competency test which have been developed over the years by courts and legislative bodies.

Hearsay Rule

One of the most important rules of evidence is the so-called "hearsay rule." The essence of the rule is that a witness may testify only to matters of which he has personal knowledge, and not to matters of which he was informed by another (or hearsay). Hearsay evidence is not competent evidence to prove an issue in court. *The rule makes inadmissible any testimony by a witness of an out-of-court statement made by another person being offered to prove the truth of the matter stated.*

It is worthwhile to note here that the rule does not forbid the introduction of all statements made out of court by a person not testifying. The phrase "offered to prove the truth of the matter stated" operates so as *not* to exclude a statement unless (1) it is expressly or in effect a statement of fact, and (2) it is being offered to prove the truth of the matter contained in it. Therefore, if the statement is offered merely to show that the words were said, it is admissible. If the statement is offered to prove a particular circumstance such as the state of mind of the person, it is admissible. Only if the statement is offered to prove the truth of the matter stated will it be inadmissible.

The basic hearsay rule is easily illustrated. Assume a witness in response to a question states, "I didn't see who fired the gun, but John Jones was there and he told me that Frank Smith fired it." If the reason this testimony was introduced was to prove that Frank Smith fired the gun, this statement would not be admissible in court for consideration by the judge or jury because the statement is hearsay. It is being offered to prove the truth of the matter stated (that Frank Smith fired the gun). If, however, the statement is introduced to prove that John Jones was at the scene of the shooting, it would no longer be hearsay and would therefore be admissible. The statement is not being offered to prove the truth of the matter stated, but to prove another fact (that John Jones was at the scene of the shooting).

The reasons why hearsay evidence is not competent evidence are clear. Human experience has demonstrated that there is a great possibility for distortion and error when one person attempts to repeat statements made by another. Also, if hearsay evidence were admissible in court, the person who made the original statements concerning the facts would not be under oath and would not be subject to cross-examination. Furthermore, the jury would have no opportunity to observe the appearance and demeanor of the person who actually made the statement. The reliability of hearsay evidence is therefore highly questionable. It would be manifestly unfair to the defendant to admit such evidence in court to prove facts against him.

Exceptions to the Hearsay Rule

There are many exceptions to the hearsay rule—many more than can be covered within the scope of this chapter. However, a few of these exceptions are of particular interest to the law enforcement officer and will be discussed briefly here.

1. Admissions and Confessions

Courts will allow a witness in a criminal proceeding to testify about an admission or confession made to him by the defendant. An *admission* is a statement by the defendant which by itself or in connection with other facts tends to show the existence of one or more, but not all of the elements of the crime for which he is being tried. A *confession* is a statement by the defendant in which he expressly admits facts revealing *all* the elements of the crime. Admissions and confessions are allowed as exceptions to the hearsay rule because persons ordinarily do not say things against their own interests unless they are true. Thus, such statements are considered reliable even though they are hearsay.

It should be noted here that before a statement made *to the police* can be admitted under this exception to the hearsay rule, the prosecution must show that the statement was voluntarily made and that the standards announced in Miranda v. Arizona, 384 U.S. 436, 86 S.Ct. 1602, 16 L.Ed.2d 694 (U. S. Supreme Court, 1966) were satisfied. These standards require the familiar *Miranda* warnings to be given to a suspect prior to any custodial interrogation. The *Miranda* decision is discussed in detail in Chapter 9.

2. Dying Declarations

At a homicide trial, it is proper to introduce testimony of words used by the victim of the homicide prior to his death concerning the facts of the offense and the identity of his slayer. However, at the time the statements are made, the victim must know or honestly believe that he is about to die and that he has no hope of recovery.

Dying declarations are allowed as an exception to the hearsay rule because it is believed that a man who knows he is facing certain death will speak only the truth. Like admissions and confessions, such statements are considered reliable even though they are hearsay.

If a dying declaration is made in the presence of a law enforcement officer, he should make careful notes not only of the victim's statement but of the surrounding circumstances. By doing this the officer will be better able to show in court that the wounded person truly believed that he was about to die.

3. Res Gestae Declarations

The Latin phrase "res gestae" means literally, "things done." It refers to every act or circumstance which makes up a criminal offense. Res gestae declarations are statements made at the time of an offense or so close thereto as to be almost automatic or impulsive. Res gestae declarations are sometimes called spontaneous exclamations or excited utterances. Such statements are considered to be an integral part of the entire criminal transaction. They are admissible as exceptions to the hearsay rule because one who speaks before he has time to reflect or deliberate is considered likely to tell the truth. Res gestae declarations are considered reliable, then, because of their spontaneity.

The res gestae exception to the hearsay rule can be illustrated by an example. Assume that during a scuffle between two men on a sidewalk, an unidentified bystander is heard to exclaim "Look out, he's got a gun!" The defendant, who runs away, is apprehended some time later. He is searched, but no gun is found upon him. At the trial of the defendant for assault, a witness testifies that he was near the place where the assault occurred—although not close enough to see if the defendant had a gun—and heard the unidentified bystander utter the words quoted above. Under the res gestae exception, the evidence of what the bystander said, would be admissible on the question of whether or not the defendant was armed as he committed the assault. Under the circumstances, the bystander's remarks would be considered a spontaneous or automatic reaction to seeing the defendant with a gun.

Courts are strict in the allowance of evidence under the res gestae exception. Only when the utterance intended to be used as evidence is clearly shown to be a part of the entire scene surrounding the crime will it be allowed to be repeated in the trial as evidence of the fact to which it refers.

4. Public Records

Public records kept by a public official who is required by law to keep the records are admissible in evidence as an exception to the hearsay rule. In order to qualify for the exception, the records must have been made by or under the general supervision of a public official in the course of his official duties. Copies of such records are admissible if they are properly certified and authenticated. If the record contains opinions of the record keeper or other information not properly before the court, the court will usually delete such material before admitting the record into evidence.

Public records are admissible as exceptions to the hearsay rule because the person making such records usually has no motive to falsify and the records are open to public scrutiny. The records are therefore presumed to be regular and accurate. Also, the person or persons who made the records are often unavailable to testify. Examples of public records that might be of interest to law enforcement officers are statutes and ordinances, judicial records, prison records, and motor vehicle records.

5. *Business Records*

Regular record entries made in the course of a business, occupation, or profession are admissible as an exception to the hearsay rule. To qualify for the exception, the entry must have been made at the time of the act, event, or transaction in question or within a reasonable time thereafter. The entry must have been made as a part of a series of transactions—a single isolated notation will not qualify. Also, the entry must be shown to have been made either with the personal knowledge of the person making it or in the course of a regular bookkeeping system. Under the Uniform Business Records as Evidence Act, in effect in most states, the court must be convinced of the fairness and reliability of the record. The original record entry must be submitted—usually a transcript or summary of the record will not be allowed in evidence.

Record entries made in the manner described above are admissible as exceptions to the hearsay rule to prove the matters recorded on the theory that, since no controversy existed at the time the entry was made, there was no motive to falsify the record. Examples of business records which might be of interest to law enforcement officers are hospital or doctor's records to prove injury or intoxication, bank records to prove the deposit or withdrawal of money, and employer's time records to prove a person was or was not at work on a given day.

6. *Previously Recorded Testimony*

Previously recorded testimony of a witness is admissible as an exception to the hearsay rule under certain conditions. First, the testimony must have been given under oath or affirmation at a previous trial or preliminary hearing. Second, the previous trial or preliminary hearing must have involved the same defendant and the same crime or act as the trial at which the testimony is sought to be introduced. This requirement ensures that the defendant against whom the testimony is to be introduced had the opportunity to cross-examine the witness. Finally, the particular witness whose former testimony is offered must be dead or otherwise wholly unavailable at the time his former testimony is offered in evidence.

7. Matters of Pedigree

Statements on matters of birth, death, marriage, and family relationship are admissible as exceptions to the hearsay rule if there is no record of the event or fact in question. Hearsay statements on these matters may be admitted only when the person who originally uttered the statement is dead or wholly unavailable. Also, the person who made the statement must have been a member of the family or someone closely connected with it such as an old friend or a servant.

Such statements are considered trustworthy and are therefore admissible because the persons who made the statements were presumably in a position to know the facts and the statements were made before any controversy arose relating to the matter stated. Matters of pedigree might be important to law enforcement officers in statutory rape cases and in cases involving juveniles.

8. State of Mind

Statements evidencing a person's state of mind are admissible as exceptions to the hearsay rule under certain conditions. If a person's mental or emotional state of mind at a particular time is an issue in a case, his declarations regarding his then-existing state of mind are admissible if made under conditions indicating no motivation to falsify or mislead. This exception is allowed largely because it is the only way to prove a person's state of mind.

A person's declarations may also be admissible in evidence to show a then-existing intent to do something in the future. Evidence of such intent is admissible to prove that the person actually accomplished the intended act. Such declarations are admissible, however, only to show that the person making the declaration, and not someone else, engaged in particular conduct.

Opinion Rule

As a general rule, witnesses are not allowed to testify concerning their opinions or conclusions. They must only state facts within their knowledge relevant to the issue in question. It is the function of the jury, or the judge (in a non-jury case), to draw conclusions from the pertinent facts placed in evidence. For example, the witness will not be allowed to state "He was driving recklessly," because "recklessly" is an opinion or conclusion. It is for the jury to decide from the witness's description of the details of his observations whether or not the driving was reckless. The basis for this rule is that once the jury has the facts, they are as able as the witness to draw the proper conclusions.

There are certain well-recognized exceptions to the opinion rule. One of these is the "qualified expert" exception. Under this exception, the court will receive opinion testimony from persons having special skill, knowledge, wisdom, or information in a particular area. For example, an officer highly experienced in traffic accident investigation might testify about skid marks and be allowed to give an opinion as to how fast a car was going. The basis for allowing this opinion is that the jury, even with all the pertinent facts, does not have sufficient knowledge or expertise in traffic accident investigation to formulate a rationally based conclusion. In order for a witness to be allowed to give expert opinion testimony, his qualifications as an expert must be proven to the satisfaction of the court.

Another exception to the opinion rule allows opinion evidence concerning certain matters of common observation that would be almost impossible to describe except in the form of an opinion. For example, a witness would be allowed to state his impression of another's manner or appearance such as that the latter was nervous or excited or angry. Other matters about which a witness may state an opinion are sobriety, mental condition, speed, size, distance, age, identity, quality, and quantity. The witness can testify only to his own impression and not to someone else's. In many cases, the witness must also state the facts which form the basis of his opinion.

Best Evidence Rule

The "best evidence" rule requires that in order to introduce the contents of a written document into court, a party must produce the original writing. Copies or oral testimony are not admissible to prove the contents of the document. For example, if a witness attempted to testify to the contents of a kidnapper's ransom letter, this testimony would be inadequate without the document itself being produced. Where it may be impossible or impracticable to produce the document itself, because it is lost, destroyed, out of the jurisdiction of the court, or in the possession of a third party, the court may allow other evidence, written or oral, to prove the document's contents.

The basis of this rule is that the exact words of a writing are often very important (especially legal documents) and a slight variation in wording may mean a great difference in the interpretation of the document. Moreover, there are substantial risks of error and inaccuracy in translating the exact terms of a document either through oral testimony from memory or through copies.

Corpus Delicti Rule

The Latin term "corpus delicti" means literally "body of the crime." When applied to a particular crime, proof of the corpus delicti means proof that the crime was actually committed and that someone was criminally responsible for it.

The corpus delicti rule states that the corpus delicti in a criminal case cannot be established by the confession of the defendant alone. No matter how complete or incriminating that confession is, it alone cannot be used by the state to prove the particular crime was actually committed by someone. The state does not have to prove the corpus delicti beyond a reasonable doubt but must produce *some evidence,* outside of the defendant's admission or confession. "Some evidence" has been defined as such independent credible evidence as will create a really substantial belief that the crime charged had actually been committed by someone. State v. Wardwell, 158 Me. 307, 183 A.2d 896 (Supreme Judicial Court of Maine, 1962). The following example illustrates the operation of the corpus delicti rule. In an appeal from a conviction for operating a motor vehicle while under the influence, the defendant objected to the admission of a statement made by him that he was driving the vehicle when it overturned. He argued that the state had failed to prove the corpus delicti by evidence other than his statement. The court found that the following facts were sufficient to establish some evidence of the corpus delicti:

1. A motor vehicle overturned while being operated upon the highway.
2. The vehicle had been in defendant's control a half-hour earlier some miles away.
3. The defendant was at the place where the overturning occurred immediately thereafter.
4. Defendant had suffered a recent injury.
5. Defendant assumed responsibility for notifying the police.
6. Earlier on the day in question, defendant had been seen drinking in a beer parlor.
7. Defendant had been warned not to drive the vehicle because he had been drinking too much. State v. Hoffses, 147 Me. 221, 85 A.2d 919 (Supreme Judicial Court of Maine, 1952).

It should be remembered that in order to *convict* the defendant of a crime, all the evidence in the case, including the confession must convince the jury *beyond a reasonable doubt* that the defendant committed the crime in question.

SUMMARY

The rules of evidence are designed to ensure that decisions made by courts in the criminal area are based only upon evidence sufficiently trustworthy and reliable to be acted upon in such vital matters. The law enforcement officer is responsible for bringing offenders against the law before the courts and presenting evidence relating to the offenses. In the areas of both criminal investigation and court testimony the officer needs a basic grasp of the rules of evidence so that he knows what evidence will be admissible in court and generally understands the terms and procedures relating to the proof of facts at a trial.

By preserving and producing evidence which complies with these rules, the officer helps to further the efficient administration of justice.

15

TESTIFYING IN COURT

Testifying in court is often overlooked in the training of law enforcement officers. The officer who investigated a case is often the most important witness in the trial of that case. He may be the only person able to give a comprehensive view of what happened. He is therefore the principal medium through whom evidence of a crime is transmitted to the finder of fact at trial.

The importance of a good presentation by law enforcement officers on the witness stand cannot be overemphasized. Hours and hours of the most competent investigation and preparation of criminal cases by investigating officers may be wasted if the results are improperly presented in court. The trier of fact (usually the jury) comes into court having no prior knowledge of the case being tried. The picture the jury gets depends largely on the ability of the investigating officer to testify truthfully and accurately. He should leave the impression that he is intelligent, honest, competent, and fair. The defense attorney will do everything legally permitted to twist the evidence in his client's favor. If the officer becomes confused, hazy, or unsure of important facts, the jury will be similarly confused or hazy. However, if the officer presents a clear-cut report containing all the elements of proof in a calm, unprejudiced manner, the jury will see the case in the same light.

A verdict of guilty will accomplish little if an officer has testified so sloppily and poorly that he affords the accused sufficient grounds for a new trial or for a reversal on appeal. Nor does a guilty verdict serve its purpose unless the trial has been conducted in such a manner that everyone in the courtroom has been impressed with the dignity and justice of the proceedings. Public confidence in our system of justice is essential to its proper function.

A law enforcement officer's testimony is important not only at the trial stage, but at various preliminary stages in a criminal proceeding. An officer may be required to testify at a preliminary hearing, at a hearing on a motion to suppress, or at some other pre-trial proceeding. An officer's testimony at a pre-trial hearing may be used later by defense counsel to confront and contradict an officer's trial testimony. For this reason, before testifying at trial, an officer should carefully review court records of statements he made at a pre-trial hearing. The officer should also consult with the prosecuting attorney regarding those records.

Unfortunately, past performance of law enforcement officers in court has not generally been of the highest quality. The reasons for this have been poor preparation, inadequate training, stage fright, and inexperience. These must be overcome if an officer is to justify an arrest or an investigation made by him. This chapter is an attempt to set forth guidelines and suggestions to help improve the quality of court testimony by law enforcement officers.

PREPARATION BEFORE TRIAL

Effective testimony in court depends to a large extent on preparation by the law enforcement officer before he enters the courtroom. As was emphasized in Chapter 12, this preparation should begin the moment the officer is notified that a possible crime has been committed. All facts, observations, and actions relating to the case should be carefully recorded in notes, reports, and photographs. Proper investigative procedures cannot be stressed strongly enough, because there are often long delays between the investigation of a case and its trial. Unless information is recorded, much of it may be forgotten.

Knowledge of the Case

As the time of trial draws near, the investigating officer should make a complete review of the case to refresh his memory of the facts. He should carefully read through all notes and reports. He should also examine real evidence which has been collected in the event that it has to be identified or referred to in court. Then he should organize his thoughts so that he can visualize the entire sequence of events as they occurred. Testimony presented to a jury as a series of events in chronological order is both interesting and convincing.

An officer may be allowed to refresh his memory on the witness stand by referring to his notes or reports. However, if he does so, the defense counsel may have a right to examine these notes and question the officer about them. Therefore, the officer should discuss with the prosecuting attorney the advisability of taking notes onto the witness stand with him.

The prosecuting attorney may want to confer with the investigating officer about the facts of the case at a pre-trial session. At this session, the prosecuting attorney may try to reawaken the officer's senses in order to recall parts of the investigation which he deems essential to the case. The prosecuting attorney may also want to review the officer's entire testimony. This is entirely proper, and at this time the officer should be sure that the prosecuting attorney knows all the facts of the case whether or not they are favorable to the prosecution. The prosecuting attorney may not tell the officer what to say or attempt to influence him to deviate from the truth in any way.

Knowledge of the Rules of Evidence

Besides knowledge of the case being tried, the law enforcement officer testifying in court should have a basic knowledge of the rules of evidence. This knowledge will help him to better understand the proceedings and will enable him to testify more intelligently, resulting in less delay and confusion in the courtroom. A discussion of some of the basic rules of evidence appears in Chapter 14.

Appearance and Attitude

When a law enforcement officer appears in court, he must observe the highest standards of conduct. The minute he walks to the witness stand, he becomes the focal point of public interest and observation. His appearance and behavior will reflect upon himself, his fellow law enforcement officers, and the entire system of criminal justice.

The key thing for a law enforcement officer to remember when testifying in court is that he is engaged in a very solemn and serious matter. He should look and act accordingly. While waiting to testify, the law enforcement officer should not linger outside the door of the courtroom, smoking gossiping, joking, laughing, or engaging in other similar conduct. This distracts attention from the proceedings and shows little regard for the serious nature of the occasion. Instead, the officer should be seated quietly in the courtroom awaiting his turn to take the stand, unless witnesses have been excluded to the witness room.

An officer's appearance while testifying should be neat and well-groomed. He should wear a clean suit and tie or a clean and neatly pressed uniform and shined shoes. He should avoid wearing a gun if possible. He should also avoid wearing dark glasses, smoking, chewing gum, or fidgeting around while on the witness stand. A favorable impression is created if the officer sits erect but at ease in the witness chair and appears confident, alert, and interested in the proceedings.

It is important to remember that the public is highly interested in its police and what they do and how they act. Their opinion of the police is often based on limited observation and experience—usually involving traffic and other motor vehicle violations. Yet, the public expects a high standard of performance all the time and especially in the courtroom. Effective and properly presented testimony can help fulfill these expectations and improve the public image of all law enforcement personnel.

TESTIMONY DURING TRIAL

Our system of securing information from a witness at a criminal trial is by questions and answers. On direct examination, each party to the proceeding (prosecution and defense), calls witnesses to the stand who that party believes will testify in its favor. The questioning by attorneys on direct examination serves merely to guide the witness in his testimony and indicate to him the information that is required. After direct examination, the witness may be subject to cross-examination by the opposing counsel. The questions on cross-examination will have the opposite purpose. Cross-examination questions may be devious, deceptive, or innocent in appearance, masking the opposing counsel's real objective, which is to discredit or minimize the effect of the witness's testimony. The law enforcement officer is almost always a witness for the state and therefore he will be directly examined by the prosecuting attorney and cross-examined by counsel for the defense.

There are no definite rules for testifying effectively in court because each case has its own peculiarities. However, general guidelines for answering questions on direct examination and on cross-examination can be provided.

Answering Questions on the Witness Stand

1. When taking the oath, the law enforcement officer should be serious. He should stand upright, facing the judicial officer administering the oath. He should say "I do" clearly and positively and then be seated to await questioning.

2. The officer should listen carefully to the questions asked and make sure he understands each question before answering. If he does not understand, he should say so, and ask to have the question

repeated. He should then pause after the question long enough to form an intelligent answer, and to allow the attorneys and the judge time to object.

3. Answers to questions should be given in a confident, straightforward, and sincere manner. The officer should speak clearly, loudly, and slowly enough so that all in the courtroom can hear and he should avoid mumbling or covering his mouth with his hand while talking. He should look at the attorney asking the question but direct his answers towards the jury. Simple conversational English should be used and all slang and unnecessary technical terms should be avoided. Most important, the officer should be respectful and courteous at all times despite his feelings toward the people involved in the case. He should address the judge as "Your Honor," the attorneys as "Sir" or "Ma'am," and the defendants as "The Defendant."

4. The essential rule to be observed above and beyond all others is to always tell the truth, even if it is favorable to the defendant. Facts should not be distorted or exaggerated to try and aid a conviction, nor should details be added to cover up personal mistakes. Once it has been shown that an officer has not truthfully testified concerning one portion of his investigation, no matter how small and unconsequential, the jury may reject the truthfulness of all other testimony which he may offer. On the other hand, an officer's testimony will appear strong if it is a truthful recital of what he did and observed, even though it reveals human error on his part and favors the defendant in some parts.

5. Answers to questions should go no further than what the questions ask for. The officer should not volunteer any information not asked for. If a question requests a "Yes" or "No" answer and the officer feels it cannot properly be answered in this manner, he should ask to have the question explained or reworded or request the right to explain his answer. He may state that he cannot answer the question by "Yes" or "No." This should alert the prosecuting attorney to come to his assistance.

6. Answers to questions should be given as specifically as possible. However, figures for time, distance, speed etc., should be approximated only, unless they were exactly measured by the officer.

7. When an officer is referring to a map or plan in his testimony, he should identify the point on the map as clearly as possible so it becomes part of the trial record. For example, he should say "the northwest corner of the room" rather than just point to the spot and say "here" or "there." If the officer does not understand the map or plan which is to be used at the trial, he should tell the prosecuting attorney before trial and go over it with the person who prepared it.

8. If a wrong or ambiguous answer is given, it should be clarified immediately. It is far better for an officer to correct his own mistakes than to have them pointed out to the jury by the defense attorney or a subsequent witness.

9. If a judge interrupts or an attorney objects to an officer's testimony, the officer should stop talking immediately. However, he should not anticipate an objection when a difficult question is asked but should only pause long enough to form an intelligent answer.

10. Under no circumstances should a law enforcement officer memorize his testimony. It will only sound rehearsed and false and will not inspire the confidence of the jury. Instead, the officer should have a thorough knowledge of the facts of the case and organize them in his mind so he can recite them as a narrative. If a particular fact or circumstance becomes hazy or is forgotten, the officer may be allowed to refresh his memory from his notes. It is worth noting again that if an officer does refer to his notes, they may be examined and used by the opposing counsel.

11. If for any reason, the judge criticizes an officer's conduct in court, the officer should not allow it to disturb his composure. The best policy is to ask the court's pardon for the error committed and proceed as though nothing had occurred.

Cross-examination

In a criminal trial, it is the duty of counsel for the defendant, as an officer of the court and as an attorney, to use every legal means to secure either the acquittal of his client or the best possible verdict for him under the circumstances. Since the arresting or investigating officer is often the chief witness for the state, the defense attorney, in order to win his case, must normally discredit or nullify the officer's testimony or at least minimize its importance in the eyes of the jury. To do this, he may use every device legally available to him. He may attempt to show that the officer did not have the proper opportunity to observe the facts, or that he was inattentive or mistaken in his observations. He may try to make it seem like the officer is lying or leaving out facts which are favorable to the defendant. In criminal trials that have been long delayed, the defense counsel may try to show that the officer's recollection of his investigation is poor and that he knows nothing without his notes. He may even try to show that the officer has a grudge against the defendant. One of the ways of doing this is to goad the officer into losing his temper so he appears personally antagonistic to the defendant. Under the proper circumstances, all these approaches are legal and available for the use of defense counsel.

The best defense against the techniques and devices of the defense attorney is thorough preparation on the part of the testifying officer. If the officer has carefully observed the facts at the time of their occurrence, made complete and sufficient notes, reviewed his notes and reports carefully to fix the events in his memory, and testified truthfully, he need have no fear of cross-examination.

Nevertheless, there are a few important suggestions regarding cross-examination which will help prevent the officer from falling into the traps laid by a clever defense attorney. Some of these suggestions have been mentioned above and others apply exclusively to cross-examination.

1. The officer should not become angry or argumentative with the defense attorney. This is exactly what the defense attorney wants and the officer will only appear to have lost his composure or to be hostile to the defendant. Rather, the officer should calmly answer all questions unless an objection to a question is sustained by the judge. If he does not remember or does not know an answer, he should simply say so.

2. The officer should make very clear by his attitudes and statements that he has no personal feelings against the accused. If an accused has been nasty, insulting, or has assaulted an officer, the defense attorney may make much of such occurrences to persuade the jury that the officer has a personal grudge in the matter and is "out to get" the accused. The jury, being only human, is quick to resent any evidence of overbearing conduct or personal animosity on the part of the police. The officer in this situation should make clear that such things are a common occurrence in his line of duty and that they have no bearing on the matter as far as the facts are concerned.

3. The officer should not be afraid to admit mistakes made either in his investigation or in his prior testimony. Everyone in the courtroom realizes that no one is perfect and by admitting his errors himself, an officer will give defense counsel less fuel for attacking his credibility.

4. If a defense attorney's question is not clear, the officer should tell the court and ask to have it restated. An answer to an ambiguous question may very likely be a set-up for a contradiction later on.

5. The officer should never be afraid to admit that he had discussed his testimony before trial with the prosecuting attorney, his superiors, or other officers. This is entirely proper and accepted procedure. However, defense counsel, in the way he asks the question, may try to make it seem improper, and thereby trick the officer-witness into a lie.

6. If defense counsel seeks to cut off an officer in the middle of his testimony, the officer may turn to the judge and request an op-

portunity to explain his answer. This request will usually be granted.

CONDUCT AFTER TRIAL

When an officer leaves the witness stand, he should do so quickly and quietly and either return to his seat or leave the courtroom if he is no longer needed. He should not linger to talk to the prosecutor. If he has additional information or ideas to tell the prosecutor, he should write them down and pass them to the prosecutor with a minimum amount of display. When an officer leaves the courtroom, he should not loiter to talk or gossip with others and, most important, he should not talk to jurors if it is a jury trial.

SUMMARY

Convincing and effective testimony by law enforcement officers is essential to the successful operation of our criminal justice system and depends on proper preparation, attitude, and experience. The suggestions outlined above are designed to familiarize the officer with court procedures and improve his approach to testimony as a witness. The preparation and individual effort required in this endeavor depends on the dedication of each law enforcement officer.

TABLE OF CASES

Major cases are in italic type. Other cases cited or discussed are in roman type. References are to pages.

A

B

C

U

V

W

Y

Z

INDEX

References are to Pages

References are to Pages

References are to Pages

References are to Pages

References are to Pages

References are to Pages

References are to Pages

References are to Pages

References are to Pages

References are to Pages

References are to Pages

References are to Pages

References are to Pages

References are to Pages

References are to Pages

References are to Pages

References are to Pages

References are to Pages

WEST PUBLISHING CO